ŚRĪMAD BHĀGAVATAM

of

KṚṢṆA-DVAIPĀYANA VYĀSA

एतन्निर्विद्यमानानामिच्छतामकुतोभयम् ।
योगिनां नृप निर्णीतं हरेर्नामानुकीर्तनम् ॥

*etan nirvidyamānānām
icchatām akuto-bhayam
yoginām nṛpa nirṇītam
harer nāmānukīrtanam* (p. 18)

Books by His Divine Grace
A.C. Bhaktivedanta Swami Prabhupāda

Bhagavad-gītā As It Is
Śrīmad-Bhāgavatam (completed by disciples)
Śrī Caitanya-caritāmṛta
Kṛṣṇa, the Supreme Personality of Godhead
Teachings of Lord Caitanya
The Nectar of Devotion
The Nectar of Instruction
Śrī Īśopaniṣad
Light of the Bhāgavata
Easy Journey to Other Planets
Teachings of Lord Kapila, the Son of Devahūti
Teachings of Queen Kuntī
Message of Godhead
The Science of Self-Realization
The Perfection of Yoga
Beyond Birth and Death
On the Way to Kṛṣṇa
Rāja-vidyā: The King of Knowledge
Elevation to Kṛṣṇa Consciousness
Kṛṣṇa Consciousness: The Matchless Gift
Kṛṣṇa Consciousness: The Topmost Yoga System
Perfect Questions, Perfect Answers
Life Comes from Life
The Nārada-bhakti-sūtra (completed by disciples)
The Mukunda-mālā-stotra (completed by disciples)
Geetār-gan (Bengali)
Vairāgya-vidyā (Bengali)
Buddhi-yoga (Bengali)
Bhakti-ratna-boli (Bengali)
Back to Godhead magazine (founder)

Books compiled from the teachings of His Divine Grace
A.C. Bhaktivedanta Swami Prabhupāda after his lifetime

Search for Liberation
A Second Chance
The Journey of Self-Discovery
Civilization and Transcendence
The Laws of Nature
Renunciation Through Wisdom
The Quest for Enlightenment
Dharma, the Way of Transcendence
Beyond Illusion and Doubt
The Hare Kṛṣṇa Challenge

Available from: www.krishna.com

ŚRĪMAD BHĀGAVATAM

Second Canto
"The Cosmic Manifestation"

(Part One—Chapters 1–6)

With the Original Sanskrit Text,
Its Roman Transliteration, Synonyms,
Translation and Elaborate Purports

by

His Divine Grace
A.C. Bhaktivedanta Swami Prabhupāda
Founder-*Ācārya* of the International Society for Krishna Consciousness

THE BHAKTIVEDANTA BOOK TRUST
New York · Los Angeles · London · Bombay

Readers interested in the subject matter of this book are invited
by the International Society for Krishna Consciousness
to correspond with its Secretary at the following address:

International Society for Krishna Consciousness
3764 Watseka Avenue
Los Angeles, California 90034
USA

www.krishna.com

Table of Contents

CHAPTER THREE
Pure Devotional Service: The Change in Heart

CHAPTER SIX
Puruṣa-sūkta Confirmed   291

Appendixes

Preface

We must know the present need of human society. And what is that need? Human society is no longer bounded by geographical limits to particular countries or communities. Human society is broader than in the Middle Ages, and the world tendency is toward one state or one human society. The ideals of spiritual communism, according to *Śrīmad-Bhāgavatam*, are based more or less on the oneness of the entire human society, nay, of the entire energy of living beings. The need is felt by great thinkers to make this a successful ideology. *Śrīmad-Bhāgavatam* will fill this need in human society. It begins, therefore, with the aphorism of Vedānta philosophy *janmādy asya yataḥ* to establish the ideal of a common cause.

Human society, at the present moment, is not in the darkness of oblivion. It has made rapid progress in the field of material comforts, education and economic development throughout the entire world. But there is a pinprick somewhere in the social body at large, and therefore there are large-scale quarrels, even over less important issues. There is need of a clue as to how humanity can become one in peace, friendship and prosperity with a common cause. *Śrīmad-Bhāgavatam* will fill this need, for it is a cultural presentation for the respiritualization of the entire human society.

Śrīmad-Bhāgavatam should be introduced also in the schools and colleges, for it is recommended by the great student-devotee Prahlāda Mahārāja in order to change the demoniac face of society.

> *kaumāra ācaret prājño*
> *dharmān bhāgavatān iha*
> *durlabhaṁ mānuṣaṁ janma*
> *tad apy adhruvam arthadam*
> (*Bhāg.* 7.6.1)

Disparity in human society is due to lack of principles in a godless civilization. There is God, or the Almighty One, from whom everything emanates, by whom everything is maintained and in whom everything is merged to rest. Material science has tried to find the ultimate source of creation very insufficiently, but it is a fact that there is one ultimate source of everything that be. This ultimate source is explained rationally and authoritatively in the beautiful *Bhāgavatam*, or *Śrīmad-Bhāgavatam*.

Śrīmad-Bhāgavatam is the transcendental science not only for knowing the ultimate source of everything but also for knowing our relation with Him and our duty toward perfection of the human society on the basis of this perfect knowledge. It is powerful reading matter in the Sanskrit language, and it is now rendered into English elaborately so that simply by a careful reading one will know God perfectly well, so much so that the reader will be sufficiently educated to defend himself from the onslaught of atheists. Over and above this, the reader will be able to convert others to accepting God as a concrete principle.

Śrīmad-Bhāgavatam begins with the definition of the ultimate source. It is a bona fide commentary on the *Vedānta-sūtra* by the same author, Śrīla Vyāsadeva, and gradually it develops into nine cantos up to the highest state of God realization. The only qualification one needs to study this great book of transcendental knowledge is to proceed step by step cautiously and not jump forward haphazardly like with an ordinary book. It should be gone through chapter by chapter, one after another. The reading matter is so arranged with its original Sanskrit text, its English transliteration, synonyms, translation and purports so that one is sure to become a God-realized soul at the end of finishing the first nine cantos.

The Tenth Canto is distinct from the first nine cantos because it deals directly with the transcendental activities of the Personality of Godhead Śrī Kṛṣṇa. One will be unable to capture the effects of the Tenth Canto without going through the first nine cantos. The book is complete in twelve cantos, each independent, but it is good for all to read them in small installments one after another.

I must admit my frailties in presenting *Śrīmad-Bhāgavatam*, but still I am hopeful of its good reception by the thinkers and leaders of society on the strength of the following statement of *Śrīmad-Bhāgavatam* (1.5.11):

> *tad-vāg-visargo janatāgha-viplavo*
> *yasmin prati-ślokam abaddhavaty api*

*nāmāny anantasya yaśo 'ṅkitāni yac
chṛṇvanti gāyanti gṛṇanti sādhavaḥ*

"On the other hand, that literature which is full with descriptions of the transcendental glories of the name, fame, form and pastimes of the unlimited Supreme Lord is a transcendental creation meant to bring about a revolution in the impious life of a misdirected civilization. Such transcendental literatures, even though irregularly composed, are heard, sung and accepted by purified men who are thoroughly honest."

Oṁ tat sat

A. C. Bhaktivedanta Swami

Introduction

"This *Bhāgavata Purāṇa* is as brilliant as the sun, and it has arisen just after the departure of Lord Kṛṣṇa to His own abode, accompanied by religion, knowledge, etc. Persons who have lost their vision due to the dense darkness of ignorance in the age of Kali shall get light from this *Purāṇa*." (*Śrīmad-Bhāgavatam* 1.3.43)

The timeless wisdom of India is expressed in the *Vedas*, ancient Sanskrit texts that touch upon all fields of human knowledge. Originally preserved through oral tradition, the *Vedas* were first put into writing five thousand years ago by Śrīla Vyāsadeva, the "literary incarnation of God." After compiling the *Vedas*, Vyāsadeva set forth their essence in the aphorisms known as *Vedānta-sūtras*. *Śrīmad-Bhāgavatam* is Vyāsadeva's commentary on his own *Vedānta-sūtras*. It was written in the maturity of his spiritual life under the direction of Nārada Muni, his spiritual master. Referred to as "the ripened fruit of the tree of Vedic literature," *Śrīmad-Bhāgavatam* is the most complete and authoritative exposition of Vedic knowledge.

After compiling the *Bhāgavatam*, Vyāsa impressed the synopsis of it upon his son, the sage Śukadeva Gosvāmī. Śukadeva Gosvāmī subsequently recited the entire *Bhāgavatam* to Mahārāja Parīkṣit in an assembly of learned saints on the bank of the Ganges at Hastināpura (now Delhi). Mahārāja Parīkṣit was the emperor of the world and was a great *rājarṣi* (saintly king). Having received a warning that he would die within a week, he renounced his entire kingdom and retired to the bank of the Ganges to fast until death and receive spiritual enlightenment. The *Bhāgavatam* begins with Emperor Parīkṣit's sober inquiry to Śukadeva Gosvāmī: "You are the spiritual master of great saints and devotees. I am therefore begging you to show the way of perfection for all persons, and especially for one who is about to die. Please let me know what a man should hear, chant, remember and worship, and also what he should not do. Please explain all this to me."

Śukadeva Gosvāmī's answer to this question, and numerous other questions posed by Mahārāja Parīkṣit, concerning everything from the nature of the self to the origin of the universe, held the assembled sages in rapt attention continuously for the seven days leading to the King's death. The sage Sūta Gosvāmī, who was present on the bank of the Ganges when Śukadeva Gosvāmī first recited Śrīmad-Bhāgavatam, later repeated the Bhāgavatam before a gathering of sages in the forest of Naimiṣāraṇya. Those sages, concerned about the spiritual welfare of the people in general, had gathered to perform a long, continuous chain of sacrifices to counteract the degrading influence of the incipient age of Kali. In response to the sages' request that he speak the essence of Vedic wisdom, Sūta Gosvāmī repeated from memory the entire eighteen thousand verses of Śrīmad-Bhāgavatam, as spoken by Śukadeva Gosvāmī to Mahārāja Parīkṣit.

The reader of Śrīmad-Bhāgavatam hears Sūta Gosvāmī relate the questions of Mahārāja Parīkṣit and the answers of Śukadeva Gosvāmī. Also, Sūta Gosvāmī sometimes responds directly to questions put by Śaunaka Ṛṣi, the spokesman for the sages gathered at Naimiṣāraṇya. One therefore simultaneously hears two dialogues: one between Mahārāja Parīkṣit and Śukadeva Gosvāmī on the bank of the Ganges, and another at Naimiṣāraṇya between Sūta Gosvāmī and the sages at Naimiṣāraṇya Forest, headed by Śaunaka Ṛṣi. Furthermore, while instructing King Parīkṣit, Śukadeva Gosvāmī often relates historical episodes and gives accounts of lengthy philosophical discussions between such great souls as the saint Maitreya and his disciple Vidura. With this understanding of the history of the Bhāgavatam, the reader will easily be able to follow its intermingling of dialogues and events from various sources. Since philosophical wisdom, not chronological order, is most important in the text, one need only be attentive to the subject matter of Śrīmad-Bhāgavatam to appreciate fully its profound message.

The translator of this edition compares the Bhāgavatam to sugar candy—wherever you taste it, you will find it equally sweet and relishable. Therefore, to taste the sweetness of the Bhāgavatam, one may begin by reading any of its volumes. After such an introductory taste, however, the serious reader is best advised to go back to Volume One of the First Canto and then proceed through the Bhāgavatam, volume after volume, in its natural order.

This edition of the Bhāgavatam is the first complete English translation of this important text with an elaborate commentary, and it is the first widely available to the English-speaking public. It is the product of

the scholarly and devotional effort of His Divine Grace A. C. Bhaktivedanta Swami Prabhupāda, the world's most distinguished teacher of
Indian religious and philosophical thought. His consummate Sanskrit
scholarship and intimate familiarity with Vedic culture and thought as
well as the modern way of life combine to reveal to the West a magnificent exposition of this important classic.

Readers will find this work of value for many reasons. For those interested in the classical roots of Indian civilization, it serves as a vast
reservoir of detailed information on virtually every one of its aspects.
For students of comparative philosophy and religion, the *Bhāgavatam*
offers a penetrating view into the meaning of India's profound spiritual
heritage. To sociologists and anthropologists, the *Bhāgavatam* reveals the
practical workings of a peaceful and scientifically organized Vedic
culture, whose institutions were integrated on the basis of a highly
developed spiritual world-view. Students of literature will discover the
Bhāgavatam to be a masterpiece of majestic poetry. For students of psychology, the text provides important perspectives on the nature of consciousness, human behavior and the philosophical study of identity.
Finally, to those seeking spiritual insight, the *Bhāgavatam* offers simple
and practical guidance for attainment of the highest self-knowledge and
realization of the Absolute Truth. The entire multivolume text, presented by the Bhaktivedanta Book Trust, promises to occupy a significant
place in the intellectual, cultural and spiritual life of modern man for a
long time to come.

—The Publishers

ŚRĪMAD
BHĀGAVATAM

CHAPTER ONE

The First Step in God Realization

INVOCATION

ॐ नमो भगवते वासुदेवाय ॥

oṁ namo bhagavate vāsudevāya

oṁ—O my Lord; *namaḥ*—my respectful obeisances unto You; *bhagavate*—unto the Personality of Godhead; *vāsudevāya*—unto Lord Kṛṣṇa, the son of Vasudeva.

TRANSLATION

O my Lord, the all-pervading Personality of Godhead, I offer my respectful obeisances unto You.

PURPORT

Vāsudevāya means "to Kṛṣṇa, the son of Vasudeva." Since by chanting the name of Kṛṣṇa, Vāsudeva, one can achieve all the good results of charity, austerity and penances, it is to be understood that by the chanting of this *mantra, oṁ namo bhagavate vāsudevāya*, the author or the speaker or any one of the readers of *Śrīmad-Bhāgavatam* is offering respectful obeisances unto the Supreme Lord, Kṛṣṇa, the reservoir of all pleasure. In the First Canto of *Śrīmad-Bhāgavatam*, the principles of creation are described, and thus the First Canto may be called "Creation."

Similarly, in the Second Canto, the postcreation cosmic manifestation is described. The different planetary systems are described in the Second Canto as different parts of the universal body of the Lord. For this reason, the Second Canto may be called "The Cosmic Manifestation." There are ten chapters in the Second Canto, and in these ten chapters the purpose of *Śrīmad-Bhāgavatam* and the different symptoms of this purpose are narrated. The first chapter describes the glories of chanting, and it hints at the process by which the neophyte devotees may perform meditation on the universal form of the Lord. In the first verse, Śukadeva Gosvāmī replies to the questions of Mahārāja Parīkṣit, who asked him about one's duties at the point of death. Mahārāja Parīkṣit was glad to receive Śukadeva Gosvāmī, and he was proud of being a descendant of Arjuna, the intimate friend of Kṛṣṇa. Personally, he was very humble and meek, but he expressed his gladness that Lord Kṛṣṇa was very kind to his grandfathers, the sons of Pāṇḍu, especially his own grandfather, Arjuna. And because Lord Kṛṣṇa was always pleased with Mahārāja Parīkṣit's family, at the verge of Mahārāja Parīkṣit's death Śukadeva Gosvāmī was sent to help him in the process of self-realization. Mahārāja Parīkṣit was a devotee of Lord Kṛṣṇa from his childhood, so he had natural affection for Kṛṣṇa. Śukadeva Gosvāmī could understand his devotion. Therefore, he welcomed the questions about the King's duty. Because the King hinted that worship of Lord Kṛṣṇa is the ultimate function of every living entity, Śukadeva Gosvāmī welcomed the suggestion and said, "Because you have raised questions about Kṛṣṇa, your question is most glorious." The translation of the first verse is as follows.

TEXT 1

श्रीशुक उवाच
वरीयानेष ते प्रश्नः कृतो लोकहितं नृप ।
आत्मवित्सम्मतः पुंसां श्रोतव्यादिषु यः परः॥ १ ॥

śrī-śuka uvāca
varīyān eṣa te praśnaḥ
kṛto loka-hitaṁ nṛpa
ātmavit-sammataḥ puṁsāṁ
śrotavyādiṣu yaḥ paraḥ

śrī-śukaḥ uvāca—Śrī Śukadeva Gosvāmī said; *varīyān*—glorious; *eṣaḥ*—this; *te*—your; *praśnaḥ*—question; *kṛtaḥ*—made by you; *loka-hitam*—beneficial for all men; *nṛpa*—O King; *ātmavit*—transcendentalist; *sammataḥ*—approved; *puṁsām*—of all men; *śrotavya-ādiṣu*—in all kinds of hearing; *yaḥ*—what is; *paraḥ*—the supreme.

TRANSLATION

Śrī Śukadeva Gosvāmī said: My dear King, your question is glorious because it is very beneficial to all kinds of people. The answer to this question is the prime subject matter for hearing, and it is approved by all transcendentalists.

PURPORT

Even the very question is so nice that it is the best subject matter for hearing. Simply by such questioning and hearing, one can achieve the highest perfectional stage of life. Because Lord Kṛṣṇa is the original Supreme Person, any question about Him is original and perfect. Lord Śrī Caitanya Mahāprabhu said that the highest perfection of life is to achieve the transcendental loving service of Kṛṣṇa. Because questions and answers about Kṛṣṇa elevate one to that transcendental position, the questions of Mahārāja Parīkṣit about Kṛṣṇa philosophy are greatly glorified. Mahārāja Parīkṣit wanted to absorb his mind completely in Kṛṣṇa, and such absorption can be effected simply by hearing about the uncommon activities of Kṛṣṇa. For instance, in the *Bhagavad-gītā* it is stated that simply by understanding the transcendental nature of Lord Kṛṣṇa's appearance, disappearance, and activities, one can immediately return home, back to Godhead, and never come back to this miserable condition of material existence. It is very auspicious, therefore, to hear always about Kṛṣṇa. So Mahārāja Parīkṣit requested Śukadeva Gosvāmī to narrate the activities of Kṛṣṇa so that he could engage his mind in Kṛṣṇa. The activities of Kṛṣṇa are nondifferent from Kṛṣṇa Himself. As long as one is engaged in hearing such transcendental activities of Kṛṣṇa, he remains aloof from the conditional life of material existence. The topics of Lord Kṛṣṇa are so auspicious that they purify the speaker, the hearer and the inquirer. They are compared to the Ganges waters, which flow from the toe of Lord Kṛṣṇa. Wherever the Ganges waters go, they purify the land and the person who bathes in them. Similarly, *kṛṣṇa-kathā*, or the topics of Kṛṣṇa, are so pure that wherever they are spoken, the place, the hearer, the inquirer, the speaker and all concerned become purified.

TEXT 2

श्रोतव्यादीनि राजेन्द्र नृणां सन्ति सहस्रशः ।
अपश्यतामात्मतत्त्वं गृहेषु गृहमेधिनाम् ॥ २ ॥

*śrotavyādīni rājendra
nṛṇāṁ santi sahasraśaḥ
apaśyatām ātma-tattvaṁ
gṛheṣu gṛha-medhinām*

śrotavya-ādīni—subject matters for hearing; *rājendra*—O Emperor; *nṛṇām*—of human society; *santi*—there are; *sahasraśaḥ*—hundreds and thousands; *apaśyatām*—of the blind; *ātma-tattvam*—knowledge of self, the ultimate truth; *gṛheṣu*—at home; *gṛha-medhinām*—of persons too materially engrossed.

TRANSLATION

Those persons who are materially engrossed, being blind to the knowledge of ultimate truth, have many subject matters for hearing in human society, O Emperor.

PURPORT

In the revealed scriptures there are two nomenclatures for the householder's life. One is *gṛhastha*, and the other is *gṛhamedhī*. The *gṛhasthas* are those who live together with wife and children but live transcendentally for realizing the ultimate truth. The *gṛhamedhīs*, however, are those who live only for the benefit of the family members, extended or centralized, and thus are envious of others. The word *medhī* indicates jealousy of others. The *gṛhamedhīs*, being interested in family affairs only, are certainly envious of others. Therefore, one *gṛhamedhī* is not on good terms with another *gṛhamedhī*, and in the extended form, one community, society or nation is not on good terms with another counterpart of selfish interest. In the age of Kali, all the householders are jealous of one another because they are blind to the knowledge of ultimate truth. They have many subject matters for hearing—political, scientific, social, economic and so on—but due to a poor fund of knowledge, they set aside the question of the ultimate miseries of life, namely miseries of birth, death, old age and disease. Factually, the human life is meant for making an ultimate solution to birth, death, old age and disease, but the *gṛhamedhīs*, being illusioned by the material nature, forget everything about self-realization. The ultimate solution to the problems of life is to go back home, back to Godhead, and thus, as stated in the *Bhagavad-gītā* (8.16), the miseries of material existence—birth, death, old age and disease—are removed.

The process of going back home, back to Godhead, is to hear about the Supreme Lord and His name, form, attributes, pastimes, paraphernalia and variegatedness. Foolish people do not know this. They want to hear something about the name, form, etc., of everything temporary, and they do not know how to utilize this propensity of hearing for the ultimate good. Misguided as they are, they also create some false literatures about the name, form, attributes, etc., of the ultimate truth. One should not, therefore, become a *gṛhamedhī* simply to exist for envying others; one should become a real householder in terms of the scriptural injunctions.

TEXT 3

निद्रया ह्रियते नक्तं व्यवायेन च वा वयः ।
दिवा चार्थेहया राजन् कुटुम्बभरणेन वा ॥ ३ ॥

nidrayā hriyate naktaṁ
vyavāyena ca vā vayaḥ
divā cārthehayā rājan
kuṭumba-bharaṇena vā

nidrayā—by sleeping; *hriyate*—wastes; *naktam*—night; *vyavāyena* —sex indulgence; *ca*—also; *vā*—either; *vayaḥ*—duration of life; *divā*—days; *ca*—and; *artha*—economic; *īhayā*—development; *rājan*— O King; *kuṭumba*—family members; *bharaṇena*—maintaining; *vā*— either.

TRANSLATION

The lifetime of such an envious householder is passed at night either in sleeping or in sex indulgence, and in the daytime either in making money or maintaining family members.

PURPORT

The present human civilization is primarily based on the principles of
sleeping and sex indulgence at night and earning money in the day and
spending the same for family maintenance. Such a form of human
civilization is condemned by the *Bhāgavata* school.

Because human life is a combination of matter and spirit soul, the
whole process of Vedic knowledge is directed at liberating the spirit soul
from the contamination of matter. The knowledge concerning this is
called *ātma-tattva*. Those men who are too materialistic are unaware of
this knowledge and are more inclined to economic development for material enjoyment. Such materialistic men are called *karmīs*, or fruitive
laborers, and they are allowed regulated economic development or association of woman for sex indulgence. Those who are above the *karmīs*,
that is, the *jñānīs*, *yogīs* and devotees, are strictly prohibited from sex indulgence. The *karmīs* are more or less devoid of *ātma-tattva* knowledge,
and as such, their life is spent without spiritual profit. The human life is
not meant for hard labor for economic development, nor is it meant for
sex indulgence like that of the dogs and hogs. It is specially meant for
making a solution to the problems of material life and the miseries
thereof. So the *karmīs* waste their valuable human life by sleeping and
sex indulgence at night, and by laboring hard in the daytime to accumulate wealth, and after doing so, they try to improve the standard of materialistic life. The materialistic way of life is described herein in a
nutshell, and how foolishly men waste the boon of human life is
described as follows.

TEXT 4

देहापत्यकलत्रादिष्वात्मसैन्येष्वसत्स्वपि ।
तेषां प्रमत्तो निधनं पश्यन्नपि न पश्यति ॥ ४ ॥

dehāpatya-kalatrādiṣv
ātma-sainyeṣv asatsv api
teṣāṁ pramatto nidhanaṁ
paśyann api na paśyati

deha—body; *apatya*—children; *kalatra*—wife; *ādiṣu*—and in everything in relation to them; *ātma*—own; *sainyeṣu*—fighting soldiers;

asatsu—fallible; *api*—in spite of; *teṣām*—of all of them; *pramattaḥ*—
too attached; *nidhanam*—destruction; *paśyan*—having been experienced; *api*—although; *na*—does not; *paśyati*—see it.

TRANSLATION

**Persons devoid of ātma-tattva do not inquire into the problems
of life, being too attached to the fallible soldiers like the body,
children and wife. Although sufficiently experienced, they still do
not see their inevitable destruction.**

PURPORT

This material world is called the world of death. Every living being,
beginning from Brahmā, whose duration of life is some thousands of
millions of years, down to the germs who live for a few seconds only,
is struggling for existence. Therefore, this life is a sort of fight with
material nature, which imposes death upon all. In the human form of
life, a living being is competent enough to come to an understanding of
this great struggle for existence, but being too attached to family members, society, country, etc., he wants to win over the invincible material
nature by the aid of bodily strength, children, wife, relatives, etc. Although he is sufficiently experienced in the matter by dint of past experience and previous examples of his deceased predecessors, he does not
see that the so-called fighting soldiers like the children, relatives, society
members and countrymen are all fallible in the great struggle. One
should examine the fact that his father or his father's father has already
died, and that he himself is therefore also sure to die, and similarly, his
children, who are the would-be fathers of their children, will also die in
due course. No one will survive in this struggle with material nature.
The history of human society definitely proves it, yet the foolish people
still suggest that in the future they will be able to live perpetually, with
the help of material science. This poor fund of knowledge exhibited by
human society is certainly misleading, and it is all due to ignoring the
constitution of the living soul. This material world exists only as a
dream, due to our attachment to it. Otherwise, the living soul is always
different from the material nature. The great ocean of material nature is
tossing with the waves of time, and the so-called living conditions are
something like foaming bubbles, which appear before us as bodily self,

wife, children, society, countrymen, etc. Due to a lack of knowledge of self, we become victimized by the force of ignorance and thus spoil the valuable energy of human life in a vain search after permanent living conditions, which are impossible in this material world.

Our friends, relatives and so-called wives and children are not only fallible, but also bewildered by the outward glamor of material existence. As such, they cannot save us. Still we think that we are safe within the orbit of family, society or country.

The whole materialistic advancement of human civilization is like the decoration of a dead body. Everyone is a dead body flapping only for a few days, and yet all the energy of human life is being wasted in the decoration of this dead body. Śukadeva Gosvāmī is pointing out the duty of the human being after showing the actual position of bewildered human activities. Persons who are devoid of the knowledge of *ātma-tattva* are misguided, but those who are devotees of the Lord and have perfect realization of transcendental knowledge are not bewildered.

TEXT 5

तस्माद्भारत सर्वात्मा भगवानीश्वरो हरिः ।
श्रोतव्यः कीर्तितव्यश्च स्मर्तव्यश्चेच्छताभयम् ॥ ५ ॥

tasmād bhārata sarvātmā
bhagavān īśvaro hariḥ
śrotavyaḥ kīrtitavyaś ca
smartavyaś cecchatābhayam

tasmāt—for this reason; *bhārata*—O descendant of Bharata; *sarvātmā*—the Supersoul; *bhagavān*—the Personality of Godhead; *īśvaraḥ*—the controller; *hariḥ*—the Lord, who vanquishes all miseries; *śrotavyaḥ*—is to be heard; *kīrtitavyaḥ*—to be glorified; *ca*—also; *smartavyaḥ*—to be remembered; *ca*—and; *icchatā*—of one who desires; *abhayam*—freedom.

TRANSLATION

O descendant of King Bharata, one who desires to be free from all miseries must hear about, glorify and also remember the Personality of Godhead, who is the Supersoul, the controller and the savior from all miseries.

PURPORT

In the previous verse, Śrī Śukadeva Gosvāmī has described how the foolish materially attached men are wasting their valuable time in the improvement of the material conditions of life by sleeping, indulging in sex life, developing economic conditions and maintaining a band of relatives who are to be vanquished in the air of oblivion. Being engaged in all these materialistic activities, the living soul entangles himself in the cycle of the law of fruitive actions. This entails the chain of birth and death in the 8,400,000 species of life: the aquatics, the vegetables, the reptiles, the birds, the beasts, the uncivilized man, and then again the human form, which is the chance for getting out of the cycle of fruitive action. Therefore, if one desires freedom from this vicious circle, then one must cease to act as a *karmī* or enjoyer of the results of one's own work, good or bad. One should not do anything, either good or bad, on his own account, but must execute everything on behalf of the Supreme Lord, the ultimate proprietor of everything that be. This process of doing work is recommended in the *Bhagavad-gītā* (9.27) also, where instruction is given for working on the Lord's account. Therefore, one should first of all hear about the Lord. When one has perfectly and scrutinizingly heard, one must glorify His acts and deeds, and thus it will become possible to remember constantly the transcendental nature of the Lord. Hearing about and glorifying the Lord are identical with the transcendental nature of the Lord, and by so doing, one will be always in the association of the Lord. This brings freedom from all sorts of fear. The Lord is the Supersoul (Paramātmā) present in the hearts of all living beings, and thus by the above hearing and glorifying process, the Lord invites the association of all in His creation. This process of hearing about and glorifying the Lord is applicable for everyone, whoever he may be, and it will lead one to the ultimate success in everything in which one may be engaged by providence. There are many classes of human beings: the fruitive workers, the empiric philosophers, the mystic *yogīs*, and ultimately, the unalloyed devotees. For all of them, one and the same process is applicable for achieving the desired success. Everyone wants to be free from all kinds of fear, and everyone wants the fullest extent of happiness in life. The perfect process for achieving this, here and now, is recommended in the *Śrīmad-Bhāgavatam*, which is uttered by such a great authority as Śrīla Śukadeva Gosvāmī. By hearing about and glorifying the Lord, all a person's activities become molded into spiritual activities, and thus all conceptions of material miseries become completely vanquished.

TEXT 6

एतावान् सांख्ययोगाभ्यां स्वधर्मपरिनिष्ठया ।
जन्मलाभः परः पुंसामन्ते नारायणस्मृतिः ॥ ६ ॥

etāvān sāṅkhya-yogābhyāṁ
sva-dharma-pariniṣṭhayā
janma-lābhaḥ paraḥ puṁsām
ante nārāyaṇa-smṛtiḥ

etāvān—all these; *sāṅkhya*—complete knowledge of matter and spirit; *yogābhyām*—knowledge of mystic power; *sva-dharma*—particular occupational duty; *pariniṣṭhayā*—by full perception; *janma*—birth; *lābhaḥ*—gain; *paraḥ*—the supreme; *puṁsām*—of a person; *ante* —at the end; *nārāyaṇa*—the Personality of Godhead; *smṛtiḥ*— remembrance.

TRANSLATION

The highest perfection of human life, achieved either by complete knowledge of matter and spirit, by practice of mystic powers, or by perfect discharge of occupational duty, is to remember the Personality of Godhead at the end of life.

PURPORT

Nārāyaṇa is the transcendental Personality of Godhead beyond the material creation. Everything that is created, sustained, and at the end annihilated is within the compass of the *mahat-tattva* (material principle) and is known as the material world. The existence of Nārāyaṇa, or the Personality of Godhead, is not within the jurisdiction of this *mahat-*

tattva, and as such, the name, form, attributes, etc. of Nārāyaṇa are beyond the jurisdiction of the material world. By the speculation of empiric philosophy, which discerns matter from spirit, or by cultivation of mystic powers, which ultimately helps the performer to reach any planet of the universe or beyond the universe, or by discharge of religious duties, one can achieve the highest perfection, provided one is able to reach the stage of *nārāyaṇa-smṛti*, or constant remembrance of the Personality of Godhead. This is possible only by the association of a pure devotee, who can give a finishing touch to the transcendental activities of all *jñānīs*, *yogīs*, or *karmīs*, in terms of prescribed duties defined in the scriptures. There are many historical instances of the achievement of spiritual perfection, such as that of the Sanakādi Ṛṣis or the nine celebrated Yogendras, who attained perfection only after being situated in the devotional service of the Lord. None of the devotees of the Lord ever deviated from the path of devotional service by taking to other methods as adopted by the *jñānīs* or *yogīs*. Everyone is anxious to achieve the highest perfection of his particular activity, and it is indicated herein that such perfection is *nārāyaṇa-smṛti*, for which everyone must endeavor his best. In other words, life should be molded in such a manner that one is able to progressively remember the Personality of Godhead in every step of life.

TEXT 7

प्रायेण मुनयो गजन्निवृत्ता विधिषेधतः ।
नैर्गुण्यस्था रमन्ते स्म गुणानुकथने हरेः ॥ ७ ॥

prāyeṇa munayo rājan
nivṛttā vidhi-ṣedhataḥ
nairguṇya-sthā ramante sma
guṇānukathane hareḥ

prāyeṇa—mainly; *munayaḥ*—all sages; *rājan*—O King; *nivṛttāḥ*—above; *vidhi*—regulative principles; *ṣedhataḥ*—from restrictions; *nairguṇya-sthāḥ*—transcendentally situated; *ramante*—take pleasure in; *sma*—distinctly; *guṇa-anukathane*—describing the glories; *hareḥ*—of the Lord.

TRANSLATION

O King Parīkṣit, mainly the topmost transcendentalists, who are above the regulative principles and restrictions, take pleasure in describing the glories of the Lord.

PURPORT

The topmost transcendentalist is a liberated soul and is therefore not within the purview of the regulative principles. A neophyte, who is intended to be promoted to the spiritual plane, is guided by the spiritual master under regulative principles. He may be compared to a patient who is treated by various restrictions under medical jurisdiction. Generally, liberated souls also take pleasure in describing the transcendental activities. As mentioned above, since Nārāyaṇa, Hari, the Personality of Godhead, is beyond the material creation, His form and attributes are not material. The topmost transcendentalists or the liberated souls realize Him by advanced experience of transcendental knowledge, and therefore they take pleasure in the discussion of the transcendental qualities of the Lord's pastimes. In the *Bhagavad-gītā* (4.9), the Personality of Godhead declares that His appearance and activities are all *divyam*, or transcendental. The common man, who is under the spell of material energy, takes it for granted that the Lord is like one of us, and therefore he refuses to accept the transcendental nature of the Lord's form, name, etc. The topmost transcendentalist is not interested in anything material, and his taking interest in the matter of the Lord's activities is definite proof that the Lord is not like one of us in the material world. In the Vedic literatures also, it is confirmed that the Supreme Lord is one, but that He is engaged in His transcendental pastimes in the company of His unalloyed devotees and that simultaneously He is present as the Supersoul, an expansion of Baladeva, in the heart of all living entities. Therefore, the highest perfection of transcendental realization is to take pleasure in hearing and describing the transcendental qualities of the Lord and not in merging into His impersonal Brahman existence, for which the impersonalist monist aspires. Real transcendental pleasure is realized in the glorification of the transcendental Lord, and not in the feeling of being situated in His impersonal feature. But there are also others who are not the topmost transcendentalists but are in a lower status, and who do not take pleasure in describing the transcendental activities of the Lord. Rather, they discuss such activities of the Lord formally with the aim of merging into His existence.

TEXT 8

इदं भागवतं नाम पुराणं ब्रह्मसम्मितम् ।
अधीतवान् द्वापरादौ पितुर्द्वैपायनादहम् ॥ ८ ॥

idaṁ bhāgavataṁ nāma
purāṇaṁ brahma-sammitam
adhītavān dvāparādau
pitur dvaipāyanād aham

idam—this; *bhāgavatam*—Śrīmad-Bhāgavatam; *nāma*—of the name; *purāṇam*—Vedic supplement; *brahma-sammitam*—approved as the essence of the *Vedas; adhītavān*—studied; *dvāpara-ādau*—at the end of the Dvāpara-yuga; *pituḥ*—from my father; *dvaipāyanāt*—Dvaipāyana Vyāsadeva; *aham*—myself.

TRANSLATION

At the end of the Dvāpara-yuga, I studied this great supplement of Vedic literature named Śrīmad-Bhāgavatam, which is equal to all the Vedas, from my father, Śrīla Dvaipāyana Vyāsadeva.

PURPORT

The statement made by Śrīla Śukadeva Gosvāmī that the topmost transcendentalist, who is beyond the jurisdiction of regulations and restrictions, mainly takes to the task of hearing about and glorifying the Personality of Godhead, is verified by his personal example. Śukadeva Gosvāmī, being a recognized liberated soul and the topmost transcendentalist, was accepted by all of the topmost sages present in the meeting during the last seven days of Mahārāja Parīkṣit. He cites from the example of his life that he himself was attracted by the transcendental activities of the Lord, and he studied *Śrīmad-Bhāgavatam* from his great father, Śrī Dvaipāyana Vyāsadeva. *Śrīmad-Bhāgavatam*, or, for that matter, any other scientific literature, cannot be studied at home by one's own intellectual capacity. Medical books of anatomy or physiology are available in the market, but no one can become a qualified medical practitioner simply by reading such books at home. One has to be admitted to the medical college and study the books under the guidance of learned professors. Similarly, *Śrīmad-Bhāgavatam, the postgraduate study of the science of Godhead,* can only be learned by studying it at the feet of a realized soul like Śrīla Vyāsadeva. Although Śukadeva Gosvāmī was a liberated soul from the very day of his birth, he still had to take lessons of *Śrīmad-Bhāgavatam* from his great father, Vyāsadeva, who compiled the *Śrīmad-Bhāgavatam* under the instruction of another great soul, Śrī Nārada Muni. Lord Śrī Caitanya Mahāprabhu instructed a learned *brāhmaṇa* to study *Śrīmad-Bhāgavatam* from a personal *bhāgavata*. *Śrīmad-Bhāgavatam* is based on the transcendental name, form, attributes, pastimes, entourage and variegatedness of the Supreme Person, and it is spoken by the incarnation of the Personality of Godhead, Śrīla Vyāsadeva. Pastimes of the Lord are executed in cooperation with His pure devotees, and consequently historical incidences are mentioned in this great literature because they are related to Kṛṣṇa. It is called *brahma-sammitam* because it is the sound representative of Lord Kṛṣṇa—like the *Bhagavad-gītā*. *Bhagavad-gītā* is the sound incarnation of the Lord because it is spoken by the Supreme Lord, and *Śrīmad-Bhāgavatam* is the sound representative of the Lord because it was spoken by the incarnation of the Lord about the activities of the Lord. As stated in the beginning of this book, it is the essence of the Vedic desire tree and the natural commentation on the *Brahma-sūtras*, the topmost philosophical thesis on the subject matter of Brahman. Vyāsadeva appeared at the end of Dvāpara-yuga as the son of Satyavatī, and therefore the word *dvāpara-ādau*, or "the beginning of Dvāpara-yuga," in this context means just prior to the beginning of the Kali-yuga. The logic of this statement, according to Śrīla Jīva Gosvāmī, is comparable to that of calling the upper portion of the tree the beginning. The root of the tree is the beginning of the tree, but in common knowledge the upper portion of the tree is first seen. In that way the end of the tree is accepted as its beginning.

TEXT 9

परिनिष्ठितोऽपि नैर्गुण्य उत्तमश्लोकलीलया ।
गृहीतचेता राजर्षे आख्यानं यदधीतवान् ॥ ९ ॥

*pariniṣṭhito 'pi nairguṇya
uttama-śloka-līlayā
gṛhīta-cetā rājarṣe
ākhyānaṁ yad adhītavān*

pariniṣṭhitaḥ—fully realized; *api*—in spite of; *nairguṇye*—in transcendence; *uttama*—enlightened; *śloka*—verse; *līlayā*—by the pastimes; *gṛhīta*—being attracted; *cetāḥ*—attention; *rājarṣe*—O saintly King; *ākhyānam*—delineation; *yat*—that; *adhītavān*—I have studied.

TRANSLATION

O saintly King, I was certainly situated perfectly in transcendence, yet I was still attracted by the delineation of the pastimes of the Lord, who is described by enlightened verses.

PURPORT

The Absolute Truth is realized as the impersonal Brahman at the first instance by philosophical speculation and later as the Supersoul by further progress of transcendental knowledge. But if, by the grace of the Lord, an impersonalist is enlightened by the superior statements of *Śrīmad-Bhāgavatam*, he is also converted into a transcendental devotee of the Personality of Godhead. With a poor fund of knowledge, we cannot adjust to the idea of the personality of the Absolute Truth, and the personal activities of the Lord are deplored by the less intelligent impersonalists; but reasons and arguments together with the transcendental process of approaching the Absolute Truth help even the staunch impersonalist to become attracted by the personal activities of the Lord. A person like Śukadeva Gosvāmī cannot be attracted by any mundane activity, but when such a devotee is convinced by a superior method, he is certainly attracted by the transcendental activities of the Lord. The Lord is transcendental, as are His activities. He is neither inactive nor impersonal.

TEXT 10

तदहं तेऽभिधास्यामि महापौरुषिको भवान् ।
यस्य श्रद्दधतामाशु स्यान्मुकुन्दे मतिः सती ॥१०॥

tad aham te 'bhidhāsyāmi
mahā-pauruṣiko bhavān
yasya śraddadhatām āśu
syān mukunde matiḥ satī

tat—that; *aham*—I; *te*—unto you; *abhidhāsyāmi*—shall recite;
mahā-pauruṣikaḥ—the most sincere devotee of Lord Kṛṣṇa; *bhavān*—
your good self; *yasya*—of which; *śraddadhatām*—of one who gives full
respect and attention; *āśu*—very soon; *syāt*—it so becomes; *mukunde*—
unto the Lord, who awards salvation; *matiḥ*—faith; *satī*—unflinching.

TRANSLATION

That very Śrīmad-Bhāgavatam I shall recite before you because
you are the most sincere devotee of Lord Kṛṣṇa. One who gives
full attention and respect to hearing Śrīmad-Bhāgavatam achieves
unflinching faith in the Supreme Lord, the giver of salvation.

PURPORT

Śrīmad-Bhāgavatam is recognized Vedic wisdom, and the system of
receiving Vedic knowledge is called *avaroha-panthā*, or the process of
receiving transcendental knowledge through bona fide disciplic succession. For advancement of material knowledge there is a need for personal
ability and researching aptitude, but in the case of spiritual knowledge,
all progress depends more or less on the mercy of the spiritual master.
The spiritual master must be satisfied with the disciple; only then is
knowledge automatically manifest before the student of spiritual science.
The process should not, however, be misunderstood to be something like
magical feats whereby the spiritual master acts like a magician and in-
jects spiritual knowledge into his disciple, as if surcharging him with an
electrical current. The bona fide spiritual master reasonably explains
everything to the disciple on the authorities of Vedic wisdom. The

disciple can receive such teachings not exactly intellectually, but by submissive inquiries and a service attitude. The idea is that both the spiritual master and the disciple must be bona fide. In this case, the spiritual master, Śukadeva Gosvāmī, is ready to recite exactly what he has learned from his great father Śrīla Vyāsadeva, and the disciple, Mahārāja Parīkṣit, is a great devotee of Lord Kṛṣṇa. A devotee of Lord Kṛṣṇa is he who believes sincerely that by becoming a devotee of the Lord one becomes fully equipped with everything spiritual. This teaching is imparted by the Lord Himself in the pages of the *Bhagavad-gītā*, in which it is clearly described that the Lord (Śrī Kṛṣṇa) is everything, and that to surrender unto Him solely and wholly makes one the most perfectly pious man. This unflinching faith in Lord Kṛṣṇa prepares one to become a student of *Śrīmad-Bhāgavatam*, and one who hears *Śrīmad-Bhāgavatam* from a devotee like Śukadeva Gosvāmī is sure to attain salvation at the end, as Mahārāja Parīkṣit did. The professional reciter of *Śrīmad-Bhāgavatam* and the pseudodevotees whose faith is based on one week's hearing are different from Śukadeva Gosvāmī and Mahārāja Parīkṣit. Śrīla Vyāsadeva explained *Śrīmad-Bhāgavatam* unto Śukadeva Gosvāmī from the very beginning of the *janmādy asya* verse, and so Śukadeva Gosvāmī also explained it to the King. Lord Kṛṣṇa is described as the Mahāpuruṣa in the *Śrīmad-Bhāgavatam* (Canto Eleven) in His devotional feature as Lord Śrī Caitanya Mahāprabhu. Śrī Caitanya Mahāprabhu is Lord Kṛṣṇa Himself in His devotional attitude, descended on earth to bestow special favors upon the fallen souls of this age of Kali. There are two verses particularly suitable to offer as prayers to this Mahāpuruṣa feature of Lord Kṛṣṇa.

> *dhyeyaṁ sadā paribhava-ghnam abhīṣṭa-dohaṁ*
> *tīrthāspadaṁ śiva-viriñci-nutaṁ śaraṇyam*
> *bhṛtyārti-haṁ praṇata-pāla bhavābdhi-potaṁ*
> *vande mahāpuruṣa te caraṇāravindam*

> *tyaktvā sudustyaja-surepsita-rājya-lakṣmīṁ*
> *dharmiṣṭha ārya-vacasā yad agād araṇyam*
> *māyā-mṛgaṁ dayitayepsitam anvadhāvad*
> *vande mahāpuruṣa te caraṇāravindam*
>   (*Bhāg.* 11.5.33–34)

In other words, *puruṣa* means the enjoyer, and *mahāpuruṣa* means the supreme enjoyer, or the Supreme Personality of Godhead Śrī Kṛṣṇa. One who deserves to approach the Supreme Lord Śrī Kṛṣṇa is called the *mahā-pauruṣika*. Anyone who hears *Śrīmad-Bhāgavatam* attentively from its bona fide reciter is sure to become a sincere devotee of the Lord, who is able to award liberation. There was none so attentive as Mahārāja Parīkṣit in the matter of hearing *Śrīmad-Bhāgavatam*, and there was none so qualified as Śukadeva Gosvāmī to recite the text of *Śrīmad-Bhāgavatam*. Therefore, anyone who follows in the footsteps of either the ideal reciter or the ideal hearer, Śukadeva Gosvāmī and Mahārāja Parīkṣit respectively, will undoubtedly attain salvation like them. Mahārāja Parīkṣit attained salvation by hearing only, and Śukadeva Gosvāmī attained salvation only by reciting. Recitation and hearing are two processes out of nine devotional activities, and by strenuously following the principles, either in all or by parts, one can attain the absolute plane. So the complete text of *Śrīmad-Bhāgavatam*, beginning with the *janmādy asya* verse up to the last one in the Twelfth Canto, was spoken by Śukadeva Gosvāmī for the attainment of salvation by Mahārāja Parīkṣit. In the *Padma Purāṇa*, it is mentioned that Gautama Muni advised Mahārāja Ambarīṣa to hear regularly *Śrīmad-Bhāgavatam* as it was recited by Śukadeva Gosvāmī, and herein it is confirmed that Mahārāja Ambarīṣa heard *Śrīmad-Bhāgavatam* from the very beginning to the end, as it was spoken by Śukadeva Gosvāmī. One who is actually interested in the *Bhāgavatam*, therefore, must not play with it by reading or hearing a portion from here and a portion from there; one must follow in the footsteps of great kings like Mahārāja Ambarīṣa or Mahārāja Parīkṣit and hear it from a bona fide representative of Śukadeva Gosvāmī.

TEXT 11

एतन्निर्विद्यमानानामिच्छतामकुतोभयम् ।
योगिनां नृप निर्णीतं हरेर्नामानुकीर्तनम् ॥११॥

etan nirvidyamānānām
icchatām akuto-bhayam
yoginām nṛpa nirṇitaṁ
harer nāmānukīrtanam

etat—it is; *nirvidyamānānām*—of those who are completely free from all material desires; *icchatām*—of those who are desirous of all sorts of material enjoyment; *akutaḥ-bhayam*—free from all doubts and fear; *yoginām*—of all who are self-satisfied; *nṛpa*—O King; *nirṇītam*—decided truth; *hareḥ*—of the Lord, Śrī Kṛṣṇa; *nāma*—holy name; *anu*—after someone, always; *kīrtanam*—chanting.

TRANSLATION

O King, constant chanting of the holy name of the Lord after the ways of the great authorities is the doubtless and fearless way of success for all, including those who are free from all material desires, those who are desirous of all material enjoyment, and also those who are self-satisfied by dint of transcendental knowledge.

PURPORT

In the previous verse, the great necessity for attaining attachment to Mukunda has been accredited. There are different types of persons who desire to attain success in different varieties of pursuits. Generally the persons are materialists who desire to enjoy the fullest extent of material gratification. Next to them are the transcendentalists, who have attained perfect knowledge about the nature of material enjoyment and thus are aloof from such an illusory way of life. More or less, they are satisfied in themselves by self-realization. Above them are the devotees of the Lord, who neither aspire to enjoy the material world nor desire to get out of it. They are after the satisfaction of the Lord, Śrī Kṛṣṇa. In other words, the devotees of the Lord do not want anything on their personal account. If the Lord desires, the devotees can accept all sorts of material facilities, and if the Lord does not desire this, the devotees can leave aside all sorts of facilities, even up to the limit of salvation. Nor are they self-satisfied, because they want the satisfaction of the Lord only. In this verse, Śrī Śukadeva Gosvāmī recommends the transcendental chanting of the holy name of the Lord. By offenseless chanting and hearing of the holy name of the Lord, one becomes acquainted with the transcendental form of the Lord, and then with the attributes of the Lord, and then with the transcendental nature of His pastimes, etc. Here it is mentioned that one should constantly chant the holy name of the Lord after hearing it from authorities. This means that hearing from the authorities is the first essential. Hearing of the holy name gradually promotes one to the stage of hearing about His form, about His attributes, His pastimes and so on, and thus the necessity of the chanting of His glories develops successively. This process is recommended not only for the successful execution of devotional service, but also even for those who are materially attached. According to Śrī Śukadeva Gosvāmī, this way of attaining success is an established fact, concluded not only by him, but also by all other previous ācāryas. Therefore, there is no need of further evidence. The process is recommended not only for the progressive students in different departments of ideological success, but also for those who are already successful in their achievement as fruitive workers, as philosophers or as devotees of the Lord.

Śrīla Jīva Gosvāmī instructs that chanting of the holy name of the Lord should be loudly done, and it should be performed offenselessly as well, as recommended in the *Padma Purāṇa*. One can deliver himself from the effects of all sins by surrendering himself unto the Lord. One can deliver himself from all offenses at the feet of the Lord by taking shelter of His holy name. But one cannot protect himself if one commits an offense at the feet of the holy name of the Lord. Such offenses are mentioned in the *Padma Purāṇa* as being ten in number. The first offense is to vilify the great devotees who have preached about the glories of the Lord. The second offense is to see the holy names of the Lord in terms of worldly distinction. The Lord is the proprietor of all the universes, and therefore He may be known in different places by different names, but that does not in any way qualify the fullness of the Lord. Any nomenclature which is meant for the Supreme Lord is as holy as the others because they are all meant for the Lord. Such holy names are as powerful as the Lord, and there is no bar for anyone in any part of the creation to chant and glorify the Lord by the particular name of the Lord as it is locally understood. They are all auspicious, and one should not distinguish such names of the Lord as material commodities. The third offense is to neglect the orders of the authorized ācāryas or spiritual masters. The fourth offense is to vilify scriptures or Vedic knowledge. The fifth offense is to define the holy name of the Lord in terms of one's mundane calculation. The holy name of the Lord is identical with the Lord Himself, and one should understand the holy name of the Lord to be nondifferent from Him. The sixth offense is to interpret the holy name. The Lord is not imaginary, nor is His holy name. There are persons with a poor fund of knowledge who think the Lord to be an imagination of the worshiper and therefore think His holy name to be imaginary. Such a chanter of the name of the Lord cannot achieve the desired success in the matter of chanting the holy name. The seventh offense is to commit sins intentionally on the strength of the holy name. In the scriptures it is said that one can be liberated from the effects of all sinful actions simply by chanting the holy name of the Lord. One who takes advantage of this transcendental method and continues to commit sins on the expectation of neutralizing the effects of sins by chanting the holy name of the Lord is the greatest offender at the feet of the holy name. Such an offender cannot purify himself by any recommended method of purification. In other words, one may be a sinful man before chanting the holy name of the Lord, but after taking shelter in the holy name of the Lord and becoming immune, one should strictly restrain oneself from committing sinful acts with a hope that his method of chanting the holy name will give him protection. The eighth offense is to consider the holy name of the Lord and His chanting method to be equal to some material auspicious activity. There are various kinds of good works for material benefits, but the holy name and His chanting are not mere auspicious holy services. Undoubtedly the holy name is holy service, but He should never be utilized for such purposes. Since the holy name and the Lord are of one and the same identity, one should not try to bring the holy name into the service of mankind. The idea is that the Supreme Lord is the supreme enjoyer. He is no one's servant or order supplier. Similarly, since the holy name of the Lord is identical with the Lord, one should not try to utilize the holy name for one's personal service.

The ninth offense is to instruct those who are not interested in chanting the holy name of the Lord about the transcendental nature of the holy name. If such instruction is imparted to an unwilling audience, the act is considered to be an offense at the feet of the holy name. The tenth offense is to become uninterested in the holy name of the Lord even after hearing of the transcendental nature of the holy name. The effect of chanting the holy name of the Lord is perceived by the chanter as liberation from the conception of false egoism. False egoism is exhibited by

thinking oneself to be the enjoyer of the world and thinking everything
in the world to be meant for the enjoyment of one's self only. The whole
materialistic world is moving under such false egoism of "I" and
"mine," but the factual effect of chanting the holy name is to become
free from such misconceptions.

TEXT 12

किं प्रमत्तस्य बहुभिः परोक्षैर्हायनैरिह ।
वरं मुहूर्तं विदितं घटते श्रेयसे यतः ॥१२॥

*kim pramattasya bahubhiḥ
parokṣair hāyanair iha
varam muhūrtam viditam
ghaṭate śreyase yataḥ*

kim—what is; *pramattasya*—of the bewildered; *bahubhiḥ*—by
many; *parokṣaiḥ*—inexperienced; *hāyanaiḥ*—years; *iha*—in this
world; *varam*—better; *muhūrtam*—a moment; *viditam*—conscious;
ghaṭate—one can try for; *śreyase*—in the matter of the supreme
interest; *yataḥ*—by that.

TRANSLATION

**What is the value of a prolonged life which is wasted, inex-
perienced by years in this world? Better a moment of full consciousness, because that gives one a start in searching after his
supreme interest.**

PURPORT

Śrīla Śukadeva Gosvāmī instructed Mahārāja Parīkṣit about the importance of the chanting of the holy name of the Lord by every progressive
gentleman. In order to encourage the King, who had only seven remaining days of life, Śrīla Śukadeva Gosvāmī asserted that there is no use in
living hundreds of years without any knowledge of the problems of
life—better to live for a moment with full consciousness of the supreme
interest to be fulfilled. The supreme interest of life is eternal, with full
knowledge and bliss. Those who are bewildered by the external features

of the material world and are engaged in the animal propensities of the
eat-drink-and-be-merry type of life are simply wasting their lives by the
unseen passing away of valuable years. We should know in perfect consciousness that human life is bestowed upon the conditioned soul to
achieve spiritual success, and the easiest possible procedure to attain this
end is to chant the holy name of the Lord. In the previous verse, we have
discussed this point to a certain extent, and we may further be enlightened on the different types of offenses committed unto the feet of
the holy name. Śrīla Jīva Gosvāmī Prabhu has quoted many passages
from authentic scriptures and has ably supported the statements in the
matter of offenses at the feet of the holy name. From *Viṣṇu-yāmala
Tantra*, Śrīla Jīva Gosvāmī has proven that one can be liberated from the
effects of all sins simply by chanting the holy name of the Lord. Quoting
from the *Mārkaṇḍeya Purāṇa*, Śrī Gosvāmījī says that one should
neither blaspheme the devotee of the Lord nor indulge in hearing others
who are engaged in belittling a devotee of the Lord. A devotee should try
to restrict the vilifier by cutting out his tongue, and being unable to do
so, one should commit suicide rather than hear the blaspheming of the
devotee of the Lord. The conclusion is that one should neither hear nor
allow vilification of a devotee of the Lord. As far as distinguishing the
Lord's holy name from the names of the demigods, the revealed scriptures disclose (Bg. 10.41) that all extraordinarily powerful beings are
but parts and parcels of the supreme energetic, Lord Kṛṣṇa. Except for
the Lord Himself, everyone is subordinate; no one is independent of the
Lord. Since no one is more powerful than or equal to the energy of the
Supreme Lord, no one's name can be as powerful as that of the Lord. By
chanting the Lord's holy name, one can derive all the stipulated energy
synchronized from all sources. Therefore, one should not equalize the
supreme holy name of the Lord with any other name. Brahmā, Śiva or
any other powerful god can never be equal to the Supreme Lord Viṣṇu.
The powerful holy name of the Lord can certainly deliver one from sinful effects, but one who desires to utilize this transcendental potency of
the holy name of the Lord in one's sinister activities is the most degraded
person in the world. Such persons are never excused by the Lord or by
any agent of the Lord. One should, therefore, utilize one's life in glorifying the Lord by all means, without any offense. Such activity of life, even
for a moment, is never to be compared to a prolonged life of ignorance,

like the lives of the tree and other living entities who may live for thousands of years without prosecuting spiritual advancement.

TEXT 13

खट्वाङ्गो नाम राजर्षिर्ज्ञात्वेयत्तामिहायुषः ।
मुहूर्तात्सर्वमुत्सृज्य गतवानभयं हरिम् ॥१३॥

khaṭvāṅgo nāma rājarṣir
jñātveyattām ihāyuṣaḥ
muhūrtāt sarvam utsṛjya
gatavān abhayaṁ harim

khaṭvāṅgaḥ—King Khaṭvāṅga; *nāma*—name; *rāja-ṛṣiḥ*—saintly king; *jñātvā*—by knowing; *iyattām*—duration; *iha*—in this world; *āyuṣaḥ*—of one's life; *muhūrtāt*—within only a moment; *sarvam*—everything; *utsṛjya*—leaving aside; *gatavān*—had undergone; *abhayam*—fully safe; *harim*—the Personality of Godhead.

TRANSLATION

The saintly King Khaṭvāṅga, after being informed that the duration of his life would be only a moment more, at once freed himself from all material activities and took shelter of the supreme safety, the Personality of Godhead.

PURPORT

A fully responsible man should always be conscious of the prime duty of the present human form of life. The activities to meet the immediate necessities of material life are not everything. One should always be alert in his duty for attainment of the best situation in the next life. Human life is meant for preparing ourselves for that prime duty. Mahārāja Khaṭvāṅga is mentioned herein as a saintly king because even within the responsibility of the state management, he was not at all forgetful of the prime duty of life. Such was the case with other *rājarṣis* (saintly kings), like Mahārāja Yudhiṣṭhira and Mahārāja Parīkṣit. They were all exemplary personalities on account of their being alert in discharging their prime duty. Mahārāja Khaṭvāṅga was invited by the demigods in the higher planets to fight demons, and as a king he fought the battles to the full satisfaction of the demigods. The demigods, being fully satisfied with him, wanted to give him some benediction for material enjoyment, but Mahārāja Khaṭvāṅga, being very much alert to his prime duty, inquired from the demigods about his remaining duration of life. This means that he was not as anxious to accumulate some material benediction from the demigods as he was to prepare himself for the next life. He was informed by the demigods, however, that his life would last only a moment longer. The king at once left the heavenly kingdom, which is always full of material enjoyment of the highest standard, and coming down to this earth, took ultimate shelter of the all-safe Personality of Godhead. He was successful in his great attempt and achieved liberation. This attempt, even for a moment, by the saintly king, was successful because he was always alert to his prime duty. Mahārāja Parīkṣit was thus encouraged by the great Śukadeva Gosvāmī, even though he had only seven days left in his life to execute the prime duty of hearing the glories of the Lord in the form of *Śrīmad-Bhāgavatam.* By the will of the Lord, Mahārāja Parīkṣit instantly met the great Śukadeva Gosvāmī, and the great treasure of spiritual success left by him is nicely mentioned in the *Śrīmad-Bhāgavatam.*

TEXT 14

तवाप्येतर्हि कौरव्य समाहं जीवितावधिः ।
उपकल्पय तत्सर्वं तावद्यत्साम्परायिकम् ॥१४॥

tavāpy etarhi kauravya
saptāhaṁ jīvitāvadhiḥ
upakalpaya tat sarvaṁ
tāvad yat sāmparāyikam

tava—your; *api*—also; *etarhi*—therefore; *kauravya*—O one born in the family of Kuru; *saptāham*—seven days; *jīvita*—duration of life; *avadhiḥ*—up to the limit of; *upakalpaya*—get them performed; *tat*—those; *sarvam*—all; *tāvat*—so long; *yat*—which are; *sāmparāyikam*—rituals for the next life.

TRANSLATION

Mahārāja Parīkṣit, now your duration of life is limited to seven more days, so during this time you can perform all those rituals which are needed for the best purpose of your next life.

PURPORT

Śukadeva Gosvāmī, after citing the example of Mahārāja Khaṭvāṅga, who prepared himself for the next life within a very short time, encouraged Mahārāja Parīkṣit by saying that since he still had seven days at his disposal, he could easily take advantage of the time to prepare himself for the next life. Indirectly, the Gosvāmī told Mahārāja Parīkṣit that he should take shelter of the sound representation of the Lord for the seven days still remaining in the duration of his life and thus get himself liberated. In other words, everyone can best prepare himself for the next life simply by hearing Śrīmad-Bhāgavatam, as it was recited by Śukadeva Gosvāmī to Mahārāja Parīkṣit. The rituals are not formal, but there are also some favorable conditions, which are required to be carried out, as instructed hereafter.

TEXT 15

अन्तकाले तु पुरुष आगते गतसाध्वसः ।
छिन्द्यादसङ्गशस्त्रेण स्पृहां देहेऽनु ये च तम् ॥१५॥

anta-kāle tu puruṣa
āgate gata-sādhvasaḥ
chindyād asaṅga-śastreṇa
spṛhāṁ dehe 'nu ye ca tam

anta-kāle—at the last stage of life; *tu*—but; *puruṣaḥ*—a person; *āgate*—having arrived; *gata-sādhvasaḥ*—without any fear of death; *chindyāt*—must cut off; *asaṅga*—nonattachment; *śastreṇa*—by the weapon of; *spṛhām*—all desires; *dehe*—in the matter of the material tabernacle; *anu*—pertaining; *ye*—all that; *ca*—also; *tam*—them.

TRANSLATION

At the last stage of one's life, one should be bold enough not to be afraid of death. But one must cut off all attachment to the material body and everything pertaining to it and all desires thereof.

PURPORT

The foolishness of gross materialism is that people think of making a permanent settlement in this world, although it is a settled fact that one has to give up everything here that has been created by valuable human energy. Great statesmen, scientists, philosophers, etc., who are foolish, without any information of the spirit soul, think that this life of a few years only is all in all and that there is nothing more after death. This poor fund of knowledge, even in the so-called learned circles of the world, is killing the vitality of human energy, and the awful result is being keenly felt. And yet the foolish materialistic men do not care about what is going to happen in the next life. The preliminary instruction in the *Bhagavad-gītā* is that one should know that the identity of the individual living entity is not lost even after the end of this present body, which is nothing but an outward dress only. As one changes an old garment, so the individual living being also changes his body, and this change of body is called death. Death is therefore a process of changing the body at the end of the duration of the present life. An intelligent person must be prepared for this and must try to have the best type of body in the next life. The best type of body is a spiritual body, which is obtained by those who go back to the kingdom of God or enter the realm of Brahman. In the second chapter of this canto, this matter will be broadly discussed, but as far as the change of body is concerned, one must prepare now for the next life. Foolish people attach more importance to the present temporary life, and thus the foolish leaders make appeals to the body and the bodily relations. The bodily relations extend not only to this body but also to the family members, wife, children, society, country and so many other things which end at the end of life. After death one forgets everything about the present bodily relations; we have a little experience of this at night when we go to sleep. While sleeping, we forget everything about this body and bodily relations, although this forgetfulness is a temporary situation for only a few hours. Death is nothing but sleeping for a few months in order to develop another term of bodily encagement, which we are awarded by the law of nature according to our aspiration. Therefore, one has only to change the aspiration during the course of this present body, and for this there is need of training in the current duration of human life. This training can be begun at any stage of life, or even a few seconds before death, but the usual procedure is for one to get the training from very early life, from the stage of *brahmacarya*, and gradually progress to the *gṛhastha*, *vānaprastha* and *sannyāsa* orders of life. The institution which gives such training is called *varṇāśrama-dharma*, or the system of *sanātana-dharma*, the best procedure for making the human life perfect. One is therefore required to give up the attachment to family or social or political life just at the age of fifty years, if not earlier, and the training in the *vānaprastha* and *sannyāsa-āśramas* is given for preparation of the next life. Foolish materialists, in the garb of leaders of the people in general, stick to family affairs without attempting to cut off relations with them, and thus they become victims of nature's law and get gross bodies again, according to their work. Such foolish leaders may have some respect from the people at the end of life, but that does not mean that such leaders will be immune to the natural laws under which everyone is tightly bound by the hands and feet. The best thing is, therefore, that everyone voluntarily give up family relations by transferring the attachment from family, society, country and everything thereof to the devotional service of the Lord. It is stated herein that one should give up all desires of family attachment. One must have a chance for better desires; otherwise there is no chance of giving up such morbid desires. Desire is the concomitant factor of the living entity. The living entity is eternal, and therefore his desires, which are natural for a living being, are also eternal. One cannot, therefore, stop desiring, but the subject matter for desires can be changed. So one must develop the desires for returning home, back to Godhead, and automatically the desires for material gain, material honor and material popularity will diminish in proportion to the development of devotional service. A living being is meant for service activities, and his desires are centered around such a service attitude. Beginning from the top executive head of the state down to the insignificant pauper in the street, all are rendering some sort of service to others. The perfection of such a ser-

vice attitude is only attained simply by transferring the desire of service
from matter to spirit, or from Satan to God.

TEXT 16

गृहात् प्रव्रजितो धीरः पुण्यतीर्थजलाप्लुतः ।
शुचौ विविक्त आसीनो विधिवत्कल्पितासने ॥१६॥

grhāt pravrajito dhīrah
puṇya-tīrtha-jalāplutah
śucau vivikta āsīno
vidhivat kalpitāsane

grhāt—from one's home; pravrajitah—having gone out; dhīrah—
self-controlled; puṇya—pious; tīrtha—sacred place; jala-āplutah—
fully washed; śucau—cleansed; vivikte—solitary; āsīnah—seated;
vidhivat—according to regulations; kalpita—having done; āsane—on a
sitting place.

TRANSLATION

One should leave home and practice self-control. In a sacred
place he should bathe regularly and sit down in a lonely place duly
sanctified.

PURPORT

To prepare oneself for the better next life, one must get out of one's
so-called home. The system of varṇāśrama-dharma, or sanātana-
dharma, prescribes retirement from family encumbrances as early as
possible after one has passed fifty years of age. Modern civilization is
based on family comforts, the highest standard of amenities, and
therefore after retirement everyone expects to live a very comfortable
life in a well-furnished home decorated with fine ladies and children,
without any desire to get out of such a comfortable home. High government officers and ministers stick to their prize posts until death, and they
neither dream nor desire to get out of homely comforts. Bound by such
hallucinations, materialistic men prepare various plans for a still more
comfortable life, but suddenly cruel death comes without mercy and

takes away the great planmaker against his desire, forcing him to give up
the present body for another body. Such a planmaker is thus forced to accept another body in one of the 8,400,000 species of life according to the
fruits of the work he has performed. In the next life, persons who are too
much attached to family comforts are generally awarded lower species of
life on account of sinful acts performed during a long duration of sinful
life, and thus all the energy of the human life is spoiled. In order to be
saved from the danger of spoiling the human form of life and being attached to unreal things, one must take warning of death at the age of
fifty, if not earlier. The principle is that one should take it for granted
that the death warning is already there, even prior to the attainment of
fifty years of age, and thus at any stage of life one should prepare himself
for a better next life. The system of the sanātana-dharma institution is
so made that the follower is trained for the better next life without any
chance that the human life will be spoiled. The holy places all over the
world are meant for the residential purposes of retired persons getting
ready for a better next life. Intelligent persons must go there at the end
of life, and for that matter, after fifty years of age, to live a life of spiritual regeneration for the sake of being freed from family attachment,
which is considered to be the shackle of material life. One is recommended to quit home just to get rid of material attachment because one
who sticks to family life until death cannot get rid of material attachment
and as long as one is materially attached one cannot understand spiritual
freedom. One should not, however, become self-complacent simply by
leaving home or by creating another home at the holy place, either law-
fully or unlawfully. Many persons leave home and go to such holy places,
but due to bad association, again become family men by illicit connection
with the opposite sex. The illusory energy of matter is so strong that one
is apt to be under such illusion at every stage of life, even after quitting
one's happy home. Therefore, it is essential that one practice self-control
by celibacy without the least desire for sex indulgence. For a man desiring to improve the condition of his existence, sex indulgence is considered suicidal, or even worse. Therefore, to live apart from family life
means to become self-controlled in regard to all sense desires, especially
sex desires. The method is that one should have a duly sanctified sitting
place made of straw, deerskin and carpet, and thus sitting on it one
should chant the holy name of the Lord without offense, as prescribed

above. The whole process is to drag the mind from material engagements
and fix it on the lotus feet of the Lord. This simple process alone will
help one advance to the highest stage of spiritual success.

TEXT 17

अभ्यसेन्मनसा शुद्धं त्रिवृद्ब्रह्माक्षरं परम् ।
मनो यच्छेज्जितश्वासो ब्रह्मबीजमविस्मरन् ॥१७॥

abhyasen manasā śuddham
trivṛd-brahmākṣaram param
mano yacchej jita-śvāso
brahma-bījam avismaran

abhyaset—one should practice; *manasā*—by the mind; *śuddham*—
sacred; *tri-vṛt*—composed of the three; *brahma-akṣaram*—transcendental letters; *param*—the supreme; *manaḥ*—mind; *yacchet*—get
under control; *jita-śvāsaḥ*—by regulating the breathing air; *brahma*—
absolute; *bījam*—seed; *avismaran*—without being forgotten.

TRANSLATION
After sitting in the above manner, make the mind remember the
three transcendental letters [a-u-m], and by regulating the
breathing process, control the mind so as not to forget the
transcendental seed.

PURPORT
Oṁkāra, or the *praṇava*, is the seed of transcendental realization, and
it is composed of the three transcendental letters *a-u-m*. By its chanting
by the mind, in conjunction with the breathing process, which is a transcendental but mechanical way of getting into trance, as devised by the
experience of great mystics, one is able to bring the mind, which is materially absorbed, under control. This is the way of changing the habit of
the mind. The mind is not to be killed. Mind or desire cannot be stopped,
but to develop a desire to function for spiritual realization, the quality of
engagement by the mind has to be changed. The mind is the pivot of the
active sense organs, and as such if the quality of thinking, feeling and

willing is changed, naturally the quality of actions by the instrumental senses will also change. *Oṁkāra* is the seed of all transcendental sound and it is only the transcendental sound which can bring about the desired change of the mind and the senses. Even a mentally deranged man can be cured by treatment of transcendental sound. In the *Bhagavad-gītā*, the *praṇava* (*oṁkāra*) has been accepted as the direct, literal representation of the Supreme Absolute Truth. One who is not able to chant directly the holy name of the Lord, as recommended above, can easily chant the *praṇava* (*oṁkāra*). This *oṁkāra* is a note of address, such as "O my Lord," just as *oṁ hari oṁ* means "O my Lord, the Supreme Personality of Godhead." As we have explained before, the Lord's holy name is identical with the Lord Himself. So also is *oṁkāra*. But persons who are unable to realize the transcendental personal form or name of the Lord on account of their imperfect senses (in other words, the neophytes) are trained to the practice of self-realization by this mechanical process of regulating the breathing function and simultaneously repeating the *praṇava* (*oṁkāra*) within the mind. As we have several times expressed, since the transcendental name, form, attributes, pastimes, etc., of the Personality of Godhead are impossible to understand with the present material senses, it is necessary that through the mind, the center of sensual activities, such transcendental realization be set into motion. The devotees directly fix their minds on the Person of the Absolute Truth. But one who is unable to accommodate such personal features of the Absolute is disciplined in impersonality to train the mind to make further progress.

TEXT 18

नियच्छेद्विषयेभ्योऽक्षान्मनसा बुद्धिसारथिः ।
मनः कर्मभिराक्षिप्तं शुभार्थे धारयेद्धिया ॥१८॥

> *niyacched viṣayebhyo 'kṣān*
> *manasā buddhi-sārathiḥ*
> *manaḥ karmabhir ākṣiptaṁ*
> *śubhārthe dhārayed dhiyā*

niyacchet—withdraw; *viṣayebhyaḥ*—from sense engagements; *akṣān*—the senses; *manasā*—by dint of the mind; *buddhi*—intelligence; *sārathiḥ*—driver; *manaḥ*—the mind; *karmabhiḥ*—by the fruitive work; *ākṣiptam*—being absorbed in; *śubha-arthe*—for the sake of the Lord; *dhārayet*—hold up; *dhiyā*—in full consciousness.

TRANSLATION

Gradually, as the mind becomes progressively spiritualized, withdraw it from sense activities, and by intelligence the senses will be controlled. The mind too absorbed in material activities can be engaged in the service of the Personality of Godhead and become fixed in full transcendental consciousness.

PURPORT

The first process of spiritualizing the mind by mechanical chanting of the *praṇava* (*oṁkāra*) and by control of the breathing system is technically called the mystic or yogic process of *prāṇāyāma*, or fully controlling the breathing air. The ultimate state of this *prāṇāyāma* system is to be fixed in trance, technically called *samādhi*. But experience has proven that even the *samādhi* stage also fails to control the materially absorbed mind. For example, the great mystic Viśvāmitra Muni, even in the stage of *samādhi*, became a victim of the senses and cohabited with Menakā. History has already recorded this. The mind, although ceasing to think of sensual activities at present, remembers past sensual activities from the subconscious status and thus disturbs one from cent percent engagement in self-realization. Therefore, Śukadeva Gosvāmī recommends the next step of assured policy, namely to fix one's mind in the service of the Personality of Godhead. Lord Śrī Kṛṣṇa, the Supreme Personality of Godhead, also recommends this direct process in the *Bhagavad-gītā* (6.47). Thus, the mind being spiritually cleansed, one should at once engage himself in the transcendental loving service of the Lord by the different devotional activities of hearing, chanting, etc. If performed under proper guidance, that is the surest path of progress, even for the disturbed mind.

TEXT 19

तत्रैकावयवं ध्यायेदव्युच्छिन्नेन चेतसा ।
मनो निर्विषयं युक्त्वा ततः किञ्चन न स्मरेत् ।
पदं तत्परमं विष्णोर्मनो यत्र प्रसीदति ॥१९॥

tatraikāvayavaṁ dhyāyed
avyucchinnena cetasā
mano nirviṣayaṁ yuktvā
tataḥ kiñcana na smaret
padaṁ tat paramaṁ viṣṇor
mano yatra prasīdati

tatra—thereafter; *eka*—one by one; *avayavam*—limbs of the body; *dhyāyet*—should be concentrated upon; *avyucchinnena*—without being deviated from the complete form; *cetasā*—by the mind; *manaḥ*—mind; *nirviṣayam*—without being contaminated by sense objects; *yuktvā*—being dovetailed; *tataḥ*—after that; *kiñcana*—anything; *na*—do not; *smaret*—think of; *padam*—personality; *tat*—that; *paramam*—Supreme; *viṣṇoḥ*—of Viṣṇu; *manaḥ*—the mind; *yatra*—whereupon; *prasīdati*—becomes reconciled.

TRANSLATION

Thereafter, you should meditate upon the limbs of Viṣṇu, one after another, without being deviated from the conception of the complete body. Thus the mind becomes free from all sense objects. There should be no other thing to be thought upon. Because the Supreme Personality of Godhead, Viṣṇu, is the Ultimate Truth, the mind becomes completely reconciled in Him only.

PURPORT

Foolish persons, bewildered by the external energy of Viṣṇu, do not know that the ultimate goal of the progressive search after happiness is to get in touch directly with Lord Viṣṇu, the Personality of Godhead. *Viṣṇu-tattva* is an unlimited expansion of different transcendental forms of the Personality of Godhead, and the supreme or original form of *viṣṇu-tattva* is Govinda, or Lord Kṛṣṇa, the supreme cause of all causes. Therefore, thinking of Viṣṇu or meditating upon the transcendental form of Viṣṇu, specifically upon Lord Kṛṣṇa, is the last word on the subject of meditation. This meditation may be begun from the lotus feet of the Lord. One should not, however, forget or be misled from the complete form of the Lord; thus one should practice thinking of the different parts of His transcendental body, one after another. Here in this verse, it is definitely assured that the Supreme Lord is not impersonal. He is a person, but His body is different from those of conditioned persons like us. Otherwise, meditation beginning from the *praṇava* (*oṁkāra*) up to the limbs of the personal body of Viṣṇu would not have been recommended by Śukadeva Gosvāmī for the attainment of complete spiritual perfection. The Viṣṇu forms of worship in great temples of India are not, therefore, arrangements of idol worship, as they are wrongly interpreted to be by a class of men with a poor fund of knowledge; rather, they are different spiritual centers of meditation on the transcendental limbs of the body of Viṣṇu. The worshipable Deity in the temple of Viṣṇu is identical with Lord Viṣṇu by the inconceivable potency of the Lord. Therefore, a neophyte's concentration or meditation upon the limbs of Viṣṇu in the temple, as contemplated in the revealed scriptures, is an easy opportunity for meditation for persons who are unable to sit down tightly at one place and then concentrate upon *praṇava oṁkāra* or the limbs of the body of Viṣṇu, as recommended herein by Śukadeva Gosvāmī, the great authority. The common man can benefit more by meditating on the form of Viṣṇu in the temple than on the *oṁkāra*, the spiritual combination of *a-u-m* as explained before. There is no difference between *oṁkāra* and the forms of Viṣṇu, but persons unacquainted with the science of Absolute Truth try to create dissension by differentiating between the forms of Viṣṇu and that of *oṁkāra*. Here it is indicated that the Viṣṇu form is the ultimate goal of meditation, and as such it is better to concentrate upon the forms of Viṣṇu than on impersonal *oṁkāra*. The latter process is also more difficult than the former.

TEXT 20

रजस्तमोभ्यामाक्षिप्तं विमूढं मन आत्मनः ।
यच्छेद्धारणया धीरो हन्ति या तत्कृतं मलम् ॥२०॥

rajas-tamobhyām ākṣiptaṁ
vimūḍhaṁ mana ātmanaḥ
yacched dhāraṇayā dhīro
hanti yā tat-kṛtaṁ malam

rajaḥ—the passionate mode of nature; *tamobhyām*—as well as by the ignorant mode of material nature; *ākṣiptam*—agitated; *vimūḍham*—bewildered; *manaḥ*—the mind; *ātmanaḥ*—of one's own; *yacchet*—get it rectified; *dhāraṇayā*—by conception (of Viṣṇu); *dhīraḥ*—the pacified; *hanti*—destroys; *yā*—all those; *tat-kṛtam*—done by them; *malam*—dirty things.

TRANSLATION

One's mind is always agitated by the passionate mode of material nature and bewildered by the ignorant mode of nature. But one can rectify such conceptions by the relation of Viṣṇu and thus become pacified by cleansing the dirty things created by them.

PURPORT

Persons generally conducted by the modes of passion and ignorance cannot be bona fide candidates for being situated in the transcendental stage of God realization. Only persons conducted by the mode of goodness can have the knowledge of the Supreme Truth. Effects of the modes of passion and ignorance are manifested by too much hankering after wealth and women. And those who are too much after wealth and women can rectify their leanings only by constant remembrance of Viṣṇu in His potential impersonal feature. Generally the impersonalists or monists are influenced by the modes of passion and ignorance. Such impersonalists think of themselves as liberated souls, but they have no knowledge of the transcendental personal feature of the Absolute Truth. Actually they are impure in heart on account of being devoid of knowledge of the personal feature of the Absolute. In the *Bhagavad-gītā*, it is said that after many hundreds of births, the impersonal philosopher surrenders unto the Personality of Godhead. To acquire such a qualification of God realization in the personal feature, the neophyte impersonalist is given a chance to realize the relation of the Lord in everything by the philosophy of pantheism.

Pantheism in its higher status does not permit the student to form an impersonal conception of the Absolute Truth, but it extends the conception of the Absolute Truth into the field of the so-called material energy. Everything created by the material energy can be dovetailed with the

Absolute by an attitude of service, which is the essential part of living
energy. The pure devotee of the Lord knows the art of converting everything into its spiritual existence by this service attitude, and only in that
devotional way can the theory of pantheism be perfected.

TEXT 21

यस्यां सन्धार्यमाणायां योगिनो भक्तिलक्षणः ।
आशु सम्पद्यते योग आश्रयं भद्रमीक्षतः ॥२१॥

*yasyāṁ sandhāryamāṇāyāṁ
yogino bhakti-lakṣaṇaḥ
āśu sampadyate yoga
āśrayaṁ bhadram īkṣataḥ*

yasyām—by such systematic remembrance; *sandhāryamāṇāyām*—
and thus being fixed in the habit of; *yoginaḥ*—the mystics; *bhakti-
lakṣaṇaḥ*—being practiced to the devotional system; *āśu*—very soon;
sampadyate—attains success; *yogaḥ*—connection by devotional service;
āśrayam—under the shelter of; *bhadram*—the all-good; *īkṣataḥ*—
which seeing that.

TRANSLATION

**O King, by this system of remembrance and by being fixed in the
habit of seeing the all-good personal conception of the Lord,
one can very soon attain devotional service to the Lord, under His
direct shelter.**

PURPORT

Success of mystic performances is achieved only by the help of the devotional attitude. Pantheism, or the system of feeling the presence of the
Almighty everywhere, is a sort of training of the mind to become accustomed to the devotional conception, and it is this devotional attitude
of the mystic that makes possible the successful termination of such
mystic attempts. One is not, however, elevated to such a successful status
without the tinge of mixture in devotional service. The devotional atmosphere created by pantheistic vision develops into devotional service

in later days, and that is the only benefit for the impersonalist. It is confirmed in the *Bhagavad-gītā* (12.5) that the impersonal way of self-realization is more troublesome because it reaches the goal in an indirect way, although the impersonalist also becomes obsessed with the personal feature of the Lord after a long time.

TEXT 22

राजोवाच

यथा सन्धार्यते ब्रह्मन् धारणा यत्र सम्मता ।
यादृशी वा हरेदाशु पुरुषस्य मनोमलम् ॥२२॥

rājovāca
yathā sandhāryate brahman
dhāraṇā yatra sammatā
yādṛśī vā hared āśu
puruṣasya mano-malam

rājā uvāca—the fortunate King said; *yathā*—as it is; *sandhāryate*—the conception is made; *brahman*—O *brāhmaṇa*; *dhāraṇā*—conception; *yatra*—where and how; *sammatā*—in a summary; *yādṛśī*—the way by which; *vā*—or; *haret*—extricated; *āśu*—without delay; *puruṣasya*—of a person; *manaḥ*—of the mind; *malam*—dirty things.

TRANSLATION

The fortunate King Parīkṣit, inquiring further, said: O *brāhmaṇa*, please describe in full detail how and where the mind has to be applied and how the conception can be fixed so that the dirty things in a person's mind can be removed.

PURPORT

The dirty things in the heart of a conditioned soul are the root cause of all troubles for him. A conditioned soul is surrounded by the manifold miseries of material existence, but on account of his gross ignorance he is unable to remove the troubles due to dirty things in the heart, accumulated during the long prison life in the material world. He is actually meant to serve the will of the Supreme Lord, but on account of the dirty things in the heart, he likes to serve his concocted desires. These desires, instead of giving him any peace of mind, create new problems and thus bind him to the cycle of repeated birth and death. These dirty things of fruitive work and empiric philosophy can be removed only by association with the Supreme Lord. The Lord, being omnipotent, can offer His association by His inconceivable potencies. Thus persons who are unable to pin their faith on the personal feature of the Absolute are given a chance to associate with His *virāṭ-rūpa*, or the cosmic impersonal feature of the Lord. The cosmic impersonal feature of the Lord is a feature of His unlimited potencies. Since the potent and potencies are identical, even the conception of His impersonal cosmic feature helps the conditioned soul to associate with the Lord indirectly and thus gradually rise to the stage of personal contact.

Mahārāja Parīkṣit was already directly connected with the personal feature of the Lord Śrī Kṛṣṇa, and as such he had no need to inquire from Śukadeva Gosvāmī about where and how to apply the mind in the impersonal *virāṭ-rūpa* of the Lord. But he inquired after a detailed description of the matter for the benefit of others, who are unable to conceive of the transcendental personal feature of the Lord as the form of eternity, knowledge and bliss. The nondevotee class of men cannot think of the personal feature of the Lord. Because of their poor fund of knowledge, the personal form of the Lord, like Rāma or Kṛṣṇa, is completely revolting to them. They have a poor estimation of the potency of the Lord. In the *Bhagavad-gītā* (9.11) it is explained by the Lord Himself that people with a poor fund of knowledge deride the supreme personality of the Lord, taking Him to be a common man. Such men are ignorant of the inconceivable potency of the Lord. By the inconceivable potency of the Lord, He can move in human society or any other society of living beings and yet remain the same omnipotent Lord, without deviating in the slightest from His transcendental position. So, for the benefit of men who are unable to accept the Lord in His personal eternal form, Mahārāja Parīkṣit inquired from Śukadeva Gosvāmī how to fix the mind on Him in the beginning, and the Gosvāmī replied in detail as follows.

TEXT 23

श्रीशुक उवाच

जितासनो जितश्वासो जितसङ्गो जितेन्द्रियः ।
स्थूले भगवतो रूपे मनः सन्धारयेद्धिया ॥२३॥

śrī-śuka uvāca
jitāsano jita-śvāso
jita-saṅgo jitendriyaḥ
sthūle bhagavato rūpe
manaḥ sandhārayed dhiyā

śrī-śukaḥ uvāca—Śukadeva Gosvāmī said; *jita-āsanaḥ*—controlled sitting posture; *jita-śvāsaḥ*—controlled breathing process; *jita-saṅgaḥ*—controlled association; *jita-indriyaḥ*—controlled senses; *sthūle*—in the gross matter; *bhagavataḥ*—unto the Personality of Godhead; *rūpe*—in the feature of; *manaḥ*—the mind; *sandhārayet*—must apply; *dhiyā*—by intelligence.

TRANSLATION

Śukadeva Gosvāmī answered: One should control the sitting posture, regulate the breathing process by the yogic prāṇāyāma and thus control the mind and senses and with intelligence apply the mind to the gross potencies of the Lord [called the virāṭ-rūpa].

PURPORT

The materially absorbed mind of the conditioned soul does not allow him to transcend the limit of the bodily conception of self, and thus the *yoga* system for meditation (controlling the sitting posture and breathing process and fixing the mind upon the Supreme) is prescribed in order to mold the character of the gross materialist. Unless such materialists are able to cleanse the materially absorbed mind, it is impossible for them to concentrate upon thoughts of transcendence. And to do so one may fix one's mind on the gross material or external feature of the Lord. The different parts of the gigantic form of the Lord are described in the following verses. The materialistic men are very anxious to have some mystic powers as a result of such a controlling process, but the real purpose of yogic regulations is to eradicate the accumulated dirty things like lust, anger, avarice and all such material contaminations. If the mystic *yogī* is diverted by the accompanying feats of mystic control, then his mission of yogic success is a failure, because the ultimate aim is God realization. He is therefore recommended to fix his gross materialistic mind by a different conception and thus realize the potency of the Lord. As soon as the potencies are understood to be instrumental manifestations of the transcendence, one automatically advances to the next step, and gradually the stage of full realization becomes possible for him.

TEXT 24

विशेषस्तस्य देहोऽयं स्थविष्ठश्च स्थवीयसाम् ।
यत्रेदं व्यज्यते विश्वं भूतं भव्यं भवच्च सत् ॥२४॥

viśeṣas tasya deho 'yaṁ
sthaviṣṭhaś ca sthavīyasām
yatredaṁ vyajyate viśvaṁ
bhūtaṁ bhavyaṁ bhavac ca sat

viśeṣaḥ—personal; *tasya*—His; *dehaḥ*—body; *ayam*—this; *sthaviṣṭhaḥ*—grossly material; *ca*—and; *sthavīyasām*—of all matter; *yatra*—wherein; *idam*—all these phenomena; *vyajyate*—is experienced; *viśvam*—universe; *bhūtam*—past; *bhavyam*—future; *bhavat*—present; *ca*—and; *sat*—resultant.

TRANSLATION

This gigantic manifestation of the phenomenal material world as a whole is the personal body of the Absolute Truth, wherein the universal resultant past, present and future of material time is experienced.

PURPORT

Anything, either material or spiritual, is but an expansion of the energy of the Supreme Personality of Godhead, and as stated in the

Bhagavad-gītā (13.13), the omnipotent Lord has His transcendental eyes, heads and other bodily parts distributed everywhere. He can see, hear, touch or manifest Himself anywhere and everywhere, for He is present everywhere as the Supersoul of all infinitesimal souls, although He has His particular abode in the absolute world. The relative world is also His phenomenal representation because it is nothing but an expansion of His transcendental energy. Although He is in His abode, His energy is distributed everywhere, just as the sun is localized as well as expanded everywhere, since the rays of the sun, being nondifferent from the sun, are accepted as expansions of the sun disc. In the *Viṣṇu Purāṇa* (1.22.52) it is said that as fire expands its rays and heat from one place, similarly the Supreme Spirit, the Personality of Godhead, expands Himself by His manifold energy everywhere and anywhere. The phenomenal manifestation of the gigantic universe is only a part of His *virāṭ* body. Less intelligent men cannot conceive of the transcendental all-spiritual form of the Lord, but they are astounded by His different energies, just as the aborigines are struck with wonder by the manifestation of lightning, a gigantic mountain or a hugely expanded banyan tree. The aborigines praise the strength of the tiger and the elephant because of their superior energy and strength. The *asuras* cannot recognize the existence of the Lord, although there are vivid descriptions of the Lord in the revealed scriptures, although the Lord incarnates and exhibits His uncommon strength and energy, and although He is accepted as the Supreme Personality of Godhead by learned scholars and saints like Vyāsadeva, Nārada, Asita and Devala in the past and by Arjuna in the *Bhāgavad-gītā*, as also by the *ācāryas* like Śaṅkara, Rāmānuja, Madhva and Lord Śrī Caitanya in the modern age. The *asuras* do not accept any evidential proof from the revealed scriptures, nor do they recognize the authority of the great *ācāryas*. They want to see with their own eyes at once. Therefore they can see the gigantic body of the Lord as *virāṭ*, which will answer their challenge, and since they are accustomed to paying homage to superior material strength like that of the tiger, elephant and lightning, they can offer respect to the *virāṭ-rūpa*. Lord Kṛṣṇa, by the request of Arjuna, exhibited His *virāṭ-rūpa* for the *asuras*. A pure devotee of the Lord, being unaccustomed to looking into such a mundane gigantic form of the Lord, requires special vision for the purpose. The Lord, therefore, favored Arjuna with special vision for looking into His *virāṭ-*

rūpa, which is described in the Eleventh Chapter of the *Bhagavad-gītā*. This *virāṭ-rūpa* of the Lord was especially manifested, not for the benefit of Arjuna, but for that unintelligent class of men who accept anyone and everyone as an incarnation of the Lord and so mislead the general mass of people. For them, the indication is that one should ask the cheap incarnation to exhibit his *virāṭ-rūpa* and thus be established as an incarnation. The *virāṭ-rūpa* manifestation of the Lord is simultaneously a challenge to the atheist and a favor for the *asuras*, who can think of the Lord as *virāṭ* and thus gradually cleanse the dirty things from their hearts in order to become qualified to actually see the transcendental form of the Lord in the near future. This is a favor of the all-merciful Lord to the atheists and the gross materialists.

TEXT 25

अण्डकोशे शरीरेऽस्मिन् सप्तावरणसंयुते ।
वैराजः पुरुषो योऽसौ भगवान् धारणाश्रयः ॥२५॥

*aṇḍa-kośe śarīre 'smin
saptāvaraṇa-saṁyute
vairājaḥ puruṣo yo 'sau
bhagavān dhāraṇāśrayaḥ*

aṇḍa-kośe—within the universal shell; *śarīre*—in the body of; *asmin*—this; *sapta*—sevenfold; *āvaraṇa*—coverings; *saṁyute*—having so done; *vairājaḥ*—the gigantic universal; *puruṣaḥ*—form of the Lord; *yaḥ*—that; *asau*—He; *bhagavān*—the Personality of Godhead; *dhāraṇā*—conception; *āśrayaḥ*—object of.

TRANSLATION

The gigantic universal form of the Personality of Godhead, within the body of the universal shell, which is covered by seven-fold material elements, is the subject for the virāṭ conception.

PURPORT

Simultaneously, the Lord has multifarious other forms, and all of them are identical with the original fountainhead form of the Lord, Śrī

Kṛṣṇa. In the *Bhagavad-gītā*, it has been proven that the original
transcendental and eternal form of the Lord is Śrī Kṛṣṇa, the Absolute
Personality of Godhead, but by His inconceivable internal potency,
ātma-māyā, He can expand Himself by multifarious forms and incarnations simultaneously, without being diminished in His full potency. He is
complete, and although innumerable complete forms emanate from Him,
He is still complete, without any loss. That is His spiritual or internal
potency. In the Eleventh Chapter of the *Bhagavad-gītā*, the Personality
of Godhead, Lord Kṛṣṇa, manifested His *virāṭ-rūpa* just to convince the
less intelligent class of men, who cannot conceive of the Lord as appearing just like a human being, that He factually has the potency of His
claim to be the Supreme Absolute Person without any rival or superior.
Materialistic men can think, although very imperfectly, of the huge universal space, comprehending an innumerable number of planets as big as
the sun. They can see only the circular sky overhead, without any information that this universe, as well as many other hundreds of thousands
of universes, are each covered by sevenfold material coverings of water,
fire, air, sky, ego, noumenon and material nature, just like a huge football, pumped and covered, floating on the water of the Causal Ocean,
wherein the Lord is lying as Mahā-Viṣṇu. All the universes in seed are
emanating from the breathing of the Mahā-Viṣṇu, who is but part of a
partial expansion of the Lord, and all the universes presided over by the
Brahmās vanish when the Mahā-Viṣṇu withdraws His great breath. In
this way, the material worlds are being created and vanished by the
supreme will of the Lord. The poor foolish materialist can just imagine
how ignorantly he puts forward an insignificant creature to become His
rival incarnation, simply on the allegations of a dying man. The *virāṭ-
rūpa* was particularly exhibited by the Lord just to give lessons to such
foolish men, so that one can accept a person as the incarnation of Godhead only if such a person is able to exhibit such a *virāṭ-rūpa* as Lord
Kṛṣṇa did. The materialistic person may concentrate his mind upon the
virāṭ or gigantic form of the Lord in his own interest and as recommended by Śukadeva Gosvāmī, but he must be on his guard not to be
misled by pretenders who claim to be the identical person as Lord Kṛṣṇa
but are not able to act like Him or exhibit the *virāṭ-rūpa*, comprehending
the whole of the universe.

TEXT 26

पातालमेतस्य हि पादमूलं
पठन्ति पार्ष्णिप्रपदे रसातलम् ।
महातलं विश्वसृजोऽथ गुल्फौ
तलातलं वै पुरुषस्य जङ्घे ॥२६॥

pātālam etasya hi pāda-mūlaṁ
paṭhanti pārṣṇi-prapade rasātalam
mahātalaṁ viśva-sṛjo 'tha gulphau
talātalaṁ vai puruṣasya jaṅghe

pātālam—the planets at the bottom of the universe; *etasya*—of His; *hi*—exactly; *pāda-mūlam*—soles of the feet; *paṭhanti*—they study it; *pārṣṇi*—the heels; *prapade*—the toes; *rasātalam*—the planets named Rasātala; *mahātalam*—the planets named Mahātala; *viśva-sṛjaḥ*—of the creator of the universe; *atha*—thus; *gulphau*—the ankles; *talātalam*—the planets named Talātala; *vai*—as they are; *puruṣasya*—of the gigantic person; *jaṅghe*—the shanks.

TRANSLATION

Persons who have realized it have studied that the planets known as Pātāla constitute the bottoms of the feet of the universal Lord, and the heels and the toes are the Rasātala planets. The ankles are the Mahātala planets, and His shanks constitute the Talātala planets.

PURPORT

Outside the bodily existence of the Supreme Personality of Godhead, the manifested cosmic existence has no reality. Everything and anything of the manifested world rests on Him, as confirmed in the *Bhagavad-gītā* (9.4), but that does not imply that everything and anything in the vision of a materialist is the Supreme Personality. The conception of the universal form of the Lord gives a chance to the materialist to think of the Supreme Lord, but the materialist must know for certain that his visualization of the world in a spirit of lording over it is not God realization.

The materialistic view of exploitation of the material resources is occa-
sioned by the illusion of the external energy of the Lord, and as such, if
anyone wants to realize the Supreme Truth by conceiving of the universal form of the Lord, he must cultivate the service attitude. Unless the
service attitude is revived, the conception of virāṭ realization will have
very little effect on the seer. The transcendental Lord, in any conception
of His form, is never a part of the material creation. He keeps His identity as Supreme Spirit in all circumstances and is never affected by the
three material qualities, for everything material is contaminated. The
Lord always exists by His internal energy.

The universe is divided into fourteen planetary systems. Seven planetary systems, called Bhūr, Bhuvar, Svar, Mahar, Janas, Tapas and Satya,
are upward planetary systems, one above the other. There are also seven
planetary systems downward, known as Atala, Vitala, Sutala, Talātala,
Mahātala, Rasātala and Pātāla, gradually, one below the other. In this
verse, the description begins from the bottom because it is in the line of
devotion that the Lord's bodily description should begin from His feet.
Śukadeva Gosvāmī is a recognized devotee of the Lord, and he is exactly
correct in the description.

TEXT 27

द्वे जानुनी सुतलं विश्वमूर्ते-
रूरुद्वयं वितलं चातलं च ।
महीतलं तज्जघनं महीपते
नभस्तलं नाभिसरो गृणन्ति ॥२७॥

dve jānunī sutalaṁ viśva-mūrter
ūru-dvayaṁ vitalaṁ cātalaṁ ca
mahītalaṁ taj-jaghanaṁ mahīpate
nabhastalaṁ nābhi-saro gṛṇanti

dve—two; *jānunī*—two knees; *sutalam*—the planetary system named
Sutala; *viśva-mūrteḥ*—of the universal form; *ūru-dvayam*—the two
thighs; *vitalam*—the planetary system named Vitala; *ca*—also;
atalam—the planets named Atala; *ca*—and; *mahītalam*—the planetary
system named Mahītala; *tat*—of that; *jaghanam*—the hips; *mahīpate*—

O King; *nabhastalam*—outer space; *nābhi-saraḥ*—the depression of the navel; *gṛṇanti*—they take it so.

TRANSLATION

The knees of the universal form are the planetary system of the name Sutala, and the two thighs are the Vitala and Atala planetary systems. The hips are Mahītala, and outer space is the depression of His navel.

TEXT 28

उरःस्थलं   ज्योतिरनीकमस्य
    ग्रीवा   महर्वदनं   वै   जनोऽस्य ।
तपो   वराटीं   विदुरादिपुंसः
    सत्यं   तु   शीर्षाणि   सहस्रशीर्ष्णः ॥२८॥

urah-sthalaṁ jyotir-anīkam asya
    grīvā mahar vadanam vai jano 'sya
tapo varāṭīṁ vidur ādi-puṁsaḥ
    satyaṁ tu śīrṣāṇi sahasra-śīrṣṇaḥ

urah—high; *sthalam*—place (the chest); *jyotiḥ-anīkam*—the luminary planets; *asya*—of Him; *grīvā*—the neck; *mahaḥ*—the planetary system above the luminaries; *vadanam*—mouth; *vai*—exactly; *janaḥ*—the planetary system above Mahar; *asya*—of Him; *tapaḥ*—the planetary system above the Janas; *varāṭīm*—forehead; *viduḥ*—is known; *ādi*—the original; *puṁsaḥ*—personality; *satyam*—the topmost planetary system; *tu*—but; *śīrṣāṇi*—the head; *sahasra*—one thousand; *śīrṣṇaḥ*—one with heads.

TRANSLATION

The chest of the Original Personality of the gigantic form is the luminary planetary system, His neck is the Mahar planets, His mouth is the Janas planets, and His forehead is the Tapas planetary system. The topmost planetary system, known as Satyaloka, is the head of He who has one thousand heads.

PURPORT

The effulgent luminary planets like the sun and the moon are situated almost in the midplace of the universe, and as such they are to be known as the chest of the original gigantic form of the Lord. And above the luminary planets, called also the heavenly places of the universal directorate demigods, are the Mahar, Janas and Tapas planetary systems, and, above all, the Satyaloka planetary system, where the chief directors of the modes of material nature reside, namely Viṣṇu, Brahmā and Śiva. This Viṣṇu is known as the Kṣīrodakaśāyī Viṣṇu, and He acts as the Supersoul in every living being. There are innumerable universes floating on the Causal Ocean, and in each of them the representation of the *virāṭ* form of the Lord is there along with innumerable suns, moons, heavenly demigods, Brahmās, Viṣṇus and Śivas, all of them situated in one part of the inconceivable potency of Lord Kṛṣṇa, as stated in the *Bhagavad-gītā* (10.42).

TEXT 29

इन्द्रादयो   बाहव   आहुरुस्राः
कर्णौ दिशः श्रोत्रमसुष्य शब्दः ।
नासत्यदस्रौ   परमस्य   नासे
घ्राणोऽस्य गन्धो मुखमग्निरिद्धः ॥२९॥

indrādayo bāhava āhur usrāḥ
karṇau diśaḥ śrotram amuṣya śabdaḥ
nāsatya-dasrau paramasya nāse
ghrāṇo 'sya gandho mukham agnir iddhaḥ

indra-ādayaḥ—demigods headed by the heavenly king, Indra; *bāhavaḥ*—arms; *āhuḥ*—are called; *usrāḥ*—the demigods; *karṇau*—the ears; *diśaḥ*—the four directions; *śrotram*—the sense of hearing; *amuṣya*—of the Lord; *śabdaḥ*—sound; *nāsatya-dasrau*—the demigods known as the Aśvinī-kumāras; *paramasya*—of the Supreme; *nāse*—nostrils; *ghrāṇaḥ*—the sense of smell; *asya*—of Him; *gandhaḥ*—fragrance; *mukham*—the mouth; *agniḥ*—fire; *iddhaḥ*—blazing.

TRANSLATION

His arms are the demigods headed by Indra, the ten directional sides are His ears, and physical sound is His sense of hearing. His nostrils are the two Aśvinī-kumāras, and material fragrance is His sense of smell. His mouth is the blazing fire.

PURPORT

The description of the gigantic form of the Personality of Godhead made in the Eleventh Chapter of the *Bhagavad-gītā* is further explained here in the *Śrīmad-Bhāgavatam*. The description in the *Bhagavad-gītā* (11.30) runs as follows: "O Viṣṇu, I see You devouring all people in Your blazing mouths and covering all the universe by Your immeasurable rays. Scorching the worlds, You are manifest." In that way, *Śrīmad-Bhāgavatam* is the postgraduate study for the student of the *Bhagavad-gītā*. Both of them are the science of Kṛṣṇa, the Absolute Truth, and so they are interdependent.

The conception of the *virāṭ-puruṣa*, or the gigantic form of the Supreme Lord, is said to include all the dominating demigods as well as the dominated living beings. Even the minutest part of a living being is controlled by the empowered agency of the Lord. Since the demigods are included in the gigantic form of the Lord, worship of the Lord, whether in His gigantic material conception or in His eternal transcendental form as Lord Śrī Kṛṣṇa, also appeases the demigods and all the other parts and parcels, as much as watering the root of a tree distributes energy to all of the tree's other parts. Consequently, for a materialist also, worship of the universal gigantic form of the Lord leads one to the right path. One need not risk being misled by approaching many demigods for fulfillment of different desires. The real entity is the Lord Himself, and all others are imaginary, for everything is included in Him only.

TEXT 30

द्यौरक्षिणी   चक्षुरभूत्पतङ्गः

पक्ष्माणि विष्णोरहनी उभे च ।

तद्भ्रूविजृम्भः   परमेष्ठिधिष्ण्य-

मापोऽस्य तालू रस एव जिह्वा ॥३०॥

dyaur akṣiṇī cakṣur abhūt pataṅgaḥ
pakṣmāṇi viṣṇor ahanī ubhe ca
tad-bhrū-vijṛmbhaḥ parameṣṭhi-dhiṣṇyam
āpo 'sya tālū rasa eva jihvā

dyauḥ—the sphere of outer space; *akṣiṇī*—the eyeballs; *cakṣuḥ*—of eyes (senses); *abhūt*—it so became; *pataṅgaḥ*—the sun; *pakṣmāṇi*—eyelids; *viṣṇoḥ*—of the Personality of Godhead, Śrī Viṣṇu; *ahanī*—day and night; *ubhe*—both; *ca*—and; *tat*—His; *bhrū*—eyebrows; *vijṛmbhaḥ*—movements; *parameṣṭhi*—the supreme entity (Brahmā); *dhiṣṇyam*—post; *āpaḥ*—Varuṇa, the director of water; *asya*—His; *tālū*—palate; *rasaḥ*—juice; *eva*—certainly; *jihvā*—the tongue.

TRANSLATION

The sphere of outer space constitutes His eyepits, and the eyeball is the sun as the power of seeing. His eyelids are both the day and night, and in the movements of His eyebrows, the Brahmā and similar supreme personalities reside. His palate is the director of water, Varuṇa, and the juice or essence of everything is His tongue.

PURPORT

To common sense the description in this verse appears to be somewhat contradictory because sometimes the sun has been described as the eyeball and sometimes as the outer space sphere. But there is no room for common sense in the injunctions of the *śāstras*. We must accept the description of the *śāstras* and concentrate more on the form of the *virāṭ-rūpa* than on common sense. Common sense is always imperfect, whereas the description in the *śāstras* is always perfect and complete. If there is any incongruity, it is due to our imperfection and not the *śāstras'*. That is the method of approaching Vedic wisdom.

TEXT 31

छन्दांस्यनन्तस्य शिरो गृणन्ति
दंष्ट्रा यमः स्नेहकला द्विजानि ।
हासो जनोन्मादकरी च माया
दुरन्तसर्गो यदपाङ्गमोक्षः ॥३१॥

chandāṁsy anantasya śiro gṛṇanti
daṁṣṭrā yamaḥ sneha-kalā dvijāni
hāso janonmāda-karī ca māyā
duranta-sargo yad-apāṅga-mokṣaḥ

chandāṁsi—the Vedic hymns; *anantasya*—of the Supreme; *śiraḥ*—the cerebral passage; *gṛṇanti*—they say; *daṁṣṭrāḥ*—the jaws of teeth; *yamaḥ*—Yamarāja, the director of sinners; *sneha-kalāḥ*—the art of affection; *dvijāni*—the set of teeth; *hāsaḥ*—smile; *jana-unmāda-karī*—the most alluring; *ca*—also; *māyā*—illusory energy; *duranta*—insurpassable; *sargaḥ*—the material creation; *yat-apāṅga*—whose glance; *mokṣaḥ*—casting over.

TRANSLATION

They say that the Vedic hymns are the cerebral passage of the Lord, and His jaws of teeth are Yama, god of death, who punishes the sinners. The art of affection is His set of teeth, and the most alluring illusory material energy is His smile. This great ocean of material creation is but the casting of His glance over us.

PURPORT

According to Vedic assertion, this material creation is the result of the Lord's casting a glance over the material energy, which is described herein as the most alluring illusory energy. The conditioned souls who are allured by such materialism should know that the material temporary creation is simply an imitation of the reality and that those who are captivated by such alluring glances of the Lord are put under the direction of the controller of sinners called Yamarāja. The Lord smiles affectionately, displaying His teeth. The intelligent person who can grasp these truths about the Lord becomes a soul fully surrendered unto Him.

TEXT 32

श्रीडोत्तरौष्ठोऽधर एव लोभो
धर्मः स्तनोऽधर्मपथोऽस्य पृष्ठम् ।
कस्तस्य मेढ्रं वृषणौ च मित्रौ
कुक्षिः समुद्रा गिरयोऽस्थिसङ्घाः ॥३२॥

vrīḍottaraüṣṭho 'dhara eva lobho
dharmaḥ stano 'dharma-patho 'sya pṛṣṭham
kas tasya meḍhraṁ vṛṣaṇau ca mitrau
kukṣiḥ samudrā girayo 'sthi-saṅghāḥ

vrīḍa—modesty; *uttara*—upper; *oṣṭha*—lip; *adharaḥ*—chin; *eva*—certainly; *lobhaḥ*—hankering; *dharmaḥ*—religion; *stanaḥ*—breast; *adharma*—irreligion; *pathaḥ*—way; *asya*—His; *pṛṣṭham*—back; *kaḥ*—Brahmā; *tasya*—His; *meḍhram*—genitals; *vṛṣaṇau*—testicles; *ca*—also; *mitrau*—the Mitrā-varuṇas; *kukṣiḥ*—waist; *samudrāḥ*—the oceans; *girayaḥ*—the hills; *asthi*—bones; *saṅghāḥ*—stack.

TRANSLATION

Modesty is the upper portion of His lips, hankering is His chin, religion is the breast of the Lord, and irreligion is His back. Brahmājī, who generates all living beings in the material world, is His genitals, and the Mitrā-varuṇas are His two testicles. The ocean is His waist, and the hills and mountains are the stacks of His bones.

PURPORT

The Supreme Lord is not impersonal, as misconceived by less intelligent thinkers. Rather, He is the Supreme Person, as confirmed in all authentic Vedic literatures. But His personality is different from what we can conceive. It is stated here that Brahmājī acts as His genitals and that the Mitrā-varuṇas are His two testicles. This means that as a person He is complete with all bodily organs, but they are of different types with different potencies. When the Lord is described as impersonal, therefore, it should be understood that His personality is not exactly the type of personality found within our imperfect speculation. One can, however, worship the Lord even by seeing the hills and mountains or the ocean and the sky as different parts and parcels of the gigantic body of the Lord, the *virāṭ-puruṣa*. The *virāṭ-rūpa*, as exhibited by Lord Kṛṣṇa to Arjuna, is a challenge to the unbelievers.

TEXT 33

नद्योऽस्य नाड्योऽथ तनूरुहाणि
महीरुहा   विश्वतनोर्नृपेन्द्र ।
अनन्तवीर्यः श्वसितं मातरिश्वा
गतिर्वयः   कर्म   गुणप्रवाहः ॥३३॥

nadyo 'sya nādyo 'tha tanū-ruhāṇi
mahī-ruhā viśva-tanor nṛpendra
ananta-vīryaḥ śvasitaṁ mātariśvā
gatir vayaḥ karma guṇa-pravāhaḥ

nadyaḥ—the rivers; *asya*—of Him; *nāḍyaḥ*—veins; *atha*—and thereafter; *tanū-ruhāṇi*—hairs on the body; *mahī-ruhāḥ*—the plants and trees; *viśva-tanoḥ*—of the universal form; *nṛpa-indra*—O King; *ananta-vīryaḥ*—of the omnipotent; *śvasitam*—breathing; *mātariśvā*—air; *gatiḥ*—movement; *vayaḥ*—passing ages; *karma*—activity; *guṇa-pravāhaḥ*—reactions of the modes of nature.

TRANSLATION

O King, the rivers are the veins of the gigantic body, the trees are the hairs of His body, and the omnipotent air is His breath. The passing ages are His movements, and His activities are the reactions of the three modes of material nature.

PURPORT

The Personality of Godhead is not a dead stone, nor is He inactive, as is poorly thought by some schools. He moves with the progress of time, and therefore He knows all about the past and future, along with His present activities. There is nothing unknown to Him. The conditioned souls are driven by the reactions of the modes of material nature, which are the activities of the Lord. As stated in the *Bhagavad-gītā* (7.12), the modes of nature act under His direction only, and as such no natural functions are blind or automatic. The power behind the activities is the supervision of the Lord, and thus the Lord is never inactive as is wrongly conceived. The *Vedas* say that the Supreme Lord has nothing to do personally, as is always the case with superiors, but everything is done by His direction. As it is said, not a blade of grass moves without His sanction. In the *Brahma-saṁhitā* (5.48), it is said that all the universes and the heads of them (the Brahmās) exist only for the duration of His breathing period. The same is confirmed here. The air on which the universes and the planets within the universes exist is nothing but a bit of the breath of the unchallengeable *virāṭ-puruṣa*. So even by studying the rivers, trees, air and passing ages, one can conceive of the Personality of Godhead without being misled by the formless conception of the Lord. In the *Bhagavad-gītā* (12.5) it is stated that those who are much inclined to the formless conception of the Supreme Truth are more troubled than those who can intelligently conceive of the personal form.

TEXT 34

ईशस्य केशान् विदुरम्बुवाहान्
वासस्तु सन्ध्यां कुरुवर्य भूम्नः ।
अव्यक्तमाहुर्हृदयं   मनश्च
स चन्द्रमाः सर्वविकारकोशः ॥३४॥

īśasya keśān vidur ambuvāhān
vāsas tu sandhyāṁ kuru-varya bhūmnaḥ
avyaktam āhur hṛdayaṁ manaś ca
sa candramāḥ sarva-vikāra-kośaḥ

īśasya—of the supreme controller; *keśān*—hairs on the head; *viduḥ*—you may know it from me; *ambu-vāhān*—the clouds which carry water; *vāsaḥ tu*—the dress; *sandhyām*—termination of day and night; *kuru-varya*—O best of the Kurus; *bhūmnaḥ*—of the Almighty; *avyaktam*—the prime cause of material creation; *āhuḥ*—it is said; *hṛdayam*—intelligence; *manaḥ ca*—and the mind; *saḥ*—He; *candramāḥ*—the moon; *sarva-vikāra-kośaḥ*—the reservoir of all changes.

TRANSLATION

O best amongst the Kurus, the clouds which carry water are the hairs on His head, the terminations of days or nights are His dress,

and the supreme cause of material creation is His intelligence. His
mind is the moon, the reservoir of all changes.

TEXT 35

विज्ञानशक्ति   महिमामनन्ति
सर्वात्मनोऽन्तःकरणं   गिरित्रम् ।
अश्वाश्वतर्युष्ट्रगजा   नखानि
सर्वे मृगाः पशवः श्रोणिदेशे ॥३५॥

vijñāna-śaktim mahim āmananti
sarvātmano 'ntaḥ-karaṇam giritram
aśvāśvatary-uṣṭra-gajā nakhāni
sarve mṛgāḥ paśavaḥ śroṇi-deśe

vijñāna-śaktim—consciousness; *mahim*—the principle of matter;
āmananti—they call it so; *sarva-ātmanaḥ*—of the omnipresent; *antaḥ-
karaṇam*—ego; *giritram*—Rudra (Śiva); *aśva*—horse; *aśvatari*—mule;
uṣṭra—camel; *gajāḥ*—elephant; *nakhāni*—nails; *sarve*—all other;
mṛgāḥ—stags; *paśavaḥ*—quadrupeds; *śroṇi-deśe*—on the region of the
belt.

TRANSLATION

The principle of matter [mahat-tattva] is the consciousness of
the omnipresent Lord, as asserted by the experts, and Rudradeva is
His ego. The horse, mule, camel and elephant are His nails, and
wild animals and all quadrupeds are situated in the belt zone of the
Lord.

TEXT 36

वयांसि   तद्व्याकरणं   विचित्रं
मनुर्मनीषा   मनुजो   निवासः ।
गन्धर्वविद्याधरचारणाप्सरः
स्वरस्मृतीरसुरानीकवीर्यः ॥३६॥

vayāṁsi tad-vyākaraṇaṁ vicitram
manur manīṣā manujo nivāsaḥ

gandharva-vidyādhara-cāraṇāpsaraḥ
svara-smṛtīr asurānīka-vīryaḥ

vayāṁsi—varieties of birds; *tat-vyākaraṇam*—vocables; *vicitram*—artistic; *manuḥ*—the father of mankind; *manīṣā*—thoughts; *manujaḥ*—mankind (the sons of Manu); *nivāsaḥ*—residence; *gandharva*—the human beings named Gandharvas; *vidyādhara*—the Vidyādharas; *cāraṇa*—the Cāraṇas; *apsaraḥ*—the angels; *svara*—musical rhythm; *smṛtīḥ*—remembrance; *asura-anīka*—the demoniac soldiers; *vīryaḥ*—prowess.

TRANSLATION

Varieties of birds are indications of His masterful artistic sense. Manu, the father of mankind, is the emblem of His standard intelligence, and humanity is His residence. The celestial species of human beings, like the Gandharvas, Vidyādharas, Cāraṇas and angels, all represent His musical rhythm, and the demoniac soldiers are representations of His wonderful prowess.

PURPORT

The aesthetic sense of the Lord is manifested in the artistic, colorful creation of varieties of birds like the peacock, parrot and cuckoo. The celestial species of human beings, like the Gandharvas and Vidyādharas, can sing wonderfully and can entice even the minds of the heavenly demigods. Their musical rhythm represents the musical sense of the Lord. How then can He be impersonal? His musical taste, artistic sense and standard intelligence, which is never fallible, are different signs of His supreme personality. The *Manu-saṁhitā* is the standard lawbook for humanity, and every human being is advised to follow this great book of social knowledge. Human society is the residential quarters for the Lord. This means that the human being is meant for God realization and association with God. This life is a chance for the conditioned soul to regain his eternal God consciousness and thus fulfill the mission of life. Mahārāja Prahlāda is the right type of representative of the Lord in the family of *asuras*. None of the living beings is away from the Lord's gigantic body. Each and every one has a particular duty in relation to the supreme body. Disruption in the matter of discharging the specific duty assigned to each and every living being is the cause of disharmony between one living being and another, but when the relation is reestablished in relation with the Supreme Lord, there is complete unity between all living beings, even up to the limit of the wild animals and human society. Lord Caitanya Mahāprabhu displayed this living unity in the jungle of Madhya Pradesh, where even the tigers, elephants and many other ferocious animals perfectly cooperated in glorifying the Supreme Lord. That is the way to peace and amity all over the world.

TEXT 37

ब्रह्माननं क्षत्रभुजो महात्मा

विड्ठुरुरङ्घ्रिश्रितकृष्णवर्णः ।

नानाभिधाभीज्यगणोपपन्नो

द्रव्यात्मकः कर्म वितानयोगः ॥३७॥

brahmānanaṁ kṣatra-bhujo mahātmā
viḍ ūrur aṅghri-śrita-kṛṣṇa-varṇaḥ
nānābhidhābhījya-gaṇopapanno
dravyātmakaḥ karma vitāna-yogaḥ

brahma—the *brāhmaṇas; ānanam*—the face; *kṣatra*—the *kṣatriyas; bhujaḥ*—the arms; *mahātmā*—the *virāṭ-puruṣa; viṭ*—the *vaiśyas; ūruḥ*—the thighs; *aṅghri-śrita*—under the protection of His feet; *kṛṣṇa-varṇaḥ*—the *śūdras; nānā*—various; *abhidhā*—by names; *abhījya-gaṇa*—the demigods; *upapannaḥ*—being overtaken; *dravya-ātmakaḥ*—with feasible goods; *karma*—activities; *vitāna-yogaḥ* —performances of sacrifice.

TRANSLATION

The virāṭ-puruṣa's face is the brāhmaṇas, His arms are the kṣatriyas, His thighs are the vaiśyas, and the śūdras are under the protection of His feet. All the worshipable demigods are also overtaken by Him, and it is the duty of everyone to perform sacrifices with feasible goods to appease the Lord.

PURPORT

Monotheism is practically suggested here. Offering sacrifices to many demigods under different names is mentioned in the Vedic literatures, but the suggestion made in this verse is that all those varieties of demigods are included in the form of the Supreme Personality of Godhead; they are only the parts and parcels of the original whole. Similarly, the divisions of the orders of human society, namely the *brāhmaṇas* (the intelligent class), the *kṣatriyas* (the administrators), the *vaiśyas* (the mercantile community) and the *śūdras* (the laborer class), are all included in the body of the Supreme. As such, sacrifice by every one of them in terms of pleasing the Supreme by feasible goods is recommended. Generally, the sacrifice is offered with clarified butter and grains, but with the progress of time, human society has produced varieties of goods by transforming materials supplied by God's material nature. Human society, therefore, *must learn to offer sacrifices not only with clarified butter, but also with other manufactured goods in the propagation of the Lord's glory, and that will bring about perfection in human society.* The intelligent class of men, or *brāhmaṇas*, may give direction for such sacrifices in consultation with the previous *ācāryas*; the administrators may give all facilities to perform such sacrifices; the *vaiśya* class or mercantile community, who produce such goods, may offer them for sacrifice; and the *śūdra* class may offer their manual labor for the successful termination of such sacrifice. Thus by the cooperation of all classes of human beings, the sacrifice recommended in this age, namely the sacrifice of congregational chanting of the holy name of the Lord, may be executed for the common welfare of all the people of the world.

TEXT 38

इयानसावीश्वरविग्रहस्य
य: सन्निवेश: कथितो मया ते ।
सन्धार्यतेऽस्मिन् वपुषि स्थविष्ठे
मन: खबुद्ध्या न यतोऽस्ति किञ्चित् ॥३८॥

iyān asāv īśvara-vigrahasya
yaḥ sanniveśaḥ kathito mayā te

sandhāryate 'smin vapuṣi sthaviṣṭhe
manaḥ sva-buddhyā na yato 'sti kiñcit

iyān—all these; *asau*—that; *īśvara*—Supreme Lord; *vigrahasya*—of
the form; *yaḥ*—whatsoever; *sanniveśaḥ*—as they are located;
kathitaḥ—explained; *mayā*—by me; *te*—unto you; *sandhāryate*—one
may concentrate; *asmin*—in this; *vapuṣi*—form of *virāṭ*; *sthaviṣṭhe*—in
the gross; *manaḥ*—mind; *sva-buddhyā*—by one's intelligence; *na*—
not; *yataḥ*—beyond Him; *asti*—there is; *kiñcit*—anything else.

TRANSLATION

I have thus explained to you the gross material gigantic conception of the Personality of Godhead. One who seriously desires
liberation concentrates his mind on this form of the Lord, because
there is nothing more than this in the material world.

PURPORT

In the *Bhagavad-gītā* (9.10), the Supreme Personality of Godhead has
verily explained that the material nature is only an order-carrying agent
of His. She is one of the different potencies of the Lord, and she acts
under His direction only. As the supreme transcendental Lord, He
simply casts a glance over the material principle, and thus the agitation
of matter begins, and the resultant actions are manifested one after
another by six kinds of gradual differentiations. All material creation is
moving in that way, and thus it appears and disappears in due course.

Less intelligent persons with a poor fund of knowledge cannot accommodate the thought of this inconceivable potency of the Lord Śrī Kṛṣṇa,
by which He appears just like a human being (Bg. 9.11). His appearance
in the material world as one of us is also His causeless mercy upon the
fallen souls. He is transcendental to all material conceptions, but by His
unbounded mercy upon His pure devotees, He comes down and
manifests Himself as the Personality of Godhead. Materialistic philosophers and scientists are too much engrossed with atomic energy and the
gigantic situation of the universal form, and they offer respect more
seriously to the external phenomenal feature of material manifestations
than to the noumenal principle of spiritual existence. The transcendental

form of the Lord is beyond the jurisdiction of such materialistic activities, and it is very difficult to conceive that the Lord can be simultaneously localized and all-pervasive, because the materialistic philosophers and scientists think of everything in terms of their own experience. Because they are unable to accept the personal feature of the Supreme Lord, the Lord is kind enough to demonstrate the *virāṭ* feature of His transcendental form, and herein Śrīla Śukadeva Gosvāmī has vividly described this form of the Lord. He concludes that there is nothing beyond this gigantic feature of the Lord. None of the materialistic thoughtful men can go beyond this conception of the gigantic form. The minds of the materialistic men are flickering and constantly changing from one aspect to another. Therefore, one is advised to think of the Lord by thinking of any part of His gigantic body, and by one's intelligence only one can think of Him in any manifestation of the material world—the forest, the hill, the ocean, the man, the animal, the demigod, the bird, the beast or anything else. Each and every item of the material manifestation entails a part of the body of the gigantic form, and thus the flickering mind can be fixed in the Lord only and nothing else. This process of concentrating on the different bodily parts of the Lord will gradually diminish the demoniac challenge of godlessness and bring about gradual development of devotional service to the Lord. Everything being a part and parcel of the Complete Whole, the neophyte student will gradually realize the hymns of *Īśopaniṣad* which state that the Supreme Lord is everywhere, and thus he will learn the art of not committing any offense to the body of the Lord. This sense of God-mindedness will diminish one's pride in challenging the existence of God. Thus one can learn to show respect to everything, for all things are parts and parcels of the supreme body.

TEXT 39

स   सर्वधीवृत्त्यनुभूतसर्वं
         आत्मा   यथा   स्वप्नजनेक्षितैकः ।
तं   सत्यमानन्दनिधिं   भजेत
         नान्यत्र सज्जेद् यत आत्मपातः ॥३९॥

sa sarva-dhī-vṛtty-anubhūta-sarva
ātmā yathā svapna-janekṣitaikaḥ
taṁ satyam ānanda-nidhiṁ bhajeta
nānyatra sajjed yata ātma-pātaḥ

saḥ—He (the Supreme Person); *sarva-dhī-vṛtti*—the process of
realization by all sorts of intelligence; *anubhūta*—cognizant; *sarve*—
everyone; *ātmā*—the Supersoul; *yathā*—as much as; *svapna-jana*—a
person dreaming; *īkṣita*—seen by; *ekaḥ*—one and the same; *tam*—unto
Him; *satyam*—the Supreme Truth; *ānanda-nidhim*—the ocean of bliss;
bhajeta—must one worship; *na*—never; *anyatra*—anything else; *sajjet*
—be attached; *yataḥ*—whereby; *ātma-pātaḥ*—degradation of oneself.

TRANSLATION

One should concentrate his mind upon the Supreme Personality
of Godhead, who alone distributes Himself in so many manifestations just as ordinary persons create thousands of manifestations
in dreams. One must concentrate the mind on Him, the only all-
blissful Absolute Truth. Otherwise one will be misled and will
cause his own degradation.

PURPORT

In this verse, the process of devotional service is indicated by the great
Gosvāmī, Śrīla Śukadeva. He tries to impress upon us that instead of
diverting our attention to several branches of self-realization, we should
concentrate upon the Supreme Personality of Godhead as the supreme
object of realization, worship and devotion. Self-realization is, as it were,
offering a fight for eternal life against the material struggle for existence, and therefore by the illusory grace of the external energy, the *yogī*
or the devotee is faced with many allurements which can entangle a great
fighter again in the bondage of material existence. A *yogī* can attain
miraculous successes in material achievements, such as *aṇimā* and
laghimā, by which one can become more minute than the minutest or
lighter than the lightest, or in the ordinary sense, one may achieve material benedictions in the shape of wealth and women. But one is warned
against such allurements because entanglement again in such illusory

pleasure means degradation of the self and further imprisonment in the material world. By this warning, one should follow one's vigilant intelligence only.

The Supreme Lord is one, and His expansions are various. He is therefore the Supersoul of everything. When a man sees anything, he must know that his seeing is secondary and the Lord's seeing is primary. One cannot see anything without the Lord's having first seen it. That is the instruction of the *Vedas* and the *Upaniṣads*. So whatever we see or do, the Supersoul of all acts of seeing or doing is the Lord. This theory of simultaneous oneness and difference between the individual soul and the Supersoul is propounded by Lord Śrī Caitanya Mahāprabhu as the philosophy of *acintya-bhedābheda-tattva*. The *virāṭ-rūpa*, or the gigantic feature of the Supreme Lord, includes everything materially manifested, and therefore the *virāṭ* or gigantic feature of the Lord is the Supersoul of all living and nonliving entities. But the *virāṭ-rūpa* is also the manifestation of Nārāyaṇa or Viṣṇu, and going further on and on one will eventually see that Lord Kṛṣṇa is the ultimate Supersoul of everything that be. The conclusion is that one should unhesitatingly become a worshiper of Lord Kṛṣṇa, or, for that matter, His plenary expansion Nārāyaṇa, and none else. In the Vedic hymns, it is clearly said that first of all Nārāyaṇa cast a glance over matter and thus there was creation. Before creation, there was neither Brahmā nor Śiva, and what to speak of others. Śrīpāda Śaṅkarācārya has definitely accepted this, that Nārāyaṇa is beyond the material creation and that all others are within the material creation. The whole material creation, therefore, is one with and different from Nārāyaṇa, simultaneously, and this supports the *acintya-bhedābheda-tattva* philosophy of Lord Śrī Caitanya Mahāprabhu. Being an emanation from the glancing potency of Nārāyaṇa, the whole material creation is nondifferent from Him. But because it is the effect of His external energy (*bahiraṅgā māyā*) and is aloof from the internal potency (*ātma-māyā*), the whole material creation is different from Him at the same time. The example given in this verse very nicely is that of the dreaming man. The dreaming man creates many things in his dream, and thus he himself becomes the entangled seer of the dream and is also affected by the consequences. This material creation is also exactly a dreamlike creation of the Lord, but He, being the transcendental Supersoul, is neither entangled nor affected by the reactions of such a dreamlike creation. He is always in His transcendental position, but essentially He is everything, and nothing is apart from Him. As a part of Him, one should therefore concentrate on Him only, without deviation; otherwise one is sure to be overcome by the potencies of the material creation, one after another. It is confirmed in the *Bhagavad-gītā* (9.7) as follows:

> *sarva-bhūtāni kaunteya*
> *prakṛtiṁ yānti māmikām*
> *kalpa-kṣaye punas tāni*
> *kalpādau visṛjāmy aham*

"O son of Kuntī, at the end of the millennium every material manifestation enters into My nature, and at the beginning of another millennium, by My potency, I again create."

The human life, however, is an opportunity to get out of this repetition of creation and annihilation. It is a means whereby one may escape the Lord's external potency and enter into His internal potency.

Thus end the Bhaktivedanta purports of the Second Canto, First Chapter, of the Śrīmad-Bhāgavatam, *entitled "The First Step in God Realization."*

CHAPTER TWO

The Lord in the Heart

TEXT 1

श्रीशुक उवाच

एवं पुरा धारणयात्मयोनि-
र्नष्टां स्मृतिं प्रत्यवरुध्य तुष्टात् ।
तथा ससर्जेदममोघदृष्टि-
र्यथाप्ययात् प्राग् व्यवसायबुद्धिः ॥ १ ॥

śrī-śuka uvāca
evaṁ purā dhāraṇayātma-yonir
naṣṭāṁ smṛtiṁ pratyavarudhya tuṣṭāt
tathā sasarjedam amogha-dṛṣṭir
yathāpyayāt prāg vyavasāya-buddhiḥ

śrī-śukaḥ uvāca—Śrī Śukadeva Gosvāmī said; evam—just in the same way; purā—prior to the manifestation of the cosmos; dhāraṇayā—by such a conception; ātma-yoniḥ—of Brahmājī; naṣṭām—lost; smṛtim—remembrance; pratyavarudhya—by regaining consciousness; tuṣṭāt—because of appeasing the Lord; tathā—thereafter; sasarja—created; idam—this material world; amogha-dṛṣṭiḥ—one who has attained clear vision; yathā—as; apyayāt—created; prāk—as formerly; vyavasāya—ascertained; buddhiḥ—intelligence.

TRANSLATION

Śrī Śukadeva Gosvāmī said: Formerly, prior to the manifestation of the cosmos, Lord Brahmā, by meditating on the virāṭ-rūpa, regained his lost consciousness by appeasing the Lord. Thus he was able to rebuild the creation as it was before.

PURPORT

The example cited herein of Śrī Brahmājī is one of forgetfulness. Brahmājī is the incarnation of one of the mundane attributes of the Lord. Being the incarnation of the passion mode of material nature, he is empowered by the Lord to generate the beautiful material manifestation. Yet due to his being one of the numerous living entities, he is apt to forget the art of his creative energy. This forgetfulness of the living being—beginning from Brahmā down to the lowest insignificant ant—is a tendency which can be counteracted by meditation on the *virāṭ-rūpa* of the Lord. This chance is available in the human form of life, and if a human being follows the instruction of *Śrīmad-Bhāgavatam* and begins to meditate upon the *virāṭ-rūpa*, then revival of his pure consciousness and counteraction of the tendency to forget his eternal relationship with the Lord can follow simultaneously. And as soon as this forgetfulness is removed, the *vyavasāya-buddhi*, as mentioned here and in the *Bhagavad-gītā* (2.41), follows at once. This ascertained knowledge of the living being leads to loving service to the Lord, which the living being requires. The kingdom of God is unlimited; therefore the number of the assisting hands of the Lord is also unlimited. The *Bhagavad-gītā* (13.14) asserts that the Lord has His hands, legs, eyes and mouths in every nook and corner of His creation. This means that the expansions of differentiated parts and parcels, called *jīvas* or living entities, are assisting hands of the Lord, and all of them are meant for rendering a particular pattern of service to the Lord. The conditioned soul, even in the position of a Brahmā, forgets this by the influence of illusory, material energy generated out of false egoism. One can counteract such false egoism by invoking God consciousness. Liberation means getting out of the slumber of forgetfulness and becoming situated in the real loving service of the Lord, as exemplified in the case of Brahmā. The service of Brahmā is the sample of service in liberation distinguished from the so-called altruistic services full of mistakes and forgetfulness. Liberation is never inaction, but service without human mistakes.

TEXT 2

शाब्दस्य हि ब्रह्मण एष पन्था
यन्नाममिथ्यार्यति धीरपार्थैः ।

परिभ्रमंस्तत्र   न   विन्दतेऽर्थान्
मायामये   वासनया   शयानः ॥ २ ॥

śabdasya hi brahmaṇa eṣa panthā
yan nāmabhir dhyāyati dhīr apārthaiḥ
paribhramaṁs tatra na vindate 'rthān
māyāmaye vāsanayā śayānaḥ

śabdasya—of the Vedic sound; hi—certainly; brahmaṇaḥ—of the
Vedas; eṣaḥ—these; panthāḥ—the way; yat—what is; nāmabhiḥ—by
different names; dhyāyati—ponders; dhīḥ—intelligence; apārthaiḥ—
by meaningless ideas; paribhraman—wandering; tatra—there; na—
never; vindate—enjoys; arthān—realities; māyā-maye—in illusory
things; vāsanayā—by different desires; śayānaḥ—as if dreaming in
sleep.

TRANSLATION

The way of presentation of the Vedic sounds is so bewildering
that it directs the intelligence of the people to meaningless things
like the heavenly kingdoms. The conditioned souls hover in
dreams of such heavenly illusory pleasures, but actually they do
not relish any tangible happiness in such places.

PURPORT

The conditioned soul is always engaged in laying out plans for happiness within the material world, even up to the end of the universal limit.
He is not even satisfied with available amenities on this planet earth,
where he has exploited the resources of nature to the best of his ability.
He wants to go to the moon or the planet Venus to exploit resources
there. But the Lord has warned us in the *Bhagavad-gītā* (8.16) about the
worthlessness of all the innumerable planets of this universe, as well as
those planets within other systems. There are innumerable universes and
also innumerable planets in each of them. But none of them is immune to
the chief miseries of material existence, namely the pangs of birth, the
pangs of death, the pangs of old age and the pangs of disease. The Lord
says that even the topmost planet, known as the Brahmaloka or

Satyaloka, (and what to speak of other planets, like the heavenly planets) is not a happy land for residential purposes, due to the presence of material pangs, as above mentioned. Conditioned souls are strictly under the laws of fruitive activities, and as such they sometimes go up to Brahmaloka and again come down to Pātālaloka, as if they were unintelligent children on a merry-go-round. The real happiness is in the kingdom of God, where no one has to undergo the pangs of material existence. Therefore, the Vedic ways of fruitive activities for the living entities are misleading. One thinks of a superior way of life in this country or that, or on this planet or another, but nowhere in the material world can he fulfill his real desire of life, namely eternal life, full intelligence and complete bliss. Indirectly, Śrīla Śukadeva Gosvāmī affirms that Mahārāja Parīkṣit, in the last stage of life, should not desire to transfer himself to the so-called heavenly planets, but should prepare himself for going back home, back to Godhead. None of the material planets, nor the amenities available there for living conditions, is everlasting; therefore one must have a factual reluctance to enjoy such temporary happiness as they afford.

TEXT 3

अतः कविर्नामसु यावदर्थः
स्यादप्रमत्तो व्यवसायबुद्धिः ।
सिद्धेऽन्यथार्थे न यतेत तत्र
परिश्रमं तत्र समीक्षमाणः ॥ ३ ॥

ataḥ kavir nāmasu yāvad arthaḥ
syād apramatto vyavasāya-buddhiḥ
siddhe 'nyathārthe na yateta tatra
pariśramaṁ tatra samīkṣamāṇaḥ

ataḥ—for this reason; *kaviḥ*—the enlightened person; *nāmasu*—in names only; *yāvat*—minimum; *arthaḥ*—necessity; *syāt*—must be; *apramattaḥ*—without being mad after them; *vyavasāya-buddhiḥ*—intelligently fixed; *siddhe*—for success; *anyathā*—otherwise; *arthe*—in the interest of; *na*—should never; *yateta*—endeavor for; *tatra*—there;

pariśramam—laboring hard; *tatra*—there; *samīkṣamāṇaḥ*—one who sees practically.

TRANSLATION

For this reason the enlightened person should endeavor only for the minimum necessities of life while in the world of names. He should be intelligently fixed and never endeavor for unwanted things, being competent to perceive practically that all such endeavors are merely hard labor for nothing.

PURPORT

The *bhāgavata-dharma*, or the cult of *Śrīmad-Bhāgavatam*, is perfectly distinct from the way of fruitive activities, which are considered by the devotees to be merely a waste of time. The whole universe, or for that matter all material existence, is moving on as *jagat*, simply for planning business to make one's position very comfortable or secure, although everyone sees that this existence is neither comfortable nor secure and can never become comfortable or secure at any stage of development. Those who are captivated by the illusory advancement of material civilization (following the way of phantasmagoria) are certainly madmen. The whole material creation is a *jugglery of names* only; in fact, it is nothing but a bewildering creation of matter like earth, water and fire. The buildings, furniture, cars, bungalows, mills, factories, industries, peace, war or even the highest perfection of material science, namely atomic energy and electronics, are all simply bewildering names of material elements with their concomitant reactions of the three modes. Since the devotee of the Lord knows them perfectly well, he is not interested in creating unwanted things for a situation which is not at all reality, but simply names of no more significance than the babble of sea waves. The great kings, leaders and soldiers fight with one another in order to perpetuate their names in history. They are forgotten in due course of time, and they make a place for another era in history. But the devotee realizes how much history and historical persons are useless products of flickering time. The fruitive worker aspires after a big fortune in the matter of wealth, woman and worldly adoration, but those who are fixed in perfect reality are not at all interested in such false things. For them it is all a waste of time. Since every second of human life is important, an enlightened man should be very careful to utilize time very cautiously. One second of human life wasted in the vain research of planning for happiness in the material world can never be replaced, even if one spends millions of coins of gold. Therefore, the transcendentalist desiring freedom from the clutches of *māyā*, or the illusory activities of life, is warned herewith not to be captivated by the external features of fruitive actors. Human life is never meant for sense gratification, but for self-realization. *Śrīmad-Bhāgavatam* instructs us solely on this subject from the very beginning to the end. Human life is simply meant for self-realization. The civilization which aims at this utmost perfection never indulges in creating unwanted things, and such a perfect civilization prepares men only to accept the bare necessities of life or to follow the principle of the best use of a bad bargain. Our material bodies and our lives in that connection are bad bargains because the living entity is actually spirit, and spiritual advancement of the living entity is absolutely necessary. Human life is intended for the realization of this important factor, and one should act accordingly, accepting only the bare necessities of life and depending more on God's gift without diversion of human energy for any other purpose, such as being mad for material enjoyment. The materialistic advancement of civilization is called "the civilization of the demons," which ultimately ends in wars and scarcity. The transcendentalist is specifically warned herewith to be fixed in mind, so that even if there is difficulty in plain living and high thinking he will not budge even an inch from his stark determination. For a transcendentalist, it is a suicidal policy to be intimately in touch with the sense gratifiers of the world, because such a policy will frustrate the ultimate gain of life. Śukadeva Gosvāmī met Mahārāja Parīkṣit when the latter felt a necessity for such a meeting. It is the duty of a transcendentalist to help persons who desire real salvation and to support the cause of salvation. One might note that Śukadeva Gosvāmī never met Mahārāja Parīkṣit while he was ruling as a great king. For a transcendentalist, the mode of activities is explained in the next *śloka*.

TEXT 4

सत्यां क्षितौ किं कशिपोः प्रयासै-
र्बाहौ स्वसिद्धे ह्युपबर्हणैः किम् ।

सत्यञ्जलौ किं पुरुधान्नपात्र्या
दिग्वल्कलादौ सति किं दुकूलैः ॥ ४ ॥

satyāṁ kṣitau kiṁ kaśipoḥ prayāsair
bāhau svasiddhe hy upabarhaṇaiḥ kim
saty añjalau kiṁ purudhānna-pātryā
dig-valkalādau sati kiṁ dukūlaiḥ

satyām—being in possession; *kṣitau*—earthly flats; *kim*—where is
the necessity; *kaśipoḥ*—of beds and cots; *prayāsaiḥ*—endeavoring for;
bāhau—the arms; *sva-siddhe*—being self-sufficient; *hi*—certainly;
upabarhaṇaiḥ—bed and bedstead; *kim*—what is the use; *sati*—being
present; *añjalau*—the palms of the hands; *kim*—what is the use;
purudhā—varieties of; *anna*—eatables; *pātryā*—by the utensils; *dik*—
open space; *valkala-ādau*—skins of trees; *sati*—being existent; *kim*—
what is the use of; *dukūlaiḥ*—clothes.

TRANSLATION

When there are ample earthly flats to lie on, what is the necessity
of cots and beds? When one can use his own arms, what is the
necessity of a pillow? When one can use the palms of his hands,
what is the necessity of varieties of utensils? When there is ample
covering, or the skins of trees, what is the necessity of clothing?

PURPORT

The necessities of life for the protection and comfort of the body must
not be unnecessarily increased. Human energy is spoiled in a vain search
after such illusory happiness. If one is able to lie down on the floor, then
why should one endeavor to get a good bedstead or soft cushion to lie on?
If one can rest without any pillow and make use of the soft arms endowed
by nature, there is no necessity of searching after a pillow. If we make a
study of the general life of the animals, we can see that they have no intelligence for building big houses, furniture, and other household
paraphernalia, and yet they maintain a healthy life by lying down on the
open land. They do not know how to cook or prepare foodstuff, yet they
still live healthy lives more easily than the human being. This does not

mean that human civilization should revert to animal life or that the human being should live naked in the jungles without any culture, education and sense of morality. An intelligent human cannot live the life of an animal; rather, man should try to utilize his intelligence in arts and science, poetry and philosophy. In such a way he can further the progressive march of human civilization. But here the idea given by Śrīla Śukadeva Gosvāmī is that the reserve energy of human life, which is far superior to that of animals, should simply be utilized for self-realization. Advancement of human civilization must be towards the goal of establishing our lost relationship with God, which is not possible in any form of life other than the human. One must realize the nullity of the material phenomenon, considering it a passing phantasmagoria, and must endeavor to make a solution to the miseries of life. Self-complacence with a polished type of animal civilization geared to sense gratification is delusion, and such a "civilization" is not worthy of the name. In pursuit of such false activities, a human being is in the clutches of māyā, or illusion. Great sages and saints in the days of yore were not living in palatial buildings furnished with good furniture and so-called amenities of life. They used to live in huts and groves and sit on the flat ground, and yet they have left immense treasures of high knowledge with all perfection. Śrīla Rūpa Gosvāmī and Śrīla Sanātana Gosvāmī were high-ranking ministers of state, but they were able to leave behind them immense writings on transcendental knowledge, while residing only for one night underneath one tree. They did not live even two nights under the same tree, and what to speak of well-furnished rooms with modern amenities. And still they were able to give us most important literatures of self-realization. So-called comforts of life are not actually helpful for progressive civilization; rather, they are detrimental to such progressive life. In the system of sanātana-dharma, of four divisions of social life and four orders of progressive realization, there are ample opportunities and sufficient directions for a happy termination of the progressive life, and the sincere followers are advised therein to accept a voluntary life of renunciation in order to achieve the desired goal of life. If one is not accustomed to abiding by the life of renunciation and self-abnegation from the beginning, one should try to get into the habit at a later stage of life as recommended by Śrīla Śukadeva Gosvāmī, and that will help one to achieve the desired success.

TEXT 5

चीराणि किं पथि न सन्ति दिशन्ति भिक्षां
नैवाङ्घ्रिपाः परभृतः सरितोऽप्यशुष्यन् ।
रुद्धा गुहाः किमजितोऽवति नोपसन्नान्
कस्माद् भजन्ति कवयो धनदुर्मदान्धान् ॥ ५ ॥

cīrāṇi kiṁ pathi na santi diśanti bhikṣāṁ
naivāṅghripāḥ para-bhṛtaḥ sarito 'py aśuṣyan
ruddhā guhāḥ kim ajito 'vati nopasannān
kasmād bhajanti kavayo dhana-durmadāndhān

cīrāṇi—torn clothes; kim—whether; pathi—on the road; na—not; santi—there is; diśanti—give in charity; bhikṣām—alms; na—not; eva—also; aṅghripāḥ—the trees; para-bhṛtaḥ—one who maintains others; saritaḥ—the rivers; api—also; aśuṣyan—have dried up; ruddhāḥ—closed; guhāḥ—caves; kim—whether; ajitaḥ—the Almighty Lord; avati—give protection; na—not; upasannān—the surrendered soul; kasmāt—what for, then; bhajanti—flatters; kavayaḥ—the learned; dhana—wealth; durmada-andhān—too intoxicated by.

TRANSLATION

Are there no torn clothes lying on the common road? Do the trees, which exist for maintaining others, no longer give alms in charity? Do the rivers, being dried up, no longer supply water to the thirsty? Are the caves of the mountains now closed, or, above all, does the Almighty Lord not protect the fully surrendered souls? Why then do the learned sages go to flatter those who are intoxicated by hard-earned wealth?

PURPORT

The renounced order of life is never meant for begging or living at the cost of others as a parasite. According to the dictionary, a parasite is a sycophant who lives at the cost of society without making any contribution to that society. The renounced order is meant for contributing something substantial to society and not depending on the earnings of the householders. On the contrary, acceptance of alms from the householders by the bona fide mendicant is an opportunity afforded by the saint for the tangible benefit of the donor. In the *sanātana-dharma* institution, alms-giving to the mendicant is part of a householder's duty, and it is advised in the scriptures that the householders should treat the mendicants as their family children and should provide them with food, clothing, etc., without being asked. Pseudomendicants, therefore, should not take advantage of the charitable disposition of the faithful householders. The first duty of a person in the renounced order of life is to contribute some literary work for the benefit of the human being in order to give him realized direction toward self-realization. Amongst the other duties in the renounced order of life of Śrīla Sanātana, Śrīla Rūpa and the other Gosvāmīs of Vṛndāvana, the foremost duty discharged by them was to hold learned discourses amongst themselves at Sevākuñja, Vṛndāvana (the spot where Śrī Rādhā-Dāmodara Temple was established by Śrīla Jīva Gosvāmī and where the actual *samādhi* tombs of Śrīla Rūpa Gosvāmī and Śrīla Jīva Gosvāmī are laid). For the benefit of all in human society, they left behind them immense literatures of transcendental importance. Similarly, all the *ācāryas* who voluntarily accepted the renounced order of life aimed at benefiting human society and not at living a comfortable or irresponsible life at the cost of others. However, those who cannot give any contribution should not go to the householders for food, for such mendicants asking bread from the householders are an insult to the highest order. Śukadeva Gosvāmī gave this warning especially for those mendicants who adopt this line of profession to solve their economic problems. Such mendicants are in abundance in the age of Kali. When a man becomes a mendicant willfully or by circumstances, he must be of firm faith and conviction that the Supreme Lord is the maintainer of all living beings everywhere in the universe. Why, then, would He neglect the maintenance of a surrendered soul who is cent percent engaged in the service of the Lord? A common master looks to the necessities of his servant, so how much more would the all-powerful, all-opulent Supreme Lord look after the necessities of life for a fully surrendered soul. The general rule is that a mendicant devotee will accept a simple small loincloth without asking anyone to give it in charity. He simply salvages it from the rejected torn cloth thrown in the street. When he is hungry he may go to a magnanimous tree which drops fruits, and when he is thirsty he may drink water from the flowing river. He does not require to live in a comfortable house, but should find a cave in the hills and not be afraid of jungle animals, keeping faith in God, who lives in everyone's heart. The Lord may dictate to tigers and other jungle animals not to disturb His devotee. Haridāsa Ṭhākura, a great devotee of Lord Śrī Caitanya, used to live in such a cave, and by chance a great venomous snake was a copartner of the cave. Some admirer of Ṭhākura Haridāsa who had to visit the Ṭhākura every day feared the snake and suggested that the Ṭhākura leave that place. Because his devotees were afraid of the snake and they were regularly visiting the cave, Ṭhākura Haridāsa agreed to the proposal on their account. But as soon as this was settled, the snake actually crawled out of its hole in the cave and left the cave for good before everyone present. By the dictation of the Lord, who lived also within the heart of the snake, the snake gave preference to Haridāsa and decided to leave the place and not disturb him. So this is a tangible example of how the Lord gives protection to a bona fide devotee like Ṭhākura Haridāsa. According to the regulations of the *sanātana-dharma* institution, one is trained from the beginning to depend fully on the protection of the Lord in all circumstances. The path of renunciation is recommended for acceptance by one who is fully accomplished and fully purified in his existence. This stage is described also in the *Bhagavad-gītā* (16.5) as *daivī sampat*. A human being is required to accumulate *daivī sampat*, or spiritual assets; otherwise, the next alternative, *āsurī sampat*, or material assets, will overcome him disproportionately, and thus one will be forced into the entanglement of different miseries of the material world. A *sannyāsī* should always live alone, without company, and he must be fearless. He should never be afraid of living alone, although he is never alone. The Lord is residing in everyone's heart, and unless one is purified by the prescribed process, one will feel that he is alone. But a man in the renounced order of life must be purified by the process; thus he will feel the presence of the Lord everywhere and will have nothing to fear (such as being without any company). Everyone can become a fearless and honest person if his very existence is purified by discharging the prescribed duty for each and every order of life. One can become fixed in one's prescribed duty by faithful aural reception of Vedic instructions and assimilation of the essence of Vedic knowledge by devotional service to the Lord.

TEXT 6

एवं खचित्ते खत एव सिद्ध
आत्मा प्रियो ऽर्थो भगवाननन्तः ।
तं निर्वृतो नियतार्थो भजेत
संसारहेतूपरमश्च   यत्र ॥ ६ ॥

evam sva-citte svata eva siddha
ātmā priyo 'rtho bhagavān anantaḥ
tam nirvṛto niyatārtho bhajeta
samsāra-hetūparamaś ca yatra

evam—thus; *sva-citte*—in one's own heart; *svataḥ*—by His omnipotency; *eva*—certainly; *siddhaḥ*—fully represented; *ātmā*—the Supersoul; *priyaḥ*—very dear; *arthaḥ*—substance; *bhagavān*—the Supreme Personality of Godhead; *anantaḥ*—the eternal unlimited; *tam*—unto Him; *nirvṛtaḥ*—being detached from the world; *niyata*—permanent; *arthaḥ*—the supreme gain; *bhajeta*—one must worship; *samsāra-hetu*—the cause of the conditioned state of existence; *uparamaḥ*—cessation; *ca*—certainly; *yatra*—in which.

TRANSLATION

Thus being fixed, one must render service unto the Supersoul situated in one's own heart by His omnipotency. Because He is the Almighty Personality of Godhead, eternal and unlimited, He is the ultimate goal of life, and by worshiping Him one can end the cause of the conditioned state of existence.

PURPORT

As confirmed in *Bhagavad-gītā* (18.61), the Supreme Personality of Godhead Śrī Kṛṣṇa is the all-pervading omnipresent Supersoul. Therefore one who is a *yogī* can worship only Him because He is the substance and not illusion. Every living creature is engaging in the service of something else. A living being's constitutional position is to render service, but in the atmosphere of *māyā*, or illusion, or the conditional state of existence, the conditioned soul seeks the service of illusion. A conditioned soul works in the service of his temporary body, bodily relatives like the wife and children, and the necessary paraphernalia for maintaining the body and bodily relations, such as the house, land, wealth, society and country, but he does not know that all such renderings of service are totally illusory. As we have discussed many times before, this material world is itself an illusion, like a mirage in the desert. In the desert there is an illusion of water, and the foolish animals become entrapped by such an illusion and run after water in the desert, although there is no water at all. But because there is no water in the desert, one does not conclude that there is no water at all. The intelligent person knows well that there is certainly water, water in the seas and oceans, but such vast reservoirs of water are far, far away from the desert. One should therefore search for water in the vicinity of seas and oceans and not in the desert. Every one of us is searching after real happiness in life, namely eternal life, eternal or unlimited knowledge and unending blissful life. But foolish people who have no knowledge of the substance search after the reality of life in the illusion. This material body does not endure eternally, and everything in relation with this temporary body, such as the wife, children, society and country, also changes along with the change of body. This is called *saṁsāra*, or repetition of birth, death, old age and disease. We would like to find a solution for all these problems of life, but we do not know the way. Herein it is suggested that anyone who wants to make an end to these miseries of life, namely repetition of birth, death, disease, and old age, must take to this process of worshiping the Supreme Lord and not others, as it is also ultimately suggested in the *Bhagavad-gītā* (18.65). If we at all want to end the cause of our conditioned life, we must take to the worship of Lord Śrī Kṛṣṇa, who is present in everyone's heart by His natural affection for all living beings, who are actually the parts and parcels of the Lord (Bg. 18.61). The baby in the lap of his mother is naturally attached to the mother, and the mother is attached to the child. But when the child grows up and becomes overwhelmed by circumstances, he gradually becomes detached from the mother, although the mother always expects some sort of service from the grown-up child and is equally affectionate toward her child, even though the child is forgetful. Similarly, because we are all part and parcel of the Lord, the Lord is always affectionate to us, and He always tries to get us back home, back to Godhead. But we, the conditioned souls, do not care for Him and run instead after the illusory bodily connections. We must therefore extricate ourselves from all illusory connections of the world and seek reunion with the Lord, trying to render service unto Him because He is the ultimate truth. Actually we are hankering after Him as the child seeks the mother. And to search out the Supreme Personality of Godhead, we need not go anywhere else, because the Lord is within our hearts. This does not suggest, however, that we should not go to the places of worship, namely the temples, churches and mosques. Such holy places of worship are also occupied by the Lord because the Lord is omnipresent. For the common man these holy places are centers of learning about the science of God. When the temples are devoid of activities, the people in general become uninterested in such places, and consequently the mass of people gradually become godless, and a godless civilization is the result. Such a hellish civilization artificially increases the conditions of life, and existence becomes intolerable for everyone. The foolish leaders of a godless civilization try to devise various plans to bring about peace and prosperity in the godless world under a patent trademark of materialism, and because such attempts are illusory only, the people elect incompetent, blind leaders, one after another, who are incapable of offering solutions. If we want at all to end this anomaly of a godless civilization, we must follow the principles of revealed scriptures like the Śrīmad-Bhāgavatam and follow the instruction of a person like Śrī Śukadeva Gosvāmī who has no attraction for material gain.

TEXT 7

कस्तां त्वनादृत्य परानुचिन्ता-
मृते पशूनसतीं नाम कुर्यात् ।
पश्यञ्जनं पतितं वैतरण्यां
स्वकर्मजान् परितापाञ्जुषाणम् ॥ ७ ॥

kas tāṁ tv anādṛtya parānucintām
ṛte paśūn asatīṁ nāma kuryāt
paśyañ janaṁ patitaṁ vaitaraṇyāṁ
sva-karmajān paritāpāñ juṣāṇam

kaḥ—who else; *tām*—that; *tu*—but; *anādṛtya*—by neglecting; *para-anucintām*—transcendental thoughts; *ṛte*—without; *paśūn*—the materialists; *asatīm*—in the nonpermanent; *nāma*—name; *kuryāt*—will adopt; *paśyan*—seeing definitely; *janam*—the general mass of people; *patitam*—fallen; *vaitaraṇyām*—in Vaitaraṇī, the river of suffering; *sva-karma-jān*—produced from one's own work; *paritāpān*—suffering; *juṣāṇam*—being overtaken by.

TRANSLATION

Who else but the gross materialists will neglect such transcendental thought and take to the nonpermanent names only, seeing the mass of people fallen in the river of suffering as the consequence of accruing the result of their own work?

PURPORT

In the *Vedas* it is said that persons who are attached to demigods to the exclusion of the Supreme Personality of Godhead are like the animals who follow the herdsman even though they are taken to the slaughterhouse. The materialists, like animals, also do not know how they are being misdirected by neglecting the transcendental thought of the Supreme Person. No one can remain vacant of thought. It is said that an idle brain is a devil's workshop because a person who cannot think in the right way must think of something which may bring about disaster. The materialists are always worshiping some minor demigods, although this is condemned in the *Bhagavad-gītā* (7.20). As long as a person is illusioned by material gains, he petitions the respective demigods to draw some particular benefit which is, after all, illusory and nonpermanent. The enlightened transcendentalist is not captivated by such illusory things; therefore he is always absorbed in the transcendental thought of the Supreme in different stages of realization, namely Brahman, Paramātmā and Bhagavān. In the previous verse it is suggested that one should think of the Supersoul, which is one step higher than the impersonal thought of Brahman, as it was suggested in the case of contemplating the *virāṭ-rūpa* of the Personality of Godhead.

Intelligent persons who can see properly may look into the general conditions of the living entities who are wandering in the cycle of the

8,400,000 species of life, as well as in different classes of human beings. It is said that there is an everlasting belt of water called the River Vaitaraṇī at the entrance of the Plutonic planet of Yamarāja, who punishes sinners in different manners. After being subjected to such sufferings, a sinner is awarded a particular species of life according to his deeds in the past. Such living entities as are punished by Yamarāja are seen in different varieties of conditioned life. Some of them are in heaven, and some of them are in hell. Some of them are brāhmaṇas, and some of them are misers. But no one is happy in this material world, and all of them are either class A, B or C prisoners suffering because of their own deeds. The Lord is impartial to all circumstances of the sufferings of the living entities, but to one who takes shelter at His lotus feet, the Lord gives proper protection, and He takes such a living entity back home, back to Himself.

TEXT 8

केचित् स्वदेहान्तर्हृदयावकाशे
प्रादेशमात्रं पुरुषं वसन्तम् ।
चतुर्भुजं कञ्जरथाङ्गशङ्ख-
गदाधरं धारणया स्मरन्ति ॥ ८ ॥

*kecit sva-dehāntar-hṛdayāvakāśe
prādeśa-mātram puruṣam vasantam
catur-bhujam kañja-rathāṅga-śaṅkha-
gadā-dharam dhāraṇayā smaranti*

kecit—others; *sva-deha-antaḥ*—within the body; *hṛdaya-avakāśe*—in the region of the heart; *prādeśa-mātram*—measuring only eight inches; *puruṣam*—the Personality of Godhead; *vasantam*—residing; *catuḥ-bhujam*—with four hands; *kañja*—lotus; *ratha-aṅga*—the wheel of a chariot; *śaṅkha*—conchshell; *gadā-dharam*—and with a club in the hand; *dhāraṇayā*—conceiving in that way; *smaranti*—do meditate upon Him.

TRANSLATION

Others conceive of the Personality of Godhead residing within the body in the region of the heart and measuring only eight inches, with four hands carrying a lotus, a wheel of a chariot, a conchshell and a club respectively.

PURPORT

The all-pervading Personality of Godhead resides as Paramātmā in the heart of each and every living entity. The measurement of the localized Personality of Godhead is estimated to expand from the ring finger to the end of the thumb, more or less eight inches. The form of the Lord described in this verse with distribution of different symbols—beginning from the lower right hand up and down to the lower left hand with lotus, wheel of a chariot, conchshell and club respectively—is called Janārdana, or the plenary portion of the Lord who controls the general mass. There are many other forms of the Lord with varied situations of the symbols of lotus, conchshell, etc., and they are differently known as Puruṣottama, Acyuta, Narasiṁha, Trivikrama, Hṛṣīkeśa, Keśava, Mādhava, Aniruddha, Pradyumna, Saṅkarṣaṇa, Śrīdhara, Vāsudeva, Dāmodara, Janārdana, Nārāyaṇa, Hari, Padmanābha, Vāmana, Madhusūdana, Govinda, Kṛṣṇa, Viṣṇumūrti, Adhokṣaja and Upendra. These twenty-four forms of the localized Personality of Godhead are worshiped in different parts of the planetary system, and in each system there is an incarnation of the Lord having a different Vaikuṇṭha planet in the spiritual sky, which is called the *paravyoma*. There are many other hundreds and scores of different forms of the Lord, and each and every one of them has a particular planet in the spiritual sky, of which this material sky is only a fragmental offshoot. The Lord exists as *puruṣa*, or the male enjoyer, although there is no comparing Him to any male form in the material world. But all such forms are *advaita*, nondifferent from one another, and each of them is eternally young. The young Lord with four hands is nicely decorated, as described below.

TEXT 9

प्रसन्नवक्त्रं　　　　नलिनायतेक्षणं

कदम्बकिञ्जल्ककपिशङ्गवाससम् ।

लसन्महारत्नहिरण्मयाङ्गदं

स्फुरन्महारत्नकिरीटकुण्डलम् ॥ ९ ॥

prasanna-vaktraṁ nalināyatekṣaṇaṁ
kadamba-kiñjalka-piśaṅga-vāsasam
lasan-mahā-ratna-hiraṇmayāṅgadaṁ
sphuran-mahā-ratna-kirīṭa-kuṇḍalam

prasanna—expresses happiness; *vaktram*—mouth; *nalina-āyata*—spread like the petals of a lotus; *īkṣaṇam*—eyes; *kadamba*—*kadamba* flower; *kiñjalka*—saffron; *piśaṅga*—yellow; *vāsasam*—garments; *lasat*—hanging; *mahā-ratna*—valuable jewels; *hiraṇmaya*—made of gold; *aṅgadam*—ornament; *sphurat*—glowing; *mahā-ratna*—valuable jewels; *kirīṭa*—headdress; *kuṇḍalam*—earrings.

TRANSLATION

His mouth expresses His happiness. His eyes spread like the petals of a lotus, and His garments, yellowish like the saffron of a kadamba flower, are bedecked with valuable jewels. His ornaments are all made of gold, set with jewels, and He wears a glowing headdress and earrings.

TEXT 10

उन्निद्रहृत्पङ्कजकर्णिकालये
योगेश्वरास्थापितपादपल्लवम् ।
श्रीलक्षणं कौस्तुभरत्नकन्धर-
मम्लानलक्ष्म्या वनमालयाचितम् ॥१०॥

unnidra-hṛt-paṅkaja-karṇikālaye
yogeśvarāsthāpita-pāda-pallavam
śrī-lakṣaṇam kaustubha-ratna-kandharam
amlāna-lakṣmyā vana-mālayācitam

unnidra—blooming; *hṛt*—heart; *paṅkaja*—lotus flower; *karṇikā-ālaye*—on the surface of the whorl; *yoga-īśvara*—the great mystics; *āsthāpita*—placed; *pāda-pallavam*—lotus feet; *śrī*—the goddess of fortune, or a beautiful calf; *lakṣaṇam*—marked in that way; *kaustubha*—the Kaustubha jewel; *ratna*—other jewels; *kandharam*—on the shoulder; *amlāna*—quite fresh; *lakṣmyā*—beauty; *vana-mālayā*—by a flower garland; *ācitam*—spread over.

TRANSLATION

His lotus feet are placed over the whorls of the lotuslike hearts of great mystics. On His chest is the Kaustubha jewel, engraved with a beautiful calf, and there are other jewels on His shoulders. His complete torso is garlanded with fresh flowers.

PURPORT

The ornaments, flowers, clothing and all the other decorations on the transcendental body of the Personality of Godhead are identical with the body of the Lord. None of them are made of material ingredients; otherwise there would be no chance of their decorating the body of the Lord. As such, in the *paravyoma*, spiritual varieties are also distinguished from the material variegatedness.

TEXT 11

विभूषितं   मेखलयाङ्गुलीयकै-
र्महाधनैर्नूपुरकङ्कणादिभिः   ।
स्निग्धामलाकुञ्चितनीलकुन्तलै-
र्विरोचमानाननहासपेशलम्   ॥११॥

vibhūṣitaṁ mekhalayāṅgulīyakair
mahā-dhanair nūpura-kaṅkaṇādibhiḥ
snigdhāmalākuñcita-nīla-kuntalair
virocamānānana-hāsa-peśalam

vibhūṣitam—well decorated; *mekhalayā*—with an ornamental wreath about the waist; *aṅgulīyakaiḥ*—by finger rings; *mahā-dhanaiḥ*—all highly valuable; *nūpura*—ringing leglets; *kaṅkaṇa-ādibhiḥ*—also by bangles; *snigdha*—slick; *amala*—spotless; *ākuñcita*—curling; *nīla*—bluish; *kuntalaiḥ*—hair; *virocamāna*—very pleasing; *ānana*—face; *hāsa*—smile; *peśalam*—beautiful.

TRANSLATION

He is well decorated with an ornamental wreath about His waist
and rings studded with valuable jewels on His fingers. His leglets,
His bangles, His oiled hair, curling with a bluish tint, and His
beautiful smiling face are all very pleasing.

PURPORT

The Supreme Personality of Godhead is the most beautiful person
amongst all others, and Śrīla Śukadeva Gosvāmī describes every part of
His transcendental beauty, one after another, in order to teach the impersonalist that the Personality of Godhead is not an imagination by the
devotee for facility of worship, but is the Supreme Person in fact and
figure. The impersonal feature of the Absolute Truth is but His radiation, as the sun rays are but radiations from the sun.

TEXT 12

अदीनलीलाहसितेक्षणोल्लसद्-
        भ्रूभङ्गसंसूचितभूर्यनुग्रहम् ।
ईक्षेत   चिन्तामयमेनमीश्वरं
यावन्मनो   धारणयावतिष्ठते ॥१२॥

adīna-līlā-hasitekṣaṇollasad-
    bhrū-bhaṅga-saṁsūcita-bhūry-anugraham
īkṣeta cintāmayam enam īśvaraṁ
    yāvan mano dhāraṇayāvatiṣṭhate

adīna—very magnanimous; līlā—pastimes; hasita—smiling; īkṣaṇa
—by glancing over; ullasat—glowing; bhrū-bhaṅga—signals of the
eyebrow; saṁsūcita—indicated; bhūri—extensive; anugraham—
benediction; īkṣeta—one must concentrate on; cintāmayam—transcendental; enam—this particular; īśvaram—the Supreme Lord; yāvat—as
long as; manaḥ—the mind; dhāraṇayā—by meditation; avatiṣṭhate—
can be fixed.

TRANSLATION

The Lord's magnanimous pastimes and the glowing glancing of His smiling face are all indications of His extensive benedictions. One must therefore concentrate on this transcendental form of the Lord, as long as the mind can be fixed on Him by meditation.

PURPORT

In *Bhagavad-gītā* (12.5) it is said that the impersonalist undergoes a series of difficult programs on account of his impersonal meditation. But the devotee, due to the Lord's personal service, progresses very easily. Impersonal meditation is therefore a source of suffering for the impersonalist. Here, the devotee has an advantage over the impersonalist philosopher. The impersonalist is doubtful about the personal feature of the Lord, and therefore he always tries to meditate upon something which is not objective. For this reason there is an authentic statement in the *Bhāgavatam* regarding the positive concentration of the mind on the factual form of the Lord.

The process of meditation recommended herein is *bhakti-yoga*, or the process of devotional service after one is liberated from the material conditions. *Jñāna-yoga* is the process of liberation from the material conditions. After one is liberated from the conditions of material existence, i.e., when one is *nivṛtta*, as previously stated herein, or when one is freed from all material necessities, one becomes qualified to discharge the process of *bhakti-yoga*. Therefore *bhakti-yoga* includes *jñāna-yoga*, or, in other words, the process of pure devotional service simultaneously serves the purpose of *jñāna-yoga*; liberation from material conditions is automatically achieved by the gradual development of pure devotional service. These effects of *bhakti-yoga* are called *anartha-nivṛtti*. Things which are artificially acquired gradually disappear along with the progress of *bhakti-yoga*. Meditation on the lotus feet of the Personality of Godhead, the first processional step, must show its effect by *anartha-nivṛtti*. The grossest type of *anartha* which binds the conditioned soul in material existence is sex desire, and this sex desire gradually develops in the union of the male and female. When the male and female are united, the sex desire is further aggravated by the accumulation of buildings, children, friends, relatives and wealth. When all these are acquired, the conditioned soul becomes overwhelmed by such entanglements, and the false sense of egoism, or the sense of "myself" and "mine," becomes prominent, and the sex desire expands to various political, social, altruistic, philanthropic and many other unwanted engagements, resembling the foam of the sea waves, which becomes very prominent at one time and at the next moment vanishes as quickly as a cloud in the sky. The conditioned soul is encircled by such products, as well as products of sex desire, and therefore *bhakti-yoga* leads to gradual evaporation of the sex desire, which is summarized in three headings, namely *profit, adoration* and *distinction*. All conditioned souls are mad after these different forms of sex desire, and one shall see for himself how much he has been freed from such material hankerings based primarily on the sex desire. As a person feels his hunger satisfied after eating each morsel of foodstuff, he must similarly be able to see the degree to which he has been freed from sex desire. The sex desire is diminished along with its various forms by the process of *bhakti-yoga* because *bhakti-yoga* automatically, by the grace of the Lord, effectively results in knowledge and renunciation, even if the devotee is not materially very well educated. Knowledge means knowing things as they are, and if by deliberation it is found that there are things which are at all unnecessary, naturally the person who has acquired knowledge leaves aside such unwanted things. When the conditioned soul finds by culture of knowledge that material necessities are unwanted things, he becomes detached from such unwanted things. This stage of knowledge is called *vairāgya*, or detachment from unwanted things. We have previously discussed that the transcendentalist is required to be self-sufficient and should not beg from the rich blind persons to fulfill the bare necessities of life. Śukadeva Gosvāmī has suggested some alternatives for the bare necessities of life, namely the problem of eating, sleeping and shelter, but he has not suggested any alternative for sex satisfaction. One who has the sex desire still with him should not at all try to accept the renounced order of life. For one who has not attained to this stage, there is no question of a renounced order of life. So by the gradual process of devotional service under the guidance of a proper spiritual master, and following the principles of the *Bhāgavatam*, one must be able at least to control the gross sex desire before one accepts the renounced order of life factually.

So purification means getting free gradually from sex desire, and this is attained by meditation on the person of the Lord as described herein, beginning from the feet. One should not try to go upwards artificially without seeing for himself how much he has been released from the sex desire. The smiling face of the Lord is the Tenth Canto of *Śrīmad-Bhāgavatam*, and there are many upstarts who at once try to begin with the Tenth Canto and especially with the five chapters which delineate the *rāsa-līlā* of the Lord. This is certainly improper. By such improper study or hearing of *Bhāgavatam*, the material opportunists have played havoc by indulgence in sex life in the name of *Bhāgavatam*. This vilification of *Bhāgavatam* is rendered by the acts of the so-called devotees; one should be free from all kinds of sex desire before he tries to make a show of recital of *Bhāgavatam*. Śrī Viśvanātha Cakravartī Ṭhākura clearly defines the import of purification as cessation from sex indulgence. He says, *yathā yathā dhīś ca śudhyati viṣaya-lāmpaṭyam tyajati, tathā tathā dhārayed iti citta-śuddhi-tāratamyenaiva dhyāna-tāratamyam uktam.* And as one gets free from the intoxication of sex indulgence by purification of intelligence, one should step forward for the next meditation, or in other words, the progress of meditation on the different limbs of the transcendental body of the Lord should be enhanced in proportion to the progress of purification of the heart. The conclusion is that those who are still entrapped by sex indulgence should never progress to meditation above the feet of the Lord; therefore recital of *Śrīmad-Bhāgavatam* by them should be restricted to the First and Second Cantos of the great literature. One must complete the purificatory process by assimilating the contents of the first nine cantos. Then one should be admitted into the realm of the Tenth Canto of *Śrīmad-Bhāgavatam*.

TEXT 13

एकैकशोऽङ्गानि धियानुभावयेत्
पादादि यावद्धसितं गदाभृतः ।
जितं जितं स्थानमपोह्य धारयेत्
परं परं शुद्ध्यति धीर्यथा यथा ॥१३॥

ekaikaśo 'ṅgāni dhiyānubhāvayet
pādādi yāvad dhasitaṁ gadābhṛtaḥ

jitaṁ jitaṁ sthānam apohya dhārayet
paraṁ paraṁ śuddhyati dhīr yathā yathā

eka-ekaśaḥ—one to one, or one after another; *aṅgāni*—limbs;
dhiyā—by attention; *anubhāvayet*—meditate upon; *pāda-ādi*—legs,
etc.; *yāvat*—until; *hasitam*—smiling; *gadā-bhṛtaḥ*—the Personality of
Godhead; *jitam jitam*—gradually controlling the mind; *sthānam*—place;
apohya—leaving; *dhārayet*—meditate upon; *param param*—higher
and higher; *śuddhyati*—purified; *dhīḥ*—intelligence; *yathā yathā*—as
much as.

TRANSLATION

The process of meditation should begin from the lotus feet of
the Lord and progress to His smiling face. The meditation should
be concentrated upon the lotus feet, then the calves, then the
thighs, and in this way higher and higher. The more the mind becomes fixed upon the different parts of the limbs, one after
another, the more the intelligence becomes purified.

PURPORT

The process of meditation recommended in the *Śrīmad-Bhāgavatam* is
not to fix one's attention on something impersonal or void. The meditation should concentrate on the Person of the Supreme Godhead, either in
His *virāṭ-rūpa*, the gigantic universal form, or in His *sac-cid-ānanda-
vigraha*, as described in the scriptures. There are authorized descriptions
of Viṣṇu forms, and there are authorized representations of Deities in
the temples. Thus one can practice meditating upon the Deity, concentrating his mind on the lotus feet of the Lord and gradually rising
higher and higher, up to His smiling face.

According to the *Bhāgavata* school, the Lord's *rāsa* dancing is the
smiling face of the Lord. Since it is recommended in this verse that one
should gradually progress from the lotus feet up to the smiling face, we
shall not jump at once to understand the Lord's pastimes in the *rāsa*
dance. It is better to practice concentrating our attention by offering
flowers and *tulasī* to the lotus feet of the Lord. In this way, we gradually
become purified by the *arcanā* process. We dress the Lord, bathe Him,
etc., and all these transcendental activities help us purify our existence.

When we reach the higher standard of purification, if we see the smiling face of the Lord or hear the *rāsa* dance pastimes of the Lord, then we can relish His activities. In the *Śrīmad-Bhāgavatam*, therefore, the *rāsa* dance pastimes are delineated in the Tenth Canto (Chapters 29–34).

The more one concentrates on the transcendental form of the Lord, either on the lotus feet, the calves, the thighs or the chest, the more one becomes purified. In this verse it is clearly stated, "the more the intelligence becomes purified," which means the more one becomes detached from sense gratification. Our intelligence in the present conditioned state of life is impure due to being engaged in sense gratification. The result of meditation on the transcendental form of the Lord will be manifested by one's detachment from sense gratification. Therefore, the ultimate purpose of meditation is purification of one's intelligence.

Those who are too engrossed in sense gratification cannot be allowed to participate in *arcanā* or to touch the transcendental form of the Rādhā-Kṛṣṇa or Viṣṇu Deities. For them it is better to meditate upon the gigantic *virāṭ-rūpa* of the Lord, as recommended in the next verse. The impersonalists and the voidists are therefore recommended to meditate upon the universal form of the Lord, whereas the devotees are recommended to meditate on the Deity worship in the temple. Because the impersonalists and the voidists are not sufficiently purified in their spiritual activities, *arcanā* is not meant for them.

TEXT 14

यावन्न जायेत परावरेऽस्मिन्
विश्वेश्वरे द्रष्टरि भक्तियोगः ।
तावत् स्थवीयः पुरुषस्य रूपं
क्रियावसाने प्रयतः स्मरेत ॥१४॥

yāvan na jāyeta parāvare 'smin
viśveśvare draṣṭari bhakti-yogaḥ
tāvat sthavīyaḥ puruṣasya rūpaṁ
kriyāvasāne prayataḥ smareta

yāvat—as long as; *na*—does not; *jāyeta*—develop; *para*—transcendental; *avare*—mundane; *asmin*—in this form of; *viśva-īśvare*—the

Lord of all worlds; *draṣṭari*—unto the seer; *bhakti-yogaḥ*—devotional service; *tāvat*—so long; *sthavīyaḥ*—the gross materialist; *puruṣasya*—of the *virāṭ-puruṣa*; *rūpam*—universal form; *kriyā-avasāne*—at the end of one's prescribed duties; *prayataḥ*—with proper attention; *smareta*—one should remember.

TRANSLATION

Unless the gross materialist develops a sense of loving service unto the Supreme Lord, the seer of both the transcendental and material worlds, he should remember or meditate upon the universal form of the Lord at the end of his prescribed duties.

PURPORT

The Supreme Lord is the seer of all worlds, both material and transcendental. In other words, the Supreme Lord is the ultimate beneficiary and enjoyer of all worlds, as confirmed in the *Bhagavad-gītā* (5.29). The spiritual world is the manifestation of His internal potency, and the material world is the manifestation of His external potency. The living entities are also His marginal potency, and by their own choice they can live in either the transcendental or material worlds. The material world is not a fit place for living entities because they are spiritually one with the Lord and in the material world the living entities become conditioned by the laws of the material world. The Lord wants all living entities, who are His parts and parcels, to live with Him in the transcendental world, and for enlightening conditioned souls in the material world, all the *Vedas* and the revealed scriptures are there—expressly to recall the conditioned souls back home, back to Godhead. Unfortunately, the conditioned living entities, although suffering continually the threefold miseries of conditioned life, are not very serious about going back to Godhead. It is due to their misguided way of living, complicated by sins and virtues. Some of them who are virtuous by deeds begin to reestablish the lost relation with the Lord, but they are unable to understand the personal feature of the Lord. The real purpose of life is to make contact with the Lord and be engaged in His service. That is the natural position of living entities. But those who are impersonalists and are unable to render any loving service to the Lord have been advised to meditate upon His impersonal feature, the *virāṭ-rūpa*, or universal form. Some way or other, one must try to re-

establish one's forgotten relation with the Lord if one at all desires to
gain real happiness in life, and to reclaim his natural unfettered condition. For the less intelligent beginners, meditation on the impersonal
feature, the *virāṭ-rūpa*, or universal form of the Lord, will gradually
qualify one to rise to personal contact. One is advised herewith to meditate upon the *virāṭ-rūpa* specified in the previous chapters in order to
understand how the different planets, seas, mountains, rivers, birds,
beasts, human beings, demigods and all that we can conceive are but different parts and limbs of the Lord's *virāṭ* form. This sort of thinking is
also a type of meditation on the Absolute Truth, and as soon as such
meditation begins, one develops one's godly qualities, and the whole
world appears to be a happy and peaceful residence for all the people of
the world. Without such meditation on God, either personal or impersonal, all good qualities of the human being become covered with misconceptions regarding his constitutional position, and without such
advanced knowledge, the whole world becomes a hell for the human
being.

TEXT 15

स्थिरं सुखं चासनमास्थितो यति-
यदा जिहासुरिममङ्ग लोकम् ।
काले च देशे च मनो न सज्जयेत्
प्राणान् नियच्छेन्मनसा जितासुः ॥१५॥

sthiraṁ sukhaṁ cāsanam āsthito yatir
yadā jihāsur imam aṅga lokam
kāle ca deśe ca mano na sajjayet
prāṇān niyacchen manasā jitāsuḥ

sthiram—without being disturbed; *sukham*—comfortable; *ca*—also;
āsanam—sitting accommodation; *āsthitaḥ*—being situated; *yatiḥ*—the
sage; *yadā*—whenever; *jihāsuḥ*—desires to give up; *imam*—this;
aṅga—O King; *lokam*—this body; *kāle*—in time; *ca*—and; *deśe*—in a
proper place; *ca*—also; *manaḥ*—the mind; *na*—not; *sajjayet*—may not
be perplexed; *prāṇān*—the senses; *niyacchet*—must control; *manasā*—
by the mind; *jita-asuḥ*—conquering the life air.

TRANSLATION

O King, whenever the yogī desires to leave this planet of human beings, he should not be perplexed about the proper time or place, but should comfortably sit without being disturbed and, regulating the life air, should control the senses by the mind.

PURPORT

In the *Bhagavad-gītā* (8.14) it is clearly stated that a person who is totally engaged in the transcendental loving service of the Lord, and who constantly remembers Him at every step, easily obtains the mercy of the Lord by entering into His personal contact. Such devotees do not need to seek an opportune moment to leave the present body. But those who are mixed devotees, alloyed with fruitive action or empirical philosophical speculation, require an opportune moment for quitting this body. For them the opportune moments are stated in the *Bhagavad-gītā* (8.23–26). But these opportune moments are not as important as one's being a successful *yogī* who is able to quit his body as he likes. Such a *yogī* must be competent to control his senses by the mind. The mind is easily conquered simply by engaging it at the lotus feet of the Lord. Gradually, by such service, all the senses become automatically engaged in the service of the Lord. That is the way of merging into the Supreme Absolute.

TEXT 16

मनः स्वबुद्ध्यामलया नियम्य
क्षेत्रज्ञ एतां निनयेत् तमात्मनि ।
आत्मानमात्मन्यवरुध्य धीरो
लब्धोपशान्तिर्विरमेत कृत्यात् ॥१६॥

manaḥ sva-buddhyāmalayā niyamya
kṣetra-jña etāṁ ninayet tam ātmani
ātmānam ātmany avarudhya dhīro
labdhopaśāntir virameta kṛtyāt

manaḥ—the mind; *sva-buddhyā*—by his own intelligence; *amalayā*—unalloyed; *niyamya*—by regulating; *kṣetra-jñe*—unto the living entity; *etām*—all of them; *ninayet*—merge; *tam*—that; *ātmani*—the self; *ātmānam*—the self; *ātmani*—in the Superself; *avarudhya*—being locked up; *dhīraḥ*—the fully satisfied; *labdha-upaśāntiḥ*—one who has attained full bliss; *virameta*—ceases from; *kṛtyāt*—all other activities.

TRANSLATION

Thereafter, the yogī should merge his mind, by his unalloyed intelligence, into the living entity, and then merge the living entity into the Superself. And by doing this, the fully satisfied living entity becomes situated in the supreme stage of satisfaction, so that he ceases from all other activities.

PURPORT

The functions of the mind are thinking, feeling and willing. When the mind is materialistic, or absorbed in material contact, it acts for material advancement of knowledge, destructively ending in discovery of nuclear weapons. But when the mind acts under spiritual urge, it acts wonderfully for going back home, back to Godhead, for life in complete bliss and eternity. Therefore the mind has to be manipulated by good and unalloyed intelligence. Perfect intelligence is to render service unto the Lord. One should be intelligent enough to understand that the living being is, in all circumstances, a servant of the circumstances. Every living being is serving the dictates of desire, anger, lust, illusion, insanity and enviousness—all materially affected. But even while executing such dictations of different temperaments, he is perpetually unhappy. When one actually feels this and turns his intelligence to inquiring about it from the right sources, he gets information of the transcendental loving service of the Lord. Instead of serving materially for the above-mentioned different humors of the body, the living entity's intelligence then becomes freed from the unhappy illusion of materialistic temperament, and thus, by unalloyed intelligence, the mind is brought into the service of the Lord. The Lord and His service are identical, being on the absolute plane. Therefore the unalloyed intelligence and the mind are merged into the Lord, and thus the living entity does not remain a seer himself but becomes seen by the Lord transcendentally. When the living entity is directly seen by the Lord, the Lord dictates to him to act according to His desire, and when the living entity follows Him perfectly, the living entity ceases to discharge any other duty for his illusory satisfaction. In his pure unalloyed state, the living being attains the stage of full bliss, labdhopaśānti, and ceases all material hankerings.

TEXT 17

न यत्र कालोऽनिमिषां परः प्रभुः
कुतो नु देवा जगतां य ईशिरे ।
न यत्र सत्त्वं न रजस्तमश्च
न वै विकारो न महान् प्रधानम् ॥१७॥

na yatra kālo 'nimiṣāṁ paraḥ prabhuḥ
kuto nu devā jagatāṁ ya īśire
na yatra sattvaṁ na rajas tamaś ca
na vai vikāro na mahān pradhānam

na—not; yatra—wherein; kālaḥ—destructive time; animiṣām—of the heavenly demigods; paraḥ—superior; prabhuḥ—controller; kutaḥ—where is there; nu—certainly; devāḥ—the demigods; jagatām—the mundane creatures; ye—those; īśire—rules; na—not; yatra—therein; sattvam—mundane goodness; na—nor; rajaḥ—mundane passion; tamaḥ—mundane ignorance; ca—also; na—nor; vai—certainly; vikāraḥ—transformation; na—nor; mahān—the material Causal Ocean; pradhānam—material nature.

TRANSLATION

In that transcendental state of labdhopaśānti, there is no supremacy of devastating time, which controls even the celestial demigods who are empowered to rule over mundane creatures. (And what to speak of the demigods themselves?) Nor is there the mode of material goodness, nor passion, nor ignorance, nor even the false ego, nor the material Causal Ocean, nor the material nature.

PURPORT

Devastating time, which controls even the celestial demigods by its manifestations of past, present and future, does not act on the transcendental plane. The influence of time is exhibited by the symptoms of birth, death, old age and disease, and these four principles of material conditions are present everywhere in any part of the material cosmos up to the planet Brahmaloka, where the duration of life of the inhabitants appears to us to be fabulous. Insurmountable time even brings about the death of Brahmā, so what to speak of other demigods like Indra, Candra, Sūrya, Vāyu and Varuṇa? The astronomical influence directed by the different demigods over mundane creatures is also conspicuous by its absence. In material existence, the living entities are afraid of Satanic influence, but for a devotee on the transcendental plane there is no such fear at all. The living entities change their material bodies in different shapes and forms under the influence of the different modes of material nature, but in the transcendental state the devotee is *guṇātīta*, or above the material modes of goodness, passion and ignorance. Thus the false ego of "I am the lord of all I survey" does not arise there. In the material world the false ego of the living being trying to lord it over the material nature is something like the moth's falling in a blazing fire. The moth is captivated by the glaring beauty of the fire, and when he comes to enjoy it, the blazing fire consumes him. In the transcendental state the living being is pure in his consciousness, and as such he has no false ego to lord it over the material nature. Rather, his pure consciousness directs him to surrender unto the Supreme Lord, as stated in the *Bhagavad-gītā* (7.19): *vāsudevaḥ sarvam iti sa mahātmā sudurlabhaḥ.* All this indicates that in the transcendental state there is neither material creation nor the Causal Ocean for material nature.

The above-mentioned state of affairs is factual on the transcendental plane, but is factually revealed in a transcendentalist's knowledge of the advanced state of pure consciousness. Such transcendentalists are of two types, namely the impersonalists and the devotees. For the impersonalist the ultimate goal or destination is the *brahmajyoti* of the spiritual sky, but for the devotees the ultimate goal is the Vaikuṇṭha planets. The devotees experience the above-mentioned state of affairs by attainment of spiritual forms for activity in the transcendental loving service of the Lord. But the impersonalist, because of his neglecting the association of the Lord, does not develop a spiritual body for spiritual activity, but remains a spiritual spark only, merged in the effulgent spiritual rays of the Supreme Personality of Godhead. The Lord is the full-fledged form

of eternity, bliss and knowledge, but the formless *brahmajyoti* is simply
eternity and knowledge. The Vaikuṇṭha planets are also forms of eternity, bliss and knowledge, and therefore the devotees of the Lord, who
are admitted into the abode of the Lord, also get bodies of eternity, bliss
and knowledge. As such there is no difference between one and another.
The Lord's abode, name, fame, entourage, etc., are of the same transcendental quality, and how this transcendental quality differs from the material world is explained herewith in this verse. In the *Bhagavad-gītā*,
three principal subjects have been explained by Lord Śrī Kṛṣṇa, namely
karma-yoga, *jñāna-yoga* and *bhakti-yoga*, but one can reach the
Vaikuṇṭha planets by the practice of *bhakti-yoga* only. The other two are
incompetent in helping one reach the Vaikuṇṭhalokas, although they
can, however, conveniently take one to the effulgent *brahmajyoti*, as
described above.

TEXT 18

परं पदं वैष्णवमामनन्ति तद्
यन्नेति नेतीत्यतदुत्सिसृक्षवः ।
विसृज्य दौरात्म्यमनन्यसौहृदा
हृदोपगुह्यार्हपदं पदे पदे ॥१८॥

param padaṁ vaiṣṇavam āmananti tad
yan neti netīty atad utsisṛkṣavaḥ
visṛjya daurātmyam ananya-sauhṛdā
hṛdopaguhyārha-padaṁ pade pade

param—the supreme; *padam*—situation; *vaiṣṇavam*—in relation
with the Personality of Godhead; *āmananti*—do they know; *tat*—that;
yat—which; *na iti*—not this; *na iti*—not this; *iti*—thus; *atat*—godless;
utsisṛkṣavaḥ—those who desire to avoid; *visṛjya*—giving it up completely; *daurātmyam*—perplexities; *ananya*—absolutely; *sauhṛdāḥ*—
in good will; *hṛdā upaguhya*—taking them into his heart; *arha*—that
which is only worshipable; *padam*—lotus feet; *pade pade*—at every
moment.

TRANSLATION

**The transcendentalists desire to avoid everything godless, for
they know that supreme situation in which everything is related**

with the Supreme Lord Viṣṇu. Therefore a pure devotee who is in absolute harmony with the Lord does not create perplexities, but worships the lotus feet of the Lord at every moment, taking them into his heart.

PURPORT

In the *Bhagavad-gītā*, *mad-dhāma* ("My abode") is mentioned several times, and according to the version of the Supreme Personality of Godhead Śrī Kṛṣṇa there exists the unlimited spiritual sky, wherein the planets are called Vaikuṇṭhas, or the abode of the Personality of Godhead. In that sky, which is far, far beyond the material sky and its sevenfold coverings, there is no need of the sun or the moon, nor is there necessity of electricity for illumination, because the planets are self-illuminating and more brilliant than the material suns. Pure devotees of the Lord are absolutely in harmony with the Personality of Godhead, or in other words, they always think of the Lord as their only dependable friend and well-wisher. They do not care for any mundane creature, up to the status of Brahmā, the lord of the universe. Only they can definitely have a clear vision of the Vaikuṇṭha planets. Such pure devotees, being perfectly directed by the Supreme Lord, do not create any artificial perplexity in the matter of transcendental understanding by wasting time in discussing what is Brahman and what is non-Brahman, or *māyā*, nor do they falsely think of themselves as one with the Lord, or argue that there is no existence of the Lord separately, or that there is no God at all, or that living beings are themselves God, or that when God incarnates Himself He assumes a material body. Nor do they concern themselves with many obscure speculative theories, which are in actuality so many stumbling blocks on the path of transcendental understanding. Apart from the class of impersonalists or nondevotees, there are also classes who pose themselves as devotees of the Lord but at heart maintain the idea of salvation by becoming one with the impersonal Brahman. They wrongly manufacture their own way of devotional service by open debauchery and mislead others who are simpletons or debauchees like themselves. All these nondevotees and debauchees are, according to Viśvanātha Cakravartī, *durātmās*, or crooked souls in the dress of *mahātmās*, or great souls. Such nondevotees and debauchees are completely excluded from the list of transcendentalists by the presentation of this particular verse by Śukadeva Gosvāmī.

So the Vaikuṇṭha planets are factually the supreme residential places called the *param padam*. The impersonal *brahmajyoti* is also called the *param padam* due to its being the rays of the Vaikuṇṭha planets, as the sun rays are the rays of the sun. In the *Bhagavad-gītā* (14.27) it is clearly said that the impersonal *brahmajyoti* rests on the person of the Lord, and because everything rests on the *brahmajyoti* directly and indirectly, everything is generated from the Lord, everything rests on Him, and after annihilation, everything is merged in Him only. Therefore, nothing is independent of Him. A pure devotee of the Lord no longer wastes valuable time in discriminating the Brahman from non-Brahman because he knows perfectly well that the Lord Parabrahman, by His Brahman energy, is interwoven in everything, and thus everything is looked upon by a devotee as the property of the Lord. The devotee tries to engage everything in His service and does not create perplexities by falsely lording it over the creation of the Lord. He is so faithful that he engages himself, as well as everything else, in the transcendental loving service of the Lord. In everything, the devotee sees the Lord, and he sees everything in the Lord. The specific disturbance created by a *durātmā*, or crooked soul, is due to his maintaining that the transcendental form of the Lord is something material.

TEXT 19

इत्थं मुनिस्तूपरमेद् व्यवस्थितो
विज्ञानदृग्वीर्यसुरन्धिताशयः ।
स्वपार्ष्णिनापीड्य गुदं ततोऽनिलं
स्थानेषु षट्सून्नमयेज्जितक्लमः ॥१९॥

ittham munis tūparamed vyavasthito
vijñāna-dṛg-vīrya-surandhitāśayaḥ
sva-pārṣṇināpīḍya gudaṁ tato 'nilaṁ
sthāneṣu ṣaṭsūnnamayej jita-klamaḥ

ittham—thus, by Brahman realization; *muniḥ*—the philosopher; *tu*—but; *uparamet*—should retire; *vyavasthitaḥ*—well situated; *vijñāna-dṛk*—by scientific knowledge; *vīrya*—strength; *su-randhita*—well regulated; *āśayaḥ*—aim of life; *sva-pārṣṇinā*—with the heel of one's foot; *āpīḍya*—by blocking; *gudam*—the air hole; *tataḥ*—thereafter; *anilam*—life air; *sthāneṣu*—in the places; *ṣaṭsu*—six primary; *unnamayet*—must be lifted; *jita-klamaḥ*—by extinguishing material desires.

TRANSLATION

By the strength of scientific knowledge, one should be well situated in absolute realization and thus be able to extinguish all material desires. One should then give up the material body by blocking the air hole [through which stool is evacuated] with the heel of one's foot and by lifting the life air from one place to another in the six primary places.

PURPORT

There are many *durātmās* who claim to have realized themselves as Brahman and yet are unable to conquer material desires. In the *Bhagavad-gītā* (18.54) it is clearly explained that an absolutely self-realized soul becomes completely aloof from all material desires. Material desires are based on the false ego of the living being and are exhibited by his childish and useless activities to conquer the laws of material nature and by his desire to lord it over the resources of the five elements. With such a mentality, one is led to believe in the strength of material science, with its discovery of atomic energy and space travel by mechanical vehicles, and by such tiny advancements in material science the false egoist tries to challenge even the strength of the Supreme Lord, who can finish all man's tiny endeavors in less than a second. The well-situated self, or Brahman-realized soul, perfectly understands that the Supreme Brahman, or the Personality of Godhead, is the all-powerful Vāsudeva and that he (the self-realized living being) is a part and parcel of the supreme whole. As such, his constitutional position is to cooperate with Him in all respects in the transcendental relation of the served and the servitor. Such a self-realized soul ceases to exhibit his useless activities of attempting to lord it over material nature. Being scientifically well informed, he fully engages himself in faithful devotion to the Lord.

The expert *yogī* who has thoroughly practiced the control of the life air by the prescribed method of the *yoga* system is advised to quit the

body as follows. He should plug up the evacuating hole with the heel of
the foot and then progressively move the life air on and on to six places:
the navel, abdomen, heart, chest, palate, eyebrows and cerebral pit. Controlling the life air by the prescribed yogic process is mechanical, and the
practice is more or less a physical endeavor for spiritual perfection. In
olden days such practice was very common for the transcendentalist, for
the mode of life and character in those days were favorable. But in
modern days, when the influence of Kali Age is so disturbing, practically
everyone is untrained in this art of bodily exercise. Concentration of the
mind is more easily attained in these days by the chanting of the holy
name of the Lord. The results are more effective than those derived from
the inner exercise of the life air.

TEXT 20

नाभ्यां स्थितं हृद्यधिरोप्य तस्मा-
दुदानगत्योरसि तं नयेन्मुनिः ।
ततोऽनुसन्धाय धिया मनस्वी
खतालुमूलं   शनकैर्नयेत ॥२०॥

nābhyāṁ sthitaṁ hṛdy adhiropya tasmād
udāna-gatyorasi taṁ nayen muniḥ
tato 'nusandhāya dhiyā manasvī
sva-tālu-mūlaṁ śanakair nayeta

nābhyām—on the navel; sthitam—situated; hṛdi—in the heart;
adhiropya—by placing; tasmāt—from there; udāna—soaring; gatya—
force; urasi—on the chest; tam—thereafter; nayet—should draw;
muniḥ—the meditative devotee; tataḥ—them; anusandhāya—just to
search out; dhiyā—by intelligence; manasvī—the meditative; sva-tālu-
mūlam—at the root of the palate; śanakaiḥ—slowly; nayeta—may be
brought in.

TRANSLATION

**The meditative devotee should slowly push up the life air from
the navel to the heart, from there to the chest and from there to**

the root of the palate. He should search out the proper places with intelligence.

PURPORT

There are six circles of the movement of the life air, and the intelligent *bhakti-yogī* should search out these places with intelligence and in a meditative mood. Among these, mentioned above is the *svādhiṣṭhāna-cakra*, or the powerhouse of the life air, and above this, just below the abdomen and navel, is the *maṇi-pūraka-cakra*. When upper space is further searched out in the heart, one reaches the *anāhata-cakra*, and further up, when the life air is placed at the root of the palate, one reaches the *viśuddhi-cakra*.

TEXT 21

तस्माद्   भ्रुवोरन्तरमुन्नयेत्
निरुद्धसप्तायतनोऽनपेक्षः   ।
स्थित्वा   मुहूर्तार्धमकुण्ठदृष्टि-
र्निर्भिद्य मूर्धन् विसृजेत्परं गतः ॥२१॥

tasmād bhruvor antaram unnayeta
niruddha-saptāyatano 'napekṣaḥ
sthitvā muhūrtārdham akuṇṭha-dṛṣṭir
nirbhidya mūrdhan visṛjet paraṁ gataḥ

tasmāt—from there; *bhruvoḥ*—of the eyebrows; *antaram*—in between; *unnayeta*—should be brought in; *niruddha*—by blocking; *sapta*—seven; *āyatanaḥ*—outlets of the life air; *anapekṣaḥ*—independent of all material enjoyment; *sthitvā*—by keeping; *muhūrta*—of a moment; *ardham*—half; *akuṇṭha*—back home, back to Godhead; *dṛṣṭiḥ*—one whose aim is targeted like that; *nirbhidya*—punching; *mūrdhan*—the cerebral hole; *visṛjet*—should give up his body; *param*—the Supreme; *gataḥ*—having gone to.

TRANSLATION

Thereafter the bhakti-yogī should push the life air up between the eyebrows, and then, blocking the seven outlets of the life air, he should maintain his aim for going back home, back to Godhead. If he is completely free from all desires for material enjoyment, he should then reach the cerebral hole and give up his material connections, having gone to the Supreme.

PURPORT

The process of giving up all material connections and returning home, back to Godhead, the Supreme, is recommended herein. The condition is that one should be completely freed from desire for material enjoyment. There are different grades of material enjoyments in respect to duration of life and sensual gratification. The highest plane of sensual enjoyment for the longest period of life is mentioned in the *Bhagavad-gītā* (9.20). All are but material enjoyments, and one should be thoroughly convinced that he has no need of such a long duration of life, even in the Brahmaloka planet. He must return home, back to Godhead, and must not be attracted by any amount of material facilities. In the *Bhagavad-gītā* (2.59) it is said that this sort of material detachment is possible to attain when one is acquainted with the supreme association of life. *Paraṁ dṛṣṭvā nivartate.* One cannot be freed from material attraction unless he has complete understanding of the nature of spiritual life. The propaganda by a certain class of impersonalists that spiritual life is void of all varieties is dangerous propaganda to mislead the living beings into becoming more and more attracted by material enjoyments. As such, persons with a poor fund of knowledge cannot have any conception of the *param*, the Supreme; they try to stick to the varieties of material enjoyments, although they may flatter themselves as being Brahman-realized souls. Such less intelligent persons cannot have any conception of the *param*, as mentioned in this verse, and therefore they cannot reach the Supreme. The devotees have full knowledge of the spiritual world, the Personality of Godhead and His transcendental association in unlimited spiritual planets called Vaikuṇṭhalokas. Herein *akuṇṭha-dṛṣṭiḥ* is mentioned. *Akuṇṭha* and *vaikuṇṭha* convey the same import, and only one who has his aim fixed upon that spiritual world and personal association with the Godhead can give up his material connections even while living in the material world. This *param* and the *paraṁ dhāma* mentioned in several places in the *Bhagavad-gītā* are one and the same thing. One who goes to the *paraṁ dhāma* does not return to the material world. This freedom is not possible even by reaching the topmost *loka* of the material world.

The life air passes through seven openings, namely two eyes, two nostrils, two ears and one mouth. Generally it passes through the mouth at the time of an ordinary man's death. But the *yogī*, as above mentioned, who controls the life air in his own way, generally releases the life air by puncturing the cerebral hole in the head. The *yogī* therefore blocks up all the above-mentioned seven openings, so that the life air will naturally burst forth through the cerebral hole. This is the sure sign of a great devotee's leaving the material connection.

TEXT 22

यदि प्रयास्यन् नृप पारमेष्ठ्यं
वैहायसानामुत यद् विहारम् ।
अष्टाधिपत्यं गुणसन्निवाये
सहैव गच्छेन्मनसेन्द्रियैश्च ॥२२॥

yadi prayāsyan nṛpa pārameṣṭhyaṁ
vaihāyasānām uta yad vihāram
aṣṭādhipatyaṁ guṇa-sannivāye
sahaiva gacchen manasendriyaiś ca

yadi—however; *prayāsyan*—maintaining a desire; *nṛpa*—O King; *pārameṣṭhyam*—the governing planet of the material world; *vaihāyasānām*—of the beings known as the Vaihāyasas; *uta*—it is said; *yat*—what is; *vihāram*—place of enjoyment; *aṣṭa-ādhipatyam*—lording it over with eightfold achievements; *guṇa-sannivāye*—in the world of three modes of nature; *saha*—along with; *eva*—certainly; *gacchet*—should go; *manasā*—accompanied by the mind; *indriyaiḥ*—and the senses; *ca*—also.

TRANSLATION

However, O King, if a yogī maintains a desire for improved material enjoyments, like transference to the topmost planet, Brahmaloka, or the achievement of the eightfold perfections, travel in outer space with the Vaihāyasas, or a situation in one of

the millions of planets, then he has to take away with him the materially molded mind and senses.

PURPORT

In the upper status of the planetary systems there are facilities thousands and thousands of times greater for material enjoyments than in the lower planetary systems. The topmost planetary systems consist of planets like Brahmaloka and Dhruvaloka (the polestar), and all of them are situated beyond Maharloka. The inhabitants of those planets are empowered with eightfold achievements of mystic perfection. They do not have to learn and practice the mystic processes of *yoga* perfection and achieve the power of becoming small like a particle (*aṇimā-siddhi*), or lighter than a soft feather (*laghimā-siddhi*). They do not have to get anything and everything from anywhere and everywhere (*prāpti-siddhi*), to become heavier than the heaviest (*mahimā-siddhi*), to act freely even to create something wonderful or to annihilate anything at will (*īśitva-siddhi*), to control all material elements (*vaśitva-siddhi*), to possess such power as will never be frustrated in any desire (*prākāmya-siddhi*), or to assume any shape or form one may even whimsically desire (*kāmāvasāyitā-siddhi*). All these expediencies are as common as natural gifts for the inhabitants of those higher planets. They do not require any mechanical help to travel in outer space, and they can move and travel at will from one planet to any other planet within no time. The inhabitants of the earth cannot move even to the nearest planet except by mechanical vehicles like spacecraft, but the highly talented inhabitants of such higher planets can do everything very easily.

Since a materialist is generally inquisitive to experience what is actually in such planetary systems, he wants to see everything personally. As inquisitive persons tour all over the world to gain direct local experience, the less intelligent transcendentalist similarly desires to have some experience of those planets about which he has heard so many wonderful things. The *yogī* can, however, easily fulfill his desire by going there with the present materialistic mind and senses. The prime inclination of the materialistic mind is to lord it over the material world, and all the *siddhis* mentioned above are features of domination over the world. The devotees of the Lord are not ambitious to dominate a false and temporary phenomenon. On the contrary, a devotee wants to be dominated by the supreme predominator, the Lord. A desire to serve the Lord, the supreme predominator, is spiritual or transcendental, and one has to attain this purification of the mind and the senses to get admission into the spiritual kingdom. With the materialistic mind one can reach the best planet in the universe, but no one can enter into the kingdom of God. Senses are called spiritually purified when they are not involved in sense gratification. Senses require engagements, and when the senses are engaged totally in the transcendental loving service of the Lord, they have no chance to become contaminated by material infections.

TEXT 23

योगेश्वराणां   गतिमाहुरन्त-

र्बहिस्त्रिलोक्याः पवनान्तरात्मनाम् ।

न कर्मभिस्तां   गतिमाप्नुवन्ति

विद्यातपोयोगसमाधिभाजाम्   ॥२३॥

yogeśvarāṇāṁ gatim āhur antar-
    bahis-tri-lokyāḥ pavanāntar-ātmanām
na karmabhis tāṁ gatim āpnuvanti
    vidyā-tapo-yoga-samādhi-bhājām

yoga-īśvarāṇām—of the great saints and devotees; gatim—destination; āhuḥ—it is said; antaḥ—within; bahiḥ—without; tri-lokyāḥ—of the three planetary systems; pavana-antaḥ—within the air; ātmanām—of the subtle body; na—never; karmabhiḥ—by fruitive activities; tām—that; gatim—speed; āpnuvanti—achieve; vidyā—devotional service; tapaḥ—austerities; yoga—mystic power; samādhi—knowledge; bhājām—of those who entertain.

TRANSLATION

The transcendentalists are concerned with the spiritual body. As such, by the strength of their devotional service, austerities, mystic power and transcendental knowledge, their movements are unrestricted, within and beyond the material worlds. The fruitive workers, or the gross materialists, can never move in such an unrestricted manner.

PURPORT

The materialistic scientist's endeavor to reach other planets by mechanical vehicles is only a futile attempt. One can, however, reach heavenly planets by virtuous activities, but one can never expect to go beyond Svarga or Janaloka by such mechanical or materialistic activities, either gross or subtle. The transcendentalists who have nothing to do with the gross material body can move anywhere within or beyond the material worlds. Within the material worlds they move in the planetary systems of the Mahar-, Janas-, Tapas- and Satya-loka, and beyond the material worlds they can move in the Vaikuṇṭhas as unrestricted spacemen. Nārada Muni is one of the examples of such spacemen, and Durvāsā Muni is one of such mystics. By the strength of devotional service, austerities, mystic powers and transcendental knowledge, everyone can move like Nārada Muni or Durvāsā Muni. It is said that Durvāsā Muni traveled throughout the entirety of material space and part of spiritual space within one year only. The speed of the transcendentalists can never be attained by the gross or subtle materialists.

TEXT 24

वैश्वानरं याति विहायसा गतः
सुषुम्णया ब्रह्मपथेन शोचिषा ।
विभूतकल्कोऽथ हरेरुदस्तात्
प्रयाति चक्रं नृप शैशुमारम् ॥२४॥

vaiśvānaraṁ yāti vihāyasā gataḥ
suṣumṇayā brahma-pathena śociṣā
vidhūta-kalko 'tha harer udastāt
prayāti cakraṁ nṛpa śaiśumāram

vaiśvānaram—the controlling deity of fire; *yāti*—goes; *vihāyasā*—by the path in the sky (the Milky Way); *gataḥ*—by passing over; *suṣumṇayā*—by the Suṣumṇā; *brahma*—Brahmaloka; *pathena*—on the way to; *śociṣā*—illuminating; *vidhūta*—being washed off; *kalkaḥ*—dirt; *atha*—thereafter; *hareḥ*—of Lord Hari; *udastāt*—upwards; *prayāti*—does reach; *cakram*—circle; *nṛpa*—O King; *śaiśumāram*—named Śiśumāra.

TRANSLATION

O King, when such a mystic passes over the Milky Way by the illuminating Suṣumṇā to reach the highest planet, Brahmaloka, he goes first to Vaiśvānara, the planet of the deity of fire, wherein he becomes completely cleansed of all contaminations, and thereafter he still goes higher, to the circle of Śiśumāra, to relate with Lord Hari, the Personality of Godhead.

PURPORT

The polar star of the universe and the circle thereof is called the Śiśumāra circle, and therein the local residential planet of the Personality of Godhead (Kṣīrodakaśāyī Viṣṇu) is situated. Before reaching there, the mystic passes over the Milky Way to reach Brahmaloka, and while going there he first reaches Vaiśvānara-loka, where the demigod controls fire. On Vaiśvānara-loka the *yogī* becomes completely cleansed of all dirty sins acquired while in contact with the material world. The Milky Way in the sky is indicated herein as the way leading to Brahmaloka, the highest planet of the universe.

TEXT 25

तद् विश्वनाभिं त्वतिवर्त्य विष्णो-
रणीयसा   विरजेनात्मनैकः ।
नमस्कृतं   ब्रह्मविदामुपैति
कल्पायुषो यद् विबुधा रमन्ते ॥२५॥

tad viśva-nābhiṁ tv ativartya viṣṇor
aṇīyasā virajenātmanaikaḥ
namaskṛtaṁ brahma-vidām upaiti
kalpāyuṣo yad vibudhā ramante

tat—that; *viśva-nābhim*—navel of the universal Personality of Godhead; *tu*—but; *ativartya*—crossing over; *viṣṇoḥ*—of Lord Viṣṇu, the Personality of Godhead; *aṇīyasā*—due to mystic perfection; *virajena*—by the purified; *ātmanā*—by the living entity; *ekaḥ*—alone; *namaskṛtam*—worshipable; *brahma-vidām*—by those who are

transcendentally situated; *upaiti*—reaches; *kalpa-āyuṣaḥ*—a period of
4,300,000,000 solar years; *yat*—the place; *vibudhāḥ*—self-realized
souls; *ramante*—do enjoy.

TRANSLATION

This Śiśumāra is the pivot for the turning of the complete universe, and it is called the navel of Viṣṇu [Garbhodakaśāyī Viṣṇu].
The yogī alone goes beyond this circle of Śiśumāra and attains the
planet [Maharloka] where purified saints like Bhṛgu enjoy a duration of life of 4,300,000,000 solar years. This planet is worshipable even for the saints who are transcendentally situated.

TEXT 26

अथो अनन्तस्य मुखानलेन
दन्दह्यमानं स निरीक्ष्य विश्वम् ।
निर्याति सिद्धेश्वरयुष्टधिष्ण्यं
यद् द्वैपरार्ध्यं तदु पारमेष्ठ्यम् ॥२६॥

atho anantasya mukhānalena
dandahyamānaṁ sa nirīkṣya viśvam
niryāti siddheśvara-yuṣṭa-dhiṣṇyaṁ
yad dvai-parārdhyaṁ tad u pārameṣṭhyam

atho—thereupon; *anantasya*—of Ananta, the resting incarnation of
Godhead; *mukha-analena*—by the fire emanating from His mouth;
dandahyamānam—burning to ashes; *saḥ*—he; *nirīkṣya*—by seeing
this; *viśvam*—the universe; *niryāti*—goes out; *siddheśvara-yuṣṭa-
dhiṣṇyam*—airplanes used by the great purified souls; *yat*—the place;
dvai-parārdhyam—15,480,000,000,000 solar years; *tat*—that; *u*—the
exalted; *pārameṣṭhyam*—Satyaloka, where Brahmā resides.

TRANSLATION

At the time of the final devastation of the complete universe [the
end of the duration of Brahmā's life], a flame of fire emanates

from the mouth of Ananta [from the bottom of the universe]. The yogī sees all the planets of the universe burning to ashes, and thus he leaves for Satyaloka by airplanes used by the great purified souls. The duration of life in Satyaloka is calculated to be 15,480,000,000,000 years.

PURPORT

It is indicated herein that the residents of Maharloka, where the purified living entities or demigods possess a duration of life calculated to be 4,300,000,000 solar years, have airships by which they reach Satyaloka, the topmost planet of the universe. In other words, the Śrīmad-Bhāgavatam gives us many clues about other planets far, far away from us which modern planes and spacecraft cannot reach, even by imaginary speeds. The statements of Śrīmad-Bhāgavatam are accepted by great ācāryas like Śrīdhara Svāmī, Rāmānujācārya and Vallabhācārya. Lord Śrī Caitanya Mahāprabhu specifically accepts Śrīmad-Bhāgavatam as the spotless Vedic authority, and as such no sane man can ignore the statements of Śrīmad-Bhāgavatam when it is spoken by the self-realized soul Śrīla Śukadeva Gosvāmī, who follows in the footsteps of his great father, Śrīla Vyāsadeva, the compiler of all Vedic literatures. In the creation of the Lord there are many wonderful things we can see with our own eyes every day and night, but we are unable to reach them equipped by modern materialistic science. We should not, therefore, depend on the fragmentary authority of materialistic science for knowing things beyond the range of scientific purview. For a common man, both modern science and Vedic wisdom are simply to be accepted because none of the statements either of modern science or of Vedic literature can be verified by him. The alternative for a common man is to believe either of them or both of them. The Vedic way of understanding, however, is more authentic because it has been accepted by the ācāryas, who are not only faithful and learned men, but are also liberated souls without any of the flaws of conditioned souls. The modern scientists, however, are conditioned souls liable to so many errors and mistakes; therefore the safe side is to accept the authentic version of Vedic literatures, like Śrīmad-Bhāgavatam, which is accepted unanimously by the great ācāryas.

TEXT 27

न यत्र शोको न जरा न मृत्यु-
र्नार्तिर्न चोद्वेग ऋते कुतश्चित् ।
यच्चित्ततोऽदः कृपयानिदंविदां
दुरन्तदुःखप्रभवानुदर्शनात् ॥२७॥

na yatra śoko na jarā na mṛtyur
nārtir na codvega ṛte kutaścit
yac cit tato 'daḥ kṛpayānidaṁ-vidāṁ
duranta-duḥkha-prabhavānudarśanāt

na—never; yatra—there are; śokaḥ—bereavement; na—nor; jarā—
old age; na—nor; mṛtyuḥ—death; na—nor; artiḥ—pains; na—nor;
ca—also; udvegaḥ—anxieties; ṛte—save and except; kutaścit—sometimes; yat—because of; cit—consciousness; tataḥ—therefore; adaḥ—
compassion; kṛpayā—out of heartfelt sympathy; an-idam-vidām—of
those who are ignorant of the process of devotional service; duranta—
unsurpassable; duḥkha—misery; prabhava—repeated birth and death;
anudarśanāt—by successive experience.

TRANSLATION

In that planet of Satyaloka, there is neither bereavement, nor
old age nor death. There is no pain of any kind, and therefore
there are no anxieties, save that sometimes, due to consciousness,
there is a feeling of compassion for those unaware of the process
of devotional service, who are subjected to unsurpassable miseries
in the material world.

PURPORT

Foolish men of materialistic temperament do not take advantage of
successive authorized knowledge. The Vedic knowledge is authorized and
is acquired not by experiment but by authentic statements of the Vedic
literatures explained by bona fide authorities. Simply by becoming an
academic scholar one cannot understand the Vedic statements; one has to

approach the real authority who has received the Vedic knowledge by disciplic succession, as clearly explained in the *Bhagavad-gītā* (4.2). Lord Kṛṣṇa affirmed that the system of knowledge as explained in the *Bhagavad-gītā* was explained to the sun-god, and the knowledge descended by disciplic succession from the sun-god to his son Manu, and from Manu to King Ikṣvāku (the forefather of Lord Rāmacandra), and thus the system of knowledge was explained down the line of great sages, one after another. But in due course of time the authorized succession was broken, and therefore, just to reestablish the true spirit of the knowledge, the Lord again explained the same knowledge to Arjuna, who was a bona fide candidate for understanding due to his being a pure devotee of the Lord. *Bhagavad-gītā*, as it was understood by Arjuna, is also explained (Bg. 10.12–13), but there are many foolish men who do not follow in the footsteps of Arjuna in understanding the spirit of *Bhagavad-gītā*. They create instead their own interpretations, which are as foolish as they themselves, and thereby only help to put a stumbling block on the path of real understanding, misdirecting the innocent followers who are less intelligent, or the *śūdras*. It is said that one should become a *brāhmaṇa* before one can understand the Vedic statements, and this stricture is as important as the stricture that no one shall become a lawyer who has not qualified himself as a graduate. Such a stricture is not an impediment in the path of progress for anyone and everyone, but it is necessary for an unqualified understanding of a particular science. Vedic knowledge is misinterpreted by those who are not qualified *brāhmaṇas*. A qualified *brāhmaṇa* is one who has undergone strict training under the guidance of a bona fide spiritual master.

The Vedic wisdom guides us to understanding our relation with the Supreme Lord Śrī Kṛṣṇa and to acting accordingly in order to achieve the desired result of returning home, back to Godhead. But materialistic men do not understand this. They want to make a plan to become happy in a place where there is no happiness. For false happiness they try to reach other planets, either by Vedic rituals or by spacecraft, but they should know for certain that any amount of materialistic adjustment for becoming happy in a place which is meant for distress cannot benefit the misguided man because, after all, the whole universe with all its paraphernalia will come to an end after a certain period. Then all plans of materialistic happiness will automatically come to an end. The intelligent person therefore makes a plan to return home, back to God-head. Such an intelligent person surpasses all the pangs of material exis-tence, like birth, death, disease and old age. He is actually happy because he has no anxieties of material existence, but as a compassionate sym-pathizer he feels unhappiness for the suffering materialistic men, and thus he occasionally comes before the materialistic men to teach them the necessity of going back to Godhead. All the bona fide ācāryas preach this truth of returning home, back to Godhead, and warn men not to make a false plan for happiness in a place where happiness is only a myth.

TEXT 28

ततो विशेषं प्रतिपद्य निर्भय-
स्तेनात्मनापोऽनलमूर्तिरत्वरन् ।
ज्योतिर्मयो वायुमुपेत्य काले
वाय्वात्मना खं बृहदात्मलिङ्गम् ॥२८॥

tato viśeṣaṁ pratipadya nirbhayas
tenātmanāpo 'nala-mūrtir atvaran
jyotirmayo vāyum upetya kāle
vāyv-ātmanā khaṁ bṛhad ātma-liṅgam

tataḥ—thereafter; *viśeṣam*—particularly; *pratipadya*—by obtaining; *nirbhayaḥ*—without any doubt; *tena*—by that; *ātmanā*—pure self; *āpaḥ*—water; *anala*—fire; *mūrtiḥ*—forms; *atvaran*—by surpass-ing; *jyotiḥ-mayaḥ*—effulgent; *vāyum*—atmosphere; *upetya*—having reached there; *kāle*—in due course of time; *vāyu*—air; *ātmanā*—by the self; *kham*—ethereal; *bṛhat*—great; *ātma-liṅgam*—the real form of the self.

TRANSLATION

After reaching Satyaloka, the devotee is specifically able to be incorporated fearlessly by the subtle body in an identity similar to that of the gross body, and one after another he gradually attains stages of existence from earthly to watery, fiery, glowing and airy, until he reaches the ethereal stage.

PURPORT

Anyone who can reach Brahmaloka, or Satyaloka, by dint of spiritual perfection and practice is qualified to attain three different types of perfection. One who has attained a specific planet by dint of pious activities attains places in terms of his comparative pious activities. One who has attained the place by dint of *virāṭ* or Hiraṇyagarbha worship is liberated along with the liberation of Brahmā. But one who attains the place by dint of devotional service is specifically mentioned here, in relation to how he can penetrate into the different coverings of the universe and thus ultimately disclose his spiritual identity in the absolute atmosphere of supreme existence.

According to Śrīla Jīva Gosvāmī, all the universes are clustered together up and down, and each and every one of them is separately sevenfold-covered. The watery portion is beyond the sevenfold coverings, and each covering is ten times more expansive than the previous covering. The Personality of Godhead who creates all such universes by His breathing period lies above the cluster of the universes. The water of the Causal Ocean is differently situated than the covering water of the universe. The water that serves as covering for the universe is material, whereas the water of the Causal Ocean is spiritual. As such, the watery covering mentioned herein is considered to be the false egoistic covering of all living entities, and the gradual process of liberation from the material coverings, one after another, as mentioned herein, is the gradual process of being liberated from false egoistic conceptions of the material gross body, and then being absorbed in the identification of the subtle body till the attainment of the pure spiritual body in the absolute realm of the kingdom of God.

Śrīla Śrīdhara Svāmī confirms that a part of the material nature, after being initiated by the Lord, is known as the *mahat-tattva*. A fractional portion of the *mahat-tattva* is called the false ego. A portion of the ego is the vibration of sound, and a portion of sound is atmospheric air. A portion of the airy atmosphere is turned into forms, and the forms constitute the power of electricity or heat. Heat produces the smell of the aroma of the earth, and the gross earth is produced by such aroma. And all these combined together constitute the cosmic phenomenon. The extent of the cosmic phenomenon is calculated to be diametrically (both ways) four billion miles. Then the coverings of the universe begin. The first stratum of the covering is calculated to extend eighty million miles, and the subsequent coverings of the universe are respectively of fire, effulgence, air and ether, one after another, each extending ten times further than the previous. The fearless devotee of the Lord penetrates each one of them and ultimately reaches the absolute atmosphere where everything is of one and the same spiritual identity. Then the devotee enters one of the Vaikuṇṭha planets, where he assumes exactly the same form as the Lord and engages in the loving transcendental service of the Lord. That is the highest perfection of devotional life. Beyond this there is nothing to be desired or achieved by the perfect yogī.

TEXT 29

घ्राणेन गन्धं रसनेन वै रसं
रूपं तु दृष्ट्या श्वसनं त्वचैव ।
श्रोत्रेण चोपेत्य नभोगुणत्वं
प्राणेन चाकूतिमुपैति योगी ॥२९॥

*ghrāṇena gandhaṁ rasanena vai rasaṁ
rūpaṁ ca dṛṣṭyā śvasanaṁ tvacaiva
śrotreṇa copetya nabho-guṇatvaṁ
prāṇena cākūtim upaiti yogī*

ghrāṇena—by smelling; *gandham*—aroma; *rasanena*—by taste; *vai*—exactly; *rasam*—palate; *rūpam*—forms; *ca*—also; *dṛṣṭyā*—by vision; *śvasanam*—contact; *tvacā*—touch; *eva*—as it were; *śrotreṇa*—by vibration of the ear; *ca*—also; *upetya*—by achieving; *nabhaḥ-guṇatvam*—identification of ether; *prāṇena*—by sense organs; *ca*—also; *ākūtim*—material activities; *upaiti*—attains; *yogī*—the devotee.

TRANSLATION

The devotee thus surpasses the subtle objects of different senses like aroma by smelling, the palate by tasting, vision by seeing forms, touch by contacting, the vibrations of the ear by ethereal identification, and the sense organs by material activities.

PURPORT

Beyond the sky there are subtle coverings, resembling the elementary coverings of the universes. The gross coverings are a development of partial ingredients of the subtle causes. So the *yogī* or devotee, along with liquidation of the gross elements, relinquishes the subtle causes like aroma by smelling. The pure spiritual spark, the living entity, thus becomes completely cleansed of all material contamination to become eligible for entrance into the kingdom of God.

TEXT 30

स   भूतसूक्ष्मेन्द्रियसंनिकर्षं
मनोमयं   देवमयं विकार्यम् ।
संसाद्य गत्या सह तेन याति
विज्ञानतच्वं गुणसंनिरोधम् ॥३०॥

sa bhūta-sūkṣmendriya-sannikarṣaṁ
manomayaṁ devamayaṁ vikāryam
saṁsādya gatyā saha tena yāti
vijñāna-tattvaṁ guṇa-sannirodham

saḥ—he (the devotee); *bhūta*—the gross; *sūkṣma*—and the subtle; *indriya*—senses; *sannikarṣam*—the point of neutralization; *manaḥ-mayam*—the mental plane; *deva-mayam*—in the mode of goodness; *vikāryam*—egoism; *saṁsādya*—surpassing; *gatyā*—by the progress; *saha*—along with; *tena*—them; *yāti*—goes; *vijñāna*—perfect knowledge; *tattvam*—truth; *guṇa*—the material modes; *sannirodham*—completely suspended.

TRANSLATION

The devotee, thus surpassing the gross and the subtle forms of coverings, enters the plane of egoism. And in that status he merges the material modes of nature [ignorance and passion] in this point of neutralization and thus reaches egoism in goodness. After this, all egoism is merged in the mahat-tattva, and he comes to the point of pure self-realization.

PURPORT

Pure self-realization, as we have several times discussed, is the pure consciousness of admitting oneself to be the eternal servitor of the Lord. Thus one is reinstated in his original position of transcendental loving service to the Lord, as will be clearly explained in the following verse. This stage of rendering transcendental loving service to the Lord without any hopes of emolument from the Lord, or any other way, can be attained when the material senses are purified and the original pure state of the senses is revived. It is suggested herein that the process of purifying the senses is by the yogic way, namely the gross senses are merged in the mode of ignorance, and the subtle senses are merged in the mode of passion. The mind belongs to the mode of goodness and therefore is called devamaya, or godly. Perfect purification of the mind is made possible when one is fixed in the conviction of being the eternal servitor of the Lord. Therefore simple attainment of goodness is also a material mode; one has to surpass this stage of material goodness and reach the point of purified goodness, or vasudeva-sattva. This vasudeva-sattva helps one to enter into the kingdom of God.

We may also remember in this connection that the process of gradual emancipation by the devotees in the manner mentioned above, although authoritative, is not viable in the present age because of people's being primarily unaware of yoga practice. The so-called yoga practice by the professional protagonists may be physiologically beneficial, but such small successes cannot help one in the attainment of spiritual emancipation as mentioned herein. Five thousand years ago, when the social status of human society was in perfect Vedic order, the yoga process mentioned herein was a common affair for everyone because everyone, and especially the brāhmaṇa and kṣatriya, was trained in the transcendental art under the care of the spiritual master far away from home, in the status of brahmacarya. Modern man, however, is incompetent to understand it perfectly.

Lord Śrī Caitanya, therefore, made it easier for the prospective devotee of the present age in the following specific manner. Ultimately there is no difference in the result. The first and foremost point is that one must understand the prime importance of *bhakti-yoga*. The living beings in different species of life are undergoing different terms of encagement according to their fruitive actions and reactions. But in the execution of different activities, one who secures some resources in *bhakti-yoga* can understand the importance of service to the Lord through the causeless mercy of the Lord, as well as that of the spiritual master. A sincere soul is helped by the Lord through meeting a bona fide spiritual master, the representative of the Lord. By the instruction of such a spiritual master, one gets the seed of *bhakti-yoga*. Lord Śrī Caitanya Mahāprabhu recommends that the devotee sow the seed of *bhakti-yoga* in his heart and nurture it by the watering of hearing and chanting the holy name, fame, etc., of the Lord. The simple process of offenselessly chanting and hearing the holy name of the Lord will gradually promote one very soon to the stage of emancipation. There are three stages in chanting the holy name of the Lord. The first stage is the offensive chanting of the holy name, and the second is the reflective stage of chanting the holy name. The third stage is the offenseless chanting of the holy name of the Lord. In the second stage only, the stage of reflection, between the offensive and offenseless stages, one automatically attains the stage of emancipation. And in the offenseless stage, one actually enters into the kingdom of God, although physically he may apparently be within the material world. To attain the offenseless stage, one must be on guard in the following manner.

When we speak of hearing and chanting, it means that not only should one chant and hear of the holy name of the Lord as Rāma, Kṛṣṇa (or systematically the sixteen names Hare Kṛṣṇa, Hare Kṛṣṇa, Kṛṣṇa Kṛṣṇa, Hare Hare/ Hare Rāma, Hare Rāma, Rāma Rāma, Hare Hare), but one should also read and hear the *Bhagavad-gītā* and *Śrīmad-Bhāgavatam* in the association of devotees. The primary practice of *bhakti-yoga* will cause the seed already sowed in heart to sprout, and by a regular watering process, as mentioned above, the *bhakti-yoga* creeper will begin to grow. By systematic nurturing, the creeper will grow to such an extent that it will penetrate the coverings of the universe, as we have heard in the previous verses, reach the effulgent sky, the *brahmajyoti*, and go farther and farther and reach the spiritual sky, where there are innumerable spiritual planets called Vaikuṇṭhalokas. Above all of them is Kṛṣṇaloka, or Goloka Vṛndāvana, wherein the growing creeper enters and takes repose at the lotus feet of Lord Śrī Kṛṣṇa, the original Personality of Godhead. When one reaches the lotus feet of Lord Kṛṣṇa at Goloka Vṛndāvana, the watering process of hearing and reading, as also chanting of the holy name in the pure devotional stage, fructifies, and the fruits grown there in the form of love of God are tangibly tasted by the devotee, even though he is here in this material world. The ripe fruits of love of God are relished only by the devotees constantly engaged in the watering process as described above. But the working devotee must always be mindful so that the creeper which has so grown will not be cut off. Therefore he should be mindful of the following considerations:

1) Offense by one at the feet of a pure devotee may be likened to the mad elephant who devastates a very good garden if it enters.

2) One must be very careful to guard himself against such offenses at the feet of pure devotees, just as one protects a creeper by all-around fencing.

3) It so happens that by the watering process some weeds are also grown, and unless such weeds are uprooted, the nurturing of the main creeper, or the creeper of *bhakti-yoga*, may be hampered.

4) Actually these weeds are material enjoyment, merging of the self in the Absolute without separate individuality, and many other desires in the field of religion, economic development, sense enjoyment and emancipation.

5) There are many other weeds, like disobedience to the tenets of the revered scriptures, unnecessary engagements, killing animals, and hankering after material gain, prestige and adoration.

6) If sufficient care is not taken, then the watering process may only help to breed the weeds, stunting the healthy growth of the main creeper and resulting in no fructification of the ultimate requirement: love of God.

7) The devotee must therefore be very careful to uproot the different weeds in the very beginning. Only then will the healthy growth of the main creeper not be stunted.

8) And by so doing, the devotee is able to relish the fruit of love of God and thus live practically with Lord Kṛṣṇa, even in this life, and be able to see the Lord in every step.

The highest perfection of life is to enjoy life constantly in the associa-

tion of the Lord, and one who can relish this does not aspire after any
temporary enjoyment of the material world via other media.

TEXT 31

तेनात्मनात्मानमुपैति शान्त-
मानन्दमानन्दमयोऽवसाने ।
एतां गतिं भागवतीं गतो यः
स वै पुनर्नेह विषज्जतेऽङ्ग ॥३१॥

tenātmanātmānam upaiti śāntam
ānandam ānandamayo 'vasāne
etāṁ gatiṁ bhāgavatīṁ gato yaḥ
sa vai punar neha viṣajjate 'ṅga

tena—by that purified; *ātmanā*—by the self; *ātmānam*—the Supersoul; *upaiti*—attains; *śāntam*—rest; *ānandam*—satisfaction; *ānanda-
mayaḥ*—naturally so being; *avasāne*—being freed from all material
contamination; *etām*—such; *gatim*—destination; *bhāgavatīm*—devotional; *gataḥ*—attained by; *yaḥ*—the person; *saḥ*—he; *vai*—certainly;
punaḥ—again; *na*—never; *iha*—in this material world; *viṣajjate*—becomes attracted; *aṅga*—O Mahārāja Parīkṣit.

TRANSLATION

Only the purified soul can attain the perfection of associating
with the Personality of Godhead in complete bliss and satisfaction
in his constitutional state. Whoever is able to renovate such devotional perfection is never again attracted by this material world,
and he never returns.

PURPORT

We should specially note in this verse the description of *gatiṁ
bhāgavatīm*. To become merged in the rays of the Parabrahman, the
Supreme Personality of Godhead, as desired by the *brahmavādī* impersonalist, is not *bhāgavatīm* perfection. The *bhāgavatas* never accept

merging in the impersonal rays of the Lord, but always aspire after personal association with the Supreme Lord in one of the Vaikuṇṭha spiritual planets in the spiritual sky. The whole of the spiritual sky, of which the total number of the material skies is only an insignificant part, is full of unlimited numbers of Vaikuṇṭha planets. The destination of the devotee (the *bhāgavata*) is to enter into one of the Vaikuṇṭha planets, in each of which the Personality of Godhead, in His unlimited personal expansions, enjoys Himself in the association of unlimited numbers of pure devotee associates. The conditioned souls in the material world, after gaining emancipation by devotional service, are promoted to these planets. But the number of ever-liberated souls is far, far greater than the number of conditioned souls in the material world, and the ever-liberated souls in the Vaikuṇṭha planets never care to visit this miserable material world.

The impersonalists, who aspire to merge in the impersonal *brahma-jyoti* effulgence of the Supreme Lord but have no conception of loving devotional service to Him in His personal form in the spiritual manifestation, may be compared to certain species of fish, who, being born in the rivers and rivulets, migrate to the great ocean. They cannot stay in the ocean indefinitely, for their urge for sense gratification brings them back to the rivers and streams to spawn. Similarly, when the materialist becomes frustrated in his attempts to enjoy himself in the limited material world, he may seek impersonal liberation by merging either with the Causal Ocean or with the impersonal *brahmajyoti* effulgence. However, as neither the Causal Ocean nor the impersonal *brahmajyoti* effulgence affords any superior substitute for association and engagement of the senses, the impersonalist will fall again into the limited material world to become entangled once more in the wheel of births and deaths, drawn on by the inextinguishable desire for sensual engagement. But any devotee who enters the kingdom of God by transcendental engagement of his senses in devotional service, and who associates with the liberated souls and the Personality of Godhead there, will never be attracted to the limited surroundings of the material world.

In the *Bhagavad-gītā* (8.15) also the same is confirmed, as the Lord says, "The great *mahātmās*, or the *bhakti-yogīs*, after attaining My association, never come back to this material world, which is full of miseries and is nonpermanent." The highest perfection of life, therefore, is to attain His association, and nothing else. The *bhakti-yogī*, being completely engaged in the Lord's service, has no attraction for any other process of liberation like *jñāna* or *yoga*. A pure devotee is a one hundred percent devotee of the Lord and nothing more.

We should further note in this verse the two words *śāntam* and *ānandam*, which denote that devotional service of the Lord can really bestow upon the devotee two important benedictions, namely peace and satisfaction. The impersonalist is desirous of becoming one with the Supreme, or in other words, he wants to become the Supreme. This is a myth only. The mystic *yogīs* become encumbered by various mystic powers and so have neither peace nor satisfaction. So neither the impersonalists nor the *yogī* can have real peace and satisfaction, but the devotee can become fully peaceful and satisfied because of his association with the complete whole. Therefore, merging in the Absolute or attaining some mystic powers has no attraction for the devotee.

Attainment of love of Godhead means complete freedom from all other attractions. The conditioned soul has many aspirations such as becoming a religious man, a rich man, or a first-class enjoyer or becoming God himself, or becoming powerful like the mystics and acting wonderfully by getting anything or doing anything, but all these aspirations should be rejected by the prospective devotee who actually wants to revive his dormant love of God. The impure devotee aspires after all of the above-mentioned material things by perfection of devotion. But a pure devotee has none of the tinges of the above contaminations, which are the influence of material desires, impersonal speculations and attainment of mystic powers. One can attain the stage of love of God by pure devotional service, or by "a learned labor of love," for the sake of the devotee's lovable object, the Personality of Godhead.

To be more clear, if one wants to attain the stage of love of Godhead, he must give up all desires for material enjoyment, he should refrain from worshiping any of the demigods, and he should devote himself only to the worship of the Supreme Personality of Godhead. He must give up the foolish idea of becoming one with the Lord and the desire to have some wonderful powers just to get the ephemeral adoration of the world. The pure devotee is only favorably engaged in the service of the Lord, without any hope of emolument. This will bring about love of Godhead, or the stage of *śāntam* and *ānandam*, as stated in this verse.

TEXT 32

एते सृती ते नृप वेदगीते
त्वयाभिपृष्टे च सनातने च ।
ये वै पुरा ब्रह्मण आह तुष्ट
आराधितो भगवान् वासुदेवः ॥३२॥

ete sṛtī te nṛpa veda-gīte
tvayābhipṛṣṭe ca sanātane ca
ye vai purā brahmaṇa āha tuṣṭa
ārādhito bhagavān vāsudevaḥ

ete—all that is described; *sṛtī*—way; *te*—unto you; *nṛpa*—O Mahārāja
Parīkṣit; *veda-gīte*—according to the version of the *Vedas*; *tvayā*—by
Your Majesty; *abhipṛṣṭe*—being properly inquired; *ca*—also;
sanātane—in the matter of eternal truth; *ca*—verily; *ye*—which; *vai*—
certainly; *purā*—before; *brahmaṇe*—unto Lord Brahmā; *āha*—said;
tuṣṭaḥ—being satisfied; *ārādhitaḥ*—being worshiped; *bhagavān*—the
Personality of Godhead; *vāsudevaḥ*—Lord Kṛṣṇa.

TRANSLATION

**Your Majesty Mahārāja Parīkṣit, know that all that I have
described in reply to your proper inquiry is just according to the
version of the Vedas, and it is eternal truth. This was described
personally by Lord Kṛṣṇa unto Brahmā, with whom the Lord was
satisfied upon being properly worshiped.**

PURPORT

The two different ways of reaching the spiritual sky and thereby getting emancipation from all material bondage, namely either the direct
process of reaching the kingdom of God or the gradual process through
the other higher planets of the universe, are set forth exactly according
to the version of the *Vedas*. The Vedic versions in this connection are,
*yadā sarve pramucyante kāmā ye 'sya hṛdi śritāḥ / atha martyo 'mṛto
bhavaty atra brahma samaśnute* (*Bṛhad-āraṇyaka Up.* 4.4.7) and *te 'rcir
abhisambhavanti* (*Bṛhad-āraṇyaka Up.* 6.2.15): "Those who are free

from all material desires, which are diseases of the heart, are able to con-
quer death and enter the kingdom of God through the Arci planets."
These Vedic versions corroborate the version of the *Śrīmad-*
Bhāgavatam, and the latter is further confirmed by Śukadeva Gosvāmī,
who affirms that the truth was disclosed by the Supreme Personality of
Godhead Lord Śrī Kṛṣṇa, Vāsudeva, to Brahmā, the first authority on the
Vedas. The disciplic succession holds that the *Vedas* were uttered by
Lord Kṛṣṇa to Brahmā, by Brahmā to Nārada, and by Nārada to
Vyāsadeva, and then by Vyāsadeva to Śukadeva Gosvāmī and so on. So
there is no difference between the versions of all the authorities. The
truth is eternal, and as such there cannot be any new opinion about the
truth. That is the way of knowing the knowledge contained in the *Vedas.*
It is not a thing to be understood by one's erudite scholarship or by the
fashionable interpretations of mundane scholars. There is nothing to be
added and nothing to be subtracted, because the truth is the truth. One
has to accept, after all, *some* authority. The modern scientists are also authorities for the common man for some scientific truths. The common
man follows the version of the scientist. This means that the common
man follows the authority. The Vedic knowledge is also received in that
way. The common man cannot argue about what is beyond the sky or
beyond the universe; he must accept the versions of the *Vedas* as they
are understood by the authorized disciplic succession. In the *Bhagavad-*
gītā also the same process of understanding the *Gītā* is stated in the
Fourth Chapter. If one does not follow the authoritative version of the
ācāryas, he will vainly search after the truth mentioned in the *Vedas.*

TEXT 33

नह्यतोऽन्यः शिवः पन्था विशतः संसृताविह ।
वासुदेवे भगवति भक्तियोगो यतो भवेत् ॥३३॥

na hy ato 'nyaḥ śivaḥ panthā
viśataḥ saṁsṛtāv iha
vāsudeve bhagavati
bhakti-yogo yato bhavet

na—never; *hi*—certainly; *ataḥ*—beyond this; *anyaḥ*—any other;
śivaḥ—auspicious; *panthāḥ*—means; *viśataḥ*—wandering; *saṁsṛtau*—

in the material world; *iha*—in this life; *vāsudeve*—unto Lord Vāsudeva, Kṛṣṇa; *bhagavati*—the Personality of Godhead; *bhakti-yogaḥ*—direct devotional service; *yataḥ*—wherein; *bhavet*—may result in.

TRANSLATION

For those who are wandering in the material universe, there is no more auspicious means of deliverance than what is aimed at in the direct devotional service of Lord Kṛṣṇa.

PURPORT

As will be clarified in the next verse, devotional service, or direct *bhakti-yoga*, is the only absolute and auspicious means of deliverance from the grip of material existence. There are many indirect methods for deliverance from the clutches of material existence, but none of them is as easy and auspicious as *bhakti-yoga*. The means of *jñāna* and *yoga* and other allied disciplines are not independent in delivering a performer. Such activities help one to reach the stage of *bhakti-yoga* after many, many years. In the *Bhagavad-gītā* (12.5) it is said that those who are attached to the impersonal feature of the Absolute are liable to many troubles in the pursuit of their desired goal, and the empiricist philosophers, searching after the Absolute Truth, realize the importance of Vāsudeva realization as all in all after many, many births (Bg. 7.19). As far as *yoga* systems are concerned, it is also said in the *Bhagavad-gītā* (6.47) that amongst the mystics who pursue the Absolute Truth, the one who is always engaged in the service of the Lord is the greatest of all. And the last instruction in the *Bhagavad-gītā* (18.66) advises fully surrendering unto the Lord, leaving aside all other engagements or different processes for self-realization and liberation from material bondage. And the purport of all Vedic literatures is to induce one to accept the transcendental loving service of the Lord by all means.

As already explained in the texts of *Śrīmad-Bhāgavatam* (First Canto), either direct *bhakti-yoga* or the means which ultimately culminate in *bhakti-yoga*, without any tinge of fruitive activity, constitutes the highest form of religion. Everything else is simply a waste of time for the performer.

Śrīla Śrīdhara Svāmī and all other *ācāryas*, like Jīva Gosvāmī, agree that *bhakti-yoga* is not only easy, simple, natural and free from trouble, but is the only source of happiness for the human being.

TEXT 34

भगवान् ब्रह्म कात्स्न्येंन त्रिरन्वीक्ष्य मनीषया ।
तदध्यवस्यत् कूटस्थो रतिरात्मन् यतो भवेत् ॥३४॥

bhagavān brahma kārtsnyena
trir anvīkṣya manīṣayā
tad adhyavasyat kūṭa-stho
ratir ātman yato bhavet

bhagavān—the great personality Brahmā; *brahma*—the *Vedas*; *kārtsnyena*—by summarization; *triḥ*—three times; *anvīkṣya*—scrutinizingly examined; *manīṣayā*—with scholarly attention; *tat*—that; *adhyavasyat*—ascertained it; *kūṭa-sthaḥ*—with concentration of the mind; *ratiḥ*—attraction; *ātman* (*ātmani*)—unto the Supreme Personality of Godhead Śrī Kṛṣṇa; *yataḥ*—by which; *bhavet*—it so happens.

TRANSLATION

The great personality Brahmā, with great attention and concentration of the mind, studied the Vedas three times, and after scrutinizingly examining them, he ascertained that attraction for the Supreme Personality of Godhead Śrī Kṛṣṇa is the highest perfection of religion.

PURPORT

Śrī Śukadeva Gosvāmī is referring to the highest Vedic authority, Lord Brahmā, who is the qualitative incarnation of Godhead. The *Vedas* were taught to Brahmājī in the beginning of the material creation. Although Brahmājī was to hear Vedic instructions directly from the Personality of Godhead, in order to satisfy the inquisitiveness of all prospective students of the *Vedas*, Brahmājī, just like a scholar, studied the *Vedas* three times, as generally done by all scholars. He studied with great attention, concentrating on the purpose of the *Vedas*, and after scrutinizingly examining the whole process, he ascertained that becoming a pure, unalloyed devotee of the Supreme Personality of Godhead Śrī Kṛṣṇa is the topmost perfection of all religious principles. And this is the last instruction of the *Bhagavad-gītā* directly presented by the Personality of Godhead. The Vedic conclusion is thus accepted by all *ācāryas*, and those who are against this conclusion are only *veda-vāda-ratas*, as explained in the *Bhagavad-gītā* (2.42).

TEXT 35

भगवान् सर्वभूतेषु लक्षितः खात्मना हरिः ।
दृस्यैर्बुद्ध्यादिभिर्द्रष्टा   लक्षणैरनुमापकैः ॥३५॥

bhagavān sarva-bhūteṣu
lakṣitaḥ svātmanā hariḥ
dṛśyair buddhy-ādibhir draṣṭā
lakṣaṇair anumāpakaiḥ

bhagavān—the Personality of Godhead; *sarva*—all; *bhūteṣu*—in the living entities; *lakṣitaḥ*—is visible; *sva-ātmanā*—along with the self; *hariḥ*—the Lord; *dṛśyaiḥ*—by what is seen; *buddhi-ādibhiḥ*—by intelligence; *draṣṭā*—one who sees; *lakṣaṇaiḥ*—by different signs; *anumāpakaiḥ*—by hypothesis.

TRANSLATION

The Personality of Godhead Lord Śrī Kṛṣṇa is in every living being along with the individual soul. And this fact is perceived and hypothesized in our acts of seeing and taking help from the intelligence.

PURPORT

The general argument of the common man is that since the Lord is not visible to our eyes, how can one either surrender unto Him or render transcendental loving service unto Him? To such a common man, here is a practical suggestion given by Śrīla Śukadeva Gosvāmī as to how one can perceive the Supreme Lord by reason and perception. Actually the Lord is not perceivable by our present materialized senses, but when one is convinced of the presence of the Lord by a practical service attitude, there is a revelation by the Lord's mercy, and such a pure devotee of the Lord can perceive the Lord's presence always and everywhere. He can perceive that intelligence is the form-direction of the Paramātmā plenary portion of the Personality of Godhead. The presence of Paramātmā in everyone's company is not very difficult to realize, even for the common man. The procedure is as follows. One can perceive one's self-identification and feel positively that he exists. He may not feel it very abruptly, but by using a little intelligence, he can feel that he is not the body. He can feel that the hand, the leg, the head, the hair and the limbs are all his bodily parts and parcels, but as such the hand, the leg, the head, etc., cannot be identified with his self. Therefore just by using intelligence he can distinguish and separate his self from other things that he sees. So the natural conclusion is that the living being, either man or beast, is the seer, and he sees besides himself all other things. So there is a difference between the seer and the seen. Now, by a little use of intelligence we can also readily agree that the living being who sees the things beyond himself by ordinary vision has no power to see or to move independently. All our ordinary actions and perceptions depend on various forms of energy supplied to us by nature in various combinations. Our senses of perception and of action, that is to say, our five perceptive senses of (1) hearing, (2) touch, (3) sight, (4) taste and (5) smell, as well as our five senses of action, namely (1) hands, (2) legs, (3) speech, (4) evacuation organs and (5) reproductive organs, and also our three subtle senses, namely (1) mind, (2) intelligence and (3) ego (thirteen senses in all), are supplied to us by various arrangements of gross or subtle forms of natural energy. And it is equally evident that our objects of perception are nothing but the products of the inexhaustible permutations and combinations of the forms taken by natural energy. As this conclusively proves that the ordinary living being has no independent power of perception or of motion, and as we undoubtedly feel our existence being conditioned by nature's energy, we conclude that he who sees is spirit, and that the senses as well as the objects of perception are material. The spiritual quality of the seer is manifest in our dissatisfaction with the limited state of materially conditioned existence. That is the difference between spirit and matter. There are some less intelligent arguments that matter develops the power of seeing and moving as a certain organic development, but such an argument cannot be accepted because there is no experimental evidence that matter has anywhere produced a living entity. Trust no future, however pleasant. Idle talks regarding future development of matter into spirit are actually foolish because no matter has ever developed the power of seeing or moving in any part of the world. Therefore it is definite that matter and spirit are two different identities, and this conclusion is arrived at by the use of intelligence. Now we come to the point that the things which are seen by a little use of intelligence cannot be animate unless we accept someone as the user of or director of the intelligence. Intelligence gives one direction like some higher authority, and the living being cannot see or move or eat or do anything without the use of intelligence. When one fails to take advantage of intelligence he becomes a deranged man, and so a living being is dependent on intelligence or the direction of a superior being. Such intelligence is all-pervading. Every living being has his intelligence, and this intelligence, being the direction of some higher authority, is just like a father giving direction to his son. The higher authority, who is present and residing within every individual living being, is the Superself.

At this point in our investigation, we may consider the following question: on the one hand we realize that all our perceptions and activities are conditioned by arrangements of material nature, yet we also ordinarily feel and say, "I am perceiving" or "I am doing." Therefore we can say that our material senses of perception and action are moving because we are identifying the self with the material body, and that the superior principle of Superself is guiding and supplying us according to our desire. By taking advantage of the guidance of Superself in the form of intelligence, we can either continue to study and to put into practice our conclusion that "I am not this body," or we can choose to remain in the false material identification, fancying ourselves to be the possessors and doers. Our freedom consists in orienting our desire either toward the ignorant, material misconception or the true, spiritual conception. We can easily attain to the true, spiritual conception by recognizing the Superself (Paramātmā) to be our friend and guide and by dovetailing our intelligence with the superior intelligence of Paramātmā. The Superself and the individual self are both spirit, and therefore the Superself and the individual self are both qualitatively one and distinct from matter. But the

Superself and the individual self cannot be on an equal level because the Superself gives direction or supplies intelligence and the individual self follows the direction, and thus actions are performed properly. The individual is completely dependent on the direction of the Superself because in every step the individual self follows the direction of the Superself in the matter of seeing, hearing, thinking, feeling, willing, etc.

So far as common sense is concerned, we come to the conclusion that there are three identities, namely matter, spirit and Superspirit. Now if we go to the *Bhagavad-gītā*, or the Vedic intelligence, we can further understand that all three identities, namely matter, individual spirit, and the Superspirit, are all dependent on the Supreme Personality of Godhead. The Superself is a partial representation or plenary portion of the Supreme Personality of Godhead. The *Bhagavad-gītā* affirms that the Supreme Personality of Godhead dominates all over the material world by His partial representation only. God is great, and He cannot be simply an order supplier of the individual selves; therefore the Superself cannot be a full representation of the Supreme Self, Puruṣottama, the Absolute Personality of Godhead. Realization of the Superself by the individual self is the beginning of self-realization, and by the progress of such self-realization one is able to realize the Supreme Personality of Godhead by intelligence, by the help of authorized scriptures, and, principally, by the grace of the Lord. The *Bhagavad-gītā* is the preliminary conception of the Personality of Godhead Śrī Kṛṣṇa, and *Śrīmad-Bhāgavatam* is the further explanation of the science of Godhead. So if we stick to our determination and pray for the mercy of the director of intelligence sitting within the same bodily tree, like a bird sitting with another bird (as explained in the *Upaniṣads*), certainly the purport of the revealed information in the *Vedas* becomes clear to our vision, and there is no difficulty in realizing the Supreme Personality of Godhead, Vāsudeva. The intelligent man therefore, after many births of such use of intelligence, surrenders himself at the lotus feet of Vāsudeva, as confirmed by the *Bhagavad-gītā* (7.19).

TEXT 36

तस्मात् सर्वात्मना राजन् हरिः सर्वत्र सर्वदा ।
श्रोतव्यः कीर्तितव्यश्च स्मर्तव्यो भगवान्नृणाम् ॥३६॥

tasmāt sarvātmanā rājan
hariḥ sarvatra sarvadā
śrotavyaḥ kīrtitavyaś ca
smartavyo bhagavān nṛṇām

tasmāt—therefore; sarva—all; ātmanā—soul; rājan—O King;
hariḥ—the Lord; sarvatra—everywhere; sarvadā—always; śrotavyaḥ—
must be heard; kīrtitavyaḥ—glorified; ca—also; smartavyaḥ—be
remembered; bhagavān—the Personality of Godhead; nṛṇām—by the
human being.

TRANSLATION

O King, it is therefore essential that every human being hear
about, glorify and remember the Supreme Lord, the Personality of
Godhead, always and everywhere.

PURPORT

Śrīla Śukadeva Gosvāmī begins this verse with the word tasmāt, or
"therefore," because in the previous verse he has already explained that
there is no auspicious means for salvation other than the sublime process
of bhakti-yoga. The bhakti-yoga process is practiced by the devotees in
different methods like hearing, chanting, remembering, serving the
lotus feet of the Lord, worshiping, praying, rendering service in love, becoming friendly, and offering all that one may possess. All nine methods
are bona fide methods, and either all of them, some of them or even one
of them can bring about the desired result for the sincere devotee. But
out of all the nine different methods, the first one, namely hearing, is the
most important function in the process of bhakti-yoga. Without hearing
sufficiently and properly, no one can make any progress by any of the
methods of practice. And for hearing only, all the Vedic literatures are
there, compiled by authorized persons like Vyāsadeva, who is the powerful incarnation of Godhead. And since it has been ascertained that the
Lord is the Supersoul of everything, He should therefore be heard and
glorified everywhere and always. That is the special duty of the human
being. When the human being gives up the process of hearing about the
all-pervading Personality of Godhead, he becomes victim to hearing rubbish transmitted by man-made machines. Machinery is not bad because

through the machine one can take advantage of hearing about the Lord, but because machinery is used for ulterior purposes, it is creating rapid degradation in the standard of human civilization. It is said here that it is incumbent upon the human beings to hear because the scriptures like *Bhagavad-gītā* and *Śrīmad-Bhāgavatam* are made for that purpose. Living beings other than human beings have no ability to hear such Vedic literatures. If human society gives itself to the process of hearing the Vedic literature, it will not become a victim to the impious sounds vibrated by impious men who degrade the standards of the total society. Hearing is solidified by the process of chanting. One who has perfectly heard from the perfect source becomes convinced about the all-pervading Personality of Godhead and thus becomes enthusiastic in glorifying the Lord. All the great *ācāryas*, like Rāmānuja, Madhva, Caitanya, Sarasvatī Ṭhākura or even, in other countries, Muhammad, Christ and others, have all extensively glorified the Lord by chanting always and in every place. Because the Lord is all-pervading, it is essential to glorify Him always and everywhere. In the process of glorifying the Lord there should be no restriction of time and space. This is called *sanātana-dharma* or *bhāgavata-dharma*. *Sanātana* means eternal, always and everywhere. *Bhāgavata* means pertaining to Bhagavān, the Lord. The Lord is the master of all time and all space, and therefore the Lord's holy name must be heard, glorified and remembered everywhere in the world. That will bring about the desired peace and prosperity so eagerly awaited by the people of the world. The word *ca* includes all the remaining processes or methods of *bhakti-yoga*, as mentioned above.

TEXT 37

पिबन्ति ये भगवत आत्मनः सतां
कथामृतं श्रवणपुटेषु सम्भृतम् ।
पुनन्ति ते विषयविदूषिताशयं
व्रजन्ति तच्चरणसरोरुहान्तिकम् ॥३७॥

pibanti ye bhagavata ātmanaḥ satāṁ
kathāmṛtaṁ śravaṇa-puṭeṣu sambhṛtam
punanti te viṣaya-vidūṣitāśayaṁ
vrajanti tac-caraṇa-saroruhāntikam

pibanti—who drink; *ye*—those; *bhagavataḥ*—of the Personality of Godhead; *ātmanaḥ*—of the most dear; *satām*—of devotees; *kathā-amṛtam*—the nectar of the messages; *śravaṇa-puṭeṣu*—within the earholes; *sambhṛtam*—fully filled; *punanti*—purify; *te*—their; *viṣaya*—material enjoyment; *vidūṣita-āśayam*—polluted aim of life; *vrajanti*—do go back; *tat*—the Lord's; *caraṇa*—feet; *saroruha-anti-kam*—near the lotus.

TRANSLATION

Those who drink through aural reception, fully filled with the nectarean message of Lord Kṛṣṇa, the beloved of the devotees, purify the polluted aim of life known as material enjoyment and thus go back to Godhead, to the lotus feet of Him [the Personality of Godhead].

PURPORT

The sufferings of human society are due to a polluted aim of life, namely lording it over the material resources. The more human society engages in the exploitation of undeveloped material resources for sense gratification, the more it will be entrapped by the illusory, material energy of the Lord, and thus the distress of the world will be intensified instead of diminished. The human necessities of life are fully supplied by the Lord in the shape of food grains, milk, fruit, wood, stone, sugar, silk, jewels, cotton, salt, water, vegetables, etc., in sufficient quantity to feed and care for the human race of the world as well as the living beings on each and every planet within the universe. The supply source is complete, and only a little energy by the human being is required to get his necessities into the proper channel. There is no need of machines and tools or huge steel plants for artificially creating comforts of life. Life is never made comfortable by artificial needs, but by plain living and high thinking. The highest perfectional thinking for human society is suggested here by Śukadeva Gosvāmī, namely, sufficiently hearing *Śrīmad-Bhāgavatam*. For men in this age of Kali, when they have lost the perfect vision of life, this *Śrīmad-Bhāgavatam* is the torchlight by which to see the real path. Śrīla Jīva Gosvāmī Prabhupāda has commented on the *kathāmṛtam* mentioned in this verse and has indicated *Śrīmad-*

Bhāgavatam to be the nectarean message of the Personality of Godhead. By sufficient hearing of *Śrīmad-Bhāgavatam*, the polluted aim of life, namely lording it over matter, will subside, and the people in general in all parts of the world will be able to live a peaceful life of knowledge and bliss.

For a pure devotee of the Lord, any topics in relation with His name, fame, quality, entourage, etc., are all pleasing, and because such topics have been approved by great devotees like Nārada, Hanumān, Nanda Mahārāja and other inhabitants of Vṛndāvana, certainly such messages are transcendental and pleasing to the heart and soul.

And by the constant hearing of the messages of the *Bhagavad-gītā*, and later of *Śrīmad-Bhāgavatam*, one is assured herein by Śrīla Śukadeva Gosvāmī that he will reach the Personality of Godhead and render Him transcendental loving service in the spiritual planet of the name Goloka Vṛndāvana, which resembles a huge lotus flower.

Thus by the process of *bhakti-yoga*, directly accepted, as suggested in this verse, by sufficient hearing of the transcendental message of the Lord, the material contamination is directly eliminated without one's attempting to contemplate the impersonal *virāṭ* conception of the Lord. And by practicing *bhakti-yoga*, if the performer is not purified from the material contamination, he must be a pseudodevotee. For such an imposter there is no remedy for being freed from material entanglement.

Thus end the Bhaktivedanta purports of the Second Canto, Second Chapter, of the Śrīmad-Bhāgavatam, *entitled "The Lord in the Heart."*

CHAPTER THREE

Pure Devotional Service:
The Change in Heart

TEXT 1

श्रीशुक उवाच

एवमेतन्निगदितं पृष्टवान् यद्भवान् मम ।
नृणां यन्म्रियमाणानां मनुष्येषु मनीषिणाम् ॥ १ ॥

śrī-śuka uvāca
evam etan nigaditaṁ
pṛṣṭavān yad bhavān mama
nṛṇāṁ yan mriyamāṇānāṁ
manuṣyeṣu manīṣiṇām

śrī-śukaḥ uvāca—Śrī Śukadeva Gosvāmī said; *evam*—so; *etat*—all these; *nigaditam*—answered; *pṛṣṭavān*—as you inquired; *yat*—what; *bhavān*—your good self; *mama*—unto me; *nṛṇām*—of the human being; *yat*—one; *mriyamāṇānām*—on the threshold of death; *manu-ṣyeṣu*—amongst the human beings; *manīṣiṇām*—of the intelligent men.

TRANSLATION

Śrī Śukadeva Gosvāmī said: Mahārāja Parīkṣit, as you have inquired from me as to the duty of the intelligent man who is on the threshold of death, so I have answered you.

PURPORT

In human society all over the world there are millions and billions of men and women, and almost all of them are less intelligent because they have very little knowledge of spirit soul. Almost all of them have a wrong conception of life, for they identify themselves with the gross and subtle material bodies, which they are not, in fact. They may be situated in different high and low positions in the estimation of human society, but one should know definitely that unless one inquires about his own self beyond the body and the mind, all his activities in human life are total failures. Therefore out of thousands and thousands of men, one may inquire about his spirit self and thus consult the revealed scriptures like *Vedānta-sūtras*, *Bhagavad-gītā* and *Śrīmad-Bhāgavatam*. But in spite of reading and hearing such scriptures, unless one is in touch with a realized spiritual master, he cannot actually realize the real nature of self, etc. And out of thousands and hundreds of thousands of men, someone may know what Lord Kṛṣṇa is in fact. In the *Caitanya-caritāmṛta* (*Madhya* 20.122–123) it is said that Lord Kṛṣṇa, out of His causeless mercy, prepared the Vedic literatures in the incarnation of Vyāsadeva for reading by the intelligent class of men in a human society which is almost totally forgetful of the genuine relation with Kṛṣṇa. Even such an intelligent class of men may be forgetful in their relation with the Lord. The whole *bhakti-yoga* process is therefore a revival of the lost relation. This revival is possible in the human form of life, which is obtained only out of the evolutionary cycle of 8,400,000 species of life. The intelligent class of human being must take a serious note of this opportunity. Not all human beings are intelligent, so the importance of human life is not always understood. Therefore *manīṣiṇām*, meaning "thoughtful," is particularly used here. A *manīṣiṇām* person, like Mahārāja Parīkṣit, must therefore take to the lotus feet of Lord Kṛṣṇa and fully engage himself in devotional service, hearing, chanting, etc., of the holy name and pastimes of the Lord, which are all *hari-kathāmṛta*. This action is especially recommended when one is preparing for death.

TEXTS 2–7

ब्रह्मवर्चसकामस्तु   यजेत   ब्रह्मणः   पतिम्   ।
इन्द्रमिन्द्रियकामस्तु   प्रजाकामः   प्रजापतीन्   ॥ २ ॥
देवीं   मायां   तु   श्रीकामस्तेजस्कामो   विभावसुम्   ।
वसुकामो   वसून्   रुद्रान्   वीर्यकामोऽथ   वीर्यवान्   ॥ ३ ॥
अन्नाद्यकामस्त्वदितिं   स्वर्गकामोऽदितेः   सुतान्   ।
विश्वान्देवान्   राज्यकामः   साध्यान्संसाधको   विशाम्   ॥ ४ ॥

आयुष्कामोऽश्विनौ देवौ पुष्टिकाम इलां यजेत् ।
प्रतिष्ठाकामः पुरुषो रोदसी लोकमातरौ ॥ ५ ॥
रूपाभिकामो गन्धर्वान् स्त्रीकामोऽप्सर उर्वशीम् ।
आधिपत्यकामः सर्वेषां यजेत परमेष्ठिनम् ॥ ६ ॥
यज्ञं यजेद् यशस्कामः कोशकामः प्रचेतसम् ।
विद्याकामस्तु गिरिशं दाम्पत्यार्थं उमां सतीम् ॥ ७ ॥

brahma-varcasa-kāmas tu
yajeta brahmaṇaḥ patim
indram indriya-kāmas tu
prajā-kāmaḥ prajāpatīn

devīṁ māyāṁ tu śrī-kāmas
tejas-kāmo vibhāvasum
vasu-kāmo vasūn rudrān
vīrya-kāmo 'tha vīryavān

annādya-kāmas tv aditiṁ
svarga-kāmo 'diteḥ sutān
viśvān devān rājya-kāmaḥ
sādhyān saṁsādhako viśām

āyuṣ-kāmo 'śvinau devau
puṣṭi-kāma ilāṁ yajet
pratiṣṭhā-kāmaḥ puruṣo
rodasī loka-mātarau

rūpābhikāmo gandharvān
strī-kāmo 'psara urvaśīm
ādhipatya-kāmaḥ sarveṣāṁ
yajeta parameṣṭhinam

yajñaṁ yajed yaśas-kāmaḥ
kośa-kāmaḥ pracetasam
vidyā-kāmas tu giriśaṁ
dāmpatyārtha umāṁ satīm

brahma—the absolute; *varcasa*—effulgence; *kāmaḥ tu*—but one who desires in that way; *yajeta*—do worship; *brahmaṇaḥ*—of the *Vedas*; *patim*—the master; *indram*—the King of heaven; *indriya-kāmaḥ tu*—but one who desires strong sense organs; *prajā-kāmaḥ*—one who desires many offspring; *prajāpatīn*—the Prajāpatis; *devīm*—the goddess; *māyām*—unto the mistress of the material world; *tu*—but; *śrī-kāmaḥ*—one who desires beauty; *tejaḥ*—power; *kāmaḥ*—one who so desires; *vibhāvasum*—the fire-god; *vasu-kāmaḥ*—one who wants wealth; *vasūn*—the Vasu demigods; *rudrān*—the Rudra expansions of Lord Śiva; *vīrya-kāmaḥ*—one who wants to be very strongly built; *atha*—therefore; *vīryavān*—the most powerful; *anna-adya*—grains; *kāmaḥ*—one who so desires; *tu*—but; *aditim*—Aditi, mother of the demigods; *svarga*—heaven; *kāmaḥ*—so desiring; *aditeḥ sutān*—the sons of Aditi; *viśvān*—Viśvadeva; *devān*—demigods; *rājya-kāmaḥ*—those who hanker for kingdoms; *sādhyān*—the Sādhya demigods; *saṁsādhakaḥ*—what fulfills the wishes; *viśām*—of the mercantile community; *āyuḥ-kāmaḥ*—desirous of long life; *aśvinau*—the two demigods known as the Aśvinī brothers; *devau*—the two demigods; *puṣṭi-kāmaḥ*—one who desires a strongly built body; *ilām*—the earth; *yajet*—must worship; *pratiṣṭhā-kāmaḥ*—one who desires good fame, or stability in a post; *puruṣaḥ*—such men; *rodasī*—the horizon; *loka-mātarau*—and the earth; *rūpa*—beauty; *abhikāmaḥ*—positively aspiring for; *gandharvān*—the residents of the Gandharva planet, who are very beautiful and are expert in singing; *strī-kāmaḥ*—one who desires a good wife; *apsaraḥ urvaśīm*—the society girls of the heavenly kingdom; *ādhipatya-kāmaḥ*—one who desires to dominate others; *sarveṣām*—everyone; *yajeta*—must worship; *parameṣṭhinam*—Brahmā, the head of the universe; *yajñam*—the Personality of Godhead; *yajet*—must worship; *yaśaḥ-kāmaḥ*—one who desires to be famous; *kośa-kāmaḥ*—one who desires a good bank balance; *pracetasam*—the treasurer of heaven, known as Varuṇa; *vidyā-kāmaḥ tu*—but one who desires education; *giriśam*—the lord of the Himalayas, Lord Śiva; *dāmpatya-arthaḥ*—and for conjugal love; *umām satīm*—the chaste wife of Lord Śiva, known as Umā.

TRANSLATION

One who desires to be absorbed in the impersonal brahmajyoti effulgence should worship the master of the Vedas [Lord Brahmā

or Bṛhaspati, the learned priest], one who desires powerful sex should worship the heavenly King, Indra, and one who desires good progeny should worship the great progenitors called the Prajāpatis. One who desires good fortune should worship Durgādevī, the superintendent of the material world. One desiring to be very powerful should worship fire, and one who aspires only after money should worship the Vasus. One should worship the Rudra incarnations of Lord Śiva if he wants to be a great hero. One who wants a large stock of grains should worship Aditi. One who desires to attain the heavenly planets should worship the sons of Aditi. One who desires a worldly kingdom should worship Viśvadeva, and one who wants to be popular with the general mass of population should worship the Sādhya demigod. One who desires a long span of life should worship the demigods known as the Aśvinī-kumāras, and a person desiring a strongly built body should worship the earth. One who desires stability in his post should worship the horizon and the earth combined. One who desires to be beautiful should worship the beautiful residents of the Gandharva planet, and one who desires a good wife should worship the Apsarās and the Urvaśī society girls of the heavenly kingdom. One who desires domination over others should worship Lord Brahmā, the head of the universe. One who desires tangible fame should worship the Personality of Godhead, and one who desires a good bank balance should worship the demigod Varuṇa. If one desires to be a greatly learned man he should worship Lord Śiva, and if one desires a good marital relation he should worship the chaste goddess Umā, the wife of Lord Śiva.

PURPORT

There are different modes of worship for different persons desiring success in particular subjects. The conditioned soul living within the purview of the material world cannot be an expert in every type of materially enjoyable asset, but one can have considerable influence over a particular matter by worshiping a particular demigod, as mentioned above. Rāvaṇa was made a very powerful man by worshiping Lord Śiva, and he used to offer severed heads to please Lord Śiva. He became so powerful by the grace of Lord Śiva that all the demigods were afraid of him, until he at last challenged the Personality of Godhead Śrī Rāma-candra and thus ruined himself. In other words, all such persons who aspire after gaining some or all of the material objects of enjoyment, or the gross materialistic persons, are on the whole less intelligent, as confirmed in the *Bhagavad-gītā* (7.20). It is said there that those who are bereft of all good sense, or those whose intelligence is withdrawn by the deluding energy of *māyā*, aspire to achieve all sorts of material enjoyment in life by pleasing the various demigods, or by advancing in material civilization under the heading of scientific progress. The real problem of life in the material world is to solve the question of birth, death, old age and disease. No one wants to change his birthright, no one wants to meet death, no one wants to be old or invalid, and no one wants diseases. But these problems are solved neither by the grace of any demigod nor by the so-called advancement of material science. In the *Bhagavad-gītā*, as well as in the *Śrīmad-Bhāgavatam*, such less intelligent persons have been described as devoid of all good sense. Śukadeva Gosvāmī said that out of the 8,400,000 species of living entities, the human form of life is rare and valuable, and out of those rare human beings those who are conscious of the material problems are rarer still, and the still more rare persons are those who are conscious of the value of the *Śrīmad-Bhāgavatam*, which contains the messages of the Lord and His pure devotees. Death is inevitable for everyone, intelligent or foolish. But Parīkṣit Mahārāja has been addressed by the Gosvāmī as the *manīṣī*, or the man of highly developed mind, because at the time of death he left all material enjoyment and completely surrendered unto the lotus feet of the Lord by hearing His messages from the right person, Śukadeva Gosvāmī. But aspirations for material enjoyment by endeavoring persons are condemned. Such aspirations are something like the intoxication of the degraded human society. Intelligent persons should try to avoid these aspirations and seek instead the permanent life by returning home, back to Godhead.

TEXT 8

धर्मार्थ उत्तमश्लोकं तन्तुः तन्वन् पितॄन् यजेत् ।
रक्षाकामः पुण्यजनानोजस्कामो मरुद्गणान् ॥ ८ ॥

> dharmārtha uttama-ślokam
> tantuḥ tanvan pitṝn yajet
> rakṣā-kāmaḥ puṇya-janān
> ojas-kāmo marud-gaṇān

dharma-arthaḥ—for spiritual advancement; *uttama-ślokam*—the Supreme Lord or persons attached to the Supreme Lord; *tantuḥ*—for offspring; *tanvan*—and for their protection; *pitṝn*—the residents of Pitṛloka; *yajet*—must worship; *rakṣā-kāmaḥ*—one who desires protection; *puṇya-janān*—pious persons; *ojaḥ-kāmaḥ*—one who desires strength should worship; *marut-gaṇān*—the demigods.

TRANSLATION

One should worship Lord Viṣṇu or His devotee for spiritual advancement in knowledge, and for protection of heredity and advancement of a dynasty one should worship the various demigods.

PURPORT

The path of religion entails making progress on the path of spiritual advancement, ultimately reviving the eternal relation with Lord Viṣṇu in His impersonal effulgence, His localized Paramātmā feature, and ultimately His personal feature by spiritual advancement in knowledge. And one who wants to establish a good dynasty and be happy in the progress of temporary bodily relations should take shelter of the Pitās and the demigods in other pious planets. Such different classes of worshipers of different demigods may ultimately reach the respective planets of those demigods within the universe, but he who reaches the spiritual planets in the *brahmajyoti* achieves the highest perfection.

TEXT 9

राज्यकामो मनून् देवान् निर्ऋतिं त्वभिचरन् यजेत् ।
कामकामो यजेत् सोममकामः पुरुषं परम् ॥ ९ ॥

> rājya-kāmo manūn devān
> nirṛtiṁ tv abhicaran yajet

kāma-kāmo yajet somam
akāmaḥ puruṣaṁ param

rājya-kāmaḥ—anyone desiring an empire or kingdom; *manūn*—the Manus, semi-incarnations of God; *devān*—demigods; *nirṛtim*—demons; *tu*—but; *abhicaran*—desiring victory over the enemy; *yajet*—should worship; *kāma-kāmaḥ*—one who desires sense gratification; *yajet*—should worship; *somam*—the demigod named Candra; *akāmaḥ*—one who has no material desires to be fulfilled; *puruṣam*—the Supreme Personality of Godhead; *param*—the Supreme.

TRANSLATION

One who desires domination over a kingdom or an empire should worship the Manus. One who desires victory over an enemy should worship the demons, and one who desires sense gratification should worship the moon. But one who desires nothing of material enjoyment should worship the Supreme Personality of Godhead.

PURPORT

For a liberated person, all the enjoyments listed above are considered to be absolutely useless. Only those who are conditioned by the material modes of external energy are captivated by different types of material enjoyment. In other words, the transcendentalist has no material desires to be fulfilled, whereas the materialist has all types of desires to be fulfilled. The Lord has proclaimed that the materialists, who desire material enjoyment and thus seek the favor of different demigods, as above mentioned, are not in control of their senses and so give themselves to nonsense. One should therefore not desire any sort of material enjoyment, being sensible enough to worship the Supreme Personality of Godhead. The leaders of nonsensical persons are still more nonsensical because they preach openly and foolishly that one can worship any form of demigod and get the same result. This sort of preaching is not only against the teachings of the *Bhagavad-gītā*, or those of the *Śrīmad-Bhāgavatam*, but is also foolish, just as it is foolish to claim that with the purchase of any travel ticket one may reach the same destination. No one can reach Bombay from Delhi by purchasing a ticket for Baroda. It is clearly defined herein that persons impregnated with different desires have different modes of worship, but one who has no desire for material enjoyment should worship the Supreme Lord, Śrī Kṛṣṇa, the Personality of Godhead. And this worshiping process is called devotional service. Pure devotional service means service to the Lord without any tinge of material desires, including desire for fruitive activity and empiric speculation. For fulfillment of material desires one may worship the Supreme Lord, but the result of such worship is different, as will be explained in the next verse. Generally the Lord does not fulfill anyone's material desires for sense enjoyment, but He awards such benedictions to worshipers of the Lord, for they ultimately come to the point of not desiring material enjoyment. The conclusion is that one must minimize the desires for material enjoyment, and for this one should worship the Supreme Personality of Godhead, who is described here as *param*, or beyond anything material. Śrīpāda Śaṅkarācārya has also stated, *nārāyaṇaḥ paro 'vyaktāt:* the Supreme Lord is beyond the material encirclement.

TEXT 10

अकामः सर्वकामो वा मोक्षकाम उदारधीः ।
तीव्रेण भक्तियोगेन यजेत पुरुषं परम् ॥१०॥

akāmaḥ sarva-kāmo vā
mokṣa-kāma udāra-dhīḥ
tīvreṇa bhakti-yogena
yajeta puruṣaṁ param

akāmaḥ—one who has transcended all material desires; *sarva-kāmaḥ*—one who has the sum total of material desires; *vā*—either; *mokṣa-kāmaḥ*—one who desires liberation; *udāra-dhīḥ*—with broader intelligence; *tīvreṇa*—with great force; *bhakti-yogena*—by devotional service to the Lord; *yajeta*—should worship; *puruṣam*—the Lord; *param*—the supreme whole.

TRANSLATION

A person who has broader intelligence, whether he be full of all material desire, without any material desire, or desiring liberation, must by all means worship the supreme whole, the Personality of Godhead.

PURPORT

The Supreme Personality of Godhead Lord Śrī Kṛṣṇa is described in the *Bhagavad-gītā* as *puruṣottama*, or the Supreme Personality. It is He only who can award liberation to the impersonalists by absorbing such aspirants in the *brahmajyoti*, the bodily rays of the Lord. The *brahma-jyoti* is not separate from the Lord, as the glowing sun ray is not independent of the sun disc. Therefore one who desires to merge into the supreme impersonal *brahmajyoti* must also worship the Lord by *bhakti-yoga*, as recommended here in the *Śrīmad-Bhāgavatam*. *Bhakti-yoga* is especially stressed here as the means of all perfection. In the previous chapters it has been stated that *bhakti-yoga* is the ultimate goal of both *karma-yoga* and *jñāna-yoga*, and in the same way in this chapter it is emphatically declared that *bhakti-yoga* is the ultimate goal of the different varieties of worship of the different demigods. *Bhakti-yoga*, thus being the supreme means of self-realization, is recommended here. Everyone must therefore seriously take up the methods of *bhakti-yoga*, even though one aspires for material enjoyment or liberation from material bondage.

Akāmaḥ is one who has no material desire. A living being, naturally being the part and parcel of the supreme whole *puruṣaṁ pūrṇam*, has as his natural function to serve the Supreme Being, just as the parts and parcels of the body, or the limbs of the body, are naturally meant to serve the complete body. Desireless means, therefore, not to be inert like the stone, but to be conscious of one's actual position and thus desire satisfaction only from the Supreme Lord. Śrīla Jīva Gosvāmī has explained this desirelessness as *bhajanīya-parama-puruṣa-sukha-mātra-sva-sukhatvam* in his *Sandarbha*. This means that one should feel happy only by experiencing the happiness of the Supreme Lord. This intuition of the living being is sometimes manifested even during the conditioned stage of a living being in the material world, and such intuition is expressed in the manner of altruism, philanthropy, socialism, communism, etc., by the undeveloped minds of less intelligent persons. In the mundane field such an outlook of doing good to others in the form of society, community, family, country or humanity is a partial manifestation of the same original feeling in which a pure living entity feels happiness by the happiness of the Supreme Lord. Such superb feelings were exhibited by the damsels of Vrajabhūmi for the happiness of the Lord.

The *gopīs* loved the Lord without any return, and this is the perfect exhibition of the *akāmaḥ* spirit. *Kāma* spirit, or the desire for one's own satisfaction, is fully exhibited in the material world, whereas the spirit of *akāmaḥ* is fully exhibited in the spiritual world.

Thoughts of becoming one with the Lord, or being merged in the *brahmajyoti*, can also be exhibitions of *kāma* spirit if they are desires for one's own satisfaction to be free from the material miseries. A pure devotee does not want liberation so that he may be relieved from the miseries of life. Even without so-called liberation, a pure devotee is aspirant for the satisfaction of the Lord. Influenced by the *kāma* spirit, Arjuna declined to fight in the Kurukṣetra battlefield because he wanted to save his relatives for his own satisfaction. But being a pure devotee, he agreed to fight on the instruction of the Lord because he came to his senses and realized that satisfaction of the Lord at the cost of his own satisfaction was his prime duty. Thus he became *akāma*. That is the perfect stage of a perfect living being.

Udāra-dhīḥ means one who has a broader outlook. People with desires for material enjoyment worship small demigods, and such intelligence is condemned in the *Bhagavad-gītā* (7.20) as *hṛta-jñāna*, the intelligence of one who has lost his senses. One cannot obtain any result from demigods without getting sanction from the Supreme Lord. Therefore a person with a broader outlook can see that the ultimate authority is the Lord, even for material benefits. Under the circumstances, one with a broader outlook, even with the desire for material enjoyment or for liberation, should take to the worship of the Lord directly. And everyone, whether an *akāma* or *sakāma* or *mokṣa-kāma*, should worship the Lord with great expedience. This implies that *bhakti-yoga* may be perfectly administered without any mixture of *karma* and *jñāna*. As the unmixed sun ray is very forceful and is therefore called *tīvra*, similarly unmixed *bhakti-yoga* of hearing, chanting, etc., may be performed by one and all regardless of inner motive.

TEXT 11

एतावानेव यजतामिह निःश्रेयसोदयः ।
भगवत्यचलो भावो यद् भागवतसंगतः ॥११॥

etāvān eva yajatām
iha niḥśreyasodayaḥ
bhagavaty acalo bhāvo
yad bhāgavata-saṅgataḥ

etāvān—all these different kinds of worshipers; *eva*—certainly; *yajatām*—while worshiping; *iha*—in this life; *niḥśreyasa*—the highest benediction; *udayaḥ*—development; *bhagavati*—unto the Supreme Personality of Godhead; *acalaḥ*—unflinching; *bhāvaḥ*—spontaneous attraction; *yat*—which; *bhāgavata*—the pure devotee of the Lord; *saṅgataḥ*—association.

TRANSLATION

All the different kinds of worshipers of multidemigods can attain the highest perfectional benediction, which is spontaneous attraction unflinchingly fixed upon the Supreme Personality of Godhead, only by the association of the pure devotee of the Lord.

PURPORT

All living entities in different statuses of life within the material creation, beginning from the first demigod, Brahmā, down to the small ant, are conditioned under the law of material nature, or the external energy of the Supreme Lord. The living entity in his pure state is conscious of the fact that he is a part and parcel of the Lord, but when he is thrown into the material world on account of his desire to lord it over material energy, he becomes conditioned by the three modes of material nature and thus struggles for existence for the highest benefit. This struggle for existence is something like following the will-o'-the-wisp under the spell of material enjoyment. All plans for material enjoyment, either by worship of different demigods as described in the previous verses of this chapter or by modernized advancement of scientific knowledge without the help of God or demigod, are illusory only, for despite all such plans for happiness, the conditioned living being within the compass of material creation can never solve the problems of life, namely birth, death, old age and disease. The history of the universe is full of such planmakers, and many kings and emperors come and go, leaving a planmaking story only. But the prime problems of life remain unsolved despite all endeavors by such planmakers.

Actually human life is meant for making a solution to the problems of life. One can never solve such problems by satisfying the different demigods, by different modes of worship, or by so-called scientific advancement in knowledge without the help of God or the demigods. Apart from the gross materialists, who care very little either for God or for the demigods, the *Vedas* recommend worship of different demigods for different benefits, and so the demigods are neither false nor imaginary. The demigods are as factual as we are, but they are much more powerful due to their being engaged in the direct service of the Lord in managing different departments in the universal government. The *Bhagavad-gītā* affirms this, and the different planets of the demigods are mentioned there, including the one of the supreme demigod, Lord Brahmā. The gross materialists do not believe in the existence of God or the demigods. Nor do they believe that different planets are dominated by different demigods. They are creating a great commotion about reaching the closest celestial body, Candraloka, or the moon, but even after much mechanical research they have only very scanty information of this moon, and in spite of much false advertisement for selling land on the moon, the puffed-up scientists or gross materialists cannot live there, and what to speak of reaching the other planets, which they are unable even to count. However, the followers of the *Vedas* have a different method of acquiring knowledge. They accept the statements of the Vedic literatures as authority *in toto*, as we have already discussed in Canto One, and therefore they have full and reasonable knowledge of God and demigods and of their different residential planets situated within the compass of the material world and beyond the limit of the material sky. The most authentic Vedic literature, accepted by the great Indian *ācāryas* like Śaṅkara, Rāmānuja, Madhva, Viṣṇusvāmī, Nimbārka and Caitanya and studied by all important personalities of the world, is the *Bhagavad-gītā*, in which the worship of the demigods and their respective residential planets are mentioned. The *Bhagavad-gītā* (9.25) affirms:

> *yānti deva-vratā devān*
> *pitṝn yānti pitṛ-vratāḥ*

bhūtāni yānti bhūtejyā
yānti mad-yājino 'pi mām

"The worshipers of demigods reach the respective planets of the demigods, and the worshipers of forefathers reach the planets of the forefathers. The gross materialist remains in the different material planets, but the devotees of the Lord reach the kingdom of God."

We also have information from the *Bhagavad-gītā* that all the planets within the material world, including Brahmaloka, are but temporarily situated, and after a fixed period they are all annihilated. Therefore the demigods and their followers are all annihilated at the period of devastation, but one who reaches the kingdom of God gets a permanent share in eternal life. That is the verdict of Vedic literature. The worshipers of the demigods have one facility more than the unbelievers due to their being convinced of the Vedic version, by which they can get information of the benefit of worshiping the Supreme Lord in the association of the devotees of the Lord. The gross materialist, however, without any faith in the Vedic version, remains eternally in darkness, driven by a false conviction on the basis of imperfect experimental knowledge, or so-called material science, which can never reach into the realm of transcendental knowledge.

Therefore unless the gross materialists or the worshipers of the temporary demigods come in contact with a transcendentalist like the pure devotee of the Lord, their attempts are simply a waste of energy. Only by the grace of the divine personalities, the pure devotees of the Lord, can one achieve pure devotion, which is the highest perfection of human life. Only a pure devotee of the Lord can show one the right way of progressive life. Otherwise both the materialistic way of life, without any information of God or the demigods, and the life engaged in the worship of demigods, in pursuit of temporary material enjoyments, are different phases of phantasmagoria. They are nicely explained in the *Bhagavad-gītā* also, but the *Bhagavad-gītā* can be understood in the association of pure devotees only, and not by the interpretations of politicians or dry philosophical speculators.

TEXT 12

ज्ञानं यदाप्रतिनिवृत्तगुणोर्मिचक्र-
मात्मप्रसाद उत यत्र गुणेष्वसङ्गः ।

कैवल्यसम्मतपथस्त्वथ भक्तियोगः
को निर्वृतो हरिकथासु रतिं न कुर्यात् ॥१२॥

jñānaṁ yad āpratinivṛtta-guṇormi-cakram
ātma-prasāda uta yatra guṇeṣv asaṅgaḥ
kaivalya-sammata-pathas tv atha bhakti-yogaḥ
ko nirvṛto hari-kathāsu ratiṁ na kuryāt

jñānam—knowledge; *yat*—that which; *ā*—up to the limit of;
pratinivṛtta—completely withdrawn; *guṇa-ūrmi*—the waves of the material modes; *cakram*—whirlpool; *ātma-prasādaḥ*—self-satisfaction;
uta—moreover; *yatra*—where there is; *guṇeṣu*—in the modes of
nature; *asaṅgaḥ*—no attachment; *kaivalya*—transcendental; *sam-
mata*—approved; *pathaḥ*—path; *tu*—but; *atha*—therefore; *bhakti-
yogaḥ*—devotional service; *kaḥ*—who; *nirvṛtaḥ*—absorbed in; *hari-
kathāsu*—in the transcendental topics of the Lord; *ratim*—attraction;
na—shall not; *kuryāt*—do.

TRANSLATION

**Transcendental knowledge in relation with the Supreme Lord
Hari is knowledge resulting in the complete suspension of the
waves and whirlpools of the material modes. Such knowledge is
self-satisfying due to its being free from material attachment, and
being transcendental it is approved by authorities. Who could fail
to be attracted?**

PURPORT

According to *Bhagavad-gītā* (10.9) the characteristics of pure
devotees are wonderful. The complete functional activities of a pure
devotee are always engaged in the service of the Lord, and thus the pure
devotees exchange feelings of ecstasy between themselves and relish
transcendental bliss. This transcendental bliss is experienced even in the
stage of devotional practice (*sādhana-avasthā*), if properly undertaken
under the guidance of a bona fide spiritual master. And in the mature
stage the developed transcendental feeling culminates in realization of
the particular relationship with the Lord by which a living entity is
originally constituted (up to the relationship of conjugal love with the
Lord, which is estimated to be the highest transcendental bliss). Thus

bhakti-yoga, being the only means of God realization, is called *kaivalya*. Śrīla Jīva Gosvāmī quotes the Vedic version (*eko nārāyaṇo devaḥ, parāvarāṇāṁ parama āste kaivalya-saṁjñitaḥ*) in this connection and establishes that Nārāyaṇa, the Personality of Godhead, is known as *kaivalya*, and the means which enables one to approach the Lord is called the *kaivalya-panthā*, or the only means of attainment of Godhead. This *kaivalya-panthā* begins from *śravaṇa*, or hearing those topics that relate to the Personality of Godhead, and the natural consequence of hearing such *hari-kathā* is attainment of transcendental knowledge, which causes detachment from all mundane topics, for which a devotee has no taste at all. For a devotee, all mundane activities, social and political, become unattractive, and in the mature state such a devotee becomes uninterested even in his own body, and what to speak of bodily relatives. In such a state of affairs one is not agitated by the waves of the material modes. There are different modes of material nature, and all mundane functions in which a common man is very much interested or in which he takes part become unattractive for the devotee. This state of affairs is described herein as *pratinivṛtta-guṇormi*, and it is possible by *ātma-prasāda*, or complete self-satisfaction without any material connection. The first-class devotee of the Lord attains this stage by devotional service, but despite his loftiness, for the Lord's satisfaction he may play the voluntary part of a preacher of the Lord's glory and dovetail all into devotional service, even mundane interest, just to give the neophytes a chance to transform mundane interest into transcendental bliss. Śrīla Rūpa Gosvāmī has described this action of a pure devotee as *nirbandhaḥ kṛṣṇa-sambandhe yuktaṁ vairāgyam ucyate*. Even mundane activities dovetailed with service to the Lord are also calculated to be transcendental or approved *kaivalya* affairs.

TEXT 13

शौनक उवाच

इत्यभिव्याहृतं राजा निशम्य भरतर्षभः ।
किमन्यत्पृष्टवान् भूयो वैयासकिमृषिं कविम् ॥१३॥

śaunaka uvāca
ity abhivyāhṛtaṁ rājā
niśamya bharatarṣabhaḥ

kim anyat pṛṣṭavān bhūyo
vaiyāsakiṁ ṛṣiṁ kavim

śaunakaḥ uvāca—Śaunaka said; *iti*—thus; *abhivyāhṛtam*—all that
was spoken; *rājā*—the King; *niśamya*—by hearing; *bharata-ṛṣabhaḥ*—
Mahārāja Parīkṣit; *kim*—what; *anyat*—more; *pṛṣṭavān*—did he inquire
from him; *bhūyaḥ*—again; *vaiyāsakim*—unto the son of Vyāsadeva;
ṛṣim—one who is well versed; *kavim*—poetic.

TRANSLATION

Śaunaka said: The son of Vyāsadeva, Śrīla Śukadeva Gosvāmī,
was a highly learned sage and was able to describe things in a poetic manner. What did Mahārāja Parīkṣit again inquire from him
after hearing all that he had said?

PURPORT

A pure devotee of the Lord automatically develops all godly qualities,
and some of the prominent features of those qualities are as follows: he is
kind, peaceful, truthful, equable, faultless, magnanimous, mild, clean,
nonpossessive, a well-wisher to all, satisfied, surrendered to Kṛṣṇa, without hankering, simple, fixed, self-controlled, a balanced eater, sane,
mannerly, prideless, grave, sympathetic, friendly, *poetic*, expert and
silent. Out of these twenty-six prominent features of a devotee, as described by Kṛṣṇadāsa Kavirāja in his *Caitanya-caritāmṛta*, the qualification of being poetic is especially mentioned herein in relation to
Śukadeva Gosvāmī. The presentation of *Śrīmad-Bhāgavatam* by his
recitation is the highest poetic contribution. He was a self-realized
learned sage. In other words, he was a poet amongst the sages.

TEXT 14

एतच्छुश्रूषतां विद्वन् सूत नोऽर्हसि भाषितुम् ।
कथा हरिकथोदर्काः सतां स्युः सदसि ध्रुवम् ॥१४॥

etac chuśrūṣatāṁ vidvan
sūta no 'rhasi bhāṣitum
kathā hari-kathodarkāḥ
satāṁ syuḥ sadasi dhruvam

etat—this; *śuśrūṣatām*—of those eager to hear; *vidvan*—O learned; *sūta*—Sūta Govāmī; *naḥ*—unto us; *arhasi*—may you do it; *bhāṣitum*—just to explain it; *kathāḥ*—topics; *hari-kathā-udarkāḥ*—result in the topics of the Lord; *satām*—of the devotees; *syuḥ*—may be; *sadasi*—in the assembly of; *dhruvam*—certainly.

TRANSLATION

O learned Sūta Gosvāmī! Please continue to explain such topics to us because we are all eager to hear. Besides that, topics which result in the discussion of the Lord Hari should certainly be discussed in the assembly of devotees.

PURPORT

As we have already quoted above from the *Bhakti-rasāmṛta-sindhu* of Rūpa Gosvāmī, even mundane things, if dovetailed in the service of the Lord Śrī Kṛṣṇa, are accepted as transcendental. For example, the epics or the histories of *Rāmāyaṇa* and *Mahābhārata*, which are specifically recommended for the less intelligent classes (women, *śūdras* and unworthy sons of the higher castes), are also accepted as Vedic literature because they are compiled in connection with the activities of the Lord. *Mahābhārata* is accepted as the fifth division of the *Vedas* after its first four divisions, namely *Sāma*, *Yajur*, *Ṛg* and *Atharva*. The less intelligent do not accept *Mahābhārata* as part of the *Vedas*, but great sages and authorities accept it as the fifth division of the *Vedas*. *Bhagavad-gītā* is also part of the *Mahābhārata*, and it is full of the Lord's instruction for the less intelligent class of men. Some less intelligent men say that *Bhagavad-gītā* is not meant for householders, but such foolish men forget that *Bhagavad-gītā* was explained to Arjuna, a *gṛhastha* (family man), and spoken by the Lord in His role as a *gṛhastha*. So *Bhagavad-gītā*, although containing the high philosophy of the Vedic wisdom, is for the beginners in the transcendental science, and *Śrīmad-Bhāgavatam* is for graduates and postgraduates in the transcendental science. Therefore literatures like *Mahābhārata*, the *Purāṇas* and similar other literatures which are full of the pastimes of the Lord, are all transcendental literatures, and they should be discussed with full confidence in the society of great devotees.

The difficulty is that such literatures, when discussed by professional

men, appear to be mundane literature like histories or epics because there are so many historical facts and figures. It is said here, therefore, that such literatures should be discussed in the assembly of devotees. Unless they are discussed by devotees, such literatures cannot be relished by the higher class of men. So the conclusion is that the Lord is not impersonal in the ultimate issue. He is the Supreme Person, and He has His different activities. He is the leader of all living entities, and He descends at His will and by His personal energy to reclaim the fallen souls. Thus He plays exactly like the social, political or religious leaders. Because such roles ultimately culminate in the discussion of topics of the Lord, all such preliminary topics are also transcendental. That is the way of spiritualizing the civic activities of human society. Men have inclinations for studying history and many other mundane literatures—stories, fiction, dramas, magazines, newspapers, etc.—so let them be dovetailed with the transcendental service of the Lord, and all of them will turn to the topics relished by all devotees. The propaganda that the Lord is impersonal, that He has no activity and that He is a dumb stone without any name and form has encouraged people to become godless, faithless demons, and the more they deviate from the transcendental activities of the Lord, the more they become accustomed to mundane activities that only clear their path to hell instead of return them home, back to Godhead.*
Śrīmad-Bhāgavatam begins from the history of the Pāṇḍavas (with necessary politics and social activities), and yet Śrīmad-Bhāgavatam is said to be the Paramahaṁsa-saṁhitā, or the Vedic literature meant for the topmost transcendentalist, and it describes paraṁ jñānam, the highest transcendental knowledge. Pure devotees of the Lord are all paramahaṁsas, and they are like the swans, who know the art of sucking milk out of a mixture of milk and water.

---

*Even fifty years ago, the social structure of all Indians was so arranged that they would not read any literature that was not connected with the activities of the Lord. They would not play any drama not connected with the Lord. They would not organize a fair or ceremony not connected with the Lord. Nor would they visit a place that was not holy and sanctified by the pastimes of the Lord. Therefore even the common man in the village would talk about Rāmāyaṇa and Mahābhārata, Gītā and Bhāgavatam, even from his very childhood. But by the influence of the age of Kali, they have been dragged to the civilization of the dogs and hogs, laboring for bread without any sense of transcendental knowledge.

TEXT 15

स वै भागवतो राजा पाण्डवेयो महारथः ।
बालक्रीडनकैः क्रीडन् कृष्णक्रीडां य आददे ॥१५॥

sa vai bhāgavato rājā
pāṇḍaveyo mahā-rathaḥ
bāla-krīḍanakaiḥ krīḍan
kṛṣṇa-krīḍāṁ ya ādade

saḥ—he; *vai*—certainly; *bhāgavataḥ*—a great devotee of the Lord;
rājā—Mahārāja Parīkṣit; *pāṇḍaveyaḥ*—grandson of the Pāṇḍavas;
mahā-rathaḥ—a great fighter; *bāla*—while a child; *krīḍanakaiḥ*—with
play dolls; *krīḍan*—playing; *kṛṣṇa*—Lord Kṛṣṇa; *krīḍām*—activities;
yaḥ—who; *ādade*—accepted.

TRANSLATION

**Mahārāja Parīkṣit, the grandson of the Pāṇḍavas, was from his
very childhood a great devotee of the Lord. Even while playing
with dolls, he used to worship Lord Kṛṣṇa by imitating the
worship of the family Deity.**

PURPORT

In the *Bhagavad-gītā* (6.41) it is stated that even a person who has
failed in the proper discharge of *yoga* practice is given a chance to take
birth in the house of devout *brāhmaṇas* or in the houses of rich men like
kṣatriya kings or rich merchants. But Mahārāja Parīkṣit was more than
that because he had been a great devotee of the Lord since his previous
birth, and as such he took his birth in an imperial family of the Kurus,
and especially that of the Pāṇḍavas. So from the very beginning of his
childhood he had the chance to know intimately the devotional service of
Lord Kṛṣṇa in his own family. The Pāṇḍavas, all being devotees of the
Lord, certainly venerated family Deities in the royal palace for worship.
Children who appear in such families fortunately generally imitate such
worship of the Deities, even in the way of childhood play. By the grace of
Lord Śrī Kṛṣṇa, we had the chance of being born in a Vaiṣṇava family,

and in our childhood we imitated the worship of Lord Kṛṣṇa by imitating our father. Our father encouraged us in all respects to observe all functions such as the Ratha-yātrā and Dola-yātrā ceremonies, and he used to spend money liberally for distributing *prasāda* to us children and our friends. Our spiritual master, who also took his birth in a Vaiṣṇava family, got all inspirations from his great Vaiṣṇava father, Ṭhākura Bhaktivinoda. That is the way of all lucky Vaiṣṇava families. The celebrated Mīrā Bāī was a staunch devotee of Lord Kṛṣṇa as the great lifter of Govardhana Hill.

The life history of many such devotees is almost the same because there is always symmetry between the early lives of all great devotees of the Lord. According to Jīva Gosvāmī, Mahārāja Parīkṣit must have heard about the childhood pastimes of Lord Kṛṣṇa at Vṛndāvana, for he used to imitate the pastimes with his young playmates. According to Śrīdhara Svāmī, Mahārāja Parīkṣit used to imitate the worship of the family Deity by elderly members. Śrīla Viśvanātha Cakravartī also confirms the viewpoint of Jīva Gosvāmī. So accepting either of them, Mahārāja Parīkṣit was naturally inclined to Lord Kṛṣṇa from his very childhood. He might have imitated either of the above-mentioned activities, and all of them establish his great devotion from his very childhood, a symptom of a *mahā-bhāgavata*. Such *mahā-bhāgavatas* are called *nitya-siddhas*, or souls liberated from birth. But there are also others, who may not be liberated from birth but who develop a tendency for devotional service by association, and they are called *sādhana-siddhas*. There is no difference between the two in the ultimate issue, and so the conclusion is that everyone can become a *sādhana-siddha*, a devotee of the Lord, simply by association with the pure devotees. The concrete example is our great spiritual master Śrī Nārada Muni. In his previous life he was simply a boy of a maidservant, but through association with great devotees he became a devotee of the Lord of his own standard, unique in the history of devotional service.

TEXT 16

वैयासकिश्च भगवान् वासुदेवपरायणः ।
उरुगायगुणोदाराः सतां स्युर्हि समागमे ॥१६॥

vaiyāsakiś ca bhagavān
vāsudeva-parāyaṇaḥ
urugāya-guṇodārāḥ
satāṁ syur hi samāgame

vaiyāsakiḥ—the son of Vyāsadeva; *ca*—also; *bhagavān*—full in transcendental knowledge; *vāsudeva*—Lord Kṛṣṇa; *parāyaṇaḥ*—attached
to; *urugāya*—of the Personality of Godhead Śrī Kṛṣṇa, who is glorified
by great philosophers; *guṇa-udārāḥ*—great qualities; *satām*—of the
devotees; *syuḥ*—must have been; *hi*—as a matter of fact; *samāgame*—
by the presence of.

TRANSLATION

Śukadeva Gosvāmī, the son of Vyāsadeva, was also full in transcendental knowledge and was a great devotee of Lord Kṛṣṇa, son
of Vasudeva. So there must have been discussion of Lord Kṛṣṇa,
who is glorified by great philosophers and in the company of great
devotees.

PURPORT

The word *satām* is very important in this verse. *Satām* means the pure
devotees, who have no other desire than to serve the Lord. Only in the
association of such devotees are the transcendental glories of Lord Kṛṣṇa
properly discussed. It is said by the Lord that His topics are all full of
spiritual significance, and once one properly hears about Him in the
association of the *satām*, certainly one senses the great potency and so
automatically attains to the devotional stage of life. As already described,
Mahārāja Parīkṣit was a great devotee of the Lord from his very birth,
and so was Śukadeva Gosvāmī. Both of them were on the same level, although it appeared that Mahārāja Parīkṣit was a great king accustomed to
royal facilities whereas Śukadeva Gosvāmī was a typical renouncer of the
world, so much so that he did not even put a cloth on his body. Superficially, Mahārāja Parīkṣit and Śukadeva Gosvāmī might seem to be op-
posites, but basically they were both unalloyed pure devotees of the Lord.
When such devotees are assembled together, there can be no topics save
discussions of the glories of the Lord, or *bhakti-yoga*. In the *Bhagavad-*

gītā also, when there were talks between the Lord and His devotee Arjuna, there could not be any topic other than *bhakti-yoga*, however the mundane scholars may speculate on it in their own ways. The use of the word *ca* after *vaiyāsakiḥ* suggests, according to Śrīla Jīva Gosvāmī, that both Śukadeva Gosvāmī and Mahārāja Parīkṣit were of the same category, settled long before, although one was playing the part of the master and the other the disciple. Since Lord Kṛṣṇa is the center of the topics, the word *vāsudeva-parāyaṇaḥ,* or "devotee of Vāsudeva," suggests devotee of Lord Kṛṣṇa, the common aim. Although there were many others who assembled at the place where Mahārāja Parīkṣit was fasting, the natural conclusion is that there was no topic other than the glorification of Lord Kṛṣṇa, because the principal speaker was Śukadeva Gosvāmī and the chief audience was Mahārāja Parīkṣit. So *Śrīmad-Bhāgavatam,* as it was spoken and heard by two principal devotees of the Lord, is only for the glorification of the Supreme Lord, the Personality of Godhead, Śrī Kṛṣṇa.

TEXT 17

आयुर्हरति वै पुंसामुद्यन्नस्तं च यन्नसौ ।
तस्यर्ते यत्क्षणो नीत उत्तमश्लोकवार्तया ॥१७॥

āyur harati vai pumsām
udyann astam ca yann asau
tasyarte yat-kṣaṇo nīta
uttama-śloka-vārtayā

āyuḥ—duration of life; *harati*—decreases; *vai*—certainly; *pumsām*—of the people; *udyan*—rising; *astam*—setting; *ca*—also; *yan*—moving; *asau*—the sun; *tasya*—of one who glorifies the Lord; *ṛte*—except; *yat*—by whom; *kṣaṇaḥ*—time; *nītaḥ*—utilized; *uttama-śloka*—the all-good Personality of Godhead; *vārtayā*—in the topics of.

TRANSLATION

Both by rising and by setting, the sun decreases the duration of life of everyone, except one who utilizes the time by discussing topics of the all-good Personality of Godhead.

PURPORT

This verse indirectly confirms the greater importance of utilizing the human form of life to realize our lost relationship with the Supreme Lord by acceleration of devotional service. Time and tide wait for no man. So the time indicated by the sunrise and the sunset will be uselessly wasted if such time is not properly utilized for realizing identification of spiritual values. Even a fraction of the duration of life wasted cannot be compensated by any amount of gold. Human life is simply awarded to a living entity (*jīva*) so that he can realize his spiritual identity and his permanent source of happiness. A living being, especially the human being, is seeking happiness because happiness is the natural situation of the living entity. But he is vainly seeking happiness in the material atmosphere. A living being is constitutionally a spiritual spark of the complete whole, and his happiness can be perfectly perceived in spiritual activities. The Lord is the complete spirit whole, and His name, form, quality, pastimes, entourage and personality are all identical with Him. Once a person comes into contact with any one of the above-mentioned energies of the Lord through the proper channel of devotional service, the door to perfection is immediately opened. In the *Bhagavad-gītā* (2.40) the Lord has explained such contact in the following words: "Endeavors in devotional service are never baffled. Nor is there failure. A slight beginning of such activities is sufficient even to deliver a person from the great ocean of material fears." As a highly potent drug injected intravenously acts at once on the whole body, the transcendental topics of the Lord injected through the ear of the pure devotee of the Lord can act very efficiently. Aural realization of the transcendental messages implies total realization, just as fructification of one part of a tree implies fructification of all other parts. This realization for a moment in the association of pure devotees like Śukadeva Gosvāmī prepares one's complete life for eternity. And thus the sun fails to rob the pure devotee of his duration of life, inasmuch as he is constantly busy in the devotional service of the Lord, purifying his existence. Death is a symptom of the material infection of the eternal living being; only due to material infection is the eternal living entity subjected to the law of birth, death, old age and disease.

The materialistic way of pious activities like charity is recommended in the *smṛti-śāstras* as quoted by Śrīla Viśvanātha Cakravartī Ṭhākura. Money given in charity to a suitable person is guaranteed bank balance in the next life. Such charity is recommended to be given to a *brāhmaṇa*. If the money is given in charity to a non-*brāhmaṇa* (without brahminical qualification) the money is returned in the next life in the same proportion. If it is given in charity to a half-educated *brāhmaṇa*, even then the money is returned double. If the money is given in charity to a learned and fully qualified *brāhmaṇa*, the money is returned a hundred and a thousand times, and if the money is given to a *veda-pāraga* (one who has factually realized the path of the *Vedas*), it is returned by unlimited multiplication. The ultimate end of Vedic knowledge is realization of the Personality of Godhead, Lord Kṛṣṇa, as stated in the *Bhagavad-gītā* (*vedaiś ca sarvair aham eva vedyaḥ*). There is a guarantee of money's being returned if given in charity, regardless of the proportion. Similarly, a moment passed in the association of a pure devotee by hearing and chanting the transcendental messages of the Lord is a perfect guarantee for eternal life, for returning home, back to Godhead. *Maddhāma gatvā punar janma na vidyate*. In other words, a devotee of the Lord is guaranteed eternal life. A devotee's old age or disease in the present life is but an impetus to such guaranteed eternal life.

TEXT 18

तरवः किं न जीवन्ति भस्त्राः किं न श्वसन्त्युत ।
न खादन्ति न मेहन्ति किं ग्रामे पशवोऽपरे ॥१८॥

taravaḥ kiṁ na jīvanti
bhastrāḥ kiṁ na śvasanty uta
na khādanti na mehanti
kiṁ grāme paśavo 'pare

taravaḥ—the trees; *kim*—whether; *na*—do not; *jīvanti*—live; *bhastrāḥ*—bellows; *kim*—whether; *na*—do not; *śvasanti*—breathe; *uta*—also; *na*—do not; *khādanti*—eat; *na*—do not; *mehanti*—discharge semen; *kim*—whether; *grāme*—in the locality; *paśavaḥ*—beastly living being; *apare*—others.

TRANSLATION

Do the trees not live? Do the bellows of the blacksmith not breathe? All around us, do the beasts not eat and discharge semen?

PURPORT

The materialistic man of the modern age will argue that life, or part of it, is never meant for discussion of theosophical or theological arguments. Life is meant for the maximum duration of existence for eating, drinking, sexual intercourse, making merry and enjoying life. The modern man wants to live forever by the advancement of material science, and there are many foolish theories for prolonging life to the maximum duration. But the *Śrīmad-Bhāgavatam* affirms that life is not meant for so-called economic development or advancement of materialistic science for the hedonistic philosophy of eating, mating, drinking and merrymaking. Life is solely meant for *tapasya*, for purifying existence so that one may enter into eternal life just after the end of the human form of life.

The materialists want to prolong life as much as possible because they have no information of the next life. They want to get the maximum comforts in this present life because they think conclusively that there is no life after death. This ignorance about the eternity of the living being and the change of covering in the material world has played havoc in the structure of modern human society. Consequently there are many problems, multiplied by various plans of modernized man. The plans for solving the problems of society have only aggravated the troubles. Even if it is possible to prolong life more than one hundred years, advancement of human civilization does not necessarily follow. The *Bhāgavatam* says that certain trees live for hundreds and thousands of years. At Vṛndāvana there is a tamarind tree (the place is known as Imlitala) which is said to have existed since the time of Lord Kṛṣṇa. In the Calcutta Botanical Garden there is a banyan tree said to be older than five hundred years, and there are many such trees all over the world. Svāmī Śaṅkarācārya lived only thirty-two years, and Lord Caitanya lived forty-eight years. Does it mean that the prolonged lives of the above-mentioned trees are more important than Śaṅkara or Caitanya? Prolonged life without spiritual value is not very important. One may doubt that trees have life because they do not breathe. But modern scientists like Bose have already proved that there is life in plants, so breathing is no sign of actual life. The *Bhāgavatam* says that the bellows of the blacksmith breathes very soundly, but that does not mean that the bellows has life. The materialist will argue that life in the tree and life in the man cannot be compared because the tree cannot enjoy life by eating palatable dishes or by enjoying sexual intercourse. In reply to this, the *Bhāgavatam* asks whether other animals like the dogs and hogs, living in the same village with human beings, do not eat and enjoy sexual life. The specific utterance of *Śrīmad-Bhāgavatam* in regard to "other animals" means that persons who are simply engaged in planning a better type of animal life consisting of eating, breathing and mating are also animals in the shape of human beings. A society of such polished animals cannot benefit suffering humanity, for an animal can easily harm another animal but rarely do good.

TEXT 19

श्वविड्वराहोष्ट्रखरैः संस्तुतः पुरुषः पशुः ।
न यत्कर्णपथोपेतो जातु नाम गदाग्रजः ॥१९॥

śva-viḍ-varāhoṣṭra-kharaiḥ
saṁstutaḥ puruṣaḥ paśuḥ
na yat-karṇa-pathopeto
jātu nāma gadāgrajaḥ

śva—a dog; *viṭ-varāha*—the village hog who eats stool; *uṣṭra*—the camel; *kharaiḥ*—and by the asses; *saṁstutaḥ*—perfectly praised; *puruṣaḥ*—a person; *paśuḥ*—animal; *na*—never; *yat*—of him; *karṇa*—ear; *patha*—path; *upetaḥ*—reached; *jātu*—at any time; *nāma*—the holy name; *gadāgrajaḥ*—Lord Kṛṣṇa, the deliver from all evils.

TRANSLATION

Men who are like dogs, hogs, camels and asses praise those men who never listen to the transcendental pastimes of Lord Śrī Kṛṣṇa, the deliverer from evils.

PURPORT

The general mass of people, unless they are trained systematically for a higher standard of life in spiritual values, are no better than animals, and in this verse they have particularly been put on the level of dogs, hogs, camels and asses. Modern university education practically prepares one to acquire a doggish mentality with which to accept the service of a greater master. After finishing a so-called education, the so-called educated persons move like dogs from door to door with applications for some service, and mostly they are driven away, informed of no vacancy. As dogs are negligible animals and serve the master faithfully for bits of bread, a man serves a master faithfully without sufficient rewards.

Persons who have no discrimination in the matter of foodstuff and who eat all sorts of rubbish are compared to hogs. Hogs are very much attached to eating stools. So stool is a kind of foodstuff for a particular type of animal. And even stones are eatables for a particular type of animal or bird. But the human being is not meant for eating everything and anything; he is meant to eat grains, vegetables, fruits, milk, sugar, etc. Animal food is not meant for the human being. For chewing solid food, the human being has a particular type of teeth meant for cutting fruits and vegetables. The human being is endowed with two canine teeth as a concession for persons who will eat animal food at any cost. It is known to everyone that one man's food is another man's poison. Human beings are expected to accept the remnants of food offered to Lord Śrī Kṛṣṇa, and the Lord accepts foodstuff from the categories of leaves, flowers, fruits, etc. (Bg. 9.26). As prescribed by Vedic scriptures, no animal food is offered to the Lord. Therefore, a human being is meant to eat a particular type of food. He should not imitate the animals to derive so-called vitamin values. Therefore, a person who has no discrimination in regard to eating is compared to a hog.

The camel is a kind of animal that takes pleasure in eating thorns. A person who wants to enjoy family life or the worldly life of so-called enjoyment is compared to the camel. Materialistic life is full of thorns, and so one should live only by the prescribed method of Vedic regulations just to make the best use of a bad bargain. Life in the material world is maintained by sucking one's own blood. The central point of attraction for material enjoyment is sex life. To enjoy sex life is to suck one's own blood, and there is not much more to be explained in this connection. The camel also sucks its own blood while chewing thorny twigs. The thorns the camel eats cut the tongue of the camel, and so blood begins to flow within the camel's mouth. The thorns, mixed with fresh blood, create a taste for the foolish camel, and so he enjoys the thorn-eating business with false pleasure. Similarly, the great business magnates, industrialists who work very hard to earn money by different ways and questionable means, eat the thorny results of their actions mixed with their own blood. Therefore the *Bhāgavatam* has situated these diseased fellows along with the camels.

The ass is an animal who is celebrated as the greatest fool, even amongst the animals. The ass works very hard and carries burdens of the maximum weight without making profit for itself.* The ass is generally

---

*Human life is meant for earning values. This life is called *arthadam*, or that which can deliver values. And what is the greatest value of life? It is to return home, back to Godhead, as indicated in the *Bhagavad-gītā* (8.15). One's selfishness must be aimed at the point of going back to Godhead. The ass does not know his self-interest, and it works very hard for others only. A person who works very hard for others only, forgetting his personal interest available in the human form of life, is compared to the ass. In the *Brahma-vaivarta Purāṇa* it is said:

> asītiṁ caturaś caiva
> lakṣāṁs tāñ jīva-jātiṣu
> bhramadbhiḥ puruṣaiḥ prāpyaṁ
> mānuṣyaṁ janma-paryayāt
>
> tad apy abhalatāṁ jātaḥ
> teṣām ātmābhimāninām
> varākāṇām anāśritya
> govinda-caraṇa-dvayam

The human life is so important that even the demigods in the higher planets sometimes aspire for a human body on this earth because in the human body only can one easily go back to Godhead. In spite of having obtained such an important body, if one does not reestablish his lost eternal relation with Govinda, Lord Kṛṣṇa, he is certainly a fool who has forgotten his self-interest. This human form of material body is obtained by a gradual process of evolution to one body after another in the cycle of 8,400,000 varieties of life. And the poor man, forgetting this importance for his own interest, involves himself in so many illusory engagements for uplifting the position of others as a leader of political emancipation and economic development. There is no harm in trying for political emancipation or economic development, but one should not forget the real aim of life: all such philanthropic activities must be dovetailed to returning to Godhead. One who does not know this is compared to the ass who works only for others, without their or his own welfare in mind.

engaged by the washerman, whose social position is not very respectable.
And the special qualification of the ass is that it is very much accustomed
to being kicked by the opposite sex. When the ass begs for sexual intercourse, he is kicked by the fair sex, yet he still follows the female for
such sexual pleasure. A henpecked man is compared, therefore, to the
ass. The general mass of people work very hard, especially in the age of
Kali. In this age the human being is actually engaged in the work of an
ass, carrying heavy burdens and driving *ṭhelā* and rickshaws. The so-
called advancement of human civilization has engaged a human being in
the work of an ass. The laborers in great factories and workshops are also
engaged in such burdensome work, and after working hard during the
day, the poor laborer has to be again kicked by the fair sex, not only for
sex enjoyment but also for so many household affairs.

So *Śrīmad-Bhāgavatam's* categorization of the common man without
any spiritual enlightenment into the society of dogs, hogs, camels and
asses is not at all an exaggeration. The leaders of such ignorant masses of
people may feel very proud of being adored by such a number of dogs
and hogs, but that is not very flattering. The *Bhāgavatam* openly
declares that although a person may be a great leader of such dogs and
hogs disguised as men, if he has no taste for being enlightened in the
science of Kṛṣṇa, such a leader is also an animal and nothing more. He
may be designated as a powerful, strong animal, or a big animal, but in
the estimation of *Śrīmad-Bhāgavatam* he is never given a place in the
category of man, on account of his atheistic temperament. Or, in other
words, such godless leaders of dogs and hoglike men are bigger animals
with the qualities of animals in greater proportion.

TEXT 20

बिले   बतोरुक्रमविक्रमान्   ये
न   शृण्वतः   कर्णपुटे   नरस्य ।
जिह्वासती   दार्दुरिकेव   सूत
न   चोपगायत्युरुगायगाथाः ॥२०॥

bile batorukrama-vikramān ye
na śṛṇvataḥ karṇa-puṭe narasya

jihvāsatī dārdurikeva sūta
na copagāyaty urugāya-gāthāḥ

bile—snake holes; *bata*—like; *urukrama*—the Lord, who acts marvelously; *vikramān*—prowess; *ye*—all these; *na*—never; *śṛṇvataḥ*—heard; *karṇa-puṭe*—the earholes; *narasya*—of the man; *jihvā*—tongue; *asatī*—useless; *dārdurikā*—of the frogs; *iva*—exactly like that; *sūta*—O Sūta Gosvāmī; *na*—never; *ca*—also; *upagāyati*—chants loudly; *urugāya*—worth singing; *gāthāḥ*—songs.

TRANSLATION

One who has not listened to the messages about the prowess and marvelous acts of the Personality of Godhead and has not sung or chanted loudly the worthy songs about the Lord is to be considered to possess earholes like the holes of snakes and a tongue like the tongue of a frog.

PURPORT

Devotional service to the Lord is rendered by all limbs or parts of the body. It is the transcendental dynamic force of the spirit soul; therefore a devotee is engaged one hundred percent in the service of the Lord. One can engage in devotional service when the senses of the body are purified in relation with the Lord, and one can render service to the Lord with the help of all the senses. As such, the senses and the action of the senses are to be considered impure or materialistic as long as they are employed only in sense gratification. The purified senses are engaged not in sense gratification but in the service of the Lord *in toto*. The Lord is the Supreme with all senses, and the servitor, who is part and parcel of the Lord, also has the same senses. Service to the Lord is the completely purified use of the senses, as described in the *Bhagavad-gītā*. The Lord imparted instructions with full senses, and Arjuna received them with full senses, and thus there was a perfect exchange of sensible and logical understanding between the master and the disciple. Spiritual understanding is nothing like an electrical charge from the master to the disciple, as foolishly claimed by some propaganda-mongers. Everything is full of sense and logic, and the exchange of views between the master and disciple is possible only when the reception is submissive and real. In the *Caitanya-caritāmṛta* it is said that one should receive the teaching of Lord Caitanya with intellect and full senses so that one can logically understand the great mission.

In the impure state of a living being, the various senses are fully engaged in mundane affairs. If the ear is not engaged in the service of the Lord by hearing about Him from *Bhagavad-gītā* or *Śrīmad-Bhāgavatam*, certainly the holes of the ear will be filled with some rubbish. Therefore the messages of *Bhagavad-gītā* and *Śrīmad-Bhāgavatam* should be preached all over the world very loudly. That is the duty of a pure devotee who has actually heard about them from the perfect sources. Many want to speak something to others, but because they are not trained to speak on the subject matter of Vedic wisdom they are all speaking nonsense, and people are receiving them with no sense. There are hundreds and thousands of sources for distributing mundane news of the world, and people of the world are also receiving it. Similarly, the people of the world should be taught to hear the transcendental topics of the Lord, and the devotee of the Lord must speak loudly so that they can hear. The frogs loudly croak, with the result that they invite the snakes to eat them. The human tongue is especially given for chanting the Vedic hymns and not for croaking like frogs. The word *asatī* used in this verse is also significant. *Asatī* means a woman who has become a prostitute. A prostitute has no reputation for good womanly qualities. Similarly, the tongue, which is given to the human being for chanting the Vedic hymns, will be considered a prostitute when engaged in chanting some mundane nonsense.

TEXT 21

भारः परं पट्टकिरीटजुष्ट-
मप्युत्तमाङ्गं न नमेन्मुकुन्दम् ।
शावौ करौ नो कुरुते सपर्यां
हरेर्लसत्काञ्चनकङ्कणौ वा ॥२१॥

bhāraḥ paraṁ paṭṭa-kirīṭa-juṣṭam
apy uttamāṅgaṁ na namen mukundam

śāvau karau no kurute saparyāṁ
harer lasat-kāñcana-kaṅkaṇau vā

bhāraḥ—a great burden; *param*—heavy; *paṭṭa*—silk; *kirīṭa*—turban; *juṣṭam*—dressed with; *api*—even; *uttama*—upper; *aṅgam*—parts of the body; *na*—never; *namet*—bow down; *mukundam*—Lord Kṛṣṇa, the deliverer; *śāvau*—dead bodies; *karau*—hands; *no*—do not; *kurute*—do; *saparyām*—worshiping; *hareḥ*—of the Personality of Godhead; *lasat*—glittering; *kāñcana*—made of gold; *kaṅkaṇau*—bangles; *vā*—even though.

TRANSLATION

The upper portion of the body, though crowned with a silk turban, is only a heavy burden if not bowed down before the Personality of Godhead who can award mukti [freedom]. And the hands, though decorated with glittering bangles, are like those of a dead man if not engaged in the service of the Personality of Godhead Hari.

PURPORT

As stated hereinbefore, there are three kinds of devotees of the Lord. The first-class devotee does not at all see anyone who is not in the service of the Lord, but the second-class devotee makes distinctions between devotees and nondevotees. The second-class devotees are therefore meant for preaching work, and as referred to in the above verse, they must loudly preach the glories of the Lord. The second-class devotee accepts disciples from the section of third-class devotees or nondevotees. Sometimes the first-class devotee also comes down to the category of the second-class devotee for preaching work. But the common man, who is expected to become at least a third-class devotee, is advised herein to visit the temple of the Lord and bow down before the Deity, even though he may be a very rich man or even a king with a silk turban or crown. The Lord is the Lord of everyone, including the great kings and emperors, and men who are rich in the estimation of mundane people must therefore make it a point to visit the temple of Lord Śrī Kṛṣṇa and regularly bow down before the Deity. The Lord in the temple in the worshipable form is never to be considered to be made of stone or wood, for the Lord in His *arcā* incarnation as the Deity in the temple shows immense favor to the fallen souls by His auspicious presence. By the hearing process, as mentioned hereinbefore, this realization of the presence of the Lord in the temple is made possible. As such, the first process in the routine work of devotional service—hearing—is the essential point. Hearing by all classes of devotees from the authentic sources like *Bhagavad-gītā* and *Śrīmad-Bhāgavatam* is essential. The common man who is puffed up with his material position and does not bow down before the Deity of the Lord in the temple, or who defies temple worship without any knowledge of the science, must know that his so-called turban or crown will only succeed in further drowning him in the water of the ocean of material existence. A drowning man with a heavy weight on his head is sure to go down more swiftly than those who have no heavy weight. A foolish, puffed-up man defies the science of God and says that God has no meaning for him, but when he is in the grip of God's law and is caught by some disease like cerebral thrombosis, that godless man sinks into the ocean of nescience by the weight of his material acquisition. Advancement of material science without God consciousness is a heavy load on the head of human society, and so one must take heed of this great warning.

The common man, if he has no time to worship the Lord, may at least engage his hands for a few seconds in washing or sweeping the Lord's temple. Mahārāja Pratāparudra, the greatly powerful king of Orissa, was always very busy with heavy state responsibilities, yet he made it a point to sweep the temple of Lord Jagannātha at Purī once a year during the festival of the Lord. The idea is that however important a man one may be he must accept the supremacy of the Supreme Lord. This God consciousness will help a man even in his material prosperity. Mahārāja Pratāparudra's subordination before Lord Jagannātha made him a powerful king, so much so that even the great Pathan in his time could not enter into Orissa on account of the powerful Mahārāja Pratāparudra. And at last Mahārāja Pratāparudra was graced by Lord Śrī Caitanya on the very grounds of his acceptance of subordination to the Lord of the universe. So even though a rich man's wife has glittering bangles made of gold on her hands, she must engage herself in rendering service to the Lord.

TEXT 22

बर्हायिते ते नयने नराणां
लिङ्गानि विष्णोर्न निरीक्षतो ये ।
पादौ नृणां तौ द्रुमजन्मभाजौ
क्षेत्राणि नानुव्रजतो हरेर्यौ ॥२२॥

barhāyite te nayane narāṇām
liṅgāni viṣṇor na nirīkṣato ye
pādau nṛṇāṁ tau druma-janma-bhājau
kṣetrāṇi nānuvrajato harer yau

barhāyite—like plumes of a peacock; te—those; nayane—eyes;
narāṇām—of men; liṅgāni—forms; viṣṇoḥ—of the Personality of Godhead; na—does not; nirīkṣataḥ—look upon; ye—all such; pādau—legs;
nṛṇām—of men; tau—those; druma-janma—being born of the tree;
bhājau—like that; kṣetrāṇi—holy places; na—never; anuvrajataḥ—
goes after; hareḥ—of the Lord; yau—which.

TRANSLATION

The eyes which do not look at the symbolic representations of
the Personality of Godhead Viṣṇu [His forms, name, quality, etc.]
are like those printed on the plumes of the peacock, and the legs
which do not move to the holy places [where the Lord is remem-
bered] are considered to be like tree trunks.

PURPORT

Especially for the householder devotees, the path of Deity worship is
strongly recommended. As far as possible, every householder, by the
direction of the spiritual master, must install the Deity of Viṣṇu, forms
like Rādhā-Kṛṣṇa, Lakṣmī-Nārāyaṇa or Sītā-Rāma especially, or any
other form of the Lord, like Nṛsiṁha, Varāha, Gaura-Nitāi, Matsya,
Kūrma, śālagrāma-śilā and many other forms of Viṣṇu, like Trivikrama, Keśava, Acyuta, Vāsudeva, Nārāyaṇa and Dāmodara, as recommended in the Vaiṣṇava-tantras or Purāṇas, and one's family should
worship strictly following the directions and regulations of arcana-vidhi.

Any member of the family who is above twelve years of age should be initiated by a bona fide spiritual master, and all the members of the household should be engaged in the daily service of the Lord, beginning from morning (4 a.m.) till night (10 p.m.) by performing *maṅgala-ārātrika, nirañjana, arcana, pūjā, kīrtana, śṛṅgāra, bhoga-vaikāli, sandhyā-ārātrika, pāṭha, bhoga* (at night), *śayana-ārātrika,* etc. Engagement in such worship of the Deity, under the direction of a bona fide spiritual master, will greatly help the householders to purify their very existence and make rapid progress in spiritual knowledge. Simple theoretical book knowledge is not sufficient for a neophyte devotee. Book knowledge is theoretical, whereas the *arcana* process is practical. Spiritual knowledge must be developed by a combination of theoretical and practical knowledge, and that is the guaranteed way for attainment of spiritual perfection. The training of devotional service for a neophyte devotee completely depends on the expert spiritual master who knows how to lead his disciple to make gradual progress towards the path back home, back to Godhead. One should not become a pseudo spiritual master as a matter of business to meet one's family expenditures; one must be an expert spiritual master to deliver the disciple from the clutches of impending death. Śrīla Viśvanātha Cakravartī Ṭhākura has defined the bona fide qualities of a spiritual master, and one of the verses in that description reads:

śrī-vigrahārādhana-nitya-nānā-
śṛṅgāra-tan-mandira-mārjanādau
yuktasya bhaktāṁś ca niyuñjato 'pi
vande guroḥ śrī-caraṇāravindam

Śrī-vigraha is the *arcā,* or suitable worshipable form of the Lord, and the disciple should be engaged in worshiping the Deity regularly by *śṛṅgāra,* by proper decoration and dressing, as also by *mandira-mārjana,* the matter of cleansing the temple. The spiritual master teaches the neophyte devotee all these kindly and personally to help him gradually in the realization of the transcendental name, quality, form, etc., of the Lord.

Only attention engaged in the service of the Lord, especially in dressing and decorating the temple, accompanied by musical *kīrtana* and spiritual instructions from scriptures, can save the common man from the hellish cinema attractions and rubbish sex-songs broadcast everywhere by radios. If one is unable to maintain a temple at home, he should go to another's temple where all the above performances are regularly executed. Visiting the temple of a devotee and looking at the profusely decorated forms of the Lord well dressed in a well-decorated, sanctified temple naturally infuse the mundane mind with spiritual inspiration. People should visit holy places like Vṛndāvana where such temples and worship of the Deity are specifically maintained. Formerly all rich men like kings and rich merchants constructed such temples under the direction of expert devotees of the Lord, like the six Gosvāmīs, and it is the duty of the common man to take advantage of these temples and festivals observed in the holy places of pilgrimage by following in the footsteps of great devotees (anuvraja). One should not visit all these sanctified pilgrimage places and temples with sightseeing in mind, but one must go to such temples and sanctified places immortalized by the transcendental pastimes of the Lord and be guided by proper men who know the science. This is called anuvraja. Anu means to follow. It is therefore best to follow the instruction of the bona fide spiritual master, even in visiting temples and the holy places of pilgrimage. One who does not move in that way is as good as a standing tree condemned by the Lord not to move. The moving tendency of the human being is misused by visiting places for sightseeing. The best purpose of such traveling tendencies could be fulfilled by visiting the holy places established by great ācāryas and thereby not being misled by the atheistic propaganda of moneymaking men who have no knowledge of spiritual matters.

TEXT 23

जीवञ्छवो   भागवताङ्घ्रिरेणुं
न जातु मर्त्योऽभिलभेत यस्तु ।
श्रीविष्णुपद्या   मनुजस्तुलस्याः
श्वसञ्छवो यस्तु न वेद गन्धम् ॥२३॥

jīvañ chavo bhāgavatāṅghri-reṇuṁ
na jātu martyo 'bhilabheta yas tu
śrī-viṣṇu-padyā manujas tulasyāḥ
śvasañ chavo yas tu na veda gandham

jīvan—while living; *śavaḥ*—a dead body; *bhāgavata-aṅghri-reṇum*—the dust of the feet of a pure devotee; *na*—never; *jātu*—at any time; *martyaḥ*—mortal; *abhilabheta*—particularly received; *yaḥ*—a person; *tu*—but; *śrī*—with opulence; *viṣṇu-padyāḥ*—of the lotus feet of Viṣṇu; *manu-jaḥ*—a descendant of Manu (a man); *tulasyāḥ*—leaves of the *tulasī* tree; *śvasan*—while breathing; *śavaḥ*—still a dead body; *yaḥ*—who; *tu*—but; *na veda*—never experienced; *gandham*—the aroma.

TRANSLATION

The person who has not at any time received the dust of the feet of the Lord's pure devotee upon his head is certainly a dead body. And the person who has never experienced the aroma of the tulasī leaves from the lotus feet of the Lord is also a dead body, although breathing.

PURPORT

According to Śrīla Viśvanātha Cakravartī Ṭhākura, the breathing dead body is a ghost. When a man dies, he is called dead, but when he again appears in a subtle form not visible to our present vision and yet acts, such a dead body is called a ghost. Ghosts are always very bad elements, always creating a fearful situation for others. Similarly, the ghostlike nondevotees who have no respect for the pure devotees, nor for the Viṣṇu Deity in the temples, create a fearful situation for the devotees at all times. The Lord never accepts any offering by such impure ghosts. There is a common saying that one should first love the dog of the beloved before one shows any loving sentiments for the beloved. The stage of pure devotion is attained by sincerely serving a pure devotee of the Lord. The first condition of devotional service to the Lord is therefore to be a servant of a pure devotee, and this condition is fulfilled by the statement "reception of the dust of the lotus feet of a pure devotee who has also served another pure devotee." That is the way of pure disciplic succession, or devotional *paramparā*.

Mahārāja Rahūgaṇa inquired from the great saint Jaḍa Bharata as to how he had attained such a liberated stage of a *paramahaṁsa*, and in answer the great saint replied as follows (*Bhāg.* 5.12.12):

rahūgaṇaitat tapasā na yāti
na cejyayā nirvapaṇād gṛhād vā

na cchandasā naiva jalāgni-sūryair
vinā mahat-pāda-rajo-'bhiṣekam

"O King Rahūgaṇa, the perfectional stage of devotional service, or the *paramahaṁsa* stage of life, cannot be attained unless one is blessed by *the dust of the feet of great devotees.* It is never attained by *tapasya* [austerity], the Vedic worshiping process, acceptance of the renounced order of life, the discharge of the duties of household life, the chanting of the Vedic hymns, or the performance of penances in the hot sun, within cold water or before the blazing fire."

In other words, Lord Śrī Kṛṣṇa is the property of His pure unconditional devotees, and as such only the devotees can deliver Kṛṣṇa to another devotee; Kṛṣṇa is never obtainable directly. Lord Caitanya therefore designated Himself as *gopī-bhartuḥ pada-kamalayor dāsa-dāsānudāsaḥ,* or "the most obedient servant of the servants of the Lord, who maintains the *gopī* damsels at Vṛndāvana." A pure devotee therefore never approaches the Lord directly, but tries to please the servant of the Lord's servants, and thus the Lord becomes pleased, and only then can the devotee relish the taste of the *tulasī* leaves stuck to His lotus feet. In the *Brahma-saṁhitā* it is said that the Lord is never to be found by becoming a great scholar of the Vedic literatures, but He is very easily approachable through His pure devotee. In Vṛndāvana all the pure devotees pray for the mercy of Śrīmatī Rādhārāṇī, the pleasure potency of Lord Kṛṣṇa. Śrīmatī Rādhārāṇī is a tenderhearted feminine counterpart of the supreme whole, resembling the perfectional stage of the worldly feminine nature. Therefore, the mercy of Rādhārāṇī is available very readily to the sincere devotees, and once She recommends such a devotee to Lord Kṛṣṇa, the Lord at once accepts the devotee's admittance into His association. The conclusion is, therefore, that one should be more serious about seeking the mercy of the devotee than that of the Lord directly, and by one's doing so (by the good will of the devotee) the natural attraction for the service of the Lord will be revived.

TEXT 24

तदश्मसारं हृदयं बतेदं
यद् गृह्यमाणैर्हरिनामधेयैः ।

न विक्रियेताथ यदा विकारो
नेत्रे जलं गात्ररुहेषु हर्षः ॥२४॥

tad aśma-sāraṁ hṛdayaṁ batedam
yad gṛhyamāṇair hari-nāma-dheyaiḥ
na vikriyetātha yadā vikāro
netre jalaṁ gātra-ruheṣu harṣaḥ

tat—that; *aśma-sāram*—is steel-framed; *hṛdayam*—heart; *bata idam*—certainly that; *yat*—which; *gṛhyamāṇaiḥ*—in spite of chanting; *hari-nāma*—the holy name of the Lord; *dheyaiḥ*—by concentration of the mind; *na*—does not; *vikriyeta*—change; *atha*—thus; *yadā*—when; *vikāraḥ*—reaction; *netre*—in the eyes; *jalam*—tears; *gātra-ruheṣu*—at the pores; *harṣaḥ*—eruptions of ecstasy.

TRANSLATION

Certainly that heart is steel-framed which, in spite of one's chanting the holy name of the Lord with concentration, does not change when ecstasy takes place, tears fill the eyes and the hairs stand on end.

PURPORT

We should note with profit that in the first three chapters of the Second Canto a gradual process of development of devotional service is being presented. In the First Chapter the first step in devotional service for God consciousness by the process of hearing and chanting has been stressed, and a gross conception of the Personality of Godhead in His universal form for the beginners is recommended. By such a gross conception of God through the material manifestations of His energy, one is enabled to spiritualize the mind and the senses and gradually concentrate the mind upon Lord Viṣṇu, the Supreme, who is present as the Supersoul in every heart and everywhere, in every atom of the material universe. The system of *pañca-upāsanā*, recommending five mental attitudes for the common man, is also enacted for this purpose, namely gradual development, worship of the superior that may be in the form of fire, electricity, the sun, the mass of living beings, Lord Śiva and, at last, the impersonal Supersoul, the partial representation of Lord Viṣṇu. They are all nicely described in the Second Chapter, but in the Third Chapter further development is prescribed after one has actually reached the stage of Viṣṇu worship, or pure devotional service, and the mature stage of Viṣṇu worship is suggested herein in relation to the change of heart.

The whole process of spiritual culture is aimed at changing the heart of the living being in the matter of his eternal relation with the Supreme Lord as subordinate servant, which is his eternal constitutional position. So with the progress of devotional service, the reaction of change in the heart is exhibited by gradual detachment from the sense of material enjoyment by a false sense of lording it over the world and an increase in the attitude of rendering loving service to the Lord. *Vidhi-bhakti*, or regulated devotional service by the limbs of the body (namely the eyes, the ears, the nose, the hands and the legs, as already explained hereinbefore), is now stressed herein in relation to the mind, which is the impetus for all activities of the limbs of the body. It is expected by all means that by discharging regulated devotional service one must manifest the change of heart. If there is no such change, the heart must be considered steel-framed, for it is not melted even when there is chanting of the holy name of the Lord. We must always remember that hearing and chanting are the basic principles of discharging devotional duties, and if they are properly performed there will follow the reactional ecstasy with signs of tears in the eyes and standing of the hairs on the body. These are natural consequences and are the preliminary symptoms of the *bhāva* stage, which occurs before one reaches the perfectional stage of *prema*, love of Godhead.

If the reaction does not take place, even after continuous hearing and chanting of the holy name of the Lord, it may be considered to be due to offenses only. That is the opinion of the *Sandarbha*. In the beginning of chanting of the holy name of the Lord, if the devotee has not been very careful about evading the ten kinds of offenses at the feet of the holy name, certainly the reaction of feelings of separation will not be visible by tears in the eyes and standing of the hair on end.

The *bhāva* stage is manifested by eight transcendental symptoms, namely inertness, perspiration, standing of hairs on end, failing in the voice, trembling, paleness of the body, tears in the eyes and finally trance. *The Nectar of Devotion*, a summary study of Śrīla Rūpa

Gosvāmī's *Bhakti-rasāmṛta-sindhu*, explains those symptoms and vividly describes other transcendental developments, both in steady and accelerating manifestations.

Śrīla Viśvanātha Cakravartī Ṭhākura has very critically discussed all these *bhāva* displays in connection with some unscrupulous neophyte's imitating the above symptoms for cheap appreciation. Not only Viśvanātha Cakravartī but also Śrīla Rūpa Gosvāmī treated them very critically. Sometimes all the above eight symptoms of ecstasy are imitated by the mundane devotees (*prākṛta-sahajiyās*), but the pseudo symptoms are at once detected when one sees the pseudodevotee addicted to so many forbidden things. Even though decorated with the signs of a devotee, a person addicted to smoking, drinking or illegitimate sex with women cannot have all the above-mentioned ecstatic symptoms. But it is seen that sometimes these symptoms are willfully imitated, and for this reason Śrīla Viśvanātha Cakravartī accuses the imitators of being stonehearted men. They are sometimes even affected by the reflection of such transcendental symptoms, yet if they still do not give up the forbidden habits, then they are hopeless cases for transcendental realization.

When Lord Caitanya met Śrīla Rāmānanda Rāya of Kavaur on the bank of the Godāvarī, the Lord developed all these symptoms, but because of the presence of some nondevotee *brāhmaṇas* who were attendants of the Rāya, the Lord suppressed these symptoms. So sometimes they are not visible even in the body of the first-class devotee for certain circumstantial reasons. Therefore real, steady *bhāva* is definitely displayed in the matter of cessation of material desires (*kṣānti*), utilization of every moment in the transcendental loving service of the Lord (*avyārtha-kālatvam*), eagerness for glorifying the Lord constantly (*nāma-gāne sadā ruci*), attraction for living in the land of the Lord (*prītis tad-vasati sthale*), complete detachment from material happiness (*virakti*), and pridelessness (*māna-śūnyatā*). One who has developed all these transcendental qualities is really possessed of the *bhāva* stage, as distinguished from the stonehearted imitator or mundane devotee.

The whole process can be summarized as follows: The advanced devotee who chants the holy name of the Lord in a perfectly offenseless manner and is friendly to everyone can actually relish the transcendental taste of glorifying the Lord. And the result of such realization is reflected in the cessation of all material desires, etc., as mentioned above. The neophytes, due to their being in the lower stage of devotional service, are invariably envious, so much so that they invent their own ways and means of devotional regulations without following the *ācāryas*. As such, even if they make a show of constantly chanting the holy name of the Lord, they cannot relish the transcendental taste of the holy name. Therefore, the show of tears in the eyes, trembling, perspiration or unconsciousness, etc., is condemned. They can, however, get in touch with a pure devotee of the Lord and rectify their bad habits; otherwise they shall continue to be stonehearted and unfit for any treatment. A complete progressive march on the return path home, back to Godhead, will depend on the instructions of the revealed scriptures directed by a realized devotee.

TEXT 25

अथाभिधेहयङ्ग   मनोऽनुकूलं
प्रभाषसे   भागवतप्रधानः ।
यदाह   वैयासकिरात्मविद्या-
विशारदो नृपतिं साधु पृष्टः ॥२५॥

athābhidhehy aṅga mano-'nukūlaṁ
prabhāṣase bhāgavata-pradhānaḥ
yad āha vaiyāsakir ātma-vidyā-
viśārado nṛpatiṁ sādhu pṛṣṭaḥ

atha—therefore; *abhidhehi*—please explain; *aṅga*—O Sūta Gosvāmī; *manaḥ*—mind; *anukūlam*—favorable to our mentality; *prabhāṣase*— you do speak; *bhāgavata*—the great devotee; *pradhānaḥ*—the chief; *yat āha*—what he spoke; *vaiyāsakiḥ*—Śukadeva Gosvāmī; *ātma-vidyā*—transcendental knowledge; *viśāradaḥ*—expert; *nṛpatim*—unto the King; *sādhu*—very good; *pṛṣṭaḥ*—being asked.

TRANSLATION

O Sūta Gosvāmī, your words are pleasing to our minds. Please therefore explain this to us as it was spoken by the great devotee Śukadeva Gosvāmī, who is very expert in transcendental knowledge, and who spoke to Mahārāja Parīkṣit upon being asked.

PURPORT

Knowledge explained by the previous ācārya like Śukadeva Gosvāmī and followed by the next like Sūta Gosvāmī is always powerful transcendental knowledge, and it is therefore penetrating and useful to all submissive students.

Thus end the Bhaktivedanta purports of the Second Canto, Third Chapter, of the Śrīmad-Bhāgavatam, *entitled "Pure Devotional Service: The Change in Heart."*

CHAPTER FOUR

The Process of Creation

TEXT 1

सूत उवाच

वैयासकेरिति वचस्तच्चनिश्चयमात्मनः ।
उपधार्य मतिं कृष्णे औत्तरेयः सतीं व्यधात् ॥ १ ॥

sūta uvāca
vaiyāsaker iti vacas
tattva-niścayam ātmanaḥ
upadhārya matiṁ kṛṣṇe
auttareyaḥ satīṁ vyadhāt

sūtaḥ uvāca—Sūta Gosvāmī said; *vaiyāsakeḥ*—of Śukadeva Gosvāmī;
iti—thus; *vacaḥ*—speeches; *tattva-niścayam*—that which verifies the
truth; *ātmanaḥ*—in the self; *upadhārya*—just having realized;
matim—concentration of the mind; *kṛṣṇe*—unto Lord Kṛṣṇa; *auttareyaḥ*—the son of Uttarā; *satīm*—chaste; *vyadhāt*—applied.

TRANSLATION

Sūta Gosvāmī said: Mahārāja Parīkṣit, the son of Uttarā, after
hearing the speeches of Śukadeva Gosvāmī, which were all about
the truth of the self, applied his concentration faithfully upon
Lord Kṛṣṇa.

PURPORT

The word *satīm* is very significant. This means "existing" and
"chaste". And both imports are perfectly applicable in the case of
Mahārāja Parīkṣit. The whole Vedic adventure is to draw one's attention
entirely unto the lotus feet of Lord Kṛṣṇa without any diversion, as

instructed in the *Bhagavad-gītā* (15.15). Fortunately Mahārāja Parīkṣit had already been attracted to the Lord from the very beginning of his body, in the womb of his mother. In the womb of his mother he was struck by the *brahmāstra* atomic bomb released by Aśvatthāmā, but by the grace of the Lord he was saved from being burnt by the fiery weapon, and since then the King continuously concentrated his mind upon Lord Kṛṣṇa, which made him perfectly chaste in devotional service. So by natural sequence he was a chaste devotee of the Lord, and when he further heard from Śrīla Śukadeva Gosvāmī that one should worship the Lord only and no one else, even though full of all desires or desireless, his natural affection for Kṛṣṇa was strengthened. We have already discussed these topics.

To become a pure devotee of Lord Kṛṣṇa, two things are very much essential, namely having a chance to be born in the family of a devotee and having the blessings of a bona fide spiritual master. By the grace of Lord Kṛṣṇa, Parīkṣit Mahārāja had both opportunities. He was born in a family of such devotees as the Pāṇḍavas, and just to continue the dynasty of the Pāṇḍavas and show them special favor, the Lord specifically saved Mahārāja Parīkṣit, who later on, by the arrangement of the Lord, was cursed by the boy of a *brāhmaṇa* and was able to get the association of such a spiritual master as Śukadeva Gosvāmī. In the *Caitanya-caritāmṛta* it is said that a fortunate person, by the mercy of the spiritual master and Lord Kṛṣṇa, achieves the path of devotional service. This was perfectly applicable in the case of Mahārāja Parīkṣit. By way of being born in a family of devotees, he automatically came in touch with Kṛṣṇa, and after being so contacted he constantly remembered Him. Consequently Lord Kṛṣṇa gave the King a further chance for development in devotional service by introducing him to Śukadeva Gosvāmī, a stalwart devotee of the Lord with perfect knowledge in self-realization. And by hearing from a bona fide spiritual master, he was perfectly able to concentrate his chaste mind further upon Lord Kṛṣṇa, as a matter of course.

TEXT 2

आत्मजायासुतागारपशुद्रविणबन्धुषु ।
राज्ये चाविकले नित्यं विरूढां ममतां जहौ ॥ २ ॥

ātma-jāyā-sutāgāra-
paśu-draviṇa-bandhuṣu
rājye cāvikale nityaṁ
virūḍhāṁ mamatāṁ jahau

ātma—body; *jāyā*—wife; *suta*—son; *āgāra*—palace; *paśu*—horses
and elephants; *draviṇa*—treasury house; *bandhuṣu*—unto friends and
relatives; *rājye*—in the kingdom; *ca*—also; *avikale*—without being
disturbed; *nityam*—constant; *virūḍhām*—deep-rooted; *mamatām*—
affinity; *jahau*—gave up.

TRANSLATION

**Mahārāja Parīkṣit, as a result of his wholehearted attraction for
Lord Kṛṣṇa, was able to give up all deep-rooted affection for his
personal body, his wife, his children, his palace, his animals like
horses and elephants, his treasury house, his friends and relatives,
and his undisputed kingdom.**

PURPORT

To become liberated means to become free from *dehātma-buddhi*, the
illusory attachment for personal bodily coverings and everything connected with the body, namely wife, children and all other entanglements.
One selects a wife for bodily comforts, and the result is children. For
wife and children one requires a dwelling place, and as such a residential
house is also necessary. Animals like horses, elephants, cows and dogs
are all household animals, and a householder has to keep them as household paraphernalia. In modern civilization the horses and elephants have
been replaced by cars and conveyances with considerable horsepower. To
maintain all the household affairs, one has to increase the bank balance
and be careful about the treasury house, and in order to display the opulence of material assets, one has to keep good relations with friends and
relatives, as well as become very careful about maintaining the status
quo. This is called material civilization of material attachment. Devotion
for Lord Kṛṣṇa means negation of all material attachments as detailed
above. By the grace of Lord Kṛṣṇa, Mahārāja Parīkṣit was awarded all
material amenities and an undisputed kingdom in which to enjoy the

undisturbed position of king, but by the grace of the Lord he was able to
give up all connections with material attachment. That is the position of a
pure devotee. Mahārāja Parīkṣit, due to his natural affection for Lord
Kṛṣṇa as a devotee of the Lord, was always executing his royal duties on
behalf of the Lord, and as a responsible king of the world he was always
careful to see that the influence of Kali would not enter his kingdom. A
devotee of the Lord never thinks of his household paraphernalia as his
own, but surrenders everything for the service of the Lord. Thereby living entities under a devotee's care get the opportunity for God realization
by the management of a devotee-master.

Attachment for household paraphernalia and for Lord Kṛṣṇa go poorly
together. One attachment is the path of darkness, and the other attachment is the path of light. Where there is light, there is no darkness, and
where there is darkness, there is no light. But an expert devotee can turn
everything to the path of light by an attitude of service to the Lord, and
the best example here is the Pāṇḍavas. Mahārāja Yudhiṣṭhira and householders like him can turn everything to light by dovetailing so-called material assets in the service of the Lord, but one who is not trained or is
unable to turn everything to the service of the Lord (nirbandhaḥ kṛṣṇa-
sambandhe) must give up all material connections before he can be fit to
hear and chant the glories of the Lord, or in other words, one who has
seriously heard Śrīmad-Bhāgavatam for even one day, like Mahārāja
Parīkṣit, from a fit personality like Śukadeva Gosvāmī, may be able
to lose all affinity for material things. There is no utility simply in imitating Mahārāja Parīkṣit and hearing Bhāgavatam from professional
men, even for seven hundred years. To take Śrīmad-Bhāgavatam as a
means of maintaining family expenditure is the grossest type of
nāmāparādha offense at the feet of the Lord (sarva-śubha-kriyā-
sāmyam api pramādaḥ).

TEXTS 3–4

पप्रच्छ चेममेवार्थं यन्मां पृच्छथ सत्तमाः ।
कृष्णानुभावश्रवणे श्रद्दधानो महामनाः ॥ ३ ॥
संख्यां विज्ञाय संन्यस्य कर्म त्रैवर्गिकं च यत् ।
वासुदेवे भगवति आत्मभावं दृढं गतः ॥ ४ ॥

> *papraccha cemam evārtham*
> *yan mām pṛcchatha sattamāḥ*
> *kṛṣṇānubhāva-śravaṇe*
> *śraddadhāno mahā-manāḥ*

> *saṁsthāṁ vijñāya sannyasya*
> *karma trai-vargikaṁ ca yat*
> *vāsudeve bhagavati*
> *ātma-bhāvaṁ dṛḍhaṁ gataḥ*

papraccha—asked; *ca*—also; *imam*—this; *eva*—exactly like; *artham*—purpose; *yat*—that; *mām*—unto me; *pṛcchatha*—you are asking; *sattamāḥ*—O great sages; *kṛṣṇa-anubhāva*—rapt in thought of Kṛṣṇa; *śravaṇe*—in hearing; *śraddadhānaḥ*—full of faith; *mahā-manāḥ*—the great soul; *saṁsthām*—death; *vijñāya*—being informed; *sannyasya*—renouncing; *karma*—fruitive activities; *trai-vargikam*—the three principles religion, economic development and sense gratification; *ca*—also; *yat*—what it may be; *vāsudeve*—unto Lord Kṛṣṇa; *bhagavati*—the Personality of Godhead; *ātma-bhāvam*—attraction of love; *dṛḍham*—firmly fixed; *gataḥ*—achieved.

TRANSLATION

O great sages, the great soul Mahārāja Parīkṣit, constantly rapt in thought of Lord Kṛṣṇa, knowing well of his imminent death, renounced all sorts of fruitive activities, namely acts of religion, economic development and sense gratification, and thus fixed himself firmly in his natural love for Kṛṣṇa and asked all these questions, exactly as you are asking me.

PURPORT

The three activities of religion, economic development and sense gratification are generally attractive for conditioned souls struggling for existence in the material world. Such regulated activities prescribed in the *Vedas* are called the *karma-kāṇḍīya* conception of life, and householders are generally recommended to follow the rules just to enjoy material prosperity both in this life and in the next. Most people are attracted by such activities. Even in the activities of their modern godless civilization, people are more concerned with economic development and sense gratification without any religious sentiments. As a great emperor of the world, Mahārāja Parīkṣit had to observe such regulations of the Vedic *karma-kāṇḍīya* section, but by his slight association with Śukadeva Gosvāmī he could perfectly understand that Lord Kṛṣṇa, the Absolute Personality of Godhead (Vāsudeva), for whom he had a natural love since his birth, is everything, and thus he fixed his mind firmly upon Him, renouncing all modes of Vedic *karma-kāṇḍīya* activities. This perfectional stage is attained by a *jñānī* after many, many births. The *jñānīs*, or the empiric philosophers endeavoring for liberation, are thousands of times better than the fruitive workers, and out of hundreds of thousands of such *jñānīs* one is liberated factually. And out of hundreds of thousands of such liberated persons, even one person is rarely found who can firmly fix his mind unto the lotus feet of Lord Śrī Kṛṣṇa, as declared by the Lord Himself in the *Bhagavad-gītā* (7.19). Mahārāja Parīkṣit is specially qualified with the word *mahā-manāḥ*, which puts him on an equal level with the *mahātmās* described in the *Bhagavad-gītā*. In the later age also there have been many *mahātmās* of this type, and they also gave up all *karma-kāṇḍīya* conceptions of life, solely and wholly depending on the Supreme Personality of Godhead Kṛṣṇa. Lord Caitanya, who is Lord Kṛṣṇa Himself, taught us in His *Śikṣāṣṭaka* (8):

> *āśliṣya vā pāda-ratāṁ pinaṣṭu mām*
> *adarśanān marma-hatāṁ karotu vā*
> *yathā tathā vā vidadhātu lampaṭo*
> *mat-prāṇa-nāthas tu sa eva nāparaḥ*

"Lord Kṛṣṇa, who is the lover of many devotees (women), may embrace this fully surrendered maidservant or may trample me with His feet, or He may render me brokenhearted by not being present before me for a long duration of time, but still He is nothing less than the Absolute Lord of my heart."

Śrīla Rūpa Gosvāmī spoke thus:

> *viracaya mayi daṇḍaṁ dīna-bandho dayāmī vā*
> *gatir iha na bhavattaḥ kācid anyā mamāsti*

nipatatu śata-koṭi-nirbharaṁ vā navāmbhaḥ
tad api kila-payodaḥ stūyate cātakena

"O Lord of the poor, do what you like with me, give me either mercy or punishment, but in this world I have none to look to except Your Lordship. The *cātaka* bird always prays for the cloud, regardless of whether it showers rains or throws a thunderbolt."

Śrīla Mādhavendra Purī, the grand–spiritual master of Lord Caitanya, took leave of all *karma-kāṇḍīya* obligations in the following words:

sandhyā-vandana bhadram astu bhavato bhoḥ snāna tubhyaṁ namo
bho devāḥ pitaraś ca tarpaṇa-vidhau nāhaṁ kṣamaḥ kṣamyatām
yatra kvāpi niṣadya yādava-kulottamasya kaṁsa-dviṣaḥ
smāraṁ smāram aghaṁ harāmi tad alaṁ manye kim anyena me

"O my evening prayer, all good unto you. O my morning bath, I bid you good-bye. O demigods and forefathers, please excuse me. I am unable to perform any more offerings for your pleasure. Now I have decided to free myself from all reactions to sins simply by remembering anywhere and everywhere the great descendant of Yadu and the great enemy of Kaṁsa [Lord Kṛṣṇa]. I think that this is sufficient for me. So what is the use of further endeavors?"

Śrīla Mādhavendra Purī said further:

mugdhaṁ māṁ nigadantu nīti-nipuṇā bhrāntaṁ muhur vaidikāḥ
mandaṁ bāndhava-sañcayā jaḍa-dhiyaṁ muktādarāḥ sodarāḥ
unmattaṁ dhanino viveka-caturāḥ kāmam mahā-dāmbhikam
moktuṁ na kṣāmate manāg api mano govinda-pāda-spṛhām

"Let the sharp moralist accuse me of being illusioned; I do not mind. Experts in Vedic activities may slander me as being misled, friends and relatives may call me frustrated, my brothers may call me a fool, the wealthy mammonites may point me out as mad, and the learned philosophers may assert that I am much too proud; still my mind does not budge an inch from the determination to serve the lotus feet of Govinda, though I be unable to do it."

And also Prahlāda Mahārāja said:

dharmārtha-kāma iti yo 'bhihitas trivarga
īkṣā trayī naya-damau vividhā ca vārtā
manye tad etad akhilaṁ nigamasya satyaṁ
svātmārpaṇaṁ sva-suhṛdaḥ paramasya puṁsaḥ

"Religion, economic development and sense gratification are celebrated as three means of attaining the path of salvation. Of these, *īkṣā trayī* especially, i.e., knowledge of the self, knowledge of fruitive acts and logic and also politics and economics, are different means of livelihood. All these are different subjects of Vedic education, and therefore I consider them temporary engagements. On the other hand, surrendering unto the Supreme Lord Viṣṇu is a factual gain in life, and I consider it the ultimate truth." (*Bhāg.* 7.6.26)

The whole matter is concluded in the *Bhagavad-gītā* (2.41) as *vyavasāyātmikā buddhiḥ*, or the absolute path of perfection. Śrī Baladeva Vidyābhūṣaṇa, a great Vaiṣṇava scholar, defines this as *bha-gavvad-arcanā-rūpaika-niṣkāma-karmabhir viśuddha-cittaḥ*—accepting transcendental loving service to the Lord as the prime duty, free from fruitive reaction.

So Mahārāja Parīkṣit was perfectly right when he firmly accepted the lotus feet of Lord Kṛṣṇa, renouncing all *karma-kāṇḍīya* conceptions of life.

TEXT 5

राजोवाच
समीचीनं वचो ब्रह्मन् सर्वज्ञस्य तवानघ ।
तमो विशीर्यते मह्यं हरेः कथयतः कथाम् ॥ ५ ॥

rājovāca
samīcīnaṁ vaco brahman
sarva-jñasya tavānagha
tamo viśīryate mahyaṁ
hareḥ kathayataḥ kathām

rājā uvāca—the King said; *samīcīnam*—perfectly right; *vacaḥ*—speeches; *brahman*—O learned *brāhmaṇa*; *sarva-jñasya*—one who knows all; *tava*—your; *anagha*—without any contamination; *tamaḥ*—

the darkness of ignorance; *viśīryate*—gradually disappearing; *mah-yam*—unto me; *hareḥ*—of the Lord; *kathayataḥ*—as you are speaking; *kathām*—topics.

TRANSLATION

Mahārāja Parīkṣit said: O learned brāhmaṇa, you know every-thing because you are without material contamination. Therefore whatever you have spoken to me appears perfectly right. Your speeches are gradually destroying the darkness of my ignorance, for you are narrating the topics of the Lord.

PURPORT

The practical experience of Mahārāja Parīkṣit is disclosed herein, revealing that transcendental topics of the Lord act like injections when received by the sincere devotee from a person who is perfectly uncon-taminated by material tinges. In other words, reception of the messages of *Śrīmad-Bhāgavatam* from professional men, heard by a *karma-kāṇḍīya* audience, never acts miraculously as stated here. Devotional hearing of the messages of the Lord is not like hearing ordinary topics; therefore the action will be felt by the sincere hearer by experience of the gradual disappearance of ignorance.

> *yasya deve parā bhaktir*
> *yathā deve tathā gurau*
> *tasyaite kathitā hy arthāḥ*
> *prakāśante mahātmanaḥ*
> (Śvetāśvatara Upaniṣad 6.23)

When a hungry man is given food to eat, he feels satiation of hunger and the pleasure of dining simultaneously. Thus he does not have to ask whether he has actually been fed or not. The crucial test of hearing *Śrīmad-Bhāgavatam* is that one should get positive enlightenment by such an act.

TEXT 6

भूय एव विवित्सामि भगवानात्ममायया ।
यथेदं सृजते विश्वं दुर्विभाव्यमधीश्वरैः ॥ ६ ॥

bhūya eva vivitsāmi
bhagavān ātma-māyayā
yathedaṁ sṛjate viśvaṁ
durvibhāvyam adhīśvaraiḥ

bhūyaḥ—again; *eva*—also; *vivitsāmi*—I wish to learn; *bhagavān*—the Personality of Godhead; *ātma*—personal; *māyayā*—by the energies; *yathā*—as; *idam*—this phenomenal world; *sṛjate*—does create; *viśvam*—universe; *durvibhāvyam*—inconceivable; *adhīśvaraiḥ*—by the great demigods.

TRANSLATION

I beg to know from you how the Personality of Godhead, by His personal energies, creates these phenomenal universes as they are, which are inconceivable even to the great demigods.

PURPORT

In every inquisitive mind the important question of the creation of the phenomenal world arises, and therefore for a personality like Mahārāja Parīkṣit, who was to know all the activities of the Lord from his spiritual master, such an inquiry is not uncommon. For every unknown thing, we have to learn and inquire from a learned personality. The question of creation is also one of such inquiries to be made to the right person. The spiritual master, therefore, must be one who is *sarva-jña*, as stated hereinbefore in connection with Śukadeva Gosvāmī. Thus all inquiries on God which are unknown to the disciple may be made from the qualified spiritual master, and here the practical example is set by Mahārāja Parīkṣit. It was, however, already known to Mahārāja Parīkṣit that everything we see is born out of the energy of the Lord, as we have all learned in the very beginning of *Śrīmad-Bhāgavatam* (*janmādy asya yataḥ*). So Mahārāja Parīkṣit wanted to know the process of creation. The origin of creation was known to him; otherwise he would not have inquired how the Personality of Godhead, by His different energies, creates this phenomenal world. The common man also knows that the creation is made by some creator and is not created automatically. We have no experience in the practical world that a thing is created automatically. Foolish people say that the creative energy is independent and acts automatically, as electrical energy works. But the intelligent man knows that even the electrical energy is generated by an expert engineer in the localized powerhouse, and thus the energy is distributed everywhere under the resident engineer's supervision. The Lord's supervision in connection with creation is mentioned even in the *Bhagavad-gītā* (9.10), and it is clearly said there that material energy is a manifestation of one of many such energies of the Supreme (*parāsya śaktir vividhaiva śrūyate*). An inexperienced boy may be struck with wonder by seeing the impersonal actions of electronics or many other wonderful things conducted by electrical energy, but an experienced man knows that behind the action is a living man who creates such energy. Similarly the so-called scholars and philosophers of the world may, by mental speculation, present so many utopian theories about the impersonal creation of the universe, but an intelligent devotee of the Lord, by studying the *Bhagavad-gītā*, can know that behind the creation is the hand of the Supreme Lord, just as in the generating electrical powerhouse there is the resident engineer. The research scholar finds out the cause and the effect of everything, but research scholars as great as Brahmā, Śiva, Indra and many other demigods are sometimes bewildered by seeing the wonderful creative energy of the Lord, so what to speak of the tiny mundane scholars dealing in petty things. As there are differences in the living conditions of different planets of the universe, and as one planet is superior to others, the brains of the living entities in those respective planets are also of different categorical values. As stated in the *Bhagavad-gītā*, one can compare the long duration of life of the inhabitants of Brahmā's planet, which is inconceivable to the inhabitants of this planet earth, to the categorical value of the brain of Brahmājī, also inconceivable to any great scientist of this planet. And with such high brain power, even Brahmājī has described in his great *saṁhitā* (*Brahma-saṁhitā* 5.1) as follows:

> *īśvaraḥ paramaḥ kṛṣṇaḥ*
> *sac-cid-ānanda-vigrahaḥ*
> *anādir ādir govindaḥ*
> *sarva-kāraṇa-kāraṇam*

"There are many personalities possessing the qualities of Bhagavān, but Kṛṣṇa is the supreme because none can excel Him. He is the Supreme

Person, and His body is eternal, full of knowledge and bliss. He is the primeval Lord Govinda and the cause of all causes."

Brahmājī admits Lord Kṛṣṇa to be the supreme cause of all causes. But persons with tiny brains within this petty planet earth think of the Lord as one of them. Thus when the Lord says in the *Bhagavad-gītā* that He (Lord Kṛṣṇa) is all in all, the speculative philosophers and the mundane wranglers deride Him, and the Lord regretfully says:

> *avajānanti māṁ mūḍhā*
> *mānuṣīṁ tanum āśritam*
> *paraṁ bhāvam ajānanto*
> *mama bhūta-maheśvaram*

"Fools deride Me when I descend in the human form. They do not know My transcendental nature and My supreme dominion over all that be." (Bg. 9.11) Brahmā and Śiva (and what to speak of other demigods) are *bhūtas*, or powerful created demigods who manage universal affairs, much like ministers appointed by a king. The ministers may be *īśvaras*, or controllers, but the Supreme Lord is *maheśvara*, or the creator of the controllers. Persons with a poor fund of knowledge do not know this, and therefore they have the audacity to deride Him because He comes before us by His causeless mercy occasionally as a human being. The Lord is not like a human being. He is *sac-cid-ānanda-vigraha*, or the Absolute Personality of Godhead, and there is no difference between His body and His soul. He is both the power and the powerful.

Mahārāja Parīkṣit did not ask his spiritual master, Śukadeva Gosvāmī, to narrate Lord Kṛṣṇa's pastimes in Vṛndāvana; he wanted to hear first about the creation of the Lord. Śukadeva Gosvāmī did not say that the King should hear about the direct transcendental pastimes of the Lord. The time was very short, and naturally Śukadeva Gosvāmī could have gone directly to the Tenth Canto to make a shortcut of the whole thing, as generally done by the professional reciters. But neither the King nor the great speaker of *Śrīmad-Bhāgavatam* jumped up like the organizers of *Bhāgavatam;* both of them proceeded systematically, so that both future readers and hearers might take lessons from the example of the procedure of reciting *Śrīmad-Bhāgavatam.* Those who are in control of the external energy of the Lord, or in other words those who are in the ma-

His Divine Grace A. C. Bhaktivedanta Swami Prabhupāda
Founder-*Ācārya* of the International Society for Krishna Consciousness

PLATE ONE

A plenary portion of the Supreme Personality of Godhead known as the Supersoul resides within the body in the region of the heart. He measures about eight inches and has four hands, carrying a lotus, a wheel of a chariot, a conchshell and a club respectively. His mouth expresses His happiness, His eyes are spread like lotus petals, and His garments, bedecked with valuable jewels, are yellowish like the saffron of a *kadamba* flower. His ornaments are all made of gold, set with jewels, and He wears a glowing headdress and earrings. On His chest He wears the Kaustubha jewel engraved with a beautiful calf, on His shoulders He wears other jewels, and around His neck He wears a garland of fresh flowers. About His waist He wears an ornamental wreath; on His fingers, rings studded with valuable jewels. His leglets, His bangles, His oiled hair curling with bluish tint and His beautiful smiling face are all very pleasing. The Lord's magnanimous pastimes and the glowing glancing of His smiling face all indicate His extensive benedictions. *(pp. 80–85)*

PLATE TWO

Because he is fixed in unbroken devotional service to the Lord, Nārada Muni has received the grace of the almighty Viṣṇu. Thus he is a liberated spaceman, and he can travel anywhere without restriction, both in the transcendental world and in the three divisions of the material world. As he travels, he constantly sings the glories of the Lord and vibrates his *vīṇā*, which is charged with transcendental sound and which was given to him by Lord Kṛṣṇa Himself. *(p. 106)*

Lord Śrī Kṛṣṇa, the original Supreme Personality of Godhead, incarnates Himself in various forms age after age to perform specific missions. Here we see His ten most prominent *līlā-avatāras* (pastime incarnations). Beginning in the lower left-hand corner and moving clockwise, we find (1) Lord Matsya, the fish incarnation, who protected Vaivasvata Manu by supporting the boat he was in during a complete inundation of the universe; (2) Lord Kūrma, the tortoise incarnation, whose shell served as a pivot for Mandara Mountain when it was being used as a churning rod by the theists and the atheists; (3) Lord Varāha, the boar incarnation, who lifted the earth up from the nether regions of the universe and slew the great demon Hiraṇyākṣa; (4) Lord Nṛsiṁhadeva, the half-man half-lion, who bifurcated the strong body of the atheist Hiraṇyakaśipu with His nails; (5) Lord Vāmanadeva, the dwarf-*brāhmaṇa* incarnation, who begged three steps of land from Bali Mahārāja; (6) Lord Paraśurāma, who annihilated the administrative class (*kṣatriyas*) twenty-one times; (7) Lord Rāmacandra, who accepted exile in the forest with His beloved consort, Sītādevī, and then exhibited superhuman powers by controlling the Indian Ocean and killing the atheist King Rāvaṇa; (8) Lord Śrī Kṛṣṇa Himself (seen here with Lord Balarāma, His first expansion), who performed such wonderful pastimes as holding Govardhana Hill aloft for seven days to protect His friends in Vṛndāvana from King Indra's inundation; (9) Lord Buddha, who appeared just to delude those who are envious of the faithful theists; and (10) Lord Kalki, who will appear at the end of the Kali-yuga to annihilate all the atheists. *(p. 197)*

PLATE FOUR

Desirous to learn the cause of all causes, Śrī Nārada Muni approached his father, the four-headed Lord Brahmā, and spoke as follows: "My dear father, whatever was created in the past, whatever will be created in the future, and whatever is being created at present, as well as everything within the universe, is within your grip, just like a walnut. As the spider very easily creates the network of its cobweb without being defeated by others, so also you yourself, by employing your self-sufficient energy, appear to create without any others' help. Yet we are moved to wonder about the existence of someone more powerful than you when we think of your great austerities and perfect discipline, although your good self is so powerful in the matter of creation. My dear father, what is the source of your knowledge, and under whom are you working?" Lord Brahmā replied, "My dear Nārada, what you have spoken about me is understandable, because unless and until one is aware of the Personality of Godhead, who is the ultimate truth beyond me, one is sure to be illusioned by observing my powerful activities. The truth is that I create only after the Lord's creation by His personal effulgence, the *brahmajyoti*, just as when the sun manifests its fire, then the moon, the firmament, the planets and the twinkling stars are also manifest. Therefore I offer my obeisances and meditate upon Lord Kṛṣṇa, the Personality of Godhead, whose invincible potency influences the less intelligent class of men to call me the supreme controller."
(pp. 238–249)

In a corner of the spiritual sky (*brahmajyoti*) a spiritual cloud sometimes appears, and the covered portion is called the *mahat-tattva*. Then, by His plenary portion known as Mahā-Viṣṇu, the Lord lies down within the water of the *mahat-tattva*. This water is called the Causal Ocean. While Mahā-Viṣṇu sleeps within the Causal Ocean, innumerable universes are generated along with His breathing. These floating universes scatter all over the Causal Ocean, remaining manifest only during the breathing period of Mahā-Viṣṇu. In each and every universal globe the same Mahā-Viṣṇu enters as Garbhodakaśāyī Viṣṇu and lies down on the serpentlike Śeṣa incarnation, and from His navel a lotus sprouts. Upon the lotus is born Brahmā, the lord of the universe, who creates the sun, the moon, the demigods and all forms of living beings of different shapes in terms of their different desires. (*p. 278*)

PLATE SIX

The universal form of the Lord is the complete whole of everything that be. This form, adorned with various crowns, clubs, discs, spears and other weapons, is difficult to look at because of its glaring, fiery effulgence, immeasurable like the sun. Many, many other forms expand without limit from this universal body of the Lord, which spreads throughout the sky and the planets and all space in between. His arms are the resting place for the great demigods and other leaders, such as Lord Brahmā, Śiva, Sūrya and Candra. Indeed, all varieties of living entities, including the birds, beasts, trees and everything that be, are all covered by the universal form of the Lord at all times, although He is transcendental to all of them, eternally existing as the Supersoul in a form not exceeding nine inches. *(pp. 280–305)*

PLATE SEVEN

The original spiritual planet, which resembles the whorl of a huge lotus flower, is called Goloka Vṛndāvana. It is the abode of Lord Kṛṣṇa, the original Personality of Godhead. This original planet of Goloka throws off a spiritual effulgence called the *brahmajyoti*, within which are unlimited numbers of spiritual planets or Vaikuṇṭhalokas. The conception of spiritual bliss (*brahmānanda*) is fully present in those planets. Each of them is eternal, indestructible and free from all kinds of inebrieties experienced in the material world. Each of them is self-illuminating and more powerfully dazzling than (if we can imagine) the total sunshine of millions of mundane

uns. The inhabitants of those planets have full knowledge of everything; they are
ll godly and free from all sorts of material hankerings. They have nothing to do
here except to render transcendental loving service to the Supreme Lord
Nārāyaṇa, who is the predominating Deity in every Vaikuṇṭha planet. The Lord
nd His eternal servitors in the transcendental kingdom all have eternal forms,
vhich are auspicious, infallible, spiritual and eternally youthful. In other words,
hey do not experience birth, death, old age or disease. Thus that eternal land is
ull of transcendental enjoyment, beauty and bliss. *(pp. 308–309)*

terial world, must first of all know how the external energy of the Lord is working under the direction of the Supreme Personality, and afterwards one may try to enter into the activities of His internal energy. The mundaners are mostly worshipers of Durgā-devī, the external energy of Kṛṣṇa, but they do not know that Durgā-devī is but the shadow energy of the Lord. Behind her astonishing display of material workings is the direction of the Lord, as confirmed in the *Bhagavad-gītā* (9.10). The *Brahma-saṁhitā* affirms that Durgā-śakti is working by the direction of Govinda, and without His sanction the powerful Durgā-śakti cannot move even a blade of grass. Therefore the neophyte devotee, instead of jumping at once to the platform of transcendental pastimes presented by the internal energy of the Lord, may know how great the Supreme Lord is by inquiring about the process of His creative energy. In the *Caitanya-caritāmṛta* also, descriptions of the creative energy and the Lord's hand in it are explained, and the author of *Caitanya-caritāmṛta* has warned the neophyte devotees to be seriously on guard against the pitfall of neglecting knowledge about Kṛṣṇa in regard to how great He is. Only when one knows Lord Kṛṣṇa's greatness can one firmly put one's unflinching faith in Him; otherwise, like the common man, even the great leaders of men will mistake Lord Kṛṣṇa for one of the many demigods, or a historical personality, or a myth only. The transcendental pastimes of the Lord in Vṛndāvana, or even at Dvārakā, are relishable for persons who have already qualified themselves in advanced spiritual techniques, and the common man may be able to attain to such a plane by the gradual process of service and inquiries, as we shall see in the behavior of Mahārāja Parīkṣit.

TEXT 7

यथा गोपायति विभुर्यथा संयच्छते पुनः ।
यां यां शक्तिमुपाश्रित्य पुरुशक्तिः परःपुमान् ।
आत्मानं क्रीडयन् क्रीडन् करोति विकरोति च ॥ ७ ॥

yathā gopāyati vibhur
yathā saṁyacchate punaḥ
yāṁ yāṁ śaktim upāśritya
puru-śaktiḥ paraḥ pumān

ātmānaṁ krīḍayan krīḍan
karoti vikaroti ca

yathā—as; gopāyati—maintains; vibhuḥ—the great; yathā—as; saṁyacchate—winds up; punaḥ—again; yām yām—as; śaktim—energies; upāśritya—by employing; puru-śaktiḥ—the all-powerful; paraḥ—the Supreme; pumān—Personality of Godhead; ātmānam—plenary expansion; krīḍayan—having engaged them; krīḍan—as also personally being engaged; karoti—does them; vikaroti—and causes to be done; ca—and.

TRANSLATION

Kindly describe how the Supreme Lord, who is all-powerful, engages His different energies and different expansions in maintaining and again winding up the phenomenal world in the sporting spirit of a player.

PURPORT

In the *Kaṭha Upaniṣad* (2.2.13) the Supreme Lord is described as the chief eternal being amongst all other eternal individual beings (*nityo nityānāṁ cetanaś cetanānām*) and the one Supreme Lord who maintains innumerable other individual living beings (*eko bahūnāṁ yo vidadhāti kāmān*). So all living entities, both in the conditioned state and in the liberated state, are maintained by the Almighty Supreme Lord. Such maintenance is effected by the Lord through His different expansions of Self and three principal energies, namely the internal, external and marginal energies. The living entities are His marginal energies, and some of them, in the confidence of the Lord, are entrusted with the work of creation also, as are Brahmā, Marīci, etc., and the acts of creation are inspired by the Lord unto them (*tene brahma hṛdā*). The external energy (*māyā*) is also impregnated with the *jīvas*, or conditioned souls. The unconditioned marginal potency acts in the spiritual kingdom, and the Lord, by His different plenary expansions, maintains them in different transcendental relations displayed in the spiritual sky. So the one Supreme Personality of Godhead manifests Himself in many (*bahu syām*), and thus all diversities are in Him, and He is in all diversities, although He is nevertheless different from all of them. That is the inconceivable mystic power of the Lord, and as such everything is simultaneously one with and different from Him by His inconceivable potencies (*acintya-bhedābheda-tattva*).

TEXT 8

नूनं भगवतो ब्रह्मन् हरेरद्भुतकर्मणः ।
दुर्विभाव्यमिवाभाति कविमिश्रापि चेष्टितम् ॥ ८ ॥

nūnaṁ bhagavato brahman
harer adbhuta-karmaṇaḥ
durvibhāvyam ivābhāti
kavibhiś cāpi ceṣṭitam

nūnam—still insufficient; *bhagavataḥ*—of the Personality of Godhead; *brahman*—O learned *brāhmaṇa*; *hareḥ*—of the Lord; *adbhuta*—wonderful; *karmaṇaḥ*—one who acts; *durvibhāvyam*—inconceivable; *iva*—like that; *ābhāti*—appears; *kavibhiḥ*—even by the highly learned; *ca*—also; *api*—in spite of; *ceṣṭitam*—being endeavored for.

TRANSLATION

O learned brāhmaṇa, the transcendental activities of the Lord are all wonderful, and they appear inconceivable because even great endeavors by many learned scholars have still proved insufficient for understanding them.

PURPORT

The acts of the Supreme Lord, in the creation of just this one universe, appear inconceivably wonderful. And there are innumerable universes, and all of them aggregated together are known as the created material world. And this part of His creation is only a fractional portion of the complete creation. The material world stands as a part only (*ekāṁśena sthito jagat*). Supposing that the material world is a display of one part of His energy, the remaining three parts consist of the *vaikuṇṭha-jagat* or

spiritual world described in the *Bhagavad-gītā* as *mad-dhāma* or
sanātana-dhāma, or the eternal world. We have marked in the previous
verse that He creates and again winds up the creation. This action is applicable only in the material world because the other, greater part of His
creation, namely the Vaikuṇṭha world, is neither created nor annihilated; otherwise the Vaikuṇṭha-dhāma would not have been called eternal. The Lord exists with *dhāma;* His eternal name, quality, pastimes,
entourage and personality are all a display of His different energies and
expansions. The Lord is called *anādi,* or having no creator, and *ādi,* or
the origin of all. We think in our own imperfect way that the Lord is also
created, but the *Vedānta* informs us that He is not created. Rather,
everything else is created by Him (*nārāyaṇaḥ paro 'vyaktāt*). Therefore,
for the common man these are all very wonderful matters for consideration. Even for great scholars they are inconceivable, and thus such
scholars present theories contradictory to one another. Even for the insignificant part of His creation, this particular universe, they have no
complete information as to how far this limited space extends, or how
many stars and planets are there, or the different conditions of those innumerable planets. Modern scientists have insufficient knowledge of all
this. Some of them assert that there are one hundred million planets scattered all over space. In a news release from Moscow dated 2/21/60, the
following piece of knowledge was relayed:

"Russia's well-known professor of astronomy Boris Vorontsov-
Veliaminov said that there must be an infinite number of planets in the
universe inhabited by beings endowed with reason.

"It could be that life similar to that on earth flourishes on such
planets.

"Doctor of Chemistry Nikolai Zhirov, covering the problem of atmosphere on other planets, pointed out that the organism of a Martian,
for instance, could very well adapt itself to normal existence with a low
body temperature.

"He said that he felt that the gaseous composition of Martian atmosphere was quite suitable to sustain life of beings which have become
adapted to it."

This adaptability of an organism to different varieties of planets is described in the *Brahma-saṁhitā* as *vibhūti-bhinnam;* i.e., each and every
one of the innumerable planets within the universe is endowed with a

particular type of atmosphere, and the living beings there are more perfectly advanced in science and psychology because of a better atmosphere. *Vibhūti* means "specific powers," and *bhinnam* means "variegated." Scientists who are attempting to explore outer space and are trying to reach other planets by mechanical arrangements must know for certain that organisms adapted to the atmosphere of earth cannot exist in the atmospheres of other planets (*Easy Journey to Other Planets*). One has to prepare himself, therefore, to be transferred to a different planet after being relieved of the present body, as it is said in the *Bhagavad-gītā* (9.25):

> *yānti deva-vratā devān*
> *pitṛn yānti pitṛ-vratāḥ*
> *bhūtāni yānti bhūtejyā*
> *yānti mad-yājino 'pi mām*

"Those who worship the demigods will take birth among the demigods, those who worship ghosts and spirits will take birth among such beings, and those who worship Me will live with Me."

Mahārāja Parīkṣit's statement regarding the workings of the creative energy of the Lord discloses that he knew everything of the process of creation. Why then did he ask Śukadeva Gosvāmī for such information? Mahārāja Parīkṣit, being a great emperor, a descendant of the Pāṇḍavas and a great devotee of Lord Kṛṣṇa, was quite able to know considerably about the creation of the world, but that much knowledge was not sufficient. He said therefore that even greatly learned scholars fail to know about that, even after great effort. The Lord is unlimited, and His activities are also unfathomed. With a limited source of knowledge and with imperfect senses, any living being, up to the standard of Brahmājī, the highest perfect living being within the universe, can never imagine knowing about the unlimited. We can know something of the unlimited when it is explained by the unlimited, as has been done by the Lord Himself in the unique statements of the *Bhagavad-gītā*, and it can also be known to some extent from realized souls like Śukadeva Gosvāmī, who learned it from Vyāsadeva, a disciple of Nārada, and thus the perfect knowledge can descend by the chain of disciplic succession only, and not by any form of experimental knowledge, old or modern.

TEXT 9

यथा गुणांस्तु प्रकृतेर्युगपत् क्रमशोऽपि वा ।
बिभर्ति भूरिशस्त्वेकः कुर्वन् कर्माणि जन्ममिः॥ ९ ॥

yathā guṇāṁs tu prakṛter
yugapat kramaśo 'pi vā
bibharti bhūriśas tv ekaḥ
kurvan karmāṇi janmabhiḥ

yathā—as they are; guṇān—the modes of; tu—but; prakṛteḥ—of the
material energy; yugapat—simultaneously; kramaśaḥ—gradually;
api—also; vā—either; bibharti—maintains; bhūriśaḥ—many forms;
tu—but; ekaḥ—the supreme one; kurvan—acting; karmāṇi—activities;
janmabhiḥ—by incarnations.

TRANSLATION

The Supreme Personality of Godhead is one, whether He alone
acts with the modes of material nature, or simultaneously expands
in many forms, or expands consecutively to direct the modes of
nature.

TEXT 10

विचिकित्सितमेतन्मे ब्रवीतु भगवान् यथा ।
शाब्दे ब्रह्मणि निष्णातः परसिंश्च भवान्खलु ॥१०॥

vicikitsitam etan me
bravītu bhagavān yathā
śābde brahmaṇi niṣṇātaḥ
parasmiṁś ca bhavān khalu

vicikitsitam—doubtful inquiry; etat—this; me—of me; bravītu—just
clear up; bhagavān—powerful like the Lord; yathā—as much as;
śābde—sound transcendental; brahmaṇi—Vedic literature; niṣṇātaḥ—
fully realized; parasmin—in transcendence; ca—also; bhavān—your
good self; khalu—as a matter of fact.

TRANSLATION

Kindly clear up all these doubtful inquiries, because you are not only vastly learned in the Vedic literatures and self-realized in transcendence, but are also a great devotee of the Lord and are therefore as good as the Personality of Godhead.

PURPORT

In the *Brahma-saṁhitā* it is said that the Supreme Absolute Truth, Govinda, the Personality of Godhead, although one without a second, is infallibly expanded by innumerable forms nondifferent from one another, and although He is the original person, He is still ever young with permanent youthful energy. He is very difficult to know simply by learning the transcendental science of the *Vedas*, but He is very easily realized by His pure devotees.

The expansions of different forms of the Lord, as from Kṛṣṇa to Baladeva to Saṅkarṣaṇa, from Saṅkarṣaṇa to Vāsudeva, from Vāsudeva to Aniruddha, from Aniruddha to Pradyumna and then again to second Saṅkarṣaṇa and from Him to the Nārāyaṇa *puruṣāvatāras*, and innumerable other forms, which are compared to the constant flowing of the uncountable waves of a river, are all one and the same. They are like lamps of equal power which kindle from one lamp to another. That is the transcendental potency of the Lord. The *Vedas* say that He is so complete that even though the whole complete identity emanates from Him, He still remains the same complete whole (*pūrṇasya pūrṇam ādāya pūrṇam evāvaśiṣyate*). As such, there is no validity in a material conception of the Lord produced by the mental speculator. Thus He remains always a mystery for the mundane scholar, even if he is vastly learned in the Vedic literatures (*vedeṣu durlabham adurlabham ātma-bhaktau*). Therefore, the Lord is beyond the limit of conception for mundane learned scholars, philosophers or scientists. He is easily understandable for the pure devotee because the Lord declares in the *Bhagavad-gītā* (18.54) that after surpassing the stage of knowledge, when one is able to be engaged in the devotional service of the Lord, then only can one know the true nature of the Lord. One cannot have any clear conception of the Lord or His holy name, form, attributes, pastimes, etc., unless one is engaged in His transcendental loving service. The statement of the *Bhagavad-gītā* that one must first of all surrender unto the Lord, being freed from all other engagements, means that one must become a pure, unconditional devotee of the Lord. Only then can one know Him by the strength of devotional service.

Mahārāja Parīkṣit admitted in the previous verse that the Lord is inconceivable even for the greatest learned scholars. Why then should he again request Śukadeva Gosvāmī to clarify his insufficient knowledge about the Lord? The reason is clear. Not only was Śukadeva Gosvāmī vastly learned in the Vedic literatures, but he was also a great self-realized soul and a powerful devotee of the Lord. A powerful devotee of the Lord is, by the grace of the Lord, more than the Lord Himself. The Personality of Godhead Śrī Rāmacandra attempted to bridge the Indian Ocean to reach the island of Laṅkā, but Śrī Hanumānjī, the unalloyed devotee of the Personality of Godhead, could cross the ocean simply by jumping over it. The Lord is so merciful upon His pure devotee that He presents His beloved devotee as more powerful than Himself. The Lord expressed Himself to be unable to save Durvāsā Muni, although the Muni was so powerful that he could reach the Lord directly under material conditions. But Durvāsā Muni was saved by Mahārāja Ambarīṣa, a devotee of the Lord. Therefore, not only is a devotee of the Lord more powerful than the Lord, but also worship of the devotee is considered more effective than direct worship of the Lord (mad-bhakta-pūjābhyadhikā).

The conclusion is, therefore, that a serious devotee must first approach a spiritual master who not only is well versed in the Vedic literatures but is also a great devotee with factual realization of the Lord and His different energies. Without the help of such a devotee spiritual master, one cannot make progress in the transcendental science of the Lord. And a bona fide spiritual master like Śukadeva Gosvāmī does not speak about the Lord only in the matter of His internal potencies, but also explains how He associates with His external potencies.

The Lord's pastimes in the internal potency are displayed in His activities in Vṛndāvana, but His external potential works are directed in His features of Kāraṇārṇavaśāyī Viṣṇu, Garbhodakaśāyī Viṣṇu and Kṣīrodakaśāyī Viṣṇu. Śrīla Viśvanātha Cakravartī offers his good counsel to the interested Vaiṣṇavas when he says that they should not be interested in hearing only about the Lord's activities (like rāsa-līlā), but

must be keenly interested in His pastimes in His features of the
purusāvatāras in connection with *sṛṣṭi-tattva*, creational functions,
following the examples of Mahārāja Parīkṣit, the ideal disciple, and
Śukadeva Gosvāmī, the ideal spiritual master.

TEXT 11

सूत उवाच

इत्युपामन्त्रितो राज्ञा गुणानुकथने हरेः ।
हृषीकेशमनुस्मृत्य प्रतिवक्तुं प्रचक्रमे ॥११॥

sūta uvāca
ity upāmantrito rājñā
guṇānukathane hareḥ
hṛṣīkeśam anusmṛtya
prativaktuṁ pracakrame

sūtaḥ uvāca—Sūta Gosvāmī said; *iti*—thus; *upāmantritaḥ*—being requested; *rājñā*—by the King; *guṇa-anukathane*—in describing the
transcendental attributes of the Lord; *hareḥ*—of the Personality of Godhead; *hṛṣīkeśam*—the master of the senses; *anusmṛtya*—properly
remembering; *prativaktum*—just to reply; *pracakrame*—executed the
preliminaries.

TRANSLATION

**Sūta Gosvāmī said: When Śukadeva Gosvāmī was thus requested
by the King to describe the creative energy of the Personality of
Godhead, he then systematically remembered the master of the
senses [Śrī Kṛṣṇa], and to reply properly he spoke thus.**

PURPORT

The devotees of the Lord, while delivering speeches and describing
the transcendental attributes of the Lord, do not think that they can do
anything independently. They think that they can speak only what they
are induced to speak by the Supreme Lord, the master of the senses. The
senses of the individual being are not his own; the devotee knows that
such senses belong to the Supreme Lord and that they can be properly

used when they are employed for the service of the Lord. The senses are instruments, and elements are ingredients, all endowed by the Lord; therefore whatever an individual can do, speak, see, etc., is under the direction of the Lord only. The *Bhagavad-gītā* (15.15) confirms this: *sarvasya cāham hṛdi sanniviṣṭo mattaḥ smṛtir jñānam apohanaṁ ca.* No one is free to act freely and independently, and as such, one should always seek the permission of the Lord to act or eat or speak, and by the blessing of the Lord everything done by a devotee is beyond the principles of the four defects typical of the conditioned soul.

TEXT 12

श्रीशुक उवाच

नमः परस्मै पुरुषाय भूयसे
सदुद्भवस्थाननिरोधलीलया ।
गृहीतशक्तित्रितयाय देहिना-
मन्तर्भवायानुपलक्ष्यवर्त्मने ॥१२॥

śrī-śuka uvāca
namaḥ parasmai puruṣāya bhūyase
sad-udbhava-sthāna-nirodha-līlayā
gṛhīta-śakti-tritayāya dehinām
antarbhavāyānupalakṣya-vartmane

śrī-śukaḥ uvāca—Śrī Śukadeva Gosvāmī said; *namaḥ*—offering obeisances; *parasmai*—the Supreme; *puruṣāya*—Personality of Godhead; *bhūyase*—unto the complete whole; *sad-udbhava*—the creation of the material world; *sthāna*—its maintenance; *nirodha*—and its winding up; *līlayā*—by the pastime of; *gṛhīta*—having accepted; *śakti*—power; *tritayāya*—three modes; *dehinām*—of all who possess material bodies; *antaḥ-bhavāya*—unto He who resides within; *anupalakṣya*—inconceivable; *vartmane*—one who has such ways.

TRANSLATION

Śukadeva Gosvāmī said: Let me offer my respectful obeisances unto the Supreme Personality of Godhead who, for the creation of the material world, accepts the three modes of nature. He is the complete whole residing within the body of everyone, and His ways are inconceivable.

PURPORT

This material world is a manifestation of the three modes goodness, passion and ignorance, and the Supreme Lord, for the creation, maintenance and destruction of the material world, accepts three predominating forms as Brahmā, Viṣṇu and Śaṅkara (Śiva). As Viṣṇu He enters into every body materially created. As Garbhodakaśāyī Viṣṇu He enters into every universe, and as Kṣīrodakaśāyī Viṣṇu He enters the body of every living being. Lord Śrī Kṛṣṇa, being the origin of all viṣṇu-tattvas, is addressed here as paraḥ pumān, or Puruṣottama, as described in the Bhagavad-gītā (15.18). He is the complete whole. The puruṣāvatāras are therefore His plenary expansions. Bhakti-yoga is the only process by which one can become competent to know Him. Because the empiric philosophers and mystic yogīs cannot conceive of the Personality of Godhead, He is called anupalakṣya-vartmane, the Lord of the inconceivable way, or bhakti-yoga.

TEXT 13

भूयो नमः सद्वृजिनच्छिदेऽसता-
मसम्भवायाखिलसत्त्वमूर्तये ।
पुंसां पुनः पारमहंस्य आश्रमे
व्यवस्थितानामनुमृग्यदाशुषे ॥१३॥

bhūyo namaḥ sad-vṛjina-cchide 'satām
asambhavāyākhila-sattva-mūrtaye
puṁsāṁ punaḥ pāramahaṁsya āśrame
vyavasthitānām anumṛgya-dāśuṣe

bhūyaḥ—again; namaḥ—my obeisances; sat—of the devotees or the pious; vṛjina—distresses; chide—the liberator; asatām—of the atheists, the nondevotee-demons; asambhavāya—cessation of further unhappiness; akhila—complete; sattva—goodness; mūrtaye—unto the Personality; puṁsām—of the transcendentalists; punaḥ—again; pāramahaṁsye—the highest stage of spiritual perfection; āśrame—in the status; *vyavasthitānām*—particularly situated; *anumṛgya*—the destination; *dāśuṣe*—one who delivers.

TRANSLATION

I again offer my respectful obeisances unto the form of complete existence and transcendence, who is the liberator of the pious devotees from all distresses and the destroyer of the further advances in atheistic temperament of the nondevotee-demons. For the transcendentalists who are situated in the topmost spiritual perfection, He grants their specific destinations.

PURPORT

Lord Śrī Kṛṣṇa is the complete form of all existence, both material and spiritual. *Akhila* means complete, or that which is not *khila*, inferior. As stated in the *Bhagavad-gītā*, there are two kinds of nature (*prakṛti*), namely the material nature and the spiritual nature, or the external and internal potencies of the Lord. The material nature is called *aparā*, or inferior, and the spiritual nature is called superior or transcendental. Therefore the form of the Lord is not of the inferior, material nature. He is complete transcendence. And He is *mūrti*, or having transcendental form. The less intelligent men, who are unaware of His transcendental form, describe Him as impersonal Brahman. But Brahman is simply the rays of His transcendental body (*yasya prabhā*). The devotees, who are aware of His transcendental form, render Him service; therefore the Lord also reciprocates by His causeless mercy and thus delivers His devotees from all distresses. The pious men who follow the rulings of the *Vedas* are also dear to Him, and therefore the pious men of this world are also protected by Him. The impious and the nondevotees are against the principles of the *Vedas*, and so such persons are always hampered from making advances in their nefarious activities. Some of them, who are specially favored by the Lord, are killed by Him personally, as in the cases of Rāvaṇa, Hiraṇyakaśipu and Kaṁsa, and thus such demons get salvation and are thereby checked from further progress in their demoniac activities. Just like a kind father, either in His favor upon the devotees or His punishment of the demons He is ever kind to everyone because He is the complete existence for all individual existence.

The *paramahaṁsa* stage of existence is the highest perfectional stage of spiritual values. According to Śrīmatī Kuntīdevī, the Lord is factually understood by the *paramahaṁsas* only. As there is gradual realization of the transcendence from impersonal Brahman to localized Paramātmā to the Personality of Godhead, Puruṣottama, Lord Kṛṣṇa, similarly there is gradual promotion of one's situation in the spiritual life of *sannyāsa*. *Kuṭīcaka*, *bahūdaka*, *parivrājakācārya* and *paramahaṁsa* are gradual progressive stages in the renounced order of life, *sannyāsa*, and Queen Kuntīdevī, the mother of the Pāṇḍavas, has spoken about them in her prayers for Lord Kṛṣṇa (Canto One, Chapter Eight). The *paramahaṁsas* are generally found among both the impersonalists and the devotees, but according to *Śrīmad-Bhāgavatam* (as clearly stated by Kuntīdevī), pure *bhakti-yoga* is understood by the *paramahaṁsas*, and Kuntīdevī has especially mentioned that the Lord descends (*paritrāṇāya sādhūnām*) especially to award *bhakti-yoga* to the *paramahaṁsas*. So ultimately the *paramahaṁsas*, in the true sense of the term, are unalloyed devotees of the Lord. Śrīla Jīva Gosvāmī has directly accepted that the highest destination is *bhakti-yoga*, by which one accepts the transcendental loving service of the Lord. Those who accept the path of *bhakti-yoga* are the factual *paramahaṁsas*.

Since the Lord is very kind to everyone, the impersonalists, who accept *bhakti* as the means of merging in the existence of the Lord in His impersonal *brahmajyoti*, are also awarded their desired destination. He has assured everyone in the *Bhagavad-gītā* (4.11): *ye yathā māṁ prapadyante*. According to Śrīla Viśvanātha Cakravartī, there are two classes of *paramahaṁsas*, namely the *brahmānandīs* (impersonalists) and the *premānandīs* (devotees), and both are awarded their desired destinations, although the *premānandīs* are more fortunate than the *brahmānandīs*. But both the *brahmānandīs* and the *premānandīs* are transcendentalists, and they have nothing to do with the inferior, material nature full of the existential miseries of life.

TEXT 14

नमो नमस्तेऽस्त्वृषभाय सात्वतां
विदूरकाष्ठाय मुहुः कुयोगिनाम् ।

निरस्तसाम्यातिशयेन   राधसा
स्वधामनि ब्रह्मणि रंस्यते नमः ॥१४॥

namo namas te 'stv ṛṣabhāya sātvatāṁ
vidūra-kāṣṭhāya muhuḥ kuyoginām
nirasta-sāmyātiśayena rādhasā
sva-dhāmani brahmaṇi raṁsyate namaḥ

namaḥ namaḥ te—let me offer my obeisances unto You; *astu*—are; *ṛṣabhāya*—unto the great associate; *sātvatām*—of the members of the Yadu dynasty; *vidūra-kāṣṭhāya*—one who is far from mundane wranglers; *muhuḥ*—always; *ku-yoginām*—of the nondevotees; *nirasta*—vanquished; *sāmya*—equal status; *atiśayena*—by greatness; *rādhasā*—by opulence; *sva-dhāmani*—in His own abode; *brahmaṇi*—in the spiritual sky; *raṁsyate*—enjoys; *namaḥ*—I do bow down.

TRANSLATION

Let me offer my respectful obeisances unto He who is the associate of the members of the Yadu dynasty and who is always a problem for the nondevotees. He is the supreme enjoyer of both the material and spiritual worlds, yet He enjoys His own abode in the spiritual sky. There is no one equal to Him because His transcendental opulence is immeasurable.

PURPORT

There are two sides of the transcendental manifestations of the Supreme Lord, Śrī Kṛṣṇa. For the pure devotees He is the constant companion, as in the case of His becoming one of the family members of the Yadu dynasty, or His becoming the friend of Arjuna, or His becoming the associate neighbor of the inhabitants of Vṛndāvana, as the son of Nanda-Yaśodā, the friend of Sudāmā, Śrīdāmā and Madhumaṅgala, or the lover of the damsels of Vrajabhūmi, etc. That is part of His personal features. And by His impersonal feature He expands the rays of the *brahmajyoti*, which is limitless and all-pervasive. Part of this all-pervasive *brahmajyoti*, which is compared to the sun rays, is covered by the darkness of the *mahat-tattva*, and this insignificant part is known as the material world. In this material world there are innumerable universes like the one we can experience, and in each of them there are hundreds of thousands of planets like the one we are inhabiting. The mundaners are more or less captivated by the unlimited expansion of the rays of the Lord, but the devotees are concerned more with His personal form, from which everything is emanating (*janmādy asya yataḥ*). As the sun rays are concentrated in the sun disc, the *brahmajyoti* is concentrated in Goloka Vṛndāvana, the topmost spiritual planet in the spiritual sky. The immeasurable spiritual sky is full of spiritual planets, named Vaikuṇṭhas, far beyond the material sky. The mundaners have insufficient information of even the mundane sky, so what can they think of the spiritual sky? Therefore the mundaners are always far, far away from Him. Even if in the future they are able to manufacture some machine whose speed may be accelerated to the velocity of the wind or mind, the mundaners will still be unable to imagine reaching the planets in the spiritual sky. So the Lord and His residential abode will always remain a myth or a mysterious problem, but for the devotees the Lord will always be available as an associate.

In the spiritual sky His opulence is immeasurable. The Lord resides in all the spiritual planets, the innumerable Vaikuṇṭha planets, by expanding His plenary portions along with His liberated devotee associates, but the impersonalists who want to merge in the existence of the Lord are allowed to merge as one of the spiritual sparks of the *brahmajyoti*. They have no qualifications for becoming associates of the Lord either in the Vaikuṇṭha planets or in the supreme planet, Goloka Vṛndāvana, described in the *Bhagavad-gītā* as *mad-dhāma* and here in this verse as the *sva-dhāma* of the Lord.

This *mad-dhāma* or *sva-dhāma* is described in the *Bhagavad-gītā* (15.6) as follows:

> *na tad bhāsayate sūryo*
> *na śaśāṅko na pāvakaḥ*
> *yad gatvā na nivartante*
> *tad dhāma paramaṁ mama*

The Lord's *sva-dhāma* does not require any sunlight or moonlight or electricity for illumination. That *dhāma*, or place, is supreme, and whoever goes there never comes back to this material world.

The Vaikuṇṭha planets and the Goloka Vṛndāvana planet are all self-illuminating, and the rays scattered by those *sva-dhāma* of the Lord constitute the existence of the *brahmajyoti*. As further confirmed in the *Vedas* like the *Muṇḍaka* (2.2.10), *Kaṭha* (2.2.15) and *Śvetāśvatara Upaniṣads* (6.14):

> na tatra sūryo bhāti na candra-tārakaṁ
> nemā vidyuto bhānti kuto 'yam agniḥ
> tam eva bhāntam anu bhāti sarvaṁ
> tasya bhāsā sarvam idaṁ vibhāti

In the *sva-dhāma* of the Lord there is no need of sun, moon or stars for illumination. Nor is there need of electricity, so what to speak of ignited lamps? On the other hand, it is because those planets are self-illuminating that all effulgence has become possible, and whatever there is that is dazzling is due to the reflection of that *sva-dhāma*.

One who is dazzled by the effulgence of the impersonal *brahmajyoti* cannot know the personal transcendence; therefore in the *Īśopaniṣad* (15) it is prayed that the Lord shift His dazzling effulgence so that the devotee can see the real reality. It is spoken thus:

> hiraṇmayena pātreṇa
> satyasyāpihitaṁ mukham
> tat tvaṁ pūṣann apāvṛṇu
> satya-dharmāya dṛṣṭaye

"O Lord, You are the maintainer of everything, both material and spiritual, and everything flourishes by Your mercy. Your devotional service, or *bhakti-yoga*, is the actual principle of religion, *satya-dharma*, and I am engaged in that service. So kindly protect me by showing Your real face. Please, therefore, remove the veil of Your *brahmajyoti* rays so that I can see Your form of eternal bliss and knowledge."

TEXT 15

यत्कीर्तनं यत्स्मरणं यदीक्षणं
यद्वन्दनं यच्छ्रवणं यदर्हणम् ।

लोकस्य सद्यो विधुनोति कल्मषं
तस्मै सुभद्रश्रवसे नमो नमः ॥१५॥

yat-kīrtanaṁ yat-smaraṇaṁ yad-īkṣaṇaṁ
yad-vandanaṁ yac-chravaṇaṁ yad-arhaṇam
lokasya sadyo vidhunoti kalmaṣaṁ
tasmai subhadra-śravase namo namaḥ

yat—whose; kīrtanam—glorification; yat—whose; smaraṇam—remembrances; yat—whose; īkṣaṇam—audience; yat—whose; vandanam—prayers; yat—whose; śravaṇam—hearing about; yat—whose; arhaṇam—worshiping; lokasya—of all people; sadyaḥ—forthwith; vidhunoti—specifically cleanses; kalmaṣam—effects of sins; tasmai—unto Him; subhadra—all-auspicious; śravase—one who is heard; namaḥ—my due obeisances; namaḥ—again and again.

TRANSLATION

Let me offer my respectful obeisances unto the all-auspicious Lord Śrī Kṛṣṇa, about whom glorification, remembrances, audience, prayers, hearing and worship can at once cleanse the effects of all sins of the performer.

PURPORT

The sublime form of religious performances to free oneself from all reactions of sins is suggested herein by the greatest authority, Śrī Śukadeva Gosvāmī. Kīrtanam, or glorifying the Lord, can be performed in very many ways, such as remembering, visiting temples to see the Deity, offering prayers in front of the Lord, and hearing recitations of glorification of the Lord as they are mentioned in the Śrīmad-Bhāgavatam or in the Bhagavad-gītā. Kīrtanam can be performed both by singing the glories of the Lord in accompaniment with melodious music and by recitation of scriptures like Śrīmad-Bhāgavatam or Bhagavad-gītā.

The devotees need not be disappointed in the physical absence of the Lord, though they may think of not being associated with Him. The devotional process of chanting, hearing, remembering, etc., (either all or some of them, or even one of them) can give us the desired result of associating with the Lord by discharging the transcendental loving service of the Lord in the above manner. Even the very sound of the holy name of Lord Kṛṣṇa or Rāma can at once surcharge the atmosphere spiritually. We must know definitely that the Lord is present wherever such pure transcendental service is performed, and thus the performer of offenseless *kīrtanam* has positive association with the Lord. Similarly, remembrance and prayers also can give us the desired result if they are properly done under expert guidance. One should not concoct forms of devotional service. One may worship the form of the Lord in a temple, or one may impersonally offer the Lord devotional prayers in a mosque or a church. One is sure to get free from the reactions of sins provided one is very careful about not committing sins willingly in expectation of getting free from the reactions of sins by worshiping in the temple or by offering prayers in the church. This mentality of committing sins willfully on the strength of devotional service is called *nāmno balād yasya hi pāpa-buddhiḥ*, and it is the greatest offense in the discharge of devotional service. Hearing, therefore, is essential in order to keep oneself strictly on guard against such pitfalls of sins. And in order to give special stress to the hearing process, the Gosvāmī invokes all auspicious fortune in this matter.

TEXT 16

विचक्षणा   यच्चरणोपसादनात्
सङ्गं व्युदस्योभयतोऽन्तरात्मनः ।
विन्दन्ति हि ब्रह्मगतिं गतक्लमा-
स्तस्मै सुभद्रश्रवसे नमो नमः ॥१६॥

vicakṣaṇā yac-caraṇopasādanāt
saṅgaṁ vyudasyobhayato 'ntar-ātmanaḥ
vindanti hi brahma-gatiṁ gata-klamās
tasmai subhadra-śravase namo namaḥ

vicakṣaṇāḥ—highly intellectual; *yat*—whose; *caraṇa-upasādanāt*—simply dedicating oneself unto the lotus feet; *saṅgam*—attachment;

vyudasya—giving up completely; *ubhayataḥ*—for present and future existence; *antaḥ-ātmanaḥ*—of the heart and soul; *vindanti*—moves progressively; *hi*—certainly; *brahma-gatim*—toward spiritual existence; *gata-klamāḥ*—without difficulty; *tasmai*—unto Him; *su-bhadra*—all-auspicious; *śravase*—unto one who is heard; *namaḥ*—my due obeisances; *namaḥ*—again and again.

TRANSLATION

Let me offer my respectful obeisances again and again unto the all-auspicious Lord Śrī Kṛṣṇa. The highly intellectual, simply by surrendering unto His lotus feet, are relieved of all attachments to present and future existences and without difficulty progress toward spiritual existence.

PURPORT

Lord Śrī Kṛṣṇa has repeatedly instructed Arjuna, or for that matter everyone concerned with becoming His unalloyed devotee. In the last phase of His instruction in the *Bhagavad-gītā* (18.64–66) He instructed most confidentially as follows:

> *sarva-guhyatamaṁ bhūyaḥ*
> *śṛṇu me paramaṁ vacaḥ*
> *iṣṭo 'si me dṛḍham iti*
> *tato vakṣyāmi te hitam*

> *man-manā bhava mad-bhakto*
> *mad-yājī māṁ namaskuru*
> *mām evaiṣyasi satyaṁ te*
> *pratijāne priyo 'si me*

> *sarva-dharmān parityajya*
> *mām ekaṁ śaraṇaṁ vraja*
> *ahaṁ tvāṁ sarva-pāpebhyo*
> *mokṣayiṣyāmi mā śucaḥ*

"My dear Arjuna, you are very dear to Me, and therefore only for your good I will disclose the most secret part of My instructions. It is simply this: become a pure devotee of Mine and give yourself unto Me only, and I promise you full spiritual existence, by which you may gain the eternal right of transcendental loving service unto Me. Just give up all other ways of religiosity and exclusively surrender unto Me and believe that I will protect you from your sinful acts, and I shall deliver you. Do not worry any more."

Persons who are intelligent take serious notice of this last instruction of the Lord. Knowledge of the self is the first step in spiritual realization, which is called confidential knowledge, and a step further is God realization, which is called more confidential knowledge. The culmination of the knowledge of *Bhagavad-gītā* is God realization, and when one attains this stage of God realization, he naturally, voluntarily becomes a devotee of the Lord to render Him loving transcendental service. This devotional service to the Lord is always based on love of God and is distinct from the nature of routine service as prescribed in *karma-yoga*, *jñāna-yoga* or *dhyāna-yoga*. In the *Bhagavad-gītā* there are different instructions for such men of different categories, and there are various descriptions for *varṇāśrama-dharma*, *sannyāsa-dharma*, *yati-dharma*, the renounced order of life, controlling the senses, meditation, perfection of mystic powers, etc., but one who fully surrenders unto the Lord to render service unto Him, out of spontaneous love for Him, factually assimilates the essence of all knowledge described in the *Vedas*. One who adopts this method very skillfully attains perfection of life at once. And this perfection of human life is called *brahma-gati*, or the progressive march in spiritual existence. As enunciated by Śrīla Jīva Gosvāmī on the basis of Vedic assurances, *brahma-gati* means to attain a spiritual form as good as that of the Lord, and in that form the liberated living being eternally lives on one of the spiritual planets situated in the spiritual sky. Attainment of this perfection of life is easily available to a pure devotee of the Lord without his undergoing any difficult method of perfection. Such a devotional life is full of *kīrtanam*, *smaraṇam*, *īkṣaṇam*, etc., as mentioned in the previous verse. One must therefore adopt this simple way of devotional life in order to attain the highest perfection available in any category of the human form of life in any part of the world. When Lord Brahmā met Lord Kṛṣṇa as a playful child at Vṛndāvana, he offered his prayer in which he said:

śreyaḥ-sṛtiṁ bhaktim udasya te vibho
kliśyanti ye kevala-bodha-labdhaye
teṣām asau kleśala eva śiṣyate
nānyad yathā sthūla-tuṣāvaghātinām
(*Bhāg.* 10.14.4)

Bhakti-yoga is the highest quality of perfection to be achieved by the intelligent person in lieu of performing a large quantity of spiritual activities. The example cited here is very appropriate. A handful of real paddy is more valuable than heaps of paddy skins without any substance within. Similarly, one should not be attracted by the jugglery of *karma-kāṇḍa* or *jñāna-kāṇḍa* or even the gymnastic performances of *yoga*, but skillfully should take to the simple performances of *kīrtanam*, *smaraṇam*, etc., under a bona fide spiritual master, and without any difficulty attain the highest perfection.

TEXT 17

तपस्विनो दानपरा यशस्विनो
मनस्विनो मन्त्रविदः सुमङ्गलाः ।
क्षेमं न विन्दन्ति विना यदर्पणं
तस्मै सुभद्रश्रवसे नमो नमः ॥१७॥

tapasvino dāna-parā yaśasvino
manasvino mantra-vidaḥ sumaṅgalāḥ
kṣemaṁ na vindanti vinā yad-arpaṇam
tasmai subhadra-śravase namo namaḥ

tapasvinaḥ—the great learned sages; *dāna-parāḥ*—the great performer of charity; *yaśasvinaḥ*—the great worker of distinction; *manasvinaḥ*—the great philosophers or mystics; *mantra-vidaḥ*—the great chanter of the Vedic hymns; *su-maṅgalāḥ*—strict followers of Vedic principles; *kṣemam*—fruitful result; *na*—never; *vindanti*—attain; *vinā*—without; *yat-arpaṇam*—dedication; *tasmai*—unto Him; *subhadra*—auspicious; *śravase*—hearing about Him; *namaḥ*—my obeisances; *namaḥ*—again and again.

TRANSLATION

Let me offer my respectful obeisances unto the all-auspicious Lord Śrī Kṛṣṇa again and again because the great learned sages, the great performers of charity, the great workers of distinction, the great philosophers and mystics, the great chanters of the Vedic hymns and the great followers of Vedic principles cannot achieve any fruitful result without dedication of such great qualities to the service of the Lord.

PURPORT

Advancement of learning, a charitable disposition, political, social or religious leadership of human society, philosophical speculations, the practice of the *yoga* system, expertise in the Vedic rituals, and all similar high qualities in man serve one in the attainment of perfection only when they are employed in the service of the Lord. Without such dovetailing, all such qualities become sources of trouble for people in general. Everything can be utilized either for one's own sense gratification or in the service of one other than oneself. There are two kinds of self-interest also, namely personal selfishness and extended selfishness. But there is no qualitative difference between personal and extended selfishness. Theft for personal interest or for the family interest is of the same quality—namely, criminal. A thief pleading not guilty because of committing theft not for personal interest but for the interest of society or country has never been excused by the established law of any country. People in general have no knowledge that the self-interest of a living being attains perfection only when such an interest coincides with the interest of the Lord. For example, what is the interest of maintaining body and soul together? One earns money for maintenance of the body (personal or social), but unless there is God consciousness, unless the body is being properly maintained to realize one's relation with God, all good efforts to maintain body and soul together are similar to the attempts of the animals to maintain body and soul together. The purpose of maintaining the human body is different from that of the animals. Similarly, advancement of learning, economic development, philosophical research, study in the Vedic literature or even the execution of pious activities (like charity, opening of hospitals, and the distribution of food grains) should be done in relation with the Lord. The aim of all such acts and endeavors must be the pleasure of the Lord and not the satisfaction of any other identity, individual or collective (*saṁsiddhir hari-toṣaṇam*). In the *Bhagavad-gītā* (9.27) the same principle is confirmed where it is said that whatever we may give in charity and whatever we may observe in austerity must be given over to the Lord or be done on His account only. The expert leaders of a godless human civilization cannot bring about a fruitful result in all their different attempts at educational advancement or economic development unless they are God conscious. And to become God conscious one has to hear about the all-auspicious Lord, as He is described in literature like the *Bhagavad-gītā* and *Śrīmad-Bhāgavatam*.

TEXT 18

किरातहूणान्ध्रपुलिन्दपुल्कशा
आभीरशुम्भा यवनाः खसादयः ।
येऽन्ये च पापा यदपाश्रयाश्रयाः
शुध्यन्ति तस्मै प्रभविष्णवे नमः ॥१८॥

kirāta-hūṇāndhra-pulinda-pulkaśā
ābhīra-śumbhā yavanāḥ khasādayaḥ
ye 'nye ca pāpā yad-apāśrayāśrayāḥ
śudhyanti tasmai prabhaviṣṇave namaḥ

kirāta—a province of old Bhārata; *hūṇa*—part of Germany and Russia; *āndhra*—a province of southern India; *pulinda*—the Greeks; *pulkaśāḥ*—another province; *ābhīra*—part of old Sind; *śumbhāḥ*—another province; *yavanāḥ*—the Turks; *khasa-ādayaḥ*—the Mongolian province; *ye*—even those; *anye*—others; *ca*—also; *pāpāḥ*—addicted to sinful acts; *yat*—whose; *apāśraya-āśrayāḥ*—having taken shelter of the devotees of the Lord; *śudhyanti*—at once purified; *tasmai*—unto Him; *prabhaviṣṇave*—unto the powerful Viṣṇu; *namaḥ*—my respectful obeisances.

TRANSLATION

Kirāta, Hūṇa, Āndhra, Pulinda, Pulkaśa, Ābhīra, Śumbha, Yavana, members of the Khasa races and even others addicted to

sinful acts can be purified by taking shelter of the devotees of the
Lord, due to His being the supreme power. I beg to offer my
respectful obeisances unto Him.

PURPORT

Kirāta: A province of old Bhārata-varṣa mentioned in the *Bhīṣma-
parva* of *Mahābhārata.* Generally the Kirātas are known as the
aboriginal tribes of India, and in modern days the Santal Parganas in
Bihar and Chota Nagpur might comprise the old province named Kirāta.

Hūṇa: The area of East Germany and part of Russia is known as the
province of the Hūṇas. Accordingly, sometimes a kind of hill tribe is
known as the Hūṇas.

Āndhra: A province in southern India mentioned in the *Bhīṣma-parva*
of *Mahābhārata.* It is still extant under the same name.

Pulinda: It is mentioned in the *Mahābhārata* (*Ādi-parva* 174.38),
viz., the inhabitants of the province of the name Pulinda. This country
was conquered by Bhīmasena and Sahadeva. The Greeks are known as
Pulindas, and it is mentioned in the *Vana-parva* of *Mahābhārata* that
the non-Vedic race of this part of the world would rule over the world.
This Pulinda province was also one of the provinces of Bhārata, and the
inhabitants were classified amongst the *kṣatriya* kings. But later on, due
to their giving up the brahminical culture, they were mentioned as
mlecchas (just as those who are not followers of the Islamic culture are
called *kafirs* and those who are not followers of the Christian culture are
called heathens).

Ābhīra: This name also appears in the *Mahābhārata,* both in the
Sabhā-parva and *Bhīṣma-parva.* It is mentioned that this province was
situated on the River Sarasvatī in Sind. The modern Sind province formerly extended on the other side of the Arabian Sea, and all the inhabitants of that province were known as the Ābhīras. They were under the
domination of Mahārāja Yudhiṣṭhira, and according to the statements of
Mārkaṇḍeya the *mlecchas* of this part of the world would also rule over
Bhārata. Later on this proved to be true, as in the case of the Pulindas.
On behalf of the Pulindas, Alexander the Great conquered India, and on
behalf of the Ābhīras, Muhammad Ghori conquered India. These
Ābhīras were also formerly *kṣatriyas* within the brahminical culture, but

they gave up the connection. The *kṣatriyas* who were afraid of Paraśurāma and had hidden themselves in the Caucasian hilly regions later on became known as the Ābhīras, and the place they inhabited was known as Ābhīradeśa.

Śumbhas or *Kaṅkas:* The inhabitants of the Kaṅka province of old Bhārata, mentioned in the *Mahābhārata.*

Yavanas: Yavana was the name of one of the sons of Mahārāja Yayāti who was given the part of the world known as Turkey to rule. Therefore the Turks are Yavanas due to being descendants of Mahārāja Yavana. The Yavanas were therefore *kṣatriyas*, and later on, by giving up the brahminical culture, they became *mleccha-yavanas*. Descriptions of the Yavanas are in the *Mahābhārata* (*Ādi-parva* 85.34). Another prince called Turvasu was also known as Yavana, and his country was conquered by Sahadeva, one of the Pāṇḍavas. The western Yavana joined with Duryodhana in the Battle of Kurukṣetra under the pressure of Karṇa. It is also foretold that these Yavanas also would conquer India, and it proved to be true.

Khasa: The inhabitants of the Khasadeśa are mentioned in the *Mahābhārata* (*Droṇa-parva*). Those who have a stunted growth of hair on the upper lip are generally called Khasas. As such, the Khasa are the Mongolians, the Chinese and others who are so designated.

The above-mentioned historical names are different nations of the world. Even those who are constantly engaged in sinful acts are all corrigible to the standard of perfect human beings if they take shelter of the devotees of the Lord. Jesus Christ and Muhammad, two powerful devotees of the Lord, have done tremendous service on behalf of the Lord on the surface of the globe. And from the version of Śrīla Śukadeva Gosvāmī it appears that instead of running a godless civilization in the present context of the world situation, if the leadership of world affairs is entrusted to the devotees of the Lord, for which a worldwide organization under the name and style of the International Society for Krishna Consciousness has already been started, then by the grace of the Almighty Lord there can be a thorough change of heart in human beings all over the world because the devotees of the Lord are able authorities to effect such a change by purifying the dust-worn minds of the people in general. The politicians of the world may remain in their respective positions because the pure devotees of the Lord are not interested in political leadership or diplomatic implications. The devotees are interested only in seeing that the people in general are not misguided by political propaganda and in seeing that the valuable life of a human being is not spoiled in following a type of civilization which is ultimately doomed. If the politicians, therefore, would be guided by the good counsel of the devotees, then certainly there would be a great change in the world situation by the purifying propaganda of the devotees, as shown by Lord Caitanya. As Śukadeva Gosvāmī began his prayer by discussing the word *yat-kīrtanam*, so also Lord Caitanya recommended that simply by glorifying the Lord's holy name, a tremendous change of heart can take place by which the complete misunderstanding between the human nations created by politicians can at once be extinguished. And after the extinction of the fire of misunderstanding, other profits will follow. The destination is to go back home, back to Godhead, as we have several times discussed in these pages.

According to the cult of devotion, generally known as the Vaiṣṇava cult, there is no bar against anyone's advancing in the matter of God realization. A Vaiṣṇava is powerful enough to turn into a Vaiṣṇava even the Kirāta, etc., as above mentioned. In the *Bhagavad-gītā* (9.32) it is said by the Lord that there is no bar to becoming a devotee of the Lord (even for those who are lowborn, or women, *śūdras* or *vaiśyas*), and by becoming a devotee everyone is eligible to return home, back to Godhead. The only qualification is that one take shelter of a pure devotee of the Lord who has thorough knowledge in the transcendental science of Kṛṣṇa (*Bhagavad-gītā* and *Śrīmad-Bhāgavatam*). Anyone from any part of the world who becomes well conversant in the science of Kṛṣṇa becomes a pure devotee and a spiritual master for the general mass of people and may reclaim them by purification of heart. Though a person be even the most sinful man, he can at once be purified by systematic contact with a pure Vaiṣṇava. A Vaiṣṇava, therefore, can accept a bona fide disciple from any part of the world without any consideration of caste and creed and promote him by regulative principles to the status of a pure Vaiṣṇava who is transcendental to brahminical culture. The system of caste, or *varṇāśrama-dharma*, is no longer regular even amongst the so-called followers of the system. Nor is it now possible to reestablish the institutional function in the present context of social, political and economic revolution. Without any reference to the particu-

lar custom of a country, one can be accepted to the Vaiṣṇava cult spiritually, and there is no hindrance in the transcendental process. So by the
order of Lord Śrī Caitanya Mahāprabhu, the cult of *Śrīmad-Bhāgavatam*
or the *Bhagavad-gītā* can be preached all over the world, reclaiming all
persons willing to accept the transcendental cult. Such cultural propaganda by the devotees will certainly be accepted by all persons who are
reasonable and inquisitive, without any particular bias for the custom of
the country. The Vaiṣṇava never accepts another Vaiṣṇava on the basis
of birthright, just as he never thinks of the Deity of the Lord in a temple
as an idol. And to remove all doubts in this connection, Śrīla Śukadeva
Gosvāmī has invoked the blessings of the Lord, who is all-powerful
(*prabhaviṣṇave namaḥ*). As the all-powerful Lord accepts the humble
service of His devotee in devotional activities of the *arcana*, His form as
the worshipable Deity in the temple, similarly the body of a pure
Vaiṣṇava changes transcendentally at once when he gives himself up to
the service of the Lord and is trained by a qualified Vaiṣṇava. The in-
junction of Vaiṣṇava regulation in this connection runs as follows: *arcye
viṣṇau śilā-dhīr guruṣu nara-matir vaiṣṇave jāti-buddhiḥ śrī-viṣṇor
nāmni śabda-sāmānya-buddhiḥ,* etc. "One should not consider the Deity
of the Lord as worshiped in the temple to be an idol, nor should one consider the authorized spiritual master an ordinary man. Nor should one
consider a pure Vaiṣṇava to belong to a particular caste, etc." (*Padma
Purāṇa*)

The conclusion is that the Lord, being all-powerful, can, under any
and every circumstance, accept anyone from any part of the world, either
personally or through His bona fide manifestation as the spiritual master.
Lord Caitanya accepted many devotees from communities other than the
varṇāśramites, and He Himself declared, to teach us, that He does not
belong to any caste or social order of life, but that He is the eternal servant of the servant of the Lord who maintains the damsels of Vṛndāvana
(Lord Kṛṣṇa). That is the way of self-realization.

TEXT 19

स एष आत्मात्मवतामधीश्वर-
त्रयीमयो धर्ममयस्तपोमयः ।

गतव्यलीकैरजशङ्कुरादिभि-
वितर्क्यलिङ्गो भगवान् प्रसीदताम् ॥१९॥

sa eṣa ātmātmavatām adhīśvaras
trayīmayo dharmamayas tapomayaḥ
gata-vyalīkair aja-śaṅkarādibhir
vitarkya-liṅgo bhagavān prasīdatām

saḥ—He; *eṣaḥ*—it is; *ātmā*—the Supersoul; *ātmavatām*—of the self-realized souls; *adhīśvaraḥ*—the Supreme Lord; *trayī-mayaḥ*—personified *Vedas*; *dharma-mayaḥ*—personified religious scripture; *tapaḥ-mayaḥ*—personified austerity; *gata-vyalīkaiḥ*—by those who are above all pretensions; *aja*—Brahmājī; *śaṅkara-ādibhiḥ*—by Lord Śiva and others; *vitarkya-liṅgaḥ*—one who is observed with awe and veneration; *bhagavān*—the Personality of Godhead; *prasīdatām*—be kind toward me.

TRANSLATION

He is the Supersoul and the Supreme Lord of all self-realized souls. He is the personification of the Vedas, religious scriptures and austerities. He is worshiped by Lord Brahmā and Śiva and all those who are transcendental to all pretensions. Being so revered with awe and veneration, may that Supreme Absolute be pleased with me.

PURPORT

The Supreme Lord, the Personality of Godhead, although the Lord of all followers of different paths of self-realization, is knowable only by those who are above all pretensions. Everyone is searching for eternal peace or eternal life, and with an aim to this destination everyone is either studying the Vedic scriptures or other religious scriptures or undergoing severe austerity as empiric philosophers, as mystics *yogīs* or as unalloyed devotees, etc. But the Supreme Lord is perfectly realized only by the devotees because they are above all pretensions. Those who are on the path of self-realization are generally classified as *karmīs*, *jñānīs*, *yogīs*, or devotees of the Lord. The *karmīs*, who are much attracted by the fruitive activities of the Vedic rituals, are called *bhukti-kāmī*, or those who desire material enjoyment. The *jñānīs*, who try to become one with the Supreme by mental speculation, are called *mukti-kāmī*, or those who desire liberation from material existence. The mystic *yogīs*, who practice different types of austerities for attainment of eight kinds of material perfection and who ultimately meet the Supersoul (Paramātmā) in trance, are called *siddhi-kāmī*, or those who desire the perfection of becoming finer than the finest, becoming heavier than the heaviest, getting everything desired, having control over everyone, creating everything liked, etc. All these are abilities of a powerful *yogī*. But the devotees of the Lord do not want anything like that for self-satisfaction. They want only to serve the Lord because the Lord is great and as living entities they are eternally subordinate parts and parcels of the Lord. This perfect realization of the self by the devotee helps him to become desireless, to desire nothing for his personal self, and thus the devotees are called *niṣkāmī*, without any desire. A living entity, by his constitutional position, cannot be void of all desires (the *bhukti-kāmī*, *mukti-kāmī* and *siddhi-kāmī* all desire something for personal satisfaction), but the *niṣkāmī* devotees of the Lord desire everything for the satisfaction of the Lord. They are completely dependent on the orders of the Lord and are always ready to discharge their duty for the satisfaction of the Lord.

In the beginning Arjuna placed himself as one of those who desire self-satisfaction, for he desired not to fight in the Battle of Kurukṣetra, but to make him desireless the Lord preached the *Bhagavad-gītā*, in which the ways of *karma-yoga*, *jñāna-yoga*, *haṭha-yoga* and also *bhakti-yoga* were explained. Because Arjuna was without any pretension, he changed his decision and satisfied the Lord by agreeing to fight (*kariṣye vacanaṁ tava*), and thus he became desireless.

The examples of Brahmā and Lord Śiva are specifically cited here because Brahmājī, Lord Śiva, Śrīmatī Lakṣmījī and the four Kumāras (Sanaka, Sanātana, etc.) are leaders of the four desireless Vaiṣṇava *sampradāyas*. They are all freed from all pretensions. Śrīla Jīva Gosvāmī interprets the word *gata-vyalīkaiḥ* as *projjhita-kaitavaiḥ*, or those who are freed from all pretensions (the unalloyed devotees only). In the *Caitanya-caritāmṛta* (*Madhya* 19.149) it is said:

> *kṛṣṇa-bhakta——niṣkāma, ata eva 'śānta'*
> *bhukti-mukti-siddhi-kāmī, sakali 'aśānta'*

Those who are after fruitive results for their pious activities, those who desire salvation and identity with the Supreme, and those who desire material perfections of mystic power are all restless because they want something for themselves, but the devotee is completely peaceful because he has no demand for himself and is always ready to serve the desire of the Lord. The conclusion is, therefore, that the Lord is for everyone because no one can achieve the result of his respective desires without His sanction, but as stated by the Lord in *Bhagavad-gītā* (8.9), all such results are awarded by Him only, for the Lord is *adhīśvara* (the original controller) of everyone, namely the Vedāntists, the great *karma-kāṇḍīyas*, the great religious leaders, the great performers of austerity and all who are striving for spiritual advancement. But ultimately He is realized by the pretensionless devotees only. Therefore special stress is given to the devotional service of the Lord by Śrīla Śukadeva Gosvāmī.

TEXT 20

श्रियः पतिर्यज्ञपतिः प्रजापति-
धियां पतिर्लोकपतिर्धरापतिः ।
पतिर्गतिश्चान्धकवृष्णिसात्वतां
प्रसीदतां मे भगवान् सतां पतिः ॥२०॥

śriyaḥ patir yajña-patiḥ prajā-patir
dhiyāṁ patir loka-patir dharā-patiḥ
patir gatiś cāndhaka-vṛṣṇi-sātvatāṁ
prasīdatāṁ me bhagavān satāṁ patiḥ

śriyaḥ—all opulence; *patiḥ*—the owner; *yajña*—of sacrifice; *patiḥ*—the director; *prajā-patiḥ*—the leader of all living entities; *dhiyām*—of intelligence; *patiḥ*—the master; *loka-patiḥ*—the proprietor of all planets; *dharā*—earth; *patiḥ*—the supreme; *patiḥ*—head; *gatiḥ*—destination; *ca*—also; *andhaka*—one of the kings of the Yadu dynasty; *vṛṣṇi*—the first king of the Yadu dynasty; *sātvatām*—the Yadus; *prasīdatām*—be merciful; *me*—upon me; *bhagavān*—Lord Śrī Kṛṣṇa; *satām*—of all devotees; *patiḥ*—the Lord.

TRANSLATION

May Lord Śrī Kṛṣṇa, who is the worshipable Lord of all devotees, the protector and glory of all the kings like Andhaka and Vṛṣṇi of the Yadu dynasty, the husband of all goddesses of fortune, the director of all sacrifices and therefore the leader of all living entities, the controller of all intelligence, the proprietor of all planets, spiritual and material, and the supreme incarnation on the earth (the supreme all in all), be merciful upon me.

PURPORT

Since Śukadeva Gosvāmī is one of the prominent *gata-vyalīkas*, who are freed from all misconceptions, he therefore expresses his own realized perception of Lord Śrī Kṛṣṇa as being the sum total of all perfection, the Personality of Godhead. Everyone is seeking the favor of the goddess of fortune, but people do not know that Lord Śrī Kṛṣṇa is the beloved husband of all goddesses of fortune. In the *Brahma-saṁhitā* it is said that the Lord, in His transcendental abode Goloka Vṛndāvana, is accustomed to herding the *surabhi* cows and is served there by hundreds of thousands of goddesses of fortune. All these goddesses of fortune are manifestations of His transcendental pleasure potency (*hlādinī-śakti*) in His internal energy, and when the Lord manifested Himself on this earth He partially displayed the activities of His pleasure potency in His *rāsa-līlā* just to attract the conditioned souls, who are all after the phantasmagoria pleasure potency in degraded sex enjoyment. The pure devotees of the Lord like Śukadeva Gosvāmī, who was completely detached from the abominable sex life of the material world, discussed this act of the Lord's pleasure potency certainly not in relation to sex, but to relish a transcendental taste inconceivable to the mundaners who are after sex life. Sex life in the mundane world is the root-cause of being conditioned by the shackles of illusion, and certainly Śukadeva Gosvāmī was never interested in the sex life of the mundane world. Nor does the manifestation of the Lord's pleasure potency have any connection with such degraded things. Lord Caitanya was a strict *sannyāsī*, so much so that He did not allow any woman to come near Him, not even to bow down and offer respects. He never even heard the prayers of the *deva-dāsīs* offered in the temple of Jagannātha because a *sannyāsī* is forbidden to hear songs sung by the fair sex. Yet even in the rigid position of a *sannyāsī* He recommended the mode of worship preferred by the *gopīs* of Vṛndāvana as the topmost loving service possible to be rendered to the Lord. And Śrīmatī Rādhārāṇī is the principal head of all such goddesses of fortune, and therefore She is the pleasure counterpart of the Lord and is nondifferent from Kṛṣṇa.

In the Vedic rituals there are recommendations for performing different types of sacrifice in order to achieve the greatest benefit in life. Such benedictions as the results of performing great sacrifices are, after all, favors given by the goddess of fortune, and the Lord, being the husband or lover of the goddess of fortune, is factually the Lord of all sacrifices also. He is the final enjoyer of all kinds of *yajña;* therefore Yajña-pati is another name of Lord Viṣṇu. It is recommended in the *Bhagavad-gītā* that everything be done for the Yajña-pati (*yajñārtāt karmaṇaḥ*), for otherwise one's acts will be the cause of conditioning by the law of material nature. Those who are not freed from all misconceptions (*vyalīkam*) perform sacrifices to please the minor demigods, but the devotees of the Lord know very well that Lord Śrī Kṛṣṇa is the supreme enjoyer of all performances of sacrifice; therefore they perform the *saṅkīrtana-yajña* (*śravaṇaṁ kīrtanaṁ viṣṇoḥ*), which is especially recommended in this age of Kali. In Kali-yuga, performance of other types of sacrifice is not feasible due to insufficient arrangements and inexpert priesthood.

We have information from the *Bhagavad-gītā* (3.10–11) that Lord Brahmā, after giving rebirth to the conditioned souls within the universe, instructed them to perform sacrifices and to lead a prosperous life. With such sacrificial performances the conditioned souls will never be in difficulty in keeping body and soul together. Ultimately they can purify their existence. They will find natural promotion into spiritual existence, the real identity of the living being. A conditioned soul should never give up the practice of sacrifice, charity and austerity, in any circumstances. The aim of all such sacrifices is to please the Yajña-pati, the Personality of Godhead; therefore the Lord is also Prajā-pati. According to the *Kaṭha Upaniṣad*, the one Lord is the leader of the innumerable living entities. The living entities are maintained by the Lord (*eko bahūnāṁ yo vidadhāti kāmān*). The Lord is therefore called the supreme Bhūta-bhṛt, or maintainer of all living beings.

Living beings are proportionately endowed with intelligence in terms of their previous activities. All living beings are not equally endowed with the same quality of intelligence because behind such development of intelligence is the control of the Lord, as declared in the *Bhagavad-gītā* (15.15). As Paramātmā, Supersoul, the Lord is living in everyone's heart, and from Him only does one's power of remembrance, knowledge and forgetfulness follow (*mattaḥ smṛtir jñānam apohanaṁ ca*). One person can sharply remember past activities by the grace of the Lord while others cannot. One is highly intelligent by the grace of the Lord, and one is a fool by the same control. Therefore the Lord is Dhiyām-pati, or the Lord of intelligence.

The conditioned souls strive to become lords of the material world. Everyone is trying to lord it over the material nature by applying his highest degree of intelligence. This misuse of intelligence by the conditioned soul is called madness. One's full intelligence should be applied to get free from the material clutches. But the conditioned soul, due to madness only, engages his full energy and intelligence in sense gratification, and to achieve this end of life he willfully commits all sorts of misdeeds. The result is that instead of attaining an unconditional life of full freedom, the mad conditioned soul is entangled again and again in different types of bondage in material bodies. Everything we see in the material manifestation is but the creation of the Lord. Therefore He is the real proprietor of everything in the universes. The conditioned soul can enjoy a fragment of this material creation under the control of the Lord, but not self-sufficiently. That is the instruction in the *Īśopaniṣad*. One should be satisfied with things awarded by the Lord of the universe. It is out of madness only that one tries to encroach upon another's share of material possessions.

The Lord of the universe, out of His causeless mercy upon the conditioned souls, descends by His own energy (*ātma-māyā*) to reestablish the eternal relation of the conditioned souls with Him. He instructs all to surrender unto Him instead of falsely claiming to be enjoyers for a certain limit under His control. When He so descends He proves how much greater is His ability to enjoy, and He exhibits His power of enjoyment by (for instance) marrying sixteen thousand wives at once. The conditioned soul is very proud of becoming the husband of even one wife, but the Lord laughs at this; the intelligent man can know who is the real husband. Factually, the Lord is the husband of all the women in His creation, but a conditioned soul under the control of the Lord feels proud to be the husband of one or two wives.

All these qualifications as the different types of *pati* mentioned in this verse are meant for Lord Śrī Kṛṣṇa, and Śukadeva Gosvāmī has therefore especially mentioned the *pati* and *gati* of the Yadu dynasty. The members of the Yadu dynasty knew that Lord Śrī Kṛṣṇa is everything, and all of them intended to return to Lord Kṛṣṇa after He had finished His transcendental pastimes on the earth. The Yadu dynasty was annihilated by the will of the Lord because its members had to return home with the Lord. The annihilation of the Yadu dynasty was a material show created by the Supreme Lord; otherwise the Lord and the members of the Yadu dynasty are all eternal associates. The Lord is therefore the guide of all devotees, and as such, Śukadeva Gosvāmī offered Him due respects with love-laden feelings.

TEXT 21

यदङ्घ्यभिध्यानसमाधिधौतया
धियानुपश्यन्ति हि तत्त्वमात्मनः ।
वदन्ति चैतत् कवयो यथारुचं
स मे मुकुन्दो भगवान् प्रसीदताम् ॥२१॥

yad-aṅghry-abhidhyāna-samādhi-dhautayā
dhiyānupaśyanti hi tattvam ātmanaḥ
vadanti caitat kavayo yathā-rucaṁ
sa me mukundo bhagavān prasīdatām

yat-aṅghri—whose lotus feet; *abhidhyāna*—thinking of, at every second; *samādhi*—trance; *dhautayā*—being washed off; *dhiyā*—by such clean intelligence; *anupaśyanti*—does see by following authorities; *hi*—certainly; *tattvam*—the Absolute Truth; *ātmanaḥ*—of the Supreme Lord and of oneself; *vadanti*—they say; *ca*—also; *etat*—this; *kavayaḥ*—philosophers or learned scholars; *yathā-rucam*—as he thinks; *saḥ*—He; *me*—mine; *mukundaḥ*—Lord Kṛṣṇa (who gives liberation); *bhagavān*—the Personality of Godhead; *prasīdatām*—be pleased with me.

TRANSLATION

It is the Personality of Godhead Śrī Kṛṣṇa who gives liberation. By thinking of His lotus feet at every second, following in the footsteps of authorities, the devotee in trance can see the Absolute Truth. The learned mental speculators, however, think of Him according to their whims. May the Lord be pleased with me.

PURPORT

The mystic *yogīs*, after a strenuous effort to control the senses, may be situated in a trance of *yoga* just to have a vision of the Supersoul within everyone, but the pure devotee, simply by remembering the Lord's lotus feet at every second, at once becomes established in real trance because by such realization his mind and intelligence are completely cleansed of the diseases of material enjoyment. The pure devotee thinks himself fallen into the ocean of birth and death and incessantly prays to the Lord to lift him up. He only aspires to become a speck of transcendental dust at the lotus feet of the Lord. The pure devotee, by the grace of the Lord, absolutely loses all attraction for material enjoyment, and to keep free from contamination he always thinks of the lotus feet of the Lord. King Kulaśekhara, a great devotee of the Lord, prayed:

kṛṣṇa tvadīya-pada-paṅkaja-pañjarāntam
adyaiva me viśatu mānasa-rāja-haṁsaḥ
prāṇa-prayāṇa-samaye kapha-vāta-pittaiḥ
kaṇṭhāvarodhana-vidhau smaraṇaṁ kutas te

"My Lord Kṛṣṇa, I pray that the swan of my mind may immediately sink down to the stems of the lotus feet of Your Lordship and be locked in their network; otherwise at the time of my final breath, when my throat is choked up with cough, how will it be possible to think of You?"

There is an intimate relationship between the swan and the lotus stem. So the comparison is very appropriate: without becoming a swan, or *paramahaṁsa*, one cannot enter into the network of the lotus feet of the Lord. As stated in the *Brahma-saṁhitā*, the mental speculators, even by dint of learned scholarship, cannot even dream of the Absolute Truth by speculating over it for eternity. The Lord reserves the right of not being exposed to such mental speculators. And because they cannot enter into the network stem of the lotus feet of the Lord, all mental speculators differ in conclusions, and at the end they make a useless compromise by saying "as many conclusions, as many ways," according to one's own inclination (yathā-rucam). But the Lord is not like a shopkeeper trying to please all sorts of customers in the mental speculator exchange. The Lord is what He is, the Absolute Personality of Godhead, and He demands absolute surrender unto Him only. The pure devotee, however, by following the ways of previous ācāryas, or authorities, can see the Supreme Lord through the transparent medium of a bona fide spiritual master (anupaśyanti). The pure devotee never tries to see the Lord by mental speculation, but by following in the footsteps of the ācāryas (mahājano yena gataḥ sa panthāḥ). Therefore there is no difference of conclusions amongst the Vaiṣṇava ācāryas regarding the Lord and the devotees. Lord Caitanya asserts that the living entity (jīva) is eternally the servitor of the Lord and that he is simultaneously one with and different from the Lord. This tattva of Lord Caitanya's is shared by all four sampradāyas of the Vaiṣṇava school (all accepting eternal servitude to the Lord even after salvation), and there is no authorized Vaiṣṇava ācārya who may think of the Lord and himself as one.

This humbleness of the pure devotee, who is one hundred percent engaged in His service, puts the devotee of the Lord in a trance by which to realize everything, because to the sincere devotee of the Lord, the Lord reveals Himself, as stated in the Bhagavad-gītā (10.10). The Lord, being the Lord of intelligence in everyone (even in the nondevotee), favors His devotee with proper intelligence so that automatically the pure devotee is enlightened with the factual truth about the Lord and His different energies. The Lord is revealed not by one's speculative power or by one's verbal jugglery over the Absolute Truth. Rather, He reveals Himself to a devotee when He is fully satisfied by the devotee's service attitude. Śukadeva Gosvāmī is not a mental speculator or compromiser of the theory of "as many ways, as many conclusions." Rather, he prays to the Lord only, invoking His transcendental pleasure. That is the way of knowing the Lord.

TEXT 22

प्रचोदिता येन पुरा सरस्वती
वितन्वताजस्य सतीं स्मृतिं हृदि ।

स्वलक्षणा प्रादुरभूत् किलास्यतः
स मे ऋषीणामृषभः प्रसीदताम् ॥२२॥

pracoditā yena purā sarasvatī
vitanvatājasya satīm smṛtim hṛdi
sva-lakṣaṇā prādurabhūt kilāsyataḥ
sa me ṛṣīṇām ṛṣabhaḥ prasīdatām

pracoditā—inspired; *yena*—by whom; *purā*—in the beginning of creation; *sarasvatī*—the goddess of learning; *vitanvatā*—amplified; *ajasya*—of Brahmā, the first created living being; *satīm smṛtim*—potent memory; *hṛdi*—in the heart; *sva*—in his own; *lakṣaṇā*—aiming at; *prādurabhūt*—was generated; *kila*—as if; *āsyataḥ*—from the mouth; *sah*—he; *me*—unto me; *ṛṣīṇām*—of the teachers; *ṛṣabhaḥ*—the chief; *prasīdatām*—be pleased.

TRANSLATION

May the Lord, who in the beginning of the creation amplified the potent knowledge of Brahmā from within his heart and inspired him with full knowledge of creation and of His own Self, and who appeared to be generated from the mouth of Brahmā, be pleased with me.

PURPORT

As we have already discussed hereinbefore, the Lord, as the Supersoul of all living beings from Brahmā to the insignificant ant, endows all with the required knowledge potent in every living being. A living being is sufficiently potent to possess knowledge from the Lord in the proportion of fifty sixty-fourths, or seventy-eight percent of the full knowledge acquirable. Since the living being is constitutionally part and parcel of the Lord, he is unable to assimilate all the knowledge that the Lord possesses Himself. In the conditioned state, the living being is subject to forget everything after a change of body known as death. This potent knowledge is again inspired by the Lord from within the heart of every living being, and it is known as the awakening of knowledge, for it is comparable to awakening from sleep or unconsciousness. This awakening of knowledge is under the full control of the Lord, and therefore we find in the practical world different grades of knowledge in different persons. This awakening of knowledge is neither an automatic nor a material interaction. The supply source is the Lord Himself (*dhiyām patiḥ*), for even Brahmā is also subject to this regulation of the supreme creator. In the beginning of the creation, Brahmā is born first without any father and mother because before Brahmā there were no other living beings. Brahmā is born from the lotus which grows from the abdomen of the Garbhodakaśāyī Viṣṇu, and therefore he is known as Aja. This Brahmā, or Aja, is also a living being, part and parcel of the Lord, but being the most pious devotee of the Lord, Brahmā is inspired by the Lord to create, subsequent to the main creation by the Lord, through the agency of material nature. Therefore neither the material nature nor Brahmā is independent of the Lord. The material scientists can merely observe the reactions of the material nature without understanding the direction behind such activities, as a child can see the action of electricity without any knowledge of the powerhouse engineer. This imperfect knowledge of the material scientist is due to a poor fund of knowledge. The Vedic knowledge was therefore first impregnated within Brahmā, and it appears that Brahmā distributed the Vedic knowledge. Brahmā is undoubtedly the speaker of the Vedic knowledge, but actually he was inspired by the Lord to receive such transcendental knowledge, as it directly descends from the Lord. The *Vedas* are therefore called *apauruṣeya*, or not imparted by any created being. Before the creation the Lord was there (*nārāyaṇaḥ paro 'vyaktāt*), and therefore the words spoken by the Lord are vibrations of transcendental sound. There is a gulf of difference between the two qualities of sound, namely *prākṛta* and *aprākṛta*. The physicist can deal only with the *prākṛta* sound, or sound vibrated in the material sky, and therefore we must know that the Vedic sounds recorded in symbolic expressions cannot be understood by anyone within the universe unless and until one is inspired by the vibration of supernatural (*aprākṛta*) sound, which descends in the chain of disciplic succession from the Lord to Brahmā, from Brahmā to Nārada, from Nārada to Vyāsa and so on. No mundane scholar can translate or reveal the true import of the Vedic *mantras* (hymns). They cannot be understood unless one is inspired or initiated by the authorized spiritual master. The original spiritual master is the Lord Himself, and the succession comes down through the sources of *paramparā*, as clearly stated in the Fourth Chapter of the *Bhagavad-gītā*. So unless one receives the transcendental knowledge from the authorized *paramparā*, one should be considered useless (*viphalā matāḥ*), even though one may be greatly qualified in the mundane advancements of arts or science.

Śukadeva Gosvāmī is praying from the Lord by dint of being inspired from within by the Lord so that he could rightly explain the facts and figures of creation as inquired by Mahārāja Parīkṣit. A spiritual master is not a theoretical speculator, like the mundane scholar, but is *śrotriyaṁ brahma-niṣṭham*.

TEXT 23

भूतैर्महद्भिर्य इमाः पुरो विभु-
र्निर्माय शेते यदमूषु पूरुषः ।
भुङ्क्ते गुणान् षोडश षोडशात्मकः
सोऽलङ्कृषीष्ट भगवान् वचांसि मे ॥२३॥

bhūtair mahadbhir ya imāḥ puro vibhur
nirmāya śete yad amūṣu pūruṣaḥ
bhuṅkte guṇān ṣoḍaśa ṣoḍaśātmakaḥ
so 'laṅkṛṣīṣṭa bhagavān vacāṁsi me

bhūtaiḥ—by the elements; *mahadbhiḥ*—of material creation; *yaḥ*—He who; *imāḥ*—all these; *puraḥ*—bodies; *vibhuḥ*—of the Lord; *nirmāya*—for being set up; *śete*—lie down; *yat amūṣu*—one who incarnated; *pūruṣaḥ*—Lord Viṣṇu; *bhuṅkte*—causes to be subjected; *guṇān*—the three modes of nature; *ṣoḍaśa*—in sixteen divisions; *ṣoḍaśa-ātmakaḥ*—being the generator of these sixteen; *saḥ*—He; *alaṅkṛṣīṣṭa*—may decorate; *bhagavān*—the Personality of Godhead; *vacāṁsi*—statements; *me*—mine.

TRANSLATION

May the Supreme Personality of Godhead, who enlivens the materially created bodies of the elements by lying down within the universe, and who in His puruṣa incarnation causes the living being to be subjected to the sixteen divisions of material modes which are his generator, be pleased to decorate my statements.

PURPORT

As a fully dependent devotee, Śukadeva Gosvāmī (unlike a mundane man who is proud of his own capability) invokes the pleasure of the Personality of Godhead so that his statements may be successful and be appreciated by the hearers. The devotee always thinks of himself as instrumental for anything successfully carried out, and he declines to take credit for anything done by himself. The godless atheist wants to take all credit for activities, not knowing that even a blade of grass cannot move without the sanction of the Supreme Spirit, the Personality of Godhead. Śukadeva Gosvāmī therefore wants to move by the direction of the Supreme Lord, who inspired Brahmā to speak the Vedic wisdom. The truths described in the Vedic literatures are not theories of mundane imagination, nor are they fictitious, as the less intelligent class of men sometimes think. The Vedic truths are all perfect descriptions of the factual truth without any mistake or illusion, and Śukadeva Gosvāmī wants to present the truths of creation not as a metaphysical theory of philosophical speculation, but as the actual facts and figures of the subject, since he would be dictated to by the Lord exactly in the same manner as Brahmājī was inspired. As stated in the *Bhagavad-gītā* (15.15), the Lord is Himself the father of the *Vedānta* knowledge, and it is He only who knows the factual purport of the *Vedānta* philosophy. So there is no greater truth than the principles of religion mentioned in the *Vedas*. Such Vedic knowledge or religion is disseminated by authorities like Śukadeva Gosvāmī because he is a humble devotional servitor of the Lord who has no desire to become a self-appointed interpreter without authority. That is the way of explaining the Vedic knowledge, technically known as the *paramparā* system, or descending process.

The intelligent man can see without mistake that any material creation (whether one's own body or a fruit or flower) cannot beautifully grow up without the spiritual touch. The greatest intelligent man of the world or the greatest man of science can present everything very beautifully only insofar as the spirit life is there or insomuch as the spiritual touch is there. Therefore the source of all truths is the Supreme Spirit, and not gross matter as wrongly conceived by the gross materialist. We get information from the Vedic literature that the Lord Himself first entered the vacuum of the material universe, and thus all things gradually developed one after another. Similarly, the Lord is situated as localized Paramātmā in every individual being; hence everything is done by Him very beautifully. The sixteen principal creative elements, namely earth, water, fire, air, sky, and the eleven sense organs, first developed from the Lord Himself and were thereby shared by the living entities. Thus the material elements were created for the enjoyment of the living entities. The beautiful arrangement behind all material manifestations is therefore made possible by the energy of the Lord, and the individual living entity can only pray to the Lord to understand it properly. Since the Lord is the supreme entity, different from Śukadeva Gosvāmī, the prayer can be offered to Him. The Lord helps the living entity to enjoy material creation, but He is aloof from such false enjoyment. Śukadeva prays for the mercy of the Lord, not only for being helped personally in presenting the truth, but also for helping others to whom he would like to speak.

TEXT 24

नमस्तस्मै भगवते वासुदेवाय वेधसे ।
पपुर्ज्ञानमयं सौम्या यन्मुखाम्बुरुहासवम् ॥२४॥

namas tasmai bhagavate
vāsudevāya vedhase
papur jñānam ayaṁ saumyā
yan-mukhāmburuhāsavam

namaḥ—my obeisances; *tasmai*—unto Him; *bhagavate*—unto the Personality of Godhead; *vāsudevāya*—unto Vāsudeva or His incarnations; *vedhase*—the compiler of the Vedic literatures; *papuḥ*—drunk; *jñānam*—knowledge; *ayam*—this Vedic knowledge; *saumyāḥ*—the devotees, especially the consorts of Lord Kṛṣṇa; *yat*—from whose; *mukha-amburuha*—the lotuslike mouth; *āsavam*—nectar from His mouth.

TRANSLATION

I offer my respectful obeisances unto Śrīla Vyāsadeva, the incarnation of Vāsudeva who compiled the Vedic scriptures. The pure devotees drink up the nectarean transcendental knowledge dropping from the lotuslike mouth of the Lord.

PURPORT

In pursuance of the specific utterance *vedhase*, or "the compiler of the system of transcendental knowledge," Śrīla Śrīdhara Svāmī has commented that the respectful obeisances are offered to Śrīla Vyāsadeva, who is the incarnation of Vāsudeva. Śrīla Jīva Gosvāmī has agreed to this, but Śrīla Viśvanātha Cakravartī Ṭhākura has made a further advance, namely that the nectar from the mouth of Lord Kṛṣṇa is transferred to His different consorts, and thus they learn the finer arts of music, dance, dressing, decorations and all such things which are relished by the Lord. Such music, dance and decorations enjoyed by the Lord are certainly not anything mundane, because the Lord is addressed in the very beginning as *para*, or transcendental. This transcendental knowledge is unknown to the forgotten conditioned souls. Śrīla Vyāsadeva, who is the incarnation of the Lord, thus compiled the Vedic literatures to revive the lost memory of the conditioned souls about their eternal relation with the Lord. One should therefore try to understand the Vedic scriptures, or the nectar transferred by the Lord to His consorts in the conjugal humor, from the lotuslike mouth of Vyāsadeva or Śukadeva. By gradual development of transcendental knowledge, one can rise to the stage of the transcendental arts of music and dance displayed by the Lord in His *rāsa-līlā*. But without having the Vedic knowledge one can hardly understand the transcendental nature of the Lord's *rāsa* dance and music. The pure devotees of the Lord, however, can equally relish the nectar in the form of the profound philosophical discourses and in the form of kissing by the Lord in the *rāsa* dance, as there is no mundane distinction between the two.

TEXT 25

एतदेवात्मभू राजन् नारदाय विपृच्छते ।
वेदगर्भोऽभ्यधात् साक्षाद् यदाह हरिरात्मनः ॥२५॥

etad evātma-bhū rājan
nāradāya vipṛcchate
veda-garbho 'bhyadhāt sākṣād
yad āha harir ātmanaḥ

etat—on this matter; *eva*—exactly; *ātma-bhūḥ*—the firstborn (Brahmājī); *rājan*—my dear King; *nāradāya*—unto Nārada Muni; *vipṛcchate*—having inquired about it from; *veda-garbhaḥ*—one who is impregnated with Vedic knowledge from birth; *abhyadhāt*—apprised; *sākṣāt*—directly; *yat āha*—what he spoke; *hariḥ*—the Lord; *ātmanaḥ* —unto His own (Brahmā).

TRANSLATION

My dear King, Brahmā, the firstborn, on being questioned by Nārada, exactly apprised him on this subject, as it was directly spoken by the Lord to His own son, who was impregnated with Vedic knowledge from his very birth.

PURPORT

As soon as Brahmā was born of the abdominal lotus petals of Viṣṇu, he was impregnated with Vedic knowledge, and therefore he is known as *veda-garbha*, or a Vedāntist from the embryo. Without Vedic knowledge, or perfect, infallible knowledge, no one can create anything. All scientific knowledge and perfect knowledge are Vedic. One can get all types of information from the *Vedas*, and as such, Brahmā was impregnated with all-perfect knowledge so that it was possible for him to create. Thus Brahmā knew the perfect description of creation, as it was exactly apprised to him by the Supreme Lord Hari. Brahmā, on being questioned by Nārada, told Nārada exactly what he had heard directly from the Lord. Nārada again told exactly the same thing to Vyāsa, and Vyāsa also told Śukadeva exactly what he heard from Nārada. And Śukadeva was going to repeat the same statements as he had heard them from Vyāsa. That is the way of Vedic understanding. The language of the *Vedas* can be revealed only by the above-mentioned disciplic succession, and not otherwise.

There is no use in theories. Knowledge must be factual. There are many things that are complicated, and one cannot understand them unless they are explained by one who knows. The Vedic knowledge is also very difficult to know and must be learned by the above-mentioned system; otherwise it is not at all understood.

Śukadeva Gosvāmī, therefore, prayed for the mercy of the Lord so that he might be able to repeat the very same message that was spoken directly by the Lord to Brahmā, or what was directly spoken by Brahmā to Nārada. Therefore the statements of creation explained by Śukadeva Gosvāmī are not at all, as the mundaners suggest, theoretical, but are perfectly correct. One who hears these messages and tries to assimilate them gets perfect information of the material creation.

Thus end the Bhaktivedanta purports of the Second Canto, Fourth Chapter, of the Śrīmad-Bhāgavatam, *entitled "The Process of Creation."*

CHAPTER FIVE

The Cause of All Causes

TEXT 1

नारद उवाच

देवदेव नमस्तेऽस्तु भूतभावन पूर्वज ।
तद् विजानीहि यज्ज्ञानमात्मतत्त्वनिदर्शनम् ॥ १ ॥

nārada uvāca
deva-deva namas te 'stu
bhūta-bhāvana pūrvaja
tad vijānīhi yaj jñānam
ātma-tattva-nidarśanam

nāradaḥ uvāca—Śrī Nārada said; *deva*—of all demigods; *deva*—the demigod; *namaḥ*—obeisances; *te*—unto you as; *astu*—are; *bhūta-bhāvana*—the generator of all living beings; *pūrva-ja*—the firstborn; *tat vijānīhi*—please explain that knowledge; *yat jñānam*—which knowledge; *ātma-tattva*—transcendental; *nidarśanam*—specifically directs.

TRANSLATION

Śrī Nārada Muni asked Brahmājī: O chief amongst the demigods, O firstborn living entity, I beg to offer my respectful obeisances unto you. Please tell me that transcendental knowledge which specifically directs one to the truth of the individual soul and the Supersoul.

PURPORT

The perfection of the *paramparā* system, or the path of disciplic succession, is further confirmed. In the previous chapter it has been established that Brahmājī, the firstborn living entity, received knowledge directly from the Supreme Lord, and the same knowledge was imparted to Nārada, the next disciple. Nārada asked to receive the knowledge, and Brahmājī imparted it upon being asked. Therefore, asking for transcendental knowledge from the right person and receiving it properly is the regulation of the disciplic succession. This process is recommended in the *Bhagavad-gītā* (4.2). The inquisitive student must approach a qualified spiritual master to receive transcendental knowledge by surrender, submissive inquiries and service. Knowledge received by submissive inquiries and service is more effective than knowledge received in exchange for money. A spiritual master in the line of disciplic succession from Brahmā and Nārada has no demand for dollars and cents. A bona fide student has to satisfy him by sincere service to obtain knowledge of the relation and nature of the individual soul and the Supersoul.

TEXT 2

यद्रूपं यदधिष्ठानं यतः सृष्टमिदं प्रभो ।
यत्संस्थं यत्परं यच्च तत् तत्त्वं वद तत्त्वतः ॥ २ ॥

yad rūpaṁ yad adhiṣṭhānam
yataḥ sṛṣṭam idaṁ prabho
yat saṁsthaṁ yat paraṁ yac ca
tat tattvaṁ vada tattvataḥ

yat—what; *rūpam*—the symptoms of manifestation; *yat*—what; *adhiṣṭhānam*—background; *yataḥ*—from where; *sṛṣṭam*—created; *idam*—this world; *prabho*—O my father; *yat*—in which; *saṁstham*—conserved; *yat*—what; *param*—under control; *yat*—what are; *ca*—and; *tat*—of this; *tattvam*—the symptoms; *vada*—please describe; *tattvataḥ*—factually.

TRANSLATION

My dear father, please describe factually the symptoms of this manifest world. What is its background? How is it created? How is it conserved? And under whose control is all this being done?

PURPORT

The inquiries by Nārada Muni on the basis of factual cause and effect appear very reasonable. The atheists, however, put forward many self-made theories without any touch of cause and effect. The manifested world, as well as the spirit soul, is still unexplained by the godless atheists through the medium of experimental knowledge, although they have put forward many theories manufactured by their fertile brains. Contrary to such mental speculative theories of creation, however, Nārada Muni wanted to know all the facts of creation in truth, and not by theories.

Transcendental knowledge regarding the soul and the Supersoul includes knowledge of the phenomenal world and the basis of its creation. In the phenomenal world three things are factually observed by any intelligent man: the living beings, the manifest world, and the ultimate control over them. The intelligent man can see that neither the living entity nor the phenomenal world are creations of chance. The symmetry of creation and its regulative actions and reactions suggests the plan of an intelligent brain behind them, and by genuine inquiry one may find out the ultimate cause with the help of one who knows them factually.

TEXT 3

सर्वं ह्येतद् भवान् वेद भूतभव्यभवत्प्रभुः ।
करामलकवद् विश्वं विज्ञानावसितं तव ॥ ३ ॥

sarvam hy etad bhavān veda
bhūta-bhavya-bhavat-prabhuḥ
karāmalaka-vad viśvam
vijñānāvasitam tava

sarvam—all and everything; *hi*—certainly; *etat*—this; *bhavān*—your good self; *veda*—know; *bhūta*—all that is created or born; *bhavya*—all that will be created or born; *bhavat*—all that is being created; *prabhuḥ*—you, the master of everything; *kara-āmalaka-vat*—just like a walnut within your grip; *viśvam*—the universe; *vijñāna-avasitam*—within your knowledge scientifically; *tava*—your.

TRANSLATION

My dear father, all this is known to you scientifically because whatever was created in the past, whatever will be created in the future, or whatever is being created at present, as well as everything within the universe, is within your grip, just like a walnut.

PURPORT

Brahmā is the direct creator of the manifested universe and everything within the universe. He therefore knows what happened in the past, what will happen in the future, and what is happening at present. Three principal items, namely the living being, the phenomenal world and the controller, are all in continuous action—past, present and future—and the direct manager is supposed to know everything of such actions and reactions, as one knows about a walnut within the grip of one's palm. The direct manufacturer of a particular thing is supposed to know how he learned the art of manufacturing, where he got the ingredients, how he set it up and how the products in the manufacturing process are being turned out. Because Brahmā is the firstborn living being, naturally he is supposed to know everything about creative functions.

TEXT 4

यद्विज्ञानो यदाधारो यत्परस्त्वं यदात्मकः ।
एकः सृजसि भूतानि भूतैरेवात्ममायया ॥ ४ ॥

yad-vijñāno yad-ādhāro
yat-paras tvaṁ yad-ātmakaḥ
ekaḥ sṛjasi bhūtāni
bhūtair evātma-māyayā

yat-vijñānaḥ—the source of knowledge; *yat-ādhāraḥ*—under whose protection; *yat-paraḥ*—under whose subordination; *tvam*—you; *yat-āt-makaḥ*—in what capacity; *ekaḥ*—alone; *sṛjasi*—you are creating; *bhūtāni*—the living entities; *bhūtaiḥ*—with the help of the material elements; *eva*—certainly; *ātma*—self; *māyayā*—by potency.

TRANSLATION

My dear father, what is the source of your knowledge? Under whose protection are you standing? And under whom are you working? What is your real position? Do you alone create all entities with material elements by your personal energy?

PURPORT

It was known to Śrī Nārada Muni that Lord Brahmā attained creative energy by undergoing severe austerities. As such, he could understand that there was someone else superior to Brahmājī who invested Brahmā with the power of creation. Therefore he asked all the above questions. Discoveries of progressive scientific achievements are therefore not independent. The scientist has to attain the knowledge of a thing already existing by means of the wonderful brain made by someone else. A scientist can work with the help of such an awarded brain, but it is not possible for the scientist to create his own or a similar brain. Therefore no one is independent in the matter of any creation, nor is such creation automatic.

TEXT 5

आत्मन् भावयसे तानि न पराभावयन् स्वयम् ।
आत्मशक्तिमवष्टभ्य   ऊर्णनाभिरिवाक्लमः ॥ ५ ॥

ātman bhāvayase tāni
na parābhāvayan svayam
ātma-śaktim avaṣṭabhya
ūrṇanābhir ivāklamaḥ

ātman (*ātmani*)—by self; *bhāvayase*—manifest; *tāni*—all those; *na*—not; *parābhāvayan*—being defeated; *svayam*—yourself; *ātma-śaktim*—self-sufficient power; *avaṣṭabhya*—being employed; *ūrṇa-nābhiḥ*—the spider; *iva*—like; *aklamaḥ*—without help.

TRANSLATION

As the spider very easily creates the network of its cobweb and manifests its power of creation without being defeated by others, so also you yourself, by employment of your self-sufficient energy, create without any other's help.

PURPORT

The best example of self-sufficiency is the sun. The sun does not require to be illuminated by any other body. Rather, it is the sun which helps all other illuminating agents, for in the presence of the sun no other illuminating agent becomes prominent. Nārada compared the position of Brahmā to the self-sufficiency of the spider, who creates its own field of activities without any other's help by employment of its own energetic creation of saliva.

TEXT 6

नाहं वेद परं ह्यस्मिन्नपरं न समं विभो ।
नामरूपगुणैर्भाव्यं सदसत् किञ्चिदन्यतः ॥ ६ ॥

nāhaṁ veda paraṁ hy asmin
nāparaṁ na samaṁ vibho
nāma-rūpa-guṇair bhāvyaṁ
sad-asat kiñcid anyataḥ

na—do not; *aham*—myself; *veda*—know; *param*—superior; *hi*—for; *asmin*—in this world; *na*—neither; *aparam*—inferior; *na*—nor; *samam*—equal; *vibho*—O great one; *nāma*—name; *rūpa*—characteristics; *guṇaiḥ*—by qualification; *bhāvyam*—all that is created; *sat*—eternal; *asat*—temporary; *kiñcit*—or anything like that; *anyataḥ*—from any other source.

TRANSLATION

Whatever we can understand by the nomenclature, characteristics and features of a particular thing—superior, inferior or equal, eternal or temporary—is not created from any source other than that of Your Lordship, thou so great.

PURPORT

The manifested world is full of varieties of created beings in 8,400,000 species of life, and some of them are superior and inferior to others. In human society the human being is considered to be the superior living being, and amongst the human beings there are also different varieties: good, bad, equal, etc. But Nārada Muni took for granted that none of them has any source of generation besides his father, Brahmājī. Therefore he wanted to know all about them from Lord Brahmā.

TEXT 7

स भवानचरद् घोरं यत् तपः सुसमाहितः ।
तेन खेदयसे नस्त्वं पराशङ्कां च यच्छसि ॥ ७ ॥

sa bhavān acarad ghoram
yat tapaḥ susamāhitaḥ
tena khedayase nas tvaṁ
parā-śaṅkāṁ ca yacchasi

saḥ—he; *bhavān*—your good self; *acarat*—undertook; *ghoram*—severe; *yat tapaḥ*—meditation; *su-samāhitaḥ*—in perfect discipline; *tena*—for that reason; *khedayase*—gives pain; *naḥ*—ourselves; *tvam*—your good self; *parā*—the ultimate truth; *śaṅkām*—doubts; *ca*—and; *yacchasi*—giving us a chance.

TRANSLATION

Yet we are moved to wonder about the existence of someone more powerful than you when we think of your great austerities in perfect discipline, although your good self is so powerful in the matter of creation.

PURPORT

Following in the footsteps of Śrī Nārada Muni, one should not blindly accept his spiritual master as God Himself. A spiritual master is duly respected on a par with God, but a spiritual master claiming to be God Himself should at once be rejected. Nārada Muni accepted Brahmā as the Supreme due to Lord Brahmā's wonderful acts in creation, but doubts arose in him when he saw that Lord Brahmā also worshiped some superior authority. The Supreme is supreme, and He has no worshipable superior. The *ahaṅgrahopāsitā*, or the one who worships himself with the idea of becoming God Himself, is misleading, but the intelligent disciple can at once detect that the Supreme God does not need to worship anyone, including Himself, in order to become God. *Ahaṅgrahopāsanā* may be one of the processes for transcendental realization, but the *ahaṅgrahopāsitā* can never be God Himself. No one becomes God by undergoing a process of transcendental realization. Nārada Muni thought of Brahmājī as the Supreme Person, but when he saw Brahmājī engaged in the process of transcendental realization, doubts arose in him. So he wanted to be clearly informed.

TEXT 8

एतन्मे पृच्छतः सर्वं सर्वज्ञ सकलेश्वर ।
विजानीहि यथैवेदमहं बुध्येऽनुशासितः ॥ ८ ॥

etan me pṛcchataḥ sarvaṁ
sarva-jña sakaleśvara
vijānīhi yathaivedam
ahaṁ budhye 'nuśāsitaḥ

etat—all those; *me*—unto me; *pṛcchataḥ*—inquisitive; *sarvam*—all that is inquired; *sarva-jña*—one who knows everything; *sakala*—over all; *īśvara*—the controller; *vijānīhi*—kindly explain; *yathā*—as; *eva*—they are; *idam*—this; *aham*—myself; *budhye*—can understand; *anuśāsitaḥ*—just learning from you.

TRANSLATION

My dear father, you know everything, and you are the controller of all. Therefore may all that I have inquired from you be kindly instructed to me so that I may be able to understand it as your student.

PURPORT

The inquiries made by Nārada Muni are very important for everyone concerned, and as such Nārada requested Brahmājī to deem them suitable so that all others who may come in the line of disciplic succession of the Brahma-sampradāya may also know them properly without any difficulty.

TEXT 9

ब्रह्मोवाच
सम्यक् कारुणिकस्येदं वत्स ते विचिकित्सितम् ।
यदहं चोदितः सौम्य भगवद्वीर्यदर्शने ॥ ९ ॥

brahmovāca
samyak kāruṇikasyedaṁ
vatsa te vicikitsitam
yad ahaṁ coditaḥ saumya
bhagavad-vīrya-darśane

brahmā uvāca—Lord Brahmā said; *samyak*—perfectly; *kāruṇi-kasya*—of you, who are very kind; *idam*—this; *vatsa*—my dear boy; *te*—your; *vicikitsitam*—inquisitiveness; *yat*—by which; *aham*—myself; *coditaḥ*—inspired; *saumya*—O gentle one; *bhagavat*—of the Personality of Godhead; *vīrya*—prowess; *darśane*—in the matter of.

TRANSLATION

Lord Brahmā said: My dear boy Nārada, being merciful to all (including me) you have asked all these questions because I have been inspired to see into the prowess of the Almighty Personality of Godhead.

PURPORT

Brahmājī, being so questioned by Nāradajī, congratulated him, for it is usual for the devotees to become very enthusiastic whenever they are questioned concerning the Almighty Personality of Godhead. That is the sign of a pure devotee of the Lord. Such discourses on the transcendental activities of the Lord purify the atmosphere in which such discussions are held, and the devotees thus become enlivened while answering such questions. It is purifying both for the questioners and for one who answers the questions. The pure devotees are not only satisfied by knowing everything about the Lord, but are also eager to broadcast the information to others, for they want to see that the glories of the Lord are known to everyone. Thus the devotee feels satisfied when such an opportunity is offered to him. This is the basic principle of missionary activities.

TEXT 10

नानृतं तव तच्चापि यथा मां प्रब्रवीषि भोः ।
अविज्ञाय परं मत्त एतावत्त्वं यतो हि मे ॥१०॥

nānṛtaṁ tava tac cāpi
yathā māṁ prabravīṣi bhoḥ
avijñāya paraṁ matta
etāvat tvaṁ yato hi me

na—not; anṛtam—false; tava—of yours; tat—that; ca—also; api—
as you have stated; yathā—in the matter of; mām—of myself;
prabravīṣi—as you describe; bhoḥ—O my son; avijñāya—without
knowing; param—the Supreme; mattaḥ—beyond myself; etāvat—all
that you have spoken; tvam—yourself; yataḥ—for the reason of; hi—
certainly; me—about me.

TRANSLATION

Whatever you have spoken about me is not false because unless
and until one is aware of the Personality of Godhead, who is the
ultimate truth beyond me, one is sure to be illusioned by observing my powerful activities.

PURPORT

"The frog in the well" logic illustrates that a frog residing in the atmosphere and boundary of a well cannot imagine the length and
breadth of the gigantic ocean. Such a frog, when informed of the gigantic
length and breadth of the ocean, first of all does not believe that there is
such an ocean, and if someone assures him that factually there is such a
thing, the frog then begins to measure it by imagination by means of
pumping its belly as far as possible, with the result that the tiny abdomen
of the frog bursts and the poor frog dies without any experience of the
actual ocean. Similarly, the material scientists also want to challenge the
inconceivable potency of the Lord by measuring Him with their froglike
brains and their scientific achievements, but at the end they simply die
unsuccessfully, like the frog.

Sometimes a materially powerful man is accepted as God or the incarnation of God without any knowledge of the factual God. Such a material assessment may be gradually extended, and the attempt may reach to the highest limit of Brahmājī, who is the topmost living being within the universe and has a duration of life unimaginable to the material scientist. As we get information from the most authentic book of knowledge, the *Bhagavad-gītā* (8.17), Brahmājī's one day and night is calculated to be some hundreds of thousands of years on our planet. This long duration of life may not be believed by "the frog in the well," but persons who have a realization of the truths mentioned in the *Bhagavad-gītā* accept the existence of a great personality who creates the variegatedness of the complete universe. It is understood from the revealed scriptures that the Brahmājī of this universe is younger than all the other Brahmās in charge of the many, many universes beyond this, but none of them can be equal to the Personality of Godhead.

Nāradajī is one of the liberated souls, and after his liberation he was known as Nārada; otherwise, before his liberation, he was simply a son of a maidservant. The questions may be asked why Nāradajī was not aware of the Supreme Lord and why he misconceived Brahmājī to be the Supreme Lord, although factually he was not. A liberated soul is never bewildered by such a mistaken idea, so why did Nāradajī ask all those questions just like an ordinary man with a poor fund of knowledge? There was such bewilderment in Arjuna also, although he is eternally the associate of the Lord. Such bewilderment in Arjuna or in Nārada takes place by the will of the Lord so that other, nonliberated persons may realize the real truth and knowledge of the Lord. The doubt arising in the mind of Nārada about Brahmājī's becoming all-powerful is a lesson for the frogs in the well, that they may not be bewildered in misconceiving the identity of the Personality of Godhead (even by comparison to a personality like Brahmā, so what to speak of ordinary men who falsely pose themselves as God or an incarnation of God). The Supreme Lord is always the Supreme, and as we have tried to establish many times in these purports, no living being, even up to the standard of Brahmā, can claim to be one with the Lord. One should not be misled when people worship a great man as God after his death as a matter of hero worship. There were many kings like Lord Rāmacandra, the King of Ayodhyā, but none of them are mentioned as God in the revealed scriptures. To be a good king is not necessarily the qualification for being Lord Rāma, but to be a great personality like Kṛṣṇa is the qualification for being the Personality of Godhead. If we scrutinize the characters who took part in the Battle of Kurukṣetra, we may find that Mahārāja Yudhiṣṭhira was no less a pious king than Lord Rāmacandra, and by character study Mahārāja Yudhiṣṭhira was a better moralist than Lord Kṛṣṇa. Lord Kṛṣṇa asked Mahārāja Yudhiṣṭhira to lie, but Mahārāja Yudhiṣṭhira protested. But that does not mean that Mahārāja Yudhiṣṭhira could be equal to Lord Rāmacandra or Lord Kṛṣṇa. The great authorities have estimated Mahārāja Yudhiṣṭhira to be a pious man, but they have accepted Lord Rāma or Kṛṣṇa as the Personality of Godhead. The Lord is therefore a different identity in all circumstances, and no idea of anthropomorphism can be applied to Him. The Lord is always the Lord, and a common living being can never be equal to Him.

TEXT 11

येन खरोचिषा विश्वं रोचितं रोचयाम्यहम् ।
यथार्कोऽग्निर्यथा सोमो यथर्क्षग्रहतारकाः ॥११॥

yena sva-rociṣā viśvaṁ
rocitaṁ rocayāmy aham
yathārko 'gnir yathā somo
yatharkṣa-graha-tārakāḥ

yena—by whom; *sva-rociṣā*—by His own effulgence; *viśvam*—all the world; *rocitam*—already created potentially; *rocayāmi*—do manifest; *aham*—I; *yathā*—as much; *arkaḥ*—the sun; *agniḥ*—fire; *yathā*—as; *somaḥ*—the moon; *yathā*—as also; *ṛkṣa*—the firmament; *graha*—the influential planets; *tārakāḥ*—the stars.

TRANSLATION

I create after the Lord's creation by His personal effulgence [known as the brahmajyoti], just as when the sun manifests its fire, the moon, the firmament, the influential planets and the twinkling stars also manifest their brightness.

PURPORT

Lord Brahmājī said to Nārada that his impression that Brahmā was not the supreme authority in the creation was correct. Sometimes less intelligent men have the foolish impression that Brahmā is the cause of all causes. But Nārada wanted to clear the matter by the statements of Brahmājī, the supreme authority in the universe. As the decision of the supreme court of a state is final, similarly the judgment of Brahmājī, the supreme authority in the universe, is final in the Vedic process of acquiring knowledge. As we have already affirmed in the previous verse, Nāradajī was a liberated soul; therefore, he was not one of the less intelligent men who accept a false god or gods in their own ways. He represented himself as less intelligent and yet intelligently presented a doubt to be cleared by the supreme authority so that the uninformed might take note of it and be rightly informed about the intracacies of the creation and the creator.

In this verse Brahmājī clears up the wrong impression held by the less intelligent and affirms that he creates the universal variegatedness after the potential creation by the glaring effulgence of Lord Śrī Kṛṣṇa. Brahmājī has also separately given this statement in the *saṁhitā* known as the *Brahma-saṁhitā* (5.40), where he says:

> *yasya prabhā prabhavato jagad-aṇḍa-koṭi-*
> *koṭiṣv aśeṣa-vasudhādi-vibhūti-bhinnam*
> *tad brahma niṣkalam anantam aśeṣa-bhūtaṁ*
> *govindam ādi-puruṣaṁ tam ahaṁ bhajāmi*

"I serve the Supreme Personality of Godhead Govinda, the primeval Lord, whose transcendental bodily effulgence, known as the *brahmajyoti*, which is unlimited, unfathomed and all-pervasive, is the cause of the creation of unlimited numbers of planets, etc., with varieties of climates and specific conditions of life."

The same statement is in the *Bhagavad-gītā* (14.27). Lord Kṛṣṇa is the background of the *brahmajyoti* (*brahmaṇo hi pratiṣṭhāham*). In the *Nirukti*, or Vedic dictionary, the import of *pratiṣṭhā* is mentioned as "that which establishes." So the *brahmajyoti* is not independent or self-sufficient. Lord Śrī Kṛṣṇa is ultimately the creator of the *brahmajyoti*,

mentioned in this verse as *sva-rociṣā*, or the effulgence of the transcendental body of the Lord. This *brahmajyoti* is all-pervading, and all creation is made possible by its potential power; therefore the Vedic hymns
declare that everything that exists is being sustained by the *brahmajyoti*
(*sarvaṁ khalv idaṁ brahma*). Therefore the potential seed of all creation
is the *brahmajyoti*, and the same *brahmajyoti*, unlimited and unfathomed, is established by the Lord. Therefore the Lord (Śrī Kṛṣṇa)
is ultimately the supreme cause of all creation (*ahaṁ sarvasya
prabhavaḥ*).

One should not expect the Lord to create like a blacksmith with a ham-
mer and other instruments. The Lord creates by His potencies. He has
His multifarious potencies (*parāsya śaktir vividhaiva śrūyate*). Just as
the small seed of a banyan fruit has the potency to create a big banyan
tree, the Lord disseminates all varieties of seeds by His potential
brahmajyoti (*sva-rociṣā*), and the seeds are made to develop by the
watering process of persons like Brahmā. Brahmā cannot create the
seeds, but he can manifest the seed into a tree, just as a gardener helps
plants and orchards to grow by the watering process. The example cited
here of the sun is very appropriate. In the material world the sun is the
cause of all illumination: fire, electricity, the rays of the moon, etc. All
luminaries in the sky are creations of the sun, the sun is the creation of
the *brahmajyoti*, and the *brahmajyoti* is the effulgence of the Lord. Thus
the ultimate cause of creation is the Lord.

TEXT 12

तस्मै नमो भगवते वासुदेवाय धीमहि ।
यन्मायया दुर्जयया मां वदन्ति जगद्गुरुम् ॥१२॥

tasmai namo bhagavate
vāsudevāya dhīmahi
yan-māyayā durjayayā
māṁ vadanti jagad-gurum

tasmai—unto Him; *namaḥ*—offer my obeisances; *bhagavate*—unto
the Personality of Godhead; *vāsudevāya*—unto Lord Kṛṣṇa; *dhīmahi*—

do meditate upon Him; *yat*—by whose; *māyayā*—potencies; *durjayayā* —invincible; *mām*—unto me; *vadanti*—they say; *jagat*—the world; *gurum*—the master.

TRANSLATION

I offer my obeisances and meditate upon Lord Kṛṣṇa [Vāsudeva], the Personality of Godhead, whose invincible potency influences them [the less intelligent class of men] to call me the supreme controller.

PURPORT

As will be more clearly explained in the next verse, the illusory potency of the Lord bewilders the less intelligent to accept Brahmājī, or for that matter any other person, as the Supreme Lord. Brahmājī, however, refuses to be called this, and he directly offers his respectful obeisances unto Lord Vāsudeva, or Śrī Kṛṣṇa, the Personality of Godhead, as he has already offered the same respects to Him in the *Brahma-saṁhitā* (5.1):

> *īśvaraḥ paramaḥ kṛṣṇaḥ*
> *sac-cid-ānanda-vigrahaḥ*
> *anādir ādir govindaḥ*
> *sarva-kāraṇa-kāraṇam*

"The Supreme Lord is the Personality of Godhead Śrī Kṛṣṇa, the primeval Lord in His transcendental body, the ultimate cause of all causes. I worship that primeval Lord Govinda."

Brahmājī is conscious of his actual position, and he knows how less intelligent persons, bewildered by the illusory energy of the Lord, whimsically accept anyone and everyone as God. A responsible personality like Brahmājī refuses to be addressed as the Supreme Lord by his disciples or subordinates, but foolish persons praised by men of the nature of dogs, hogs, camels and asses feel flattered to be addressed as the Supreme Lord. Why such persons take pleasure in being addressed as God, or why such persons are addressed as God by foolish admirers, is explained in the following verse.

TEXT 13

विलज्जमानया यस्य स्थातुमीक्षापथेऽमुया ।
विमोहिता विकत्थन्ते ममाहमिति दुर्धियः ॥१३॥

vilajjamānayā yasya
sthātum īkṣā-pathe 'muyā
vimohitā vikatthante
mamāham iti durdhiyaḥ

vilajjamānayā—by one who is ashamed; *yasya*—whose; *sthātum*—to stay; *īkṣā-pathe*—in front; *amuyā*—by the bewildering energy; *vimohitāḥ*—those who are bewildered; *vikatthante*—talk nonsense; *mama*—it is mine; *aham*—I am everything; *iti*—thus vituperating; *durdhiyaḥ*—thus ill conceived.

TRANSLATION

The illusory energy of the Lord cannot take precedence, being ashamed of her position, but those who are bewildered by her always talk nonsense, being absorbed in thoughts of "It is I" and "It is mine."

PURPORT

The invincibly powerful deluding energy of the Personality of God, or the third energy, representing nescience, can bewilder the entire world of animation, but still she is not strong enough to be able to stand in front of the Supreme Lord. Nescience is behind the Personality of Godhead, where she is powerful enough to mislead the living beings, and the primary symptom of bewildered persons is that they talk nonsense. Nonsensical talks are not supported by the principles of Vedic literatures, and first-grade nonsense talk is "It is I, it is mine." A godless civilization is exclusively conducted by such false ideas, and such persons, without any factual realization of God, accept a false God or falsely declare themselves to be God to mislead persons who are already bewildered by the deluding energy. Those who are before the Lord, however, and who surrender unto Him, cannot be influenced by the deluding energy; therefore they are free from the misconception of "It is I, it is mine," and therefore they do not accept a false God or pose themselves as equal to the Supreme Lord. Identification of the bewildered person is distinctly given in this verse.

TEXT 14

द्रव्यं कर्म च कालश्च खभावो जीव एव च ।
वासुदेवात्परो ब्रह्मन् चान्योऽर्थोऽस्ति तत्त्वतः॥१४॥

dravyaṁ karma ca kālaś ca
svabhāvo jīva eva ca
vāsudevāt paro brahman
na cānyo 'rtho 'sti tattvataḥ

dravyam—the ingredients (earth, water, fire, air and sky); *karma*— the interaction; *ca*—and; *kālaḥ*—eternal time; *ca*—also; *sva-bhāvaḥ*— intuition or nature; *jīvaḥ*—the living being; *eva*—certainly; *ca*—and; *vāsudevāt*—from Vāsudeva; *paraḥ*—differentiated parts; *brahman*—O *brāhmaṇa*; *na*—never; *ca*—also; *anyaḥ*—separate; *arthaḥ*—value; *asti*—there is; *tattvataḥ*—in truth.

TRANSLATION

The five elementary ingredients of creation, the interaction thereof set up by eternal time, and the intuition or nature of the individual living beings are all differentiated parts and parcels of the Personality of Godhead, Vāsudeva, and in truth there is no other value in them.

PURPORT

This phenomenal world is impersonally the representation of Vāsudeva because the ingredients of its creation, their interaction and the enjoyer of the resultant action, the living being, are all produced by the external and internal energies of Lord Kṛṣṇa. This is confirmed in the *Bhagavad-gītā* (7.4–5). The ingredients, namely earth, water, fire, air and sky, as well as the conception of material identity, intelligence and the mind, are produced of the external energy of the Lord. The

living entity who enjoys the interaction of the above gross and subtle ingredients, as set up by eternal time, is an offshoot of internal potency,
with freedom to remain either in the material world or in the spiritual
world. In the material world the living entity is enticed by deluding nescience, but in the spiritual world he is in the normal condition of spiritual existence without any delusion. The living entity is known as the
marginal potency of the Lord. But in all circumstances, neither the material ingredients nor the spiritual parts and parcels are independent of
the Personality of Godhead Vāsudeva, for all things, whether products of
the external, internal or marginal potencies of the Lord, are simply displays of the same effulgence of the Lord, just as light, heat and smoke are
displays of fire. None of them are separate from the fire—all of them
combine together to be called fire; similarly, all phenomenal manifestations, as well as the effulgence of the body of Vāsudeva, are His impersonal features, whereas He eternally exists in His transcendental form
called *sac-cid-ānanda-vigrahaḥ*, distinct from all conceptions of the material ingredients mentioned above.

TEXT 15

नारायणपरा वेदा देवा नारायणाङ्गजाः ।
नारायणपरा लोका नारायणपरा मखाः ॥१५॥

nārāyaṇa-parā vedā
devā nārāyaṇāṅgajāḥ
nārāyaṇa-parā lokā
nārāyaṇa-parā makhāḥ

nārāyaṇa—the Supreme Lord; *parāḥ*—is the cause and is meant for;
vedāḥ—knowledge; *devāḥ*—the demigods; *nārāyaṇa*—the Supreme
Lord; *aṅga-jāḥ*—assisting hands; *nārāyaṇa*—the Personality of Godhead; *parāḥ*—for the sake of; *lokāḥ*—the planets; *nārāyaṇa*—the
Supreme Lord; *parāḥ*—just to please Him; *makhāḥ*—all sacrifices.

TRANSLATION

**The Vedic literatures are made by and are meant for the
Supreme Lord, the demigods are also meant for serving the Lord**

as parts of His body, the different planets are also meant for the sake of the Lord, and different sacrifices are performed just to please Him.

PURPORT

According to the *Vedānta-sūtras* (*śāstra-yonitvāt*), the Supreme Lord is the author of all revealed scriptures, and all revealed scriptures are for knowing the Supreme Lord. *Veda* means knowledge that leads to the Lord. The *Vedas* are made just to revive the forgotten consciousness of the conditioned souls, and any literature not meant for reviving God consciousness is rejected at once by the *nārāyaṇa-para* devotees. Such deluding books of knowledge, not having Nārāyaṇa as their aim, are not at all knowledge, but are the playgrounds for crows who are interested in the rejected refuse of the world. Any book of knowledge (science or art) must lead to the knowledge of Nārāyaṇa; otherwise it must be rejected. That is the way of advancement of knowledge. The supreme worshipable Deity is Nārāyaṇa. The demigods are recommended secondarily for worship in relation to Nārāyaṇa because the demigods are assisting hands in the management of the universal affairs. As the officers of a kingdom are respected due to their relation to the king, the demigods are worshiped due to their relation to the Lord. Without the Lord's relation, worship of the demigods is unauthorized (*avidhi-pūrvakam*), just as it is improper to water the leaves and branches of a tree without watering its root. Therefore the demigods are also dependent on Nārāyaṇa. The *lokas*, or different planets, are attractive because they have different varieties of life and bliss partially representing the *sac-cid-ānanda-vigraha*. Everyone wants the eternal life of bliss and knowledge. In the material world such an eternal life of bliss and knowledge is progressively realized in the upper planets, but after reaching there one is inclined to achieve further progress along the path back to Godhead. Duration of life, with a proportionate quantity of bliss and knowledge, may be increased from one planet to another. One can increase the duration of life to thousands and hundreds of thousands of years in different planets, but nowhere is there eternal life. But one who can reach the highest planet, that of Brahmā, can aspire to reach the planets in the spiritual sky, where life is eternal. Therefore, the progressive journey from one planet to another culminates in reaching the supreme planet of the Lord (*mad-dhāma*), where life is eternal and full of bliss and knowledge. All different kinds of sacrifice are performed just to satisfy Lord Nārāyaṇa with a view to reach Him, and the best sacrifice recommended in this age of Kali is *saṅkīrtana-yajña*, the mainstay of the devotional service of a *nārāyaṇa-para* devotee.

TEXT 16

नारायणपरो योगो नारायणपरं तपः ।
नारायणपरं ज्ञानं नारायणपरा गतिः ॥१६॥

nārāyaṇa-paro yogo
nārāyaṇa-paraṁ tapaḥ
nārāyaṇa-paraṁ jñānaṁ
nārāyaṇa-parā gatiḥ

nārāyaṇa-paraḥ—just to know Nārāyaṇa; *yogaḥ*—concentration of mind; *nārāyaṇa-param*—just with an aim to achieve Nārāyaṇa; *tapaḥ*—austerity; *nārāyaṇa-param*—just to realize a glimpse of Nārāyaṇa; *jñānam*—culture of transcendental knowledge; *nārāyaṇa-parā*—the path of salvation ends by entering the kingdom of Nārāyaṇa; *gatiḥ*—progressive path.

TRANSLATION

All different types of meditation or mysticism are means for realizing Nārāyaṇa. All austerities are aimed at achieving Nārāyaṇa. Culture of transcendental knowledge is for getting a glimpse of Nārāyaṇa, and ultimately salvation is entering the kingdom of Nārāyaṇa.

PURPORT

In meditation, there are two systems of *yoga*, namely *aṣṭāṅga-yoga* and *sāṅkhya-yoga*. *Aṣṭāṅga-yoga* is practice in concentrating the mind, releasing oneself from all engagements by the regulative processes of meditation, concentration, sitting postures, blocking the movements of the internal circulation of air, etc. *Sāṅkhya-yoga* is meant to distinguish the truth from ephemerals. But ultimately both the systems are meant for realizing the impersonal Brahman, which is but a partial representation of Nārāyaṇa, the Personality of Godhead. As we have explained before, the impersonal Brahman effulgence is only a part of the Personality of Godhead. Impersonal Brahman is situated on the person of the Supreme Personality of Godhead, and as such, Brahman is the glorification of the Personality of the Godhead. This is confirmed both in the *Bhagavad-gītā* and in the *Matsya Purāṇa*. *Gati* refers to the ultimate destination, or the last word in liberation. Oneness with the impersonal *brahmajyoti* is not ultimate liberation; superior to that is the sublime association of the Personality of Godhead in one of the innumerable spiritual planets in the Vaikuṇṭha sky. Therefore the conclusion is that Nārāyaṇa, or the Personality of Godhead, is the ultimate destination for all kinds of *yoga* systems as well as all kinds of liberation.

TEXT 17

तस्यापि द्रष्टुरीशस्य कूटस्थस्याखिलात्मनः ।
सृज्यं सृजामि सृष्टोऽहमीक्षयैवाभिचोदितः ॥१७॥

tasyāpi draṣṭur īśasya
kūṭa-sthasyākhilātmanaḥ
sṛjyaṁ sṛjāmi sṛṣṭo 'ham
īkṣayaivābhicoditaḥ

tasya—His; *api*—certainly; *draṣṭuḥ*—of the seer; *īśasya*—of the controller; *kūṭa-sthasya*—of the one who is over everyone's intelligence; *akhila-ātmanaḥ*—of the Supersoul; *sṛjyam*—that which is already created; *sṛjāmi*—do I discover; *sṛṣṭaḥ*—created; *aham*—myself; *īkṣayā*—by glance over; *eva*—exactly; *abhicoditaḥ*—being inspired by Him.

TRANSLATION

Inspired by Him only, I discover what is already created by Him [Nārāyaṇa] under His vision as the all-pervading Supersoul, and I also am created by Him only.

PURPORT

Even Brahmā, the creator of the universe, admits that he is not the actual creator but is simply inspired by the Lord Nārāyaṇa and therefore creates under His superintendence those things already created by Him, the Supersoul of all living entities. Two identities of soul, the Supersoul and the individual soul, are admitted to be in the living entity, even by the greatest authority of the universe. The Supersoul is the Supreme Lord, the Personality of Godhead, whereas the individual soul is the eternal servitor of the Lord. The Lord inspires the individual soul to create what is already created by the Lord, and by the good will of the Lord a discoverer of something in the world is accredited as the discoverer. It is said that Columbus discovered the Western Hemisphere, but actually the tract of land was not created by Columbus. The vast tract of land was already there by the omnipotency of the Supreme Lord, and Columbus, by dint of his past service unto the Lord, was blessed with the credit of discovering America. Similarly, no one can create anything without the sanction of the Lord, since everyone sees according to his ability. This ability is also awarded by the Lord according to one's willingness to render service unto the Lord. One must therefore be voluntarily willing to render service unto the Lord, and thus the Lord will empower the doer in proportion to his surrender unto the lotus feet of the Lord. Lord Brahmā is a great devotee of the Lord; therefore he has been empowered or inspired by the Lord to create such a universe as the one manifested before us. The Lord also inspired Arjuna to fight in the field of Kurukṣetra as follows:

> tasmāt tvam uttiṣṭha yaśo labhasva
> jitvā śatrūn bhuṅkṣva rājyaṁ samṛddham
> mayaivaite nihatāḥ pūrvam eva
> nimitta-mātraṁ bhava savyasācin
>
> (Bg. 11.33)

The Battle of Kurukṣetra, or any other battle at any place or at any time, is made by the will of the Lord, for no one can arrange such mass annihilation without the sanction of the Lord. The party of Duryodhana insulted Draupadī, a great devotee of Kṛṣṇa, and she appealed to the Lord as well as to all the silent observers of this unwarranted insult. Arjuna was then advised by the Lord to fight and take credit; otherwise the party of Duryodhana would be killed anyway by the will of the Lord.

So Arjuna was advised just to become the agent and take the credit for killing great generals like Bhīṣma and Karṇa.

In the Vedic writings such as the *Kaṭha Upaniṣad,* the Lord is described as the *sarva-bhūta-antarātmā,* or the Personality of Godhead who resides in everyone's body and who directs everything for one who is a soul surrendered unto Him. Those who are not surrendered souls are put under the care of the material nature (*bhrāmayan sarva-bhūtāni yantrārūḍhāni māyayā*); therefore, they are allowed to do things on their own account and suffer the consequences themselves. Devotees like Brahmā and Arjuna do not do anything on their own account, but as fully surrendered souls they always await indications from the Lord; therefore they attempt to do something which appears very wonderful to ordinary vision. One of the Lord's names is Urukrama, or one whose actions are very wonderful and are beyond the imagination of the living being, so the actions of His devotees sometimes appear very wonderful due to the direction of the Lord. Beginning from Brahmā, the topmost intelligent living entity within the universe, down to the smallest ant, every living entity's intelligence is overseen by the Lord in His transcendental position as the witness of all actions. The subtle presence of the Lord is felt by the intelligent man who can study the psychic effects of thinking, feeling and willing.

TEXT 18

सत्त्वं रजस्तम इति निर्गुणस्य गुणात्रयः ।
स्थितिसर्गनिरोधेषु गृहीता मायया विभोः ॥१८॥

sattvaṁ rajas tama iti
nirguṇasya guṇās trayaḥ
sthiti-sarga-nirodheṣu
gṛhītā māyayā vibhoḥ

sattvam—the mode of goodness; *rajaḥ*—the mode of passion; *tamaḥ*—the mode of ignorance; *iti*—all these; *nirguṇasya*—of the Transcendence; *guṇāḥ trayaḥ*—are three qualities; *sthiti*—maintenance; *sarga*—creation; *nirodheṣu*—in destruction; *gṛhītāḥ*—accepted; *māyayā*—by the external energy; *vibhoḥ*—of the Supreme.

TRANSLATION

The Supreme Lord is pure spiritual form, transcendental to all
material qualities, yet for the sake of the creation of the material
world and its maintenance and annihilation, He accepts through
His external energy the material modes of nature called goodness,
passion and ignorance.

PURPORT

The Supreme Lord is the master of the external energy manifested by
the three material modes, namely goodness, passion and ignorance, and
as master of this energy He is ever unaffected by the influence of such
bewildering energy. The living entities, the *jīvas*, however, are affected
by or susceptible to being influenced by such modes of material nature—
that is the difference between the Lord and the living entities. The living
entities are subjected by those qualities, although originally the living
entities are qualitatively one with the Lord. In other words, the material
modes of nature, being products of the energy of the Lord, are certainly
connected with the Lord, but the connection is just like that between the
master and the servants. The Supreme Lord is the controller of the material energy, whereas the living entities, who are entangled in the material world, are neither masters nor controllers. Rather, they become
subordinate to or controlled by such energy. Factually the Lord is eternally manifested by His internal potency or spiritual energy just like the
sun and its rays in the clear sky, but at times He creates the material energy, as the sun creates a cloud in the clear sky. As the sun is ever in-
creasingly unaffected by a spot of cloud, so also the unlimited Lord is
unaffected by the spot of material energy manifested at times in the unlimited span of the Lord's rays of *brahmajyoti*.

TEXT 19

कार्यकारणकर्तृत्वे   द्रव्यज्ञानक्रियाश्रयाः ।
बध्नन्ति नित्यदा मुक्तं मायिनं पुरुषं गुणाः ॥१९॥

kārya-kāraṇa-kartṛtve
dravya-jñāna-kriyāśrayāḥ

badhnanti nityadā muktaṁ
māyinaṁ puruṣaṁ guṇāḥ

kārya—effect; *kāraṇa*—cause; *kartṛtve*—in activities; *dravya*—material; *jñāna*—knowledge; *kriyā-āśrayāḥ*—manifested by such symptoms; *badhnanti*—conditions; *nityadā*—eternally; *muktam*—transcendental; *māyinam*—affected by material energy; *puruṣam*—the living entity; *guṇāḥ*—the material modes.

TRANSLATION

These three modes of material nature, being further manifested as matter, knowledge and activities, put the eternally transcendental living entity under conditions of cause and effect and make him responsible for such activities.

PURPORT

Because they are between the internal and external potencies, the eternally transcendental living entities are called the marginal potency of the Lord. Factually, the living entities are not meant to be so conditioned by material energy, but due to their being affected by the false sense of lording it over the material energy, they come under the influence of such potency and thus become conditioned by the three modes of material nature. This external energy of the Lord covers up the pure knowledge of the living entity's eternally existing with Him, but the covering is so constant that it appears that the conditioned soul is eternally ignorant. Such is the wonderful action of *māyā*, or external energy manifested as if materially produced. By the covering power of the material energy, the material scientist cannot look beyond the material causes, but factually, behind the material manifestations, there are *adhibhūta*, *adhyātma* and *adhidaiva* actions, which the conditioned soul in the mode of ignorance cannot see. The *adhibhūta* manifestation entails repetitions of births and deaths with old age and diseases, the *adhyātma* manifestation conditions the spirit soul, and the *adhidaiva* manifestation is the controlling system. These are the material manifestations of cause and effect and the sense of responsibility of the conditioned actors. They are, after all, manifestations of the conditioned state, and the human being's freedom from such a conditioned state is the highest perfectional attainment.

TEXT 20

स एष भगवाल्लिङ्गैस्त्रिभिरेतैरधोक्षजः ।
स्वलक्षितगतिर्ब्रह्मन् सर्वेषां मम चेश्वरः ॥२०॥

sa eṣa bhagavāl liṅgais
tribhir etair adhokṣajaḥ
svalakṣita-gatir brahman
sarveṣāṁ mama ceśvaraḥ

saḥ—He; *eṣaḥ*—this; *bhagavān*—the Personality of Godhead; *liṅgaiḥ*—by the symptoms; *tribhiḥ*—by the three; *etaiḥ*—by all these; *adhokṣajaḥ*—the Superseer Transcendence; *su-alakṣita*—veritably unseen; *gatiḥ*—movement; *brahman*—O Nārada; *sarveṣām*—of everyone; *mama*—mine; *ca*—as also; *īśvaraḥ*—the controller.

TRANSLATION

O Brāhmaṇa Nārada, the Superseer, the transcendent Lord, is beyond the perception of the material senses of the living entities because of the above-mentioned three modes of nature. But He is the controller of everyone, including me.

PURPORT

In the *Bhagavad-gītā* (7.24–25) the Lord has declared very clearly that the impersonalist, who gives more importance to the transcendental rays of the Lord as *brahmajyoti* and who concludes that the Absolute Truth is ultimately impersonal and only manifests a form at a time of necessity, is less intelligent than the personalist, however much the impersonalist may be engaged in studying the *Vedānta*. The fact is that such impersonalists are covered by the above-mentioned three modes of material nature; therefore, they are unable to approach the transcendental Personality of the Lord. The Lord is not approachable by everyone because He is curtained by His *yogamāyā* potency. But one should not wrongly conclude that the Lord was formerly unmanifested and has now manifested Himself in the human form. This misconception of the formlessness of the Supreme Personality of Godhead is due to the *yogamāyā* curtain of the Lord and can be removed only by the Supreme Will, as soon as the conditioned soul surrenders unto Him. The devotees of the Lord who are transcendental to the above-mentioned three modes of material nature can see the all-blissful transcendental form of the Lord with their vision of love in the attitude of pure devotional service.

TEXT 21

कालं कर्म खभावं च मायेशो मायया खया ।
आत्मन् यदृच्छया प्राप्तं विबुभूषुरुपाददे ॥२१॥

kālaṁ karma svabhāvaṁ ca
māyeśo māyayā svayā
ātman yadṛcchayā prāptaṁ
vibubhūṣur upādade

kālam—eternal time; *karma*—the fate of the living entity; *sva-bhāvam*—nature; *ca*—also; *māyā*—potency; *īśaḥ*—the controller; *māyayā*—by the energy; *svayā*—of His own; *ātman (ātmani)*—unto His Self; *yadṛcchayā*—independently; *prāptam*—being merged in; *vibubhūṣuḥ*—appearing differently; *upādade*—accepted for being created again.

TRANSLATION

The Lord, who is the controller of all energies, thus creates, by His own potency, eternal time, the fate of all living entities, and their particular nature, for which they were created, and He again merges them independently.

PURPORT

The creation of the material world, wherein the conditioned souls are allowed to act subordinately by the Supreme Lord, takes place again and again after being repeatedly annihilated. The material creation is something like a cloud in the unlimited sky. The real sky is the spiritual sky, eternally filled with the rays of the *brahmajyoti*, and a portion of this unlimited sky is covered by the *mahat-tattva* cloud of the material creation, in which the conditioned souls, who want to lord it against the will of the Lord, are put into play as they desire under the control of the Lord by the agency of His external energy. As the rainy season appears and disappears regularly, the creation takes place and is again annihilated under the control of the Lord, as confirmed in the *Bhagavad-gītā* (8.19). So the creation and annihilation of the material worlds is a regular action of the Lord just to allow the conditioned souls to play as they like and thereby create their own fate of being differently created again in terms of their independent desires at the time of annihilation. The creation, therefore, takes place at a historical date (as we are accustomed to think of everything which has a beginning in our tiny experience). The process of creation and annihilation is called *anādi*, or without reference to date regarding the time the creation first took place, because the duration of even a partial creation is 8,640,000,000 years. The law of creation is, however, as mentioned in the Vedic literatures, that it is created at certain intervals and is again annihilated by the will of the Lord. The whole material or even the spiritual creation is a manifestation of the energy of the Lord, just as the light and heat of a fire are different manifestations of the fire's energy. The Lord therefore exists in His impersonal form by such expansion of energy, and the complete creation rests on His impersonal feature. Nonetheless He keeps Himself distinct from such creation as the *pūrṇam* (or complete), and so no one should wrongly think that His personal feature is not existent due to His impersonal unlimited expansions. The impersonal expansion is a manifestation of His energy, and He is always in His personal feature despite His innumerable unlimited expansions of impersonal energies (Bg. 9.5–7). For human intelligence it is very difficult to conceive how the whole creation rests on His expansion of energy, but the Lord has given a very good example in the *Bhagavad-gītā*. It is said that although the air and the atoms rest within the huge expansion of the sky, which is like the resting reservoir of everything materially created, still the sky remains separate and unaffected. Similarly although the Supreme Lord maintains everything created by His expansion of energy, He always remains separate. This is accepted even by Śaṅkarācārya, the great advocate of the impersonal form of the Absolute. He says *nārāyaṇaḥ paro 'vyaktāt*, or Nārāyaṇa exists separately, apart from the impersonal creative energy. The whole creation thus merges within the body of transcendental Nārāyaṇa at the time of annihilation, and the creation emanates from His body again with the same unchanging categories of fate and individual nature. The individual living entities, being parts and parcels of the Lord, are sometimes described as *ātmā*, qualitatively one in spiritual constitution. But because such living entities are apt to be attracted to the material creation, actively and subjectively, they are therefore different from the Lord.

TEXT 22

कालाद् गुणव्यतिकरः परिणामः खभावतः ।
कर्मणो जन्म महतः पुरुषाधिष्ठितादभूत् ॥२२॥

kālād guṇa-vyatikaraḥ
pariṇāmaḥ svabhāvataḥ
karmaṇo janma mahataḥ
puruṣādhiṣṭhitād abhūt

kālāt—from eternal time; *guṇa-vyatikaraḥ*—transformation of the modes by reaction; *pariṇāmaḥ*—transformation; *svabhāvataḥ*—from the nature; *karmaṇaḥ*—of activities; *janma*—creation; *mahataḥ*—of the *mahat-tattva*; *puruṣa-adhiṣṭhitāt*—because of the *puruṣa* incarnation of the Lord; *abhūt*—it took place.

TRANSLATION

After the incarnation of the first puruṣa [Kāraṇārṇavaśāyī Viṣṇu], the mahat-tattva, or the principles of material creation, take place, and then time is manifested, and in course of time the three qualities appear. Nature means the three qualitative appearances. They transform into activities.

PURPORT

By the omnipotency of the Supreme Lord, the whole material creation evolves by the process of transformation and reactions one after another, and by the same omnipotency, they are wound up again one after another and conserved in the body of the Supreme. *Kāla*, or time, is the synonym of nature and is the transformed manifestation of the principles of material creation. As such, *kāla* may be taken as the first cause of all creation, and by transformation of nature different activities of the material world become visible. These activities may be taken up as the natural instinct of each and every living being, or even of the inert objects, and after the manifestation of activities there are varieties of products and by-products of the same nature. Originally these are all due to the Supreme Lord. The *Vedānta-sūtras* and the *Bhāgavatam* thus begin with the Absolute Truth as the beginning of all creations (*janmādy asya yataḥ*).

TEXT 23

महतस्तु विकुर्वाणाद्रजःसत्त्वोपबृंहितात् ।
तमःप्रधानस्त्वभवद् द्रव्यज्ञानक्रियात्मकः ॥२३॥

mahatas tu vikurvāṇād
rajaḥ-sattvopabṛṁhitāt
tamaḥ-pradhānas tv abhavad
dravya-jñāna-kriyātmakaḥ

mahataḥ—of the *mahat-tattva*; *tu*—but; *vikurvāṇāt*—being transformed; *rajaḥ*—the material mode of passion; *sattva*—the mode of goodness; *upabṛṁhitāt*—because of being increased; *tamaḥ*—the mode of darkness; *pradhānaḥ*—being prominent; *tu*—but; *abhavat*—took place; *dravya*—matter; *jñāna*—material knowledge; *kriyā-ātmakaḥ*—predominantly material activities.

TRANSLATION

Material activities are caused by the mahat-tattva's being agitated. At first there is transformation of the modes of goodness and passion, and later—due to the mode of ignorance—matter, its knowledge, and different activities of material knowledge come into play.

PURPORT

Material creations of every description are more or less due to the development of the mode of passion (*rajas*). The *mahat-tattva* is the

principle of material creation, and when it is agitated by the will of the
Supreme at first the modes of passion and goodness are prominent, and
afterwards the mode of passion, being generated in due course by material activities of different varieties, becomes prominent, and the living
entities are thus involved more and more in ignorance. Brahmā is the
representation of the mode of passion, and Viṣṇu is the representation of
the mode of goodness, while the mode of ignorance is represented by
Lord Śiva, the father of material activities. Material nature is called the
mother, and the initiator for materialistic life is the father, Lord Śiva. All
material creation by the living entities is therefore initiated by the mode
of passion. With the advancement of the duration of life in a particular
millennium, the different modes act by gradual development. In the age
of Kali (when the mode of passion is most prominent) material activities
of different varieties, in the name of advancement of human civilization,
take place, and the living entities become more and more involved in
forgetting their real identity—the spiritual nature. By a slight cultivation of the mode of goodness, a glimpse of spiritual nature is perceived,
but due to the prominence of the mode of passion, the mode of goodness
becomes adulterated. Therefore one cannot transcend the limits of the
material modes, and therefore realization of the Lord, who is always
transcendental to the modes of material nature, becomes very difficult
for the living entities, even though prominently situated in the mode of
goodness through cultivation of the various methods. In other words, the
gross matters are *adhibhūtam*, their maintenance is *adhidaivam*, and the
initiator of material activities is called *adhyātmam*. In the material world
these three principles act as prominent features, namely as raw material,
its regular supplies, and its use in different varieties of material creations
for sense enjoyment by the bewildered entities.

TEXT 24

सोऽहङ्कार इति प्रोक्तो विकुर्वन् समभूत्त्रिधा ।
वैकारिकस्तैजसश्च तामसश्चेति यत्त्रिदा ।
द्रव्यशक्तिः क्रियाशक्तिर्ज्ञानशक्तिरिति प्रभो ॥२४॥

so 'haṅkāra iti prokto
vikurvan samabhūt tridhā

vaikārikas taijasaś ca
tāmasaś ceti yad-bhidā
dravya-śaktiḥ kriyā-śaktir
jñāna-śaktir iti prabho

saḥ—the very same thing; *ahaṅkāraḥ*—ego; *iti*—thus; *proktaḥ*—said; *vikurvan*—being transformed; *samabhūt*—became manifested; *tridhā*—in three features; *vaikārikaḥ*—in the mode of goodness; *taijasaḥ*—in the mode of passion; *ca*—and; *tāmasaḥ*—in the mode of ignorance; *ca*—also; *iti*—thus; *yat*—what is; *bhidā*—divided; *dravya-śaktiḥ*—powers that evolve matter; *kriyā-śaktiḥ*—initiation that creates; *jñāna-śaktiḥ*—intelligence that guides; *iti*—thus; *prabho*—O master.

TRANSLATION

The self-centered materialistic ego, thus being transformed into three features, becomes known as the modes of goodness, passion and ignorance in three divisions, namely the powers that evolve matter, knowledge of material creations, and the intelligence that guides such materialistic activities. Nārada, you are quite competent to understand this.

PURPORT

Materialistic ego, or the sense of identification with matter, is grossly self-centered, devoid of clear knowledge of the existence of God. And this self-centered egoism of the materialistic living entities is the cause of their being conditioned by the other paraphernalia and continuing their bondage of material existence. In the *Bhagavad-gītā* this self-centered egoism is very nicely explained in the Seventh Chapter (verses 24 through 27). The self-centered impersonalist, without a clear conception of the Personality of Godhead, concludes in his own way that the Personality of Godhead takes a material shape from His original impersonal spiritual existence for a particular mission. And this misleading conception of the Supreme Lord by the self-centered impersonalist continues, even though he is seen to be very interested in the Vedic literatures such as the *Brahma-sūtras* and other highly intellectual sources of knowledge. This ignorance of the personal feature of the Lord is due simply to ignorance of the mixture of different modes. The impersonalist thus cannot conceive of the Lord's eternal spiritual form of eternal knowledge, bliss and existence. The reason is that the Lord reserves the right of not exposing Himself to the nondevotee who, even after a thorough study of literature like the *Bhagavad-gītā*, remains an impersonalist simply by obstinacy. This obstinacy is due to the action of *yogamāyā*, a personal energy of the Lord that acts like an aide-de-camp by covering the vision of the obstinate impersonalist. Such a bewildered human being is described as *mūḍha*, or grossly ignorant, because he is unable to understand the transcendental form of the Lord as being unborn and unchangeable. If the Lord takes a form or material shape from His original impersonal feature, then it means that He is born and changeable from impersonal to personal. But He is not changeable. Nor does He ever take a new birth like a conditioned soul. The conditioned soul may take a form birth after birth due to his conditional existence in matter, but the self-centered impersonalists, by their gross ignorance, accept the Lord as one of them because of self-centered egoism, even after so-called advancement of knowledge in the *Vedānta*. The Lord, being situated in the heart of every individual living entity, knows very well the tendency of such conditioned souls in terms of past, present and future, but the bewildered conditioned soul hardly can know Him in His eternal form. By the will of the Lord, therefore, the impersonalist, even after knowing the Brahman and Paramātmā features of the Lord, remains ignorant of His eternal personal feature as ever-existent Nārāyaṇa, transcendental to all material creation.

The cause of such gross ignorance is constant engagement by the materialistic man in the matter of artificially increasing material demands. To realize the Supreme Personality of Godhead, one has to purify the materialistic senses by devotional service. The mode of goodness, or the brahminical culture recommended in the Vedic literatures, is helpful to such spiritual realization, and thus the *jñāna-śakti* stage of the conditioned soul is comparatively better than the other two stages, namely *dravya-śakti* and *kriyā-śakti*. The whole material civilization is manifested by a huge accumulation of materials, or, in other words, raw materials for industrial purposes, and the industrial enterprises (*kriyā-śakti*) are all due to gross ignorance of spiritual life. In order to rectify this great anomaly of materialistic civilization, based on the principles of *dravya-śakti* and *kriyā-śakti*, one has to adopt the process of devotional service of the Lord by adoption of the principles of *karma-yoga*, mentioned in the *Bhagavad-gītā* (9.27) as follows:

> yat karoṣi yad aśnāsi
> yaj juhoṣi dadāsi yat
> yat tapasyasi kaunteya
> tat kuruṣva mad-arpaṇam

"O son of Kuntī, all that you do, all that you eat, all that you offer and give away, as well as all austerities that you may perform, should be done as an offering unto Me."

TEXT 25

तामसादपि भूतादेर्विकुर्वाणादभूत्रभः ।
तस्य मात्रा गुणः शब्दो लिङ्गं यद् द्रष्टृदृश्ययोः ॥२५॥

> tāmasād api bhūtāder
> vikurvāṇād abhūn nabhaḥ
> tasya mātrā guṇaḥ śabdo
> liṅgaṁ yad draṣṭṛ-dṛśyayoḥ

tāmasāt—from the darkness of false ego; *api*—certainly; *bhūta-ādeḥ*—of the material elements; *vikurvāṇāt*—because of transformation; *abhūt*—generated; *nabhaḥ*—the sky; *tasya*—its; *mātrā*—subtle form; *guṇaḥ*—quality; *śabdaḥ*—sound; *liṅgam*—characteristics; *yat*—as its; *draṣṭṛ*—the seer; *dṛśyayoḥ*—of what is seen.

TRANSLATION

From the darkness of false ego, the first of the five elements, namely the sky, is generated. Its subtle form is the quality of sound, exactly as the seer is in relationship with the seen.

PURPORT

The five elements, namely sky, air, fire, water and earth, are all but different qualities of the darkness of false ego. This means that the false ego in the sum total form of *mahat-tattva* is generated from the marginal potency of the Lord, and due to this false ego of lording it over the material creation, ingredients are generated for the false enjoyment of the living being. The living being is practically the dominating factor over the material elements as the enjoyer, though the background is the Supreme Lord. Factually, save and except the Lord, no one can be called the enjoyer, but the living entity falsely desires to become the enjoyer. This is the origin of false ego. When the bewildered living being desires this, the shadow elements are generated by the will of the Lord, and the living entities are allowed to run after them as after a phantasmagoria.

It is said that first the *tan-mātrā* sound is created and then the sky, and in this verse it is confirmed that actually it is so, but sound is the subtle form of the sky, and the distinction is like that between the seer and the seen. The sound is the representation of the actual object, as the sound produced speaking of the object gives an idea of the description of the object. Therefore sound is the subtle characteristic of the object. Similarly, sound representation of the Lord, in terms of His characteristics, is the complete form of the Lord, as was seen by Vasudeva and Mahārāja Daśaratha, the fathers of Lord Kṛṣṇa and Lord Rāma. The sound representation of the Lord is nondifferent from the Lord Himself because the Lord and His representation in sound are absolute knowledge. Lord Caitanya has instructed us that in the holy name of the Lord, as sound representation of the Lord, all the potencies of the Lord are invested. Thus one can immediately enjoy the association of the Lord by the pure vibration of the sound representation of His holy name, and the concept of the Lord is immediately manifested before the pure devotee. A pure devotee, therefore, is not aloof from the Lord even for a moment. The holy name of the Lord, as recommended in the *śāstras*—Hare Kṛṣṇa, Hare Kṛṣṇa, Kṛṣṇa Kṛṣṇa, Hare Hare/ Hare Rāma, Hare Rāma, Rāma Rāma, Hare Hare—may therefore be constantly chanted by the devotee aspiring to be constantly in touch with the Supreme Lord. One who is thus able to associate with the Lord is sure to be delivered from the darkness of the created world, which is a product of false ego (*tamasi mā jyotir gama*).

TEXTS 26–29

नमसोऽथ विकुर्वाणादभूत् स्पर्शगुणोऽनिलः ।
परान्वयाच्छब्दवांश्च प्राण ओजः सहो बलम् ॥२६॥

वायोरपि विकुर्वाणात् कालकर्मस्वभावतः ।
उदपद्यत तेजो वै रूपवत् स्पर्शशब्दवत् ॥२७॥
तेजसस्तु विकुर्वाणादासीदम्भो रसात्मकम् ।
रूपवत् स्पर्शवच्चाम्भो घोषवच्च परान्वयात् ॥२८॥
विशेषस्तु विकुर्वाणादम्भसो गन्धवानभूत् ।
परान्वयाद् रसस्पर्शशब्दरूपगुणान्वितः ॥२९॥

nabhaso 'tha vikurvāṇād
abhūt sparśa-guṇo 'nilaḥ
parānvayāc chabdavāṁś ca
prāṇa ojaḥ saho balam

vāyor api vikurvāṇāt
kāla-karma-svabhāvataḥ
udapadyata tejo vai
rūpavat sparśa-śabdavat

tejasas tu vikurvāṇād
āsīd ambho rasātmakam
rūpavat sparśavac cāmbho
ghoṣavac ca parānvayāt

viśeṣas tu vikurvāṇād
ambhaso gandhavān abhūt
parānvayād rasa-sparśa-
śabda-rūpa-guṇānvitaḥ

nabhasaḥ—of the sky; *atha*—thus; *vikurvāṇāt*—being transformed; *abhūt*—generated; *sparśa*—touch; *guṇaḥ*—quality; *anilaḥ*—air; *para*—previous; *anvayāt*—by succession; *śabdavān*—full of sound; *ca*—also; *prāṇaḥ*—life; *ojaḥ*—sense perception; *sahaḥ*—fat; *balam*—strength; *vāyoḥ*—of the air; *api*—also; *vikurvāṇāt*—by transformation; *kāla*—time; *karma*—reaction of the past; *svabhāvataḥ*—on the basis of nature; *udapadyata*—generated; *tejaḥ*—fire; *vai*—duly; *rūpavat*—with form; *sparśa*—touch; *śabdavat*—with sound also; *tejasaḥ*—of the fire;

tu—but; *vikurvāṇāt*—on being transformed; *āsīt*—it so happened; *ambhaḥ*—water; *rasa-ātmakam*—composed of juice; *rūpavat*—with form; *sparśavat*—with touch; *ca*—and; *ambhaḥ*—water; *ghoṣavat*—with sound; *ca*—and; *para*—previous; *anvayāt*—by succession; *viśeṣaḥ*—variegatedness; *tu*—but; *vikurvāṇāt*—by transformation; *ambhasaḥ*—of water; *gandhavān*—odorous; *abhūt*—became; *para*—previous; *anvayāt*—by succession; *rasa*—juice; *sparśa*—touch; *śabda*—sound; *rūpa-guṇa-anvitaḥ*—qualitative.

TRANSLATION

Because the sky is transformed, the air is generated with the quality of touch, and by previous succession the air is also full of sound and the basic principles of duration of life: sense perception, mental power and bodily strength. When the air is transformed in course of time and nature's course, fire is generated, taking shape with the sense of touch and sound. Since fire is also transformed, there is a manifestation of water, full of juice and taste. As previously, it also has form and touch and is also full of sound. And water, being transformed from all variegatedness on earth, appears odorous and, as previously, becomes qualitatively full of juice, touch, sound and form respectively.

PURPORT

The whole process of creation is an act of gradual evolution and development from one element to another, reaching up to the variegatedness of the earth as so many trees, plants, mountains, rivers, reptiles, birds, animals and varieties of human beings. The quality of sense perception is also evolutionary, namely generated from sound, then touch, and from touch to form. Taste and odor are also generated along with the gradual development of sky, air, fire, water and earth. They are all mutually the cause and effect of one another, but the original cause is the Lord Himself in plenary portion, as Mahā-Viṣṇu lying in the causal water of the *mahat-tattva*. As such, Lord Kṛṣṇa is described in the *Brahma-saṁhitā* as the cause of all causes, and this is confirmed in the *Bhagavad-gītā* (10.8) as follows:

aham sarvasya prabhavo
mattaḥ sarvaṁ pravartate
iti matvā bhajante māṁ
budhā bhāva-samanvitāḥ

The qualitites of sense perception are fully represented in the earth, and they are manifested in other elements to a lesser extent. In the sky there is sound only, whereas in the air there are sound and touch. In the fire there are sound, touch and shape, and in the water there is taste also, along with the other perceptions, namely sound, touch and shape. In the earth, however, there are all the above-mentioned qualities with an extra development of odor also. Therefore on the earth there is a full display of variegatedness of life, which is originally started with the basic principle of air. Diseases of the body take place due to derangement of air within the earthly body of the living beings. Mental diseases result from special derangement of the air within the body, and as such, yogic exercise is especially beneficial to keep the air in order so that diseases of the body become almost nil by such exercises. When they are properly done the duration of life also increases, and one can have control over death also by such practices. A perfect *yogī* can have command over death and quit the body at the right moment, when he is competent to transfer himself to a suitable planet. The *bhakti-yogī*, however, surpasses all the *yogīs* because, by dint of his devotional service, he is promoted to the region beyond the material sky and is placed in one of the planets in the spiritual sky by the supreme will of the Lord, the controller of everything.

TEXT 30

वैकारिकान्मनो जज्ञे देवा वैकारिका दश ।
दिग्वातार्कप्रचेतोऽश्विवह्नीन्द्रोपेन्द्रमित्रकाः ॥३०॥

vaikārikān mano jajñe
devā vaikārikā daśa
dig-vātārka-praceto 'śvi-
vahnīndropendra-mitra-kāḥ

vaikārikāt—from the mode of goodness; *manaḥ*—the mind; *jajñe*—generated; *devāḥ*—demigods; *vaikārikāḥ*—in the mode of goodness;

daśa—ten; *dik*—the controller of directions; *vāta*—the controller of air; *arka*—the sun; *pracetaḥ*—Varuṇa; *aśvi*—the Aśvinī-kumāras; *vahni*—the fire-god; *indra*—the King of heaven; *upendra*—the deity in heaven; *mitra*—one of the twleve Ādityas; *kāḥ*—Prajāpati Brahmā.

TRANSLATION

From the mode of goodness the mind is generated and becomes manifest, as also the ten demigods controlling the bodily movements. Such demigods are known as the controller of directions, the controller of air, the sun-god, the father of Dakṣa Prajāpati, the Aśvinī-kumāras, the fire-god, the King of heaven, the worshipable deity in heaven, the chief of the Ādityas, and Brahmājī, the Prajāpati. All come into existence.

PURPORT

Vaikārika is the neutral stage of creation, and *tejas* is the initiative of creation, while *tamas* is the full display of material creation under the spell of the darkness of ignorance. Manufacture of the "necessities of life" in factories and workshops, excessively prominent in the age of Kali, or in the age of the machine, is the summit stage of the quality of darkness. Such manufacturing enterprises by human society are in the mode of darkness because factually there is no necessity for the commodities manufactured. Human society primarily requires food for subsistance, shelter for sleeping, defense for protection, and commodities for satisfaction of the senses. The senses are the practical signs of life, as will be explained in the next verse. Human civilization is meant for purifying the senses, and objects of sense satisfaction should be supplied as much as absolutely required, but not for aggravating artificial sensory needs. Food, shelter, defense and sense gratification are all needs in material existence. Otherwise, in his pure, uncontaminated state of original life, the living entity has no such needs. The needs are therefore artificial, and in the pure state of life there are no such needs. As such, increasing the artificial needs, as is the standard of material civilization, or advancing the economic development of human society, is a sort of engagement in darkness, without knowledge. By such engagement, human energy is spoiled, because human energy is primarily meant for purifying the senses in order to engage them in satisfying the senses of the Supreme Lord. The Supreme Lord, being the supreme possessor of spiritual senses, is the master of the senses, Hṛṣīkeśa. Hṛṣīka means the senses, and īśa means the master. The Lord is not the servant of the senses, or, in other words, He is not directed by the dictation of the senses, but the conditioned souls or the individual living entities are servants of the senses. They are conducted by the direction or dictation of the senses, and therefore material civilization is a kind of engagement in sense gratification only. The standard of human civilization should be to cure the disease of sense gratification, and one can do this simply by becoming an agent for satisfying the spiritual senses of the Lord. The senses are never to be stopped in their engagements, but one should purify them by engaging them in the pure service of sense gratification of the master of the senses. This is the instruction of the whole Bhagavad-gītā. Arjuna wanted first of all to satisfy his own senses by his decision not to fight with his kinsmen and friends, but Lord Śrī Kṛṣṇa taught him the Bhagavad-gītā just to purify Arjuna's decision for sense gratification. Therefore Arjuna agreed to satisfy the senses of the Lord, and thus he fought the Battle of Kurukṣetra, as the Lord desired.

The Vedas instruct us to get out of the existence of darkness and go forward on the path of light (tamasi mā jyotir gama). The path of light is therefore to satisfy the senses of the Lord. Misguided men, or less intelligent men, follow the path of self-realization without any attempt to satisfy the transcendental senses of the Lord by following the path shown by Arjuna and other devotees of the Lord. On the contrary, they artificially try to stop the activities of the senses (yoga system), or they deny the transcendental senses of the Lord (jñāna system). The devotees, however, are above the yogīs and the jñānīs because pure devotees do not deny the senses of the Lord; they want to satisfy the senses of the Lord. Only because of the darkness of ignorance do the yogīs and jñānīs deny the senses of the Lord and thus artificially try to control the activities of the diseased senses. In the diseased condition of the senses there is too much engagement of the senses in increasing material needs. When one comes to see the disadvantage of aggravating the sense activities, one is called a jñānī, and when one tries to stop the activities of the senses by the practice of yogic principles, he is called a yogī, but when one is fully aware of the transcendental senses of the Lord and tries to satisfy His senses, one is called a devotee of the Lord. The devotees of the Lord do not try to deny the senses of the Lord, nor do they artificially stop the actions of the senses. But they do voluntarily engage the purified senses in the service of the master of the senses, as was done by Arjuna, thereby easily attaining the perfection of satisfying the Lord, the ultimate goal of all perfection.

TEXT 31

तैजसात् तु विकुर्वाणादिन्द्रियाणि दशाभवन् ।
ज्ञानशक्तिः क्रियाशक्तिर्बुद्धिः प्राणश्च तैजसौ ।
श्रोत्रं त्वग्घ्राणदृग्जिह्वा वाग्दोर्मेढ्राङ्घ्रिपायवः॥३१॥

taijasāt tu vikurvāṇād
indriyāṇi daśābhavan
jñāna-śaktiḥ kriyā-śaktir
buddhiḥ prāṇaś ca taijasau
śrotraṁ tvag-ghrāṇa-dṛg-jihvā
vāg-dor-meḍhrāṅghri-pāyavaḥ

taijasāt—by the passionate egoism; *tu*—but; *vikurvāṇāt*—transformation of; *indriyāṇi*—the senses; *daśa*—ten; *abhavan*—generated; *jñāna-śaktiḥ*—the five senses for acquiring knowledge; *kriyā-śaktiḥ*—the five senses of activities; *buddhiḥ*—intelligence; *prāṇaḥ*—the living energy; *ca*—also; *taijasau*—all products of the mode of passion; *śrotram*—the sense for hearing; *tvak*—the sense for touching; *ghrāṇa*—the sense for smelling; *dṛk*—the sense for seeing; *jihvāḥ*—the sense for tasting; *vāk*—the sense for speaking; *doḥ*—the sense for handling; *meḍhra*—the genitals; *aṅghri*—the legs; *pāyavaḥ*—the sense for evacuating.

TRANSLATION

By further transformation of the mode of passion, the sense organs like the ear, skin, nose, eyes, tongue, mouth, hands, genitals, legs, and the outlet for evacuating, together with intelligence and living energy, are all generated.

PURPORT

The living condition in material existence depends more or less on
one's intelligence and powerful living energy. Intelligence to counteract
the hard struggle for existence is assisted by the senses for acquiring
knowledge, and the living energy maintains himself by manipulating the
active organs, like the hands and legs. But on the whole, the struggle for
existence is an exertion of the mode of passion. Therefore all the sense
organs, headed by intelligence and the living energy, *prāṇa*, are different products and by-products of the second mode of nature, called
passion. This mode of passion, however, is the product of the air
element, as described before.

TEXT 32

यदैतेऽसङ्गता भावा भूतेन्द्रियमनोगुणाः ।
यदायतननिर्माणे न शेकुर्ब्रह्मवित्तम ॥३२॥

*yadaite 'saṅgatā bhāvā
bhūtendriya-mano-guṇāḥ
yadāyatana-nirmāṇe
na śekur brahma-vittama*

yadā—as long as; *ete*—all these; *asaṅgatāḥ*—without being
assembled; *bhāvāḥ*—remained so situated; *bhūta*—elements; *indriya*—
senses; *manaḥ*—mind; *guṇāḥ*—modes of nature; *yadā*—so long;
āyatana—the body; *nirmāṇe*—in being formed; *na śekuḥ*—was not
possible; *brahma-vit-tama*—O Nārada, the best knower of transcendental knowledge.

TRANSLATION

O Nārada, best of the transcendentalists, the forms of the body
cannot take place as long as these created parts, namely the elements, senses, mind and modes of nature, are not assembled.

PURPORT

The different types of bodily construction of the living entities are exactly like different types of motorcars manufactured by assembling the

allied motor parts. When the car is ready, the driver sits in the car and moves it as he desires. This is also confirmed in the *Bhagavad-gītā* (18.61): the living entity is as if seated on the machine of the body, and the car of the body is moving by the control of material nature, just as the railway trains are moving under the direction of the controller. The living entities, however, are not the bodies; they are separate from the cars of the body. But the less intelligent material scientist cannot understand the process of assembling the parts of the body, namely the senses, the mind and the qualities of the material modes. Every living entity is a spiritual spark, part and parcel of the Supreme Being, and by the kindness of the Lord, for the Father is kind to His sons, the individual living beings are given a little freedom to act according to their will to lord it over the material nature. Just as a father gives some playthings to the crying child to satisfy him, the whole material creation is made possible by the will of the Lord to allow the bewildered living entities to lord it over things as they desire, although under the control of the agent of the Lord. The living entities are exactly like small children playing the material field under the control of the maidservant of the Lord (nature). They accept the *māyā*, or the maidservant, as all in all and thus wrongly conceive the Supreme Truth to be feminine (goddess Durgā, etc.). The foolish, childlike materialists cannot reach beyond the conception of the maidservant, material nature, but the intelligent grown-up sons of the Lord know well that all the acts of material nature are controlled by the Lord, just as a maidservant is under the control of the master, the father of the undeveloped children.

The parts of the body, such as the senses, are the creation of the *mahat-tattva*, and when they are assembled by the will of the Lord, the material body comes into existence, and the living entity is allowed to use it for further activities. This is explained as follows.

TEXT 33

तदा संहत्य चान्योन्यं भगवच्छक्तिचोदिताः ।
सदसत्त्वमुपादाय चोभयं ससृजुर्बुदः ॥३३॥

tadā saṁhatya cānyonyaṁ
bhagavac-chakti-coditāḥ

sad-asattvam upādāya
cobhayaṁ sasrjur hy adaḥ

tadā—all those; *saṁhatya*—being assembled; *ca*—also; *anyonyam*—
one another; *bhagavat*—by the Personality of Godhead; *śakti*—energy;
coditāḥ—being applied; *sat-asattvam*—primarily and secondarily;
upādāya—accepting; *ca*—also; *ubhayam*—both; *sasrjuḥ*—came into
existence; *hi*—certainly; *adaḥ*—this universe.

TRANSLATION

**Thus when all these became assembled by force of the energy of
the Supreme Personality of Godhead, this universe certainly came
into being by accepting both the primary and secondary causes of
creation.**

PURPORT

In this verse it is clearly mentioned that the Supreme Personality of
Godhead exerts His different energies in the creation; it is not that He
Himself is transformed into material creations. He expands Himself by
His different energies, as well as by His plenary portions. In a corner of
the spiritual sky of *brahmajyoti* a spiritual cloud sometimes appears, and
the covered portion is called the *mahat-tattva*. The Lord then, by His
plenary portion as Mahā-Viṣṇu, lies down within the water of the *mahat-
tattva*, and the water is called the Causal Ocean (Kāraṇa-jala). While
Mahā-Viṣṇu sleeps within the Causal Ocean, innumerable universes are
generated along with His breathing. These universes are floating, and
they are scattered all over the Causal Ocean. They stay only during the
breathing period of Mahā-Viṣṇu. In each and every universal globe, the
same Mahā-Viṣṇu enters again as Garbhodakaśāyī Viṣṇu and lies there
on the serpentlike Śeṣa incarnation. From His navel sprouts a lotus stem,
and on the lotus, Brahmā, the lord of the universe, is born. Brahmā creates all forms of living beings of different shapes in terms of different
desires within the universe. He also creates the sun, moon and other
demigods.

Therefore the chief engineer of the material creation is the Lord Himself, as confirmed in the *Bhagavad-gītā* (9.10). It is He only who directs
the material nature to produce all sorts of moving and nonmoving
creations.

There are two modes of material creation: the creation of the collective universes, as stated above, done by the Mahā-Viṣṇu, and the creation of the single universe. Both are done by the Lord, and thus the universal shape, as we can see, takes place.

TEXT 34

वर्षपूगसहस्रान्ते   तदण्डमुदके शयम् ।
कालकर्मस्वभावस्थो   जीवोऽजीवमजीवयत् ॥३४॥

varṣa-pūga-sahasrānte
tad aṇḍam udake śayam
kāla-karma-svabhāva-stho
jīvo 'jīvam ajīvayat

varṣa-pūga—many years; *sahasra-ante*—of thousands of years; *tat*—that; *aṇḍam*—the universal globe; *udake*—in the causal water; *śayam*—being drowned; *kāla*—eternal time; *karma*—action; *svabhāva-sthaḥ*—according to the modes of nature; *jīvaḥ*—the Lord of the living beings; *ajīvam*—nonanimated; *ajīvayat*—caused to be animated.

TRANSLATION

Thus all the universes remained thousands of aeons within the water [the Causal Ocean], and the Lord of living beings, entering in each of them, caused them to be fully animated.

PURPORT

The Lord is described here as the *jīva* because He is the leader of all other *jīvas* (living entities). In the *Vedas* He is described as the *nitya*, the leader of all other *nityas*. The Lord's relation with the living entities is like that of the father with the sons. The sons and the father are qualitatively equal, but the father is never the son, nor is the son ever the father who begets. So, as described above, the Lord as Garbhodakaśāyī Viṣṇu or Hiraṇyagarbha Supersoul enters into each and every universe and causes it to be animated by begetting the living entities within the womb of the material nature, as confirmed in the *Bhagavad-gītā* (14.3). After each annihilation of the material creation, all the living entities are merged within the body of the Lord, and after creation they are again impregnated within the material energy. In material existence, therefore, the material energy is seemingly the mother of the living entities, and the Lord is the father. When, however, the animation takes place, the living entities revive their own natural activities under the spell of time and energy, and thus the varieties of living beings are manifested. The Lord, therefore, is ultimately the cause of all animation in the material world.

TEXT 35

स एव पुरुषस्तसादण्डं निर्भिद्य निर्गतः ।
सहस्रोर्वेङ्घ्रिबाह्वक्षः सहस्राननशीर्षवान् ॥३५॥

sa eva puruṣas tasmād
aṇḍaṁ nirbhidya nirgataḥ
sahasrorv-aṅghri-bāhv-akṣaḥ
sahasrānana-śīrṣavān

saḥ—He (the Lord); *eva*—Himself; *puruṣaḥ*—the Supreme Personality of Godhead; *tasmāt*—from within the universe; *aṇḍam*—Hiraṇyagarbha; *nirbhidya*—dividing; *nirgataḥ*—came out; *sahasra*—thousands; *ūru*—thighs; *aṅghri*—legs; *bāhu*—arms; *akṣaḥ*—eyes; *sahasra*—thousands of; *ānana*—mouths; *śīrṣavān*—with heads also.

TRANSLATION

The Lord [Mahā-Viṣṇu], although lying in the Causal Ocean, came out of it, and dividing Himself as Hiraṇyagarbha, He entered into each universe and assumed the virāṭ-rūpa, with thousands of legs, arms, mouths, heads, etc.

PURPORT

The expansions of the planetary systems within each and every universe are situated in the different parts of the virāṭ-rūpa (universal form) of the Lord, and they are described as follows.

TEXT 36

यस्येहावयवैर्लोकान् कल्पयन्ति मनीषिणः ।
कट्यादिभिरधः सप्त सप्तोर्ध्वं जघनादिभिः ॥३६॥

yasyehāvayavair lokān
kalpayanti manīṣiṇaḥ
kaṭya-ādibhir adhaḥ sapta
saptordhvaṁ jaghanādibhiḥ

yasya—whose; *iha*—in the universe; *avayavaiḥ*—by the limbs of the body; *lokān*—all the planets; *kalpayanti*—imagine; *manīṣiṇaḥ*—great philosophers; *kaṭi-ādibhiḥ*—down from the waist; *adhaḥ*—downwards; *sapta*—seven systems; *sapta ūrdham*—and seven systems upwards; *jaghana-ādibhiḥ*—front portion.

TRANSLATION

Great philosophers imagine that the complete planetary systems in the universe are displays of the different upper and lower limbs of the universal body of the Lord.

PURPORT

The word *kalpayanti*, or "imagine," is significant. The *virāṭ* universal form of the Absolute is an imagination of the speculative philosophers who are unable to adjust to the eternal two-handed form of Lord Śrī Kṛṣṇa. Although the universal form, as imagined by the great philosophers, is one of the features of the Lord, it is more or less imaginary. It is said that the seven upper planetary systems are situated above the waist of the universal form, whereas the lower planetary systems are situated below His waist. The idea impressed herein is that the Supreme Lord is conscious of every part of His body, and nowhere in the creation is there anything beyond His control.

TEXT 37

पुरुषस्य मुखं ब्रह्म क्षत्रमेतस्य बाहवः ।
ऊर्वोर्वैश्यो भगवतः पद्भ्यां शूद्रो व्यजायत ॥३७॥

*puruṣasya mukhaṁ brahma
kṣatram etasya bāhavaḥ
ūrvor vaiśyo bhagavataḥ
padbhyāṁ śūdro vyajāyata*

puruṣasya—of the Supreme Personality of Godhead; *mukham*—mouth; *brahma*—is the *brāhmaṇas*; *kṣatram*—the royal order; *etasya*—of Him; *bāhavaḥ*—the arms; *ūrvoḥ*—the thighs; *vaiśyaḥ*—are the mercantile men; *bhagavataḥ*—of the Personality of Godhead; *padbhyām*—from His legs; *śūdraḥ*—the laborer class; *vyajāyata*—became manifested.

TRANSLATION

The brāhmaṇas represent His mouth, the kṣatriyas His arms, the vaiśyas His thighs, and the śūdras are born of His legs.

PURPORT

All living beings are stated to be the parts and parcels of the Supreme Lord, and how they are so is explained in this verse. The four divisions of human society, namely the intelligent class (the *brāhmaṇas*), the administrative class (the *kṣatriyas*), the mercantile class (the *vaiśyas*), and the laborer class (the *śūdras*), are all in different parts of the body of the Lord. As such, no one is different from the Lord. The mouth of the body and the legs of the body are nondifferent constitutionally, but the mouth or the head of the body is qualitatively more important than the legs. At the same time, the mouth, the legs, the arms and the thighs are all component parts of the body. These limbs of the body of the Lord are meant to serve the complete whole. The mouth is meant for speaking and eating, the arms are meant for the protection of the body, the legs are meant for carrying the body, and the waist of the body is meant for maintaining the body. The intelligent class in society, therefore, must speak on behalf of the body, as well as accept foodstuff to satisfy the hunger of the body. The hunger of the Lord is to accept the fruits of sacrifice. The *brāhmaṇas*, or the intelligent class, must be very expert in performing such sacrifices, and the subordinate classes must join in such sacrifices. To speak for the Supreme Lord means to glorify the Lord by means of propagating the knowledge of the Lord as it is, broadcasting the factual nature of the Lord and the factual position of all other parts of the whole body. The *brāhmaṇas*, therefore, are required to know the *Vedas*, or the ultimate source of knowledge. *Veda* means knowledge, and *anta* means the end of it. According to *Bhagavad-gītā*, the Lord is the source of everything (*ahaṁ sarvasya prabhavaḥ*), and thus the end of all knowledge (*Vedānta*) is to know the Lord, to know our relationship with Him and to act according to that relationship only. The parts of the body are related to the body; similarly, the living being must know his relationship with the Lord. The human life is especially meant for this purpose, namely to know the factual relationship of every living being with the Supreme Lord. Without knowing this relationship, the human life is spoiled. The intelligent class of men, the *brāhmaṇas*, are therefore especially responsible for broadcasting this knowledge of our relationship with the Lord and leading the general mass of people to the right path. The administrative class is meant for protecting the living beings so that they can serve this purpose; the mercantile class is meant for producing food grains and distributing them to the complete human society so that the whole population is given a chance to live comfortably and discharge the duties of human life. The mercantile class is also required to give protection to the cows in order to get sufficient milk and milk products, which alone can give the proper health and intelligence to maintain a civilization perfectly meant for knowledge of the ultimate truth. And the laborer class, who are neither intelligent nor powerful, can help by physical services to the other higher classes and thus be benefited by their cooperation. Therefore the universe is a complete unit in relationship with the Lord, and without this relationship with the Lord the whole human society is disturbed and is without any peace and prosperity. This is confirmed in the *Vedas: brāhmaṇo 'sya mukham āsīd, bāhū rājanyaḥ kṛtaḥ.*

TEXT 38

भूर्लोकः कल्पितः पद्भ्यां भुवर्लोकोऽस्य नाभितः ।
हृदा खर्लोक उरसा महर्लोको महात्मनः   ॥३८॥

bhūrlokaḥ kalpitaḥ padbhyāṁ
bhuvarloko 'sya nābhitaḥ

hṛdā svarloka urasā
maharloko mahātmanaḥ

bhūḥ—the lower planetary systems up to the stratum of the earth; *lokaḥ*—the planets; *kalpitaḥ*—it is so imagined or said; *padbhyām*—out of the legs; *bhuvaḥ*—the upper; *lokaḥ*—the planetary system; *asya*—of Him (the Lord); *nābhitaḥ*—from the navel abdomen; *hṛdā*—by the heart; *svarlokaḥ*—the planetary systems occupied by the demigods; *urasā*—by the chest; *maharlokaḥ*—the planetary system occupied by great sages and saints; *mahā-ātmanaḥ*—of the Supreme Personality of Godhead.

TRANSLATION

The lower planetary systems, up to the limit of the earthly stratum, are said to be situated in His legs. The middle planetary systems, beginning from Bhuvarloka, are situated in His navel. And the still higher planetary systems, occupied by the demigods and highly cultured sages and saints, are situated in the chest of the Supreme Lord.

PURPORT

There are fourteen spheres of planetary systems within this universe. The lower systems are called Bhūrloka, the middle systems are called Bhuvarloka, and the higher planetary systems, up to Brahmaloka, the highest planetary system of the universe, are called Svarloka. And all of them are situated on the body of the Lord. In other words, no one within this universe is without a relationship with the Lord.

TEXT 39

ग्रीवायां जनलोकोऽस्य तपोलोक: स्तनद्वयात् ।
मूर्धभि: सत्यलोकस्तु ब्रह्मलोक: सनातन: ॥३९॥

grīvāyāṁ janaloko 'sya
tapolokaḥ stana-dvayāt
mūrdhabhiḥ satyalokas tu
brahmalokaḥ sanātanaḥ

grīvāyām—up to the neck; *janalokaḥ*—the Janaloka planetary system; *asya*—of Him; *tapolokaḥ*—the Tapoloka planetary system; *stana-dvayāt*—beginning from the breast; *mūrdhabhiḥ*—by the head; *satyalokaḥ*—the Satyaloka planetary system; *tu*—but; *brahmalokaḥ*—the spiritual planets; *sanātanaḥ*—eternal.

TRANSLATION

From the forefront of the chest up to the neck of the universal form of the Lord are situated the planetary systems named Janaloka and Tapoloka, whereas Satyaloka, the topmost planetary system, is situated on the head of the form. The spiritual planets, however, are eternal.

PURPORT

Many times in these pages we have discussed the spiritual planets situated beyond the material sky, and the description is corroborated in this verse . The word *sanātana* is significant. This very idea of eternity is expressed in the *Bhagavad-gītā* (8.20), where it is said that beyond the material creation is the spiritual sky, where everything is eternal. Sometimes Satyaloka, the planet in which Brahmā resides, is also called Brahmaloka. But the Brahmaloka mentioned here is not the same as the Satyaloka planetary system. This Brahmaloka is eternal, whereas the Satyaloka planetary system is not eternal. And to distinguish between the two, the adjective *sanātana* has been used in this case. According to Śrīla Jīva Gosvāmī, this Brahmaloka is the *loka* or abode of Brahman, or the Supreme Lord. In the spiritual sky all the planets are as good as the Lord Himself. The Lord is all spirit, and His name, fame, glories, qualities, pastimes, etc., are all nondifferent from Him because He is absolute. As such, the planets in the kingdom of God are also nondifferent from Him. In those planets there is no difference between the body and the soul, nor is there any influence of time as we experience it in the material world. And in addition to there being no influence of time, the planets in Brahmaloka, due to being spiritual, are never annihilated. All variegatedness in the spiritual planets is also one with the Lord, and therefore the Vedic aphorism *ekam evādvitīyam* is fully realized in that *sanātana* atmosphere of spiritual variegatedness. This material world is only a shadow phantasmagoria of the spiritual kingdom of the Lord, and because it is a shadow it is never eternal; the variegatedness in the material world of duality (spirit and matter) cannot be compared to that of the spiritual world. Because of a poor fund of knowledge, less intelligent persons sometimes mistake the conditions of the shadow world to be equivalent to those of the spiritual world, and thus they mistake the Lord and His pastimes in the material world to be one with the conditioned souls and their activities. The Lord condemns such less intelligent persons in the *Bhagavad-gītā* (9.11):

> avajānanti māṁ mūḍhā
> mānuṣīṁ tanum āśritam
> paraṁ bhāvam ajānanto
> mama bhūta-maheśvaram

Whenever the Lord incarnates, He does so in His full internal potency (*ātma-māyā*), and less intelligent persons mistake Him to be one of the material creations. Śrīla Śrīdhara Svāmī, therefore, rightly commenting on this verse, says that the Brahmaloka mentioned here is Vaikuṇṭha, the kingdom of God, which is *sanātana*, or eternal, and is therefore not exactly like the material creations described above. The *virāṭ* universal form of the Lord is an imagination for the material world. It has nothing to do with the spiritual world, or the kingdom of God.

TEXTS 40–41

तत्कट्यां चातलं क्लृप्तं वितलं विभोः ।
जानुभ्यां सुतलं शुद्धं जङ्घाभ्यां तु तलातलम् ॥४०॥
महातलं तु गुल्फाभ्यां प्रपदाभ्यां रसातलम् ।
पातालं पादतलत इति लोकमयः पुमान् ॥४१॥

> tat-kaṭyāṁ cātalaṁ klptam
> ūrubhyāṁ vitalaṁ vibhoḥ
> jānubhyāṁ sutalaṁ śuddhaṁ
> jaṅghābhyāṁ tu talātalam
>
> mahātalaṁ tu gulphābhyāṁ
> prapadābhyāṁ rasātalam

pātālaṁ pāda-talata
iti lokamayaḥ pumān

tat—in His; *katyām*—waist; *ca*—also; *atalam*—the first planetary system below the earth; *klptam*—situated; *ūrubhyām*—on the thighs; *vitalam*—the second planetary system below; *vibhoḥ*—of the Lord; *jānubhyām*—on the ankles; *sutalam*—the third planetary system below; *śuddham*—purified; *jaṅghābhyām*—on the joints; *tu*—but; *talātalam*—the fourth planetary system below; *mahātalam*—the fifth planetary system below; *tu*—but; *gulphābhyām*—situated on the calves; *prapadābhyām*—on the upper or front portion of the feet; *rasātalam*—the sixth planetary system below; *pātālam*—the seventh planetary system below; *pāda-talataḥ*—on the bottom or soles of the feet; *iti*—thus; *loka-mayaḥ*—full of planetary systems; *pumān*—the Lord.

TRANSLATION

My dear son Nārada, know from me that there are seven lower planetary systems out of the total fourteen. The first planetary system, known as Atala, is situated on the waist; the second, Vitala, is situated on the thighs; the third, Sutala, on the knees; the fourth, Talātala, on the shanks; the fifth, Mahātala, on the ankles; the sixth, Rasātala, on the upper portion of the feet; and the seventh, Pātāla, on the soles of the feet. Thus the virāṭ form of the Lord is full of all planetary systems.

PURPORT

Modern enterprisers (the astronauts who travel in space) may take information from *Śrīmad-Bhāgavatam* that in space there are fourteen divisions of planetary systems. The situation is calculated from the earthly planetary system, which is called Bhūrloka. Above Bhūrloka is Bhuvarloka, and the topmost planetary system is called Satyaloka. These are the upper seven *lokas*, or planetary systems. And similarly, there are seven lower planetary systems, known as Atala, Vitala, Sutala, Talātala, Mahātala, Rasātala and Pātāla *lokas*. All these planetary systems are scattered over the complete universe, which occupies an area of two billion times two billion square miles. The modern astronauts can travel only a few thousand miles away from the earth, and therefore their attempt to travel in the sky is something like child's play on the shore of an expansive ocean. The moon is situated in the third status of the upper planetary system, and in the Fifth Canto of *Śrīmad-Bhāgavatam* we shall be able to know the distant situation of the various planets scattered over the vast material sky. There are innumerable universes beyond the one in which we are put, and all these material universes cover only an insignificant portion of the spiritual sky, which is described above as *sanātana* Brahmaloka. The Supreme Lord very kindly invites the intelligent human beings to return home, back to Godhead, in the following verse of the *Bhagavad-gītā* (8.16):

> *ābrahma-bhuvanāl lokāḥ*
> *punar āvartino 'rjuna*
> *mām upetya tu kaunteya*
> *punar janma na vidyate*

Beginning from Satyaloka, the topmost planet of the universe, situated just below the eternal Brahmaloka, as described above, all the planets are material. And one's situation in any of the many material planets is still subject to the laws of material nature, namely birth, death, old age and disease. But one can get complete liberation from all the above-mentioned material pangs when one enters into the eternal Brahmaloka *sanātana* atmosphere, the kingdom of God. Therefore liberation, as contemplated by the speculative philosophers and the mystics, is possible only when one becomes a devotee of the Lord. Anyone who is not a devotee cannot enter into the kingdom of God. Only by attainment of a service attitude in the transcendental position can one enter into the kingdom of Godhead. Therefore the speculative philosophers, as well as the mystics, must first of all be attracted to the devotional cult before they can factually attain liberation.

TEXT 42

भूर्लोकः कल्पितः पद्भ्यां भुवर्लोकोऽस्य नाभितः ।
खर्लोकः कल्पितो मूर्ध्नेति वा लोककल्पना ॥४२॥

bhūrlokaḥ kalpitaḥ padbhyāṁ
bhuvarloko 'sya nābhitaḥ
svarlokaḥ kalpito mūrdhnā
iti vā loka-kalpanā

bhūrlokaḥ—the entire planetary system from Pātāla to the earthly planetary system; *kalpitaḥ*—imagined; *padbhyām*—situated on the legs; *bhuvarlokaḥ*—the Bhuvarloka planetary system; *asya*—of the universal form of the Lord; *nābhitaḥ*—out of the navel abdomen; *svarlokaḥ*—the higher planetary system, beginning with the heavenly planets; *kalpitaḥ*—imagined; *mūrdhnā*—from the chest to the head; *iti*—thus; *vā*—either; *loka*—the planetary systems; *kalpanā*—imagination.

TRANSLATION

Others may divide the whole planetary system into three divisions, namely the lower planetary systems on the legs [up to the earth], the middle planetary systems on the navel, and the upper planetary systems [Svarloka] from the chest to the head of the Supreme Personality.

PURPORT

The three divisions of the complete planetary systems are here mentioned; fourteen are imagined by others, and that is also explained.

Thus end the Bhaktivedanta purports of the Second Canto, Fifth Chapter, of the Śrīmad-Bhāgavatam, entitled "The Cause of All Causes."

CHAPTER SIX

Puruṣa-sūkta Confirmed

TEXT 1

ब्रह्मोवाच

वाचां वह्नेर्मुखं क्षेत्रं छन्दसां सप्त धातवः ।
हव्यकव्यामृतान्नानां जिह्वा सर्वरसस्य च ॥ १ ॥

brahmovāca

vācāṁ vahner mukhaṁ kṣetraṁ
chandasāṁ sapta dhātavaḥ
havya-kavyāmṛtānnānāṁ
jihvā sarva-rasasya ca

brahmā uvāca—Lord Brahmā said; *vācām*—of the voice; *vahneḥ*—of fire; *mukham*—the mouth; *kṣetram*—the generating center; *chandasām*—of the Vedic hymns, such as Gāyatrī; *sapta*—seven; *dhātavaḥ*—skin and six other layers; *havya-kavya*—offerings for the demigods and the forefathers; *amṛta*—food for human beings; *annānām*—of all sorts of foodstuffs; *jihvā*—the tongue; *sarva*—all; *rasasya*—of all delicacies; *ca*—also.

TRANSLATION

Lord Brahmā said: The mouth of the virāṭ-puruṣa [the universal form of the Lord] is the generating center of the voice, and the controlling deity is Fire. His skin and six other layers are the generating centers of the Vedic hymns, and His tongue is the productive center of different foodstuffs and delicacies for offering to the demigods, the forefathers and the general mass of people.

PURPORT

The opulences of the universal form of the Lord are described herein. It is said that His mouth is the generating center of all kinds of voices, and its controlling deity is the fire demigod. And His skin and other six layers of bodily construction are the representative generating centers of the seven kinds of Vedic hymns, like the Gāyatrī. Gāyatrī is the beginning of all Vedic *mantras*, and it is explained in the first volume of *Śrīmad-Bhāgavatam*. Since the generating centers are the different parts of the universal form of the Lord, and since the form of the Lord is transcendental to the material creation, it is to be understood that the voice, the tongue, the skin, etc., suggest that the Lord in His transcendental form is not without them. The material voice, or the energy of taking in foodstuff, is generated originally from the Lord; such actions are but perverted reflections of the original reservoirs—the transcendental situation is not without spiritual variegatedness. In the spiritual world, all the perverted forms of material variegatedness are fully represented in their original spiritual identity. The only difference is that material activities are contaminated by the three modes of material nature, whereas the potencies in the spiritual world are all pure because they are engaged in the unalloyed transcendental loving service of the Lord. In the spiritual world, the Lord is the sublime enjoyer of everything, and the living entities there are all engaged in His transcendental loving service without any contamination of the modes of material nature. The activities in the spiritual world are without any of the inebrieties of the material world, but there is no question of impersonal voidness on the spiritual platform, as suggested by the impersonalists. Devotional service is defined in the *Nārada-pañcarātra* as follows:

> *sarvopādhi-vinirmuktaṁ*
> *tat-paratvena nirmalam*
> *hṛṣīkeṇa hṛṣīkeśa-*
> *sevanaṁ bhaktir ucyate*

Originally, since all the senses are produced of the Lord's reservoir of senses, the sensual activities of the material world are to be purified by the process of devotional service, and thus the perfection of life can be attained simply by purifying the present position of our material activities. And the purifying process begins from the stage of being liberated from the conception of different designations. Every living entity is engaged in some sort of service, either for the self, or for the family, or for the society, country, etc., but, unfortunately, all such services are rendered due to material attachment. The attachments of the material affinity may be simply changed to the service of the Lord, and thus the treatment of being freed from material attachment begins automatically. The process of liberation is therefore easier through devotional service than by any other methods, for in the *Bhagavad-gītā* (12.5) it is said that one is subjected to various kinds of tribulations if one is impersonally attached: *kleśo 'dhikataras teṣām avyaktāsakta-cetasām.*

TEXT 2

सर्वासूनां च वायोश्च तन्नासे परमायणे ।
अश्विनोरोषधीनां च घ्राणो मोदप्रमोदयोः ॥ २ ॥

sarvāsūnāṁ ca vāyoś ca
tan-nāse paramāyaṇe
aśvinor oṣadhīnāṁ ca
ghrāṇo moda-pramodayoḥ

sarva—all; *asūnām*—different kinds of life air; *ca*—and; *vāyoḥ*—of the air; *ca*—also; *tat*—His; *nāse*—in the nose; *parama-āyaṇe*—in the transcendental generating center; *aśvinoḥ*—of the Aśvinī-kumāra demigods; *oṣadhīnām*—of all medicinal herbs; *ca*—also; *ghrāṇaḥ*—His smelling power; *moda*—pleasure; *pramodayoḥ*—specific sport.

TRANSLATION

His two nostrils are the generating centers of our breathing and of all other airs, His smelling powers generate the Aśvinī-kumāra demigods and all kinds of medicinal herbs, and His breathing energies produce different kinds of fragrance.

TEXT 3

रूपाणां तेजसां चक्षुर्दिवः सूर्यस्य चाक्षिणी ।
कर्णौ दिशां च तीर्थानां श्रोत्रमाकाशशब्दयोः ॥ ३ ॥

rūpāṇāṁ tejasāṁ cakṣur
divaḥ sūryasya cākṣiṇī

karṇau diśāṁ ca tīrthānāṁ
śrotram ākāśa-śabdayoḥ

rūpāṇām—for all kinds of forms; *tejasām*—of all that is illuminating; *cakṣuḥ*—the eyes; *divaḥ*—that which glitters; *sūryasya*—of the sun; *ca*—also; *akṣiṇī*—the eyeballs; *karṇau*—the ears; *diśām*—of all directions; *ca*—and; *tīrthānām*—of all the *Vedas*; *śrotram*—the sense of hearing; *ākāśa*—the sky; *śabdayoḥ*—of all sounds.

TRANSLATION

His eyes are the generating centers of all kinds of forms, and they glitter and illuminate. His eyeballs are like the sun and the heavenly planets. His ears hear from all sides and are receptacles for all the Vedas, and His sense of hearing is the generating center of the sky and of all kinds of sound.

PURPORT

The word *tīrthānām* is sometimes interpreted to mean the places of pilgrimage, but Śrīla Jīva Gosvāmī says that it means the reception of the Vedic transcendental knowledge. The propounders of the Vedic knowledge are also known as the *tīrthas*.

TEXT 4

तद्गात्रं वस्तुसाराणां सौभगस्य च भाजनम् ।
त्वगस्य स्पर्शवायोश्च सर्वमेधस्य चैव हि ॥ ४ ॥

tad-gātram vastu-sārāṇām
saubhagasya ca bhājanam
tvag asya sparśa-vāyoś ca
sarva-medhasya caiva hi

tat—His; *gātram*—bodily surface; *vastu-sārāṇām*—of the active principles of all articles; *saubhagasya*—of all auspicious opportunities; *ca*—and; *bhājanam*—the field of production; *tvak*—skin; *asya*—His; *sparśa*—touch; *vāyoḥ*—of the moving airs; *ca*—also; *sarva*—all kinds of; *medhasya*—of sacrifices; *ca*—also; *eva*—certainly; *hi*—exactly.

TRANSLATION

His bodily surface is the breeding ground for the active principles of everything and for all kinds of auspicious opportunities. His skin, like the moving air, is the generating center for all kinds of sense of touch and is the place for performing all kinds of sacrifice.

PURPORT

The air is the moving agent of all the planets, and as such the generating centers for promotion to the deserving planets, the sacrifices, are His bodily surface and are naturally the origin of all auspicious opportunities.

TEXT 5

रोमाण्युद्भिज्जजातीनां यैर्वा यज्ञस्तु सम्भृतः ।
केशश्मश्रुनखान्यस्य शिलालोहाभ्रविद्युताम् ॥ ५ ॥

romāṇy udbhijja-jātīnām
yair vā yajñas tu sambhṛtaḥ
keśa-śmaśru-nakhāny asya
śilā-lohābhra-vidyutām

romāṇi—hairs on the body; udbhijja—vegetables; jātīnām—of the kingdoms; yaiḥ—by which; vā—either; yajñaḥ—sacrifices; tu—but; sambhṛtaḥ—particularly served; keśa—hairs on the head; śmaśru—facial hair; nakhāni—nails; asya—of Him; śilā—stones; loha—iron ores; abhra—clouds; vidyutām—electricity.

TRANSLATION

The hairs on His body are the cause of all vegetation, particularly of those trees which are required as ingredients for sacrifice. The hairs on His head and face are reservoirs for the clouds, and His nails are the breeding ground of electricity, stones and iron ores.

PURPORT

The polished nails of the Lord generate electricity, and the clouds rest on the hairs of His head. One can therefore collect all sorts of necessities of life from the person of the Lord, and therefore the *Vedas* affirm that everything that is produced is caused by the Lord. The Lord is the supreme cause of all causes.

TEXT 6

बाहवो लोकपालानां प्रायशः क्षेमकर्मणाम् ॥ ६ ॥

bāhavo loka-pālānāṁ
prāyaśaḥ kṣema-karmaṇām

bāhavaḥ—arms; *loka-pālānām*—of the governing deities of the planets, the demigods; *prāyaśaḥ*—almost always; *kṣema-karmaṇām*—of those who are leaders and protectors of the general mass.

TRANSLATION

The Lord's arms are the productive fields for the great demigods and other leaders of the living entities who protect the general mass.

PURPORT

This important verse of *Śrīmad-Bhāgavatam* is corroborated and nicely explained in the *Bhagavad-gītā* (10.41–42) as follows:

yad yad vibhūtimat sattvam
śrīmad ūrjitam eva vā
tat tad evāvagaccha tvaṁ
mama tejo-'ṁśa-sambhavam

athavā bahunaitena
kiṁ jñātena tavārjuna
viṣṭabhyāham idaṁ kṛtsnam
ekāṁśena sthito jagat

There are many powerful kings, leaders, learned scholars, scientists, artists, engineers, inventors, excavators, archaeologists, industrialists, politicians, economists, business magnates, and many more powerful

deities or demigods like Brahmā, Śiva, Indra, Candra, Sūrya, Varuṇa and
Marut, who are all protecting the interest of the universal affairs of
maintenance, in different positions, and all of them are different powerful parts and parcels of the Supreme Lord. The Supreme Lord Śrī Kṛṣṇa
is the father of all living entities, who are placed in different high and
low positions according to their desires or aspirations. Some of them, as
particularly mentioned above, are specifically endowed with powers by
the will of the Lord. A sane person must know for certain that a living
being, however powerful he may be, is neither absolute nor independent.
All living beings must accept the origin of their specific power as
mentioned in this verse. And if they act accordingly, then simply by
discharging their respective occupational duties they can achieve the
highest perfection of life, namely eternal life, complete knowledge and
inexhaustible blessings. As long as the powerful men of the world do not
accept the origin of their respective powers, namely the Personality of
Godhead, the actions of *māyā* (illusion) will continue to act. The actions
of *māyā* are such that a powerful person, misled by the illusory, material
energy, wrongly accepts himself as all in all and does not develop God
consciousness. As such, the false sense of egoism (namely myself and
mine) has become overly prominent in the world, and there is a hard
struggle for existence in human society. The intelligent class of men,
therefore, must admit the Lord as the ultimate source of all energies and
thus pay tribute to the Lord for His good blessings. Simply by accepting
the Lord as the supreme proprietor of everything, since He is actually so,
one can achieve the highest perfection of life. Whatever a person may be
in the estimation of the social order of things, if a person tries to recipro-
cate a feeling of love towards the Supreme Personality of Godhead and is
satisfied with the blessings of the Lord, he will at once feel the highest
peace of mind for which he is hankering life after life. Peace of mind, or
in other words the healthy state of mind, can be achieved only when the
mind is situated in the transcendental loving service of the Lord. The
parts and parcels of the Lord are endowed with specific powers for rendering service unto the Lord, just as a big business magnate's sons are
empowered with specific powers of administration. The obedient son of
the father never goes against the will of the father and therefore passes
life very peacefully in concurrence with the head of the family, the
father. Similarly, the Lord being the father, all living beings should fully

and satisfactorily discharge the duty and will of the father, as faithful sons. This very mentality will at once bring peace and prosperity to human society.

TEXT 7

विक्रमो भूर्भुवः खश्च क्षेमस्य शरणस्य च ।
सर्वकामवरस्यापि हरेश्चरण आस्पदम् ॥ ७ ॥

vikramo bhūr bhuvaḥ svaś ca
kṣemasya śaraṇasya ca
sarva-kāma-varasyāpi
hareś caraṇa āspadam

vikramaḥ—forward steps; *bhūḥ bhuvaḥ*—of the lower and upper planets; *svaḥ*—as well as of heaven; *ca*—also; *kṣemasya*—of protection of all that we have; *śaraṇasya*—of fearlessness; *ca*—also; *sarva-kāma*—all that we need; *varasya*—of all benedictions; *api*—exactly; *hareḥ*—of the Lord; *caraṇaḥ*—the lotus feet; *āspadam*—shelter.

TRANSLATION

Thus the forward steps of the Lord are the shelter for the upper, lower and heavenly planets, as well as for all that we need. His lotus feet serve as protection from all kinds of fear.

PURPORT

For absolute protection from all sorts of fear, as well as for all our needs of life, we must take shelter of the lotus feet of the Lord, not only in this planet but also in all the upper, lower and heavenly planets. This absolute dependence on the lotus feet of the Lord is called pure devotional service, and it is directly hinted at within this passage. No one should have any kind of doubt in this matter, nor should one be inclined to seek the help of any other demigods, because all of them are dependent on Him only. Everyone, except the Lord Himself, is dependent on the mercy of the Lord; even the all-pervading Supersoul is also dependent on the supreme aspect of Bhagavān, the Personality of Godhead.

TEXT 8

अपां वीर्यस्य सर्गस्य पर्जन्यस्य प्रजापतेः ।
पुंसः शिश्न उपस्थस्तु प्रजात्यानन्दनिर्वृतेः ॥ ८ ॥

apāṁ vīryasya sargasya
parjanyasya prajāpateḥ
puṁsaḥ śiśna upasthas tu
prajāty-ānanda-nirvṛteḥ

apām—of water; *vīryasya*—of the semen; *sargasya*—of the generative; *parjanyasya*—of rains; *prajāpateḥ*—of the creator; *puṁsaḥ*—of
the Lord; *śiśnaḥ*—the genitals; *upasthaḥ tu*—the place where the
genitals are situated; *prajāti*—due to begetting; *ānanda*—pleasure;
nirvṛteḥ—cause.

TRANSLATION

From the Lord's genitals originate water, semen, generatives,
rains, and the procreators. His genitals are the cause of a pleasure
that counteracts the distress of begetting.

PURPORT

The genitals and the pleasure of begetting counteract the distresses of
family encumbrances. One would cease to generate altogether if there
were not, by the grace of the Lord, a coating, a pleasure-giving substance, on the surface of the generative organs. This substance gives a
pleasure so intense that it counteracts fully the distress of family encumbrances. A person is so captivated by this pleasure-giving substance
that he is not satisfied by begetting a single child, but increases the number of children, with great risk in regard to maintaining them, simply for
this pleasure-giving substance. This pleasure-giving substance is not
false, however, because it originates from the transcendental body of the
Lord. In other words, the pleasure-giving substance is a reality, but it has
taken on an aspect of pervertedness on account of material contamination. In the material world, sex life is the cause of many distresses on account of material contact. Therefore, the sex life in the material world
should not be encouraged beyond the necessity. There is a necessity for

generating progency even in the material world, but such generation of children must be carried out with full responsibility for spiritual values. The spiritual values of life can be realized in the human form of material existence, and the human being must adopt family planning with reference to the context of spiritual values, and not otherwise. The degraded form of family restriction by use of contraceptives, etc., is the grossest type of material contamination. Materialists who use these devices want to fully utilize the pleasure potency of the coating on the genitals by artificial means, without knowing the spiritual importance. And without knowledge of spiritual values, the less intelligent man tries to utilize only the material sense pleasure of the genitals.

TEXT 9

पायुर्यमस्य मित्रस्य परिमोक्षस्य नारद ।
हिंसाया निर्ऋतेर्मृत्योर्निरयस्य गुदं स्मृतः ॥ ९ ॥

pāyur yamasya mitrasya
parimokṣasya nārada
himsāyā nirṛter mṛtyor
nirayasya gudaṁ smṛtaḥ

pāyuḥ—the evacuating outlet; *yamasya*—the controlling deity of death; *mitrasya*—of Mitra; *parimokṣasya*—of the evacuating hole; *nārada*—O Nārada; *himsāyāḥ*—of envy; *nirṛteḥ*—of misfortune; *mṛtyoḥ*—of death; *nirayasya*—of hell; *gudam*—the rectum; *smṛtaḥ*—is understood.

TRANSLATION

O Nārada, the evacuating outlet of the universal form of the Lord is the abode of the controlling deity of death, Mitra, and the evacuating hole and the rectum of the Lord is the place of envy, misfortune, death, hell, etc.

TEXT 10

पराभूतेरधर्मस्य तमसश्चापि पश्चिमः ।
नाड्यो नदनदीनां च गोत्राणामस्थिसंहतिः ॥१०॥

parābhūter adharmasya
tamasaś cāpi paścimaḥ
nāḍyo nada-nadīnāṁ ca
gotrāṇām asthi-saṁhatiḥ

parābhūteḥ—of frustration; *adharmasya*—of immorality; *tamasaḥ*—of ignorance; *ca*—and; *api*—as also; *paścimaḥ*—the back; *nāḍyaḥ*—of the intestines; *nada*—of the great rivers; *nadīnām*—of the rivulets; *ca*—also; *gotrāṇām*—of the mountains; *asthi*—bones; *saṁhatiḥ*—accumulation.

TRANSLATION

The back of the Lord is the place for all kinds of frustration and ignorance, as well as for immorality. From His veins flow the great rivers and rivulets, and on His bones are stacked the great mountains.

PURPORT

In order to defy the impersonal conception of the Supreme Personality of Godhead, a systematic analysis of the physiological and anatomical constitution of His transcendental body is given here. It is clear from the available description of the body of the Lord (His universal form) that the form of the Lord is distinct from the forms of ordinary mundane conception. In any case, He is never a formless void. Ignorance is the back of the Lord, and therefore the ignorance of the less intelligent class of men is also not separate from His bodily conception. Since His body is the complete whole of everything that be, one cannot assert that He is impersonal only. On the contrary, the perfect description of the Lord holds that He is both impersonal and personal simultaneously. The Personality of Godhead is the original feature of the Lord, and His impersonal emanation is but the reflection of His transcendental body. Those who are fortunate enough to have a view of the Lord from the front can realize His personal feature, whereas those who are frustrated and are thus kept on the ignorance side of the Lord, or, in other words, those who have the view of the Lord from the back, realize Him in His impersonal feature.

TEXT 11

अव्यक्तरससिन्धूनां भूतानां निधनस्य च ।
उदरं विदितं पुंसो हृदयं मनसः पदम् ॥११॥

avyakta-rasa-sindhūnāṁ
bhūtānāṁ nidhanasya ca
udaraṁ viditaṁ puṁso
hṛdayaṁ manasaḥ padam

avyakta—the impersonal feature; *rasa-sindhūnām*—of the seas and oceans of water; *bhūtānām*—of those who take birth in the material world; *nidhanasya*—of the annihilation; *ca*—also; *udaram*—His belly; *viditam*—is known by the intelligent class of men; *puṁsaḥ*—of the great personality; *hṛdayam*—the heart; *manasaḥ*—of the subtle body; *padam*—the place.

TRANSLATION

The impersonal feature of the Lord is the abode of great oceans, and His belly is the resting place for the materially annihilated living entities. His heart is the abode of the subtle material bodies of living beings. Thus it is known by the intelligent class of men.

PURPORT

In the *Bhagavad-gītā* (8.17-18) it is stated that according to human calculations one day of Brahmā is equal to one thousand ages of four millenniums (4,300,000 years) each, and the same period is calculated to be his night also. A Brahmā lives for one hundred such years and then dies. A Brahmā, who is generally a great devotee of the Lord, attains liberation after such a downfall. The universe (called the *brahmāṇḍa*, or the round football-like domain controlled by a Brahmā) is thus annihilated, and thus the inhabitants of a particular planet, or of the whole universe, are also annihilated. *Avyakta*, mentioned here in this verse, means the night of Brahmā, when partial annihilation takes place and the living entities of that particular *brahmāṇḍa*, up to the planets of Brahmaloka, along with the big oceans, etc., all repose in the belly of the *virāṭ-puruṣa*. At the end of a Brahmā's night, the creation again takes place, and the

living entities, reserved within the belly of the Lord, are let loose to play
their respective parts as if being awakened from a deep slumber. Since
the living entities are never destroyed, the annihilation of the material
world does not annihilate the existence of the living entities, but until
liberation is attained one has to accept one material body after another,
again and again. The human life is meant for making a solution to this
repeated change of bodies and thereby attaining a place in the spiritual
sky, where everything is eternal, blissful and full of knowledge. In other
words, the subtle forms of the living entities take place in the heart of
the Supreme Being, and such forms take tangible shape at the time of
creation.

TEXT 12

धर्मस्य मम तुभ्यं च कुमाराणां भवस्य च ।
विज्ञानस्य च सत्त्वस्य परस्यात्मा परायणम् ॥१२॥

dharmasya mama tubhyaṁ ca
kumārāṇāṁ bhavasya ca
vijñānasya ca sattvasya
parasyātmā parāyaṇam

dharmasya—of religious principles, or of Yamarāja; mama—mine;
tubhyam—of yours; ca—and; kumārāṇām—of the four Kumāras;
bhavasya—Lord Śiva; ca—and also; vijñānasya—of transcendental
knowledge; ca—also; sattvasya—of truth; parasya—of the great personality; ātmā—consciousness; parāyaṇam—dependent.

TRANSLATION

Also, the consciousness of that great personality is the abode of
religious principles—mine, yours, and those of the four bachelors
Sanaka, Sanātana, Sanat-kumāra and Sanandana. That consciousness is also the abode of truth and transcendental knowledge.

TEXTS 13–16

अहं भवान् भवश्चैव त इमे मुनयोऽग्रजाः ।
सुरासुरनरा नागाः खगा मृगसरीसृपाः ॥१३॥

गन्धर्वाप्सरसो यक्षा रक्षोभूतगणोरगाः ।
पशवः पितरः सिद्धा विद्याध्राश्चरणा द्रुमाः ॥१४॥
अन्ये च विविधा जीवा जलस्थलनभौकसः ।
ग्रहर्क्षकेतवस्तारास्तडितः स्तनयित्नवः ॥१५॥
सर्वं पुरुष एवेदं भूतं भव्यं भवच्च यत् ।
तेनेदमावृतं विश्वं वितस्तिमधितिष्ठति ॥१६॥

aham bhavān bhavaś caiva
ta ime munayo 'grajāḥ
surāsura-narā nāgāḥ
khagā mṛga-sarīsṛpāḥ

gandharvāpsaraso yakṣā
rakṣo-bhūta-gaṇoragāḥ
paśavaḥ pitaraḥ siddhā
vidyādhrāś cāraṇā drumāḥ

anye ca vividhā jīvā
jala-sthala-nabhaukasaḥ
graharkṣa-ketavas tārās
taḍitaḥ stanayitnavaḥ

sarvam puruṣa evedam
bhūtam bhavyam bhavac ca yat
tenedam āvṛtam viśvam
vitastim adhitiṣṭhati

aham—myself; bhavān—yourself; bhavaḥ—Lord Śiva; ca—also; eva—certainly; te—they; ime—all; munayaḥ—the great sages; agra-jāḥ—born before you; sura—the demigods; asura—the demons; narāḥ—the human beings; nāgāḥ—the inhabitants of the Nāga planet; khagāḥ—birds; mṛga—beasts; sarīsṛpāḥ—reptiles; gandharva-apsarasaḥ, yakṣāḥ, rakṣaḥ-bhūta-gaṇa-uragāḥ, paśavaḥ, pitaraḥ, siddhāḥ, vidyādhrāḥ, cāraṇāḥ—all inhabitants of different planets; drumāḥ—the vegetable kingdom; anye—many others; ca—also; vividhāḥ—of different varieties; *jīvāḥ*—living entities; *jala*—water; *sthala*—land; *nabha-okasaḥ*—the inhabitants of the sky, or the birds; *graha*—the asteroids; *ṛkṣa*—the influential stars; *ketavaḥ*—the comets; *tārāḥ*—the luminaries; *taḍitaḥ*—the lightning; *stanayitnavaḥ*—the sound of the clouds; *sarvam*—everything; *puruṣaḥ*—the Personality of Godhead; *eva idam*—certainly all these; *bhūtam*—whatever is created; *bhavyam*—whatever will be created; *bhavat*—and whatever was created in the past; *ca*—also; *yat*—whatever; *tena idam*—it is all by Him; *āvṛtam*—covered; *viśvam*—universally comprehending; *vitastim*—half a cubit; *adhitiṣṭhati*—situated.

TRANSLATION

Beginning from me [Brahmā] down to you and Bhava [Śiva], all the great sages who were born before you, the demigods, the demons, the Nāgas, the human beings, the birds, the beasts, as well as the reptiles, etc., and all phenomenal manifestations of the universes, namely the planets, stars, asteroids, luminaries, lightning, thunder, and the inhabitants of the different planetary systems, namely the Gandharvas, Apsarās, Yakṣas, Rakṣas, Bhūtagaṇas, Uragas, Paśus, Pitās, Siddhas, Vidyādharas, Cāraṇas, and all other different varieties of living entities, including the birds, beasts, trees and everything that be, are all covered by the universal form of the Lord at all times, namely past, present and future, although He is transcendental to all of them, eternally existing in a form not exceeding nine inches.

PURPORT

The Supreme Personality of Godhead, by His partial representation, measuring not more than nine inches as Supersoul, expands by His potential energy in the shape of the universal form, which includes everything manifested in different varieties of organic and inorganic materials. The manifested varieties of the universe are therefore not different from the Lord, just as golden ornaments of different shapes and forms are nondifferent from the original stock reserve of gold. In other words, the Lord is the Supreme Person who controls everything within the creation, and still He remains the supreme separate identity, distinct from all manifested material creation. In the *Bhagavad-gītā* (9.4–5) He is therefore said to be Yogeśvara. Everything rests on the potency of Lord Śrī Kṛṣṇa, and still the Lord is different from and transcendental to all such identities. In the Vedic *Puruṣa-sūkta* of the *Ṛg mantra*, this is also confirmed. This philosophical truth of simultaneous oneness and difference was propounded by Lord Śrī Caitanya Mahāprabhu, and it is known as *acintya-bhedābheda-tattva*. Brahmā, Nārada and all others are simultaneously one with the Lord and different from the Supreme Lord. We are all one with Him, just as the gold ornaments are one in quality with the stock gold, but the individual gold ornament is never equal in quantity with the stock gold. The stock gold is never exhausted even if there are innumerable ornaments emanating from the stock because the stock is *pūrṇam*, complete; even if *pūrṇam* is deducted from the *pūrṇam*, still the supreme *pūrṇam* remains the same *pūrṇam*. This fact is inconceivable to our present imperfect senses. Lord Caitanya therefore defined His theory of philosophy as *acintya* (inconceivable), and as confirmed in the *Bhagavad-gītā* as well as in the *Bhāgavatam*, Lord Caitanya's theory of *acintya-bhedābheda-tattva* is the perfect philosophy of the Absolute Truth.

TEXT 17

स्वधिष्ण्यं प्रतपन् प्राणो बहिश्च प्रतपत्यसौ ।
एवं विराजं प्रतपंस्तपत्यन्तर्बहिः पुमान् ॥१७॥

sva-dhiṣṇyaṁ pratapan prāṇo
bahiś ca pratapaty asau
evaṁ virājaṁ pratapaṁs
tapaty antar bahiḥ pumān

sva-dhiṣṇyam—radiation; *pratapan*—by expansion; *prāṇaḥ*—living energy; *bahiḥ*—external; *ca*—also; *pratapati*—illuminated; *asau*—the sun; *evam*—in the same way; *virājam*—the universal form; *pratapan*—by expansion of; *tapati*—enlivens; *antaḥ*—internally; *bahiḥ*—externally; *pumān*—the Supreme Personality.

TRANSLATION

The sun illuminates both internally and externally by expanding its radiation; similarly, the Supreme Personality of Godhead, by expanding His universal form, maintains everything in the creation both internally and externally.

PURPORT

The universal form of the Lord, or the impersonal feature of the Lord known as the *brahmajyoti*, is clearly explained here and compared to the radiation of the sun. The sunshine may expand all over the universe, but the source of the sunshine, namely the sun planet or the deity known as Sūrya-nārāyaṇa, is the basis of such radiation. Similarly, the Supreme Personality of Godhead Lord Kṛṣṇa is the basis of the impersonal *brahmajyoti* radiation, or the impersonal feature of the Lord. This is confirmed in the *Bhagavad-gītā* (14.27). So the universal form of the Lord is the secondary imagination of the impersonal form of the Lord, but the primary form of the Lord is Śyāmasundara, with two hands, playing on His eternal flute. Seventy-five percent of the expansive radiation of the Lord is manifested in the spiritual sky (*tripād-vibhūti*), and twenty-five percent of His personal radiation comprehends the entire expansion of the material universes. This is also explained and stated in the *Bhagavad-gītā* (10.42). Thus the seventy-five percent expansion of His radiation is called His internal energy, whereas the twenty-five percent expansion is called the external energy of the Lord. The living entities, who are residents of the spiritual as well as the material expansions, are His marginal energy (*taṭastha-śakti*), and they are at liberty to live in either of the energies, external or internal. Those who live within the spiritual expansion of the Lord are called liberated souls, whereas the residents of the external expansion are called the conditioned souls. We can just make an estimate of the number of the residents of the internal expansions in comparison with the number of residents in the external energy and may easily conclude that the liberated souls are far more numerous than the conditioned souls.

TEXT 18

सोऽमृतस्याभयस्येशो मर्त्येमन्नं यदत्यगात् ।
महिमैष ततो ब्रह्मन् पुरुषस्य दुरत्ययः ॥१८॥

so 'mṛtasyābhayasyeśo
martyam annaṁ yad atyagāt

mahimaiṣa tato brahman
puruṣasya duratyayaḥ

saḥ—He (the Lord); *amṛtasya*—of deathlessness; *abhayasya*—of
fearlessness; *īśaḥ*—the controller; *martyam*—dying; *annam*—fruitive
action; *yat*—one who has; *atyagāt*—has transcended; *mahimā*—the glories; *eṣaḥ*—of Him; *tataḥ*—therefore; *brahman*—O brāhmaṇa Nārada;
puruṣasya—of the Supreme Personality; *duratyayaḥ*—immeasurable.

TRANSLATION

The Supreme Personality of Godhead is the controller of immortality and fearlessness, and He is transcendental to death and
the fruitive actions of the material world. O Nārada, O brāhmaṇa,
it is therefore difficult to measure the glories of the Supreme
Person.

PURPORT

The glories of the Lord, in the transcendental seventy-five percent of
the Lord's internal potency, are stated in the *Padma Purāṇa* (*Uttara-
khaṇḍa*). It is said there that those planets in the spiritual sky, which
comprises the seventy-five percent expansion of the internal potency of
the Lord, are far, far greater than those planets in the total universes
composed of the external potency of the Lord. In the *Caitanya-
caritāmṛta*, the total universes in the external potency of the Lord are
compared to a bucketful of mustard seeds. One mustard seed is calculated to be a universe itself. In one of the universes, in which we are now
living, the number of planets cannot be counted by human energy, and
so how can we think of the sum total in all the universes, which are compared to a bucketful of mustard seeds? And the planets in the spiritual
sky are at least three times the number of those in the material sky. Such
planets, being spiritual, are in fact transcendental to the material modes;
therefore they are constituted in the mode of unalloyed goodness only.
The conception of spiritual bliss (*brahmānanda*) is fully present in those
planets. Each of them is eternal, indestructible and free from all kinds of
inebrieties experienced in the material world. Each of them is self-
illuminating and more powerfully dazzling than (if we can imagine) the

total sunshine of millions of mundane suns. The inhabitants of those planets are liberated from birth, death, old age and diseases and have full knowledge of everything; they are all godly and free from all sorts of material hankerings. They have nothing to do there except to render transcendental loving service to the Supreme Lord Nārāyaṇa, who is the predominating Deity of such Vaikuṇṭha planets. Those liberated souls are engaged incessantly in singing songs mentioned in the *Sāma Veda* (*vedaiḥ sāṅga-pada-kramopaniṣadair gāyanti yaṁ sāmagāḥ*). All of them are personifications of the five *Upaniṣads*. *Tripād-vibhūti*, or the seventy-five percent known as the internal potency of the Lord, is to be understood as the kingdom of God far beyond the material sky; and when we speak of *pāda-vibhūti*, or the twenty-five percent comprising His external energy, we should understand that this refers to the sphere of the material world. It is also said in the *Padma Purāṇa* that the kingdom of *tripād-vibhūti* is transcendental, whereas the *pāda-vibhūti* is mundane; *tripād-vibhūti* is eternal, whereas the *pāda-vibhūti* is transient. The Lord and His eternal servitors in the transcendental kingdom all have eternal forms which are auspicious, infallible, spiritual and eternally youthful. In other words, there is no birth, death, old age and disease. That eternal land is full of transcendental enjoyment and full of beauty and bliss. This very fact is also corroborated in this verse of *Śrīmad-Bhāgavatam*, and the transcendental nature is described as *amṛta*. As described in the *Vedas*, *utāmṛtatvasyeśānaḥ:* the Supreme Lord is the Lord of immortality, or in other words, the Lord is immortal, and because He is the Lord of immortality He can award immortality to His devotees. In the *Bhagavad-gītā* (8.16) the Lord also assures that whoever may go to His abode of immortality shall never return to this mortal land of threefold miseries. The Lord is not like the mundane lord. The mundane master or lord never enjoys equally with his subordinates, nor is a mundane lord immortal, nor can he award immortality to his subordinate. The Supreme Lord, who is the leader of all living entities, can award all the qualities of His personality unto His devotees, including immortality and spiritual bliss. In the material world there is always anxiety or fearfulness in the hearts of all living entities, but the Lord, being Himself the supreme fearless, also awards the same quality of fearlessness to His pure devotees. Mundane existence is itself a kind of fear because in all mundane bodies the effects of birth, death, old age and disease always keep a living being compact in fear. In the mundane world, there is always the influence of time, which changes things from one stage to another, and the living entity, originally being *avikāra*, or unchangeable, suffers a great deal on account of changes due to the influence of time. The changing effects of eternal time are conspicuously absent in the immortal kingdom of God, which should therefore be understood to have no influence of time and therefore no fear whatsoever. In the material world, so-called happiness is the result of one's own work. One can become a rich man by dint of one's own hard labor, and there are always fear and doubts as to the duration of such acquired happiness. But in the kingdom of God, no one has to endeavor to attain a standard of happiness. Happiness is the nature of the spirit, as stated in the *Vedānta-sūtras: ānandamayo 'bhyāsāt*—the spirit is by nature full of happiness. Happiness in spiritual nature always increases in volume with a new phase of appreciation; there is no question of decreasing the bliss. Such unalloyed spiritual bliss is nowhere to be found within the orbit of the material universe, including the Janaloka planets, or, for that matter, the Maharloka or Satyaloka planets, because even Lord Brahmā is subject to the laws of fruitive actions and the law of birth and death. It is therefore stated here: *duratyayaḥ*, or, in other words, spiritual happiness in the eternal kingdom of God cannot be imagined even by the great *brahmacārīs* or *sannyāsīs* who are eligible to be promoted to the planets beyond the region of heaven. Or, the greatness of the Supreme Lord is so great that it cannot be imagined even by the great *brahmacārīs* or *sannyāsīs*, but such happiness is factually attained by the unalloyed devotees of the Lord, by His divine grace.

TEXT 19

पादेषु सर्वभूतानि पुंसः स्थितिपदो विदुः ।
अमृतं क्षेममभयं त्रिमूर्ध्नोऽधायि मूर्धसु ॥१९॥

pādeṣu sarva-bhūtāni
puṁsaḥ sthiti-pado viduḥ
amṛtaṁ kṣemam abhayaṁ
tri-mūrdhno 'dhāyi mūrdhasu

pādeṣu—in the one fourth; *sarva*—all; *bhūtāni*—living entities; *puṁsaḥ*—of the Supreme Person; *sthiti-padaḥ*—the reservoir of all material opulence; *viduḥ*—you should know; *amṛtam*—deathlessness; *kṣemam*—all happiness, free from the anxiety of old age, diseases, etc.; *abhayam*—fearlessness; *tri-mūrdhnaḥ*—beyond the three higher planetary systems; *adhāyi*—exist; *mūrdhasu*—beyond the material coverings.

TRANSLATION

The Supreme Personality of Godhead is to be known as the supreme reservoir of all material opulences by the one fourth of His energy in which all the living entities exist. Deathlessness, fearlessness and freedom from the anxieties of old age and disease exist in the kingdom of God, which is beyond the three higher planetary systems and beyond the material coverings.

PURPORT

Out of the total manifestations of the *sandhinī* energy of the Lord, one fourth is displayed in the material world, and three fourths are displayed in the spiritual world. The Lord's energy is divided into three component parts, namely *sandhinī*, *saṁvit* and *hlādinī*; in other words, He is the full manifestation of existence, knowledge and bliss. In the material world such a sense of existence, knowledge and pleasure is meagerly exhibited, and all living entities, who are minute parts and parcels of the Lord, are eligible to relish such consciousness of existence, knowledge and bliss very minutely in the liberated stage, whereas in the conditioned stage of material existence they can hardly appreciate what is the factual, existential, cognizable and pure happiness of life. The liberated souls, who exist in far greater numerical strength than those souls in the material world, can factually experience the potency of the above-mentioned *sandhinī*, *saṁvit* and *hlādinī* energies of the Lord in the matter of deathlessness, fearlessness and freedom from old age and disease.

In the material world, the planetary systems are arranged in three spheres, called *triloka*, or Svarga, Martya and Pātāla, and all of them constitute only one fourth of the total *sandhinī* energy. Beyond that is the spiritual sky where the Vaikuṇṭha planets exist beyond the coverings of seven material strata. In none of the *triloka* planetary systems can one experience the status of immortality, full knowledge and full bliss. The upper three planetary systems are called *sāttvika* planets because they provide facilities for a long duration of life and relative freedom from disease and old age, as well as a sense of fearlessness. The great sages and saints are promoted beyond the heavenly planets to Maharloka, but that also is not the place of complete fearlessness because at the end of one *kalpa* the Maharloka is annihilated and the inhabitants have to transport themselves to still higher planets. Yet even on these planets no one is immune to death. There may be a comparative extension of life, expansion of knowledge and sense of full bliss, but factual deathlessness, fearlessness and freedom from old age, diseases, etc., are possible only beyond the material spheres of the coverings of the material sky. Such things are situated on the head (*adhāyi mūrdhasu*).

TEXT 20

पादास्त्रयो बहिश्चासन्नप्रजानां य आश्रमाः ।
अन्तस्त्रिलोक्यास्त्वपरो गृह्मेधोऽबृहद्व्रतः ॥२०॥

pādās trayo bahiś cāsann
aprajānāṁ ya āśramāḥ
antas tri-lokyās tv aparo
gṛha-medho 'bṛhad-vrataḥ

pādāḥ trayaḥ—the cosmos of three fourths of the Lord's energy; *bahiḥ*—thus situated beyond; *ca*—and for all; *āsan*—were; *aprajānām*—of those who are not meant for rebirth; *ye*—those; *āśramāḥ*—status of life; *antaḥ*—within; *tri-lokyāḥ*—of the three worlds; *tu*—but; *aparaḥ*—others; *gṛha-medhaḥ*—attached to family life; *abṛhat-vrataḥ*—without strictly following a vow of celibacy.

TRANSLATION

The spiritual world, which consists of three fourths of the Lord's energy, is situated beyond this material world, and it is especially meant for those who will never be reborn. Others, who are attached to family life and who do not strictly follow celibacy vows, must live within the three material worlds.

PURPORT

The climax of the system of *varṇāśrama-dharma*, or *sanātana-dharma*, is clearly expressed here in this particular verse of *Śrīmad-Bhāgavatam*. The highest benefit that can be awarded to a human being is to train him to be detached from sex life, particularly because it is only due to sex indulgence that the conditioned life of material existence continues birth after birth. Human civilization in which there is no control of sex life is a fourth-class civilization because in such an atmosphere there is no liberation of the soul encaged in the material body. Birth, death, old age and disease are related to the material body, and they have nothing to do with the spirit soul. But as long as the bodily attachment for sensual enjoyment is encouraged, the individual spirit soul is forced to continue the repetition of birth and death on account of the material body, which is compared to garments subjected to the law of deterioration.

In order to award the highest benefit of human life, the *varṇāśrama* system trains the follower to adopt the vow of celibacy beginning from the order of *brahmacārī*. The *brahmacārī* life is for students who are educated to follow strictly the vow of celibacy. Youngsters who have had no taste of sex life can easily follow the vow of celibacy, and once fixed in the principle of such a life, one can very easily continue to the highest perfectional stage, attaining the kingdom of the three-fourths energy of the Lord. It is already explained that in the cosmos of three-fourths energy of the Lord there is neither death nor fear, and one is full of the blissful life of happiness and knowledge. A householder attached to family life can easily give up such a life of sex indulgence if he has been trained in the principles of the life of a *brahmacārī*. A householder is recommended to quit home at the end of fifty years (*pañcaśordhvaṁ vanaṁ vrajet*) and live a life in the forest; then, being fully detached from family affection, he may accept the order of renunciation as a *sannyāsī* fully engaged in the service of the Lord. Any form of religious principles in which the followers are trained to pursue the vow of celibacy is good for the human being because only those who are trained in that way can end the miserable life of material existence. The principles of *nirvāṇa*, as recommended by Lord Buddha, are also meant for ending the miserable life of material existence. And this process, in the highest degree, is recommended here in the *Śrīmad-Bhāgavatam*, with clear perception of ideal perfection, although basically there is no difference between the process of Buddhists, Śaṅkarites and Vaiṣṇavites. For promotion to the highest status of perfection, namely freedom from birth and death, anxiety and fearfulness, not one of these processes allows the follower to break the vow of celibacy.

The householders and persons who have deliberately broken the vow of celibacy cannot enter into the kingdom of deathlessness. The pious householders or the fallen *yogīs* or the fallen transcendentalists can be promoted to the higher planets within the material world (one fourth of the energy of the Lord), but they will fail to enter into the kingdom of deathlessness. *Abṛhad-vratas* are those who have broken the vow of celibacy. The *vānaprasthas*, or those retired from family life, and the *sannyāsīs*, or the renounced persons, cannot break the vow of celibacy if they want success in the process. The *brahmacārīs*, *vānaprasthas* and *sannyāsīs* do not intend to take rebirth (*apraja*), nor are they meant for secretly indulging in sex life. Such a falldown by the spiritualist may be compensated by another chance for human life in good families of learned *brāhmaṇas* or of rich merchants for another term of elevation, but the best thing is to attain the highest perfection of deathlessness as soon as the human form of life is attained; otherwise the whole policy of human life will prove to be a total failure. Lord Caitanya was very strict in advising His followers in this matter of celibacy. One of His personal attendants, Choṭa Haridāsa, was severly punished by Lord Caitanya because of his failure to observe the vow of celibacy. For a transcendentalist, therefore, who at all wants to be promoted to the kingdom beyond material miseries, it is worse than suicide to deliberately indulge in sex life, especially in the renounced order of life. Sex life in the renounced order of life is the most perverted form of religious life, and such a misguided person can only be saved if, by chance, he meets a pure devotee.

TEXT 21

सृती विचक्रमे विश्वङ् साश्नानशने उभे ।
यदविद्या च विद्या च पुरुषस्तूभयाश्रयः ॥२१॥

srṭī vicakrame viśvaṅ
śāsānānaśane ubhe
yad avidyā ca vidyā ca
puruṣas tūbhayāśrayaḥ

srṭī—the destination of the living entities; *vicakrame*—exists comprehensively; *viśvaṅ*—the all-pervading Personality of Godhead; *śāsana*—activities of lording it over; *anaśane*—activities in devotional service; *ubhe*—both; *yat*—what is; *avidyā*—nescience; *ca*—as well as; *vidyā*—factual knowledge; *ca*—and; *puruṣaḥ*—the Supreme Person; *tu*—but; *ubhaya*—for both of them; *āśrayaḥ*—the master.

TRANSLATION

By His energies, the all-pervading Personality of Godhead is thus comprehensively the master in the activities of controlling and in devotional service. He is the ultimate master of both nescience and factual knowledge of all situations.

PURPORT

The word *viśvaṅ* is significant in this verse. One who travels perfectly in every field of activity is called the *puruṣa* or *kṣetrajña*. These two terms, *kṣetrajña* and *puruṣa*, are equally applicable to both the individual self and the Supreme Self, the Lord. In the *Bhagavad-gītā* (13.3) the matter is explained as follows:

kṣetrajñaṁ cāpi māṁ viddhi
sarva-kṣetreṣu bhārata
kṣetra-kṣetrajñayor jñānaṁ
yat taj jñānaṁ matam mama

Kṣetra means the place, and one who knows the place is called the *kṣetrajña*. The individual self knows about his limited field of activities, but the Supreme Self, the Lord, knows about the unlimited field of activities. The individual soul knows about his own thinking, feeling and willing activities, but the Supersoul, or the Paramātmā, the supreme controller, being present everywhere, knows everyone's thinking, feeling and willing activities, and as such the individual living entity is the

minute master of his personal affairs whereas the Supreme Personality
of Godhead is the master of everyone's affairs, past, present and future
(*vedāhaṁ samatītāni*, etc.). Only the ignorant person does not know this
difference between the Lord and the living entities. The living entities,
as distinguished from incognizant matter, may be qualitatively equal to
the Lord in cognizance, but the living entity can never be equal to the
Lord in full knowledge of past, present and future.

And because the living entity is partially cognizant, he is therefore
sometimes forgetful of his own identity. This forgetfulness is specifically
manifested in the field of the *ekapād-vibhūti* of the Lord, or in the material world, but in the *tripād-vibhūti* field of actions, or in the spiritual
world, there is no forgetfulness by the living entities, who are free from
all kinds of contaminations resulting from the forgetful state of existence. The material body is the symbol of the gross and subtle form of
forgetfulness; therefore the whole atmosphere of the material world is
called *avidyā*, or nescience, whereas the whole atmosphere of the spiritual world is called *vidyā*, or full of knowledge. There are different
stages of *avidyā*, and they are called *dharma, artha* and *mokṣa*. The idea
of *mokṣa*, or liberation, held by the monist in the matter of oneness of
the living entity and the Lord by ultimate merging in one, is also the last
stage of materialism or forgetfulness. Knowledge of the qualitative oneness of the self and Superself is partial knowledge and ignorance also because there is no knowledge of quantitative difference, as explained
above. The individual self can never be equal to the Lord in cognizance;
otherwise he could not be placed in the state of forgetfulness. So, because
there is a stage of forgetfulness of the individual selves, or the living entities, there is always a gulf of difference between the Lord and the living
entity, as between the part and the whole. The part is never equal to the
whole. So the conception of one hundred percent equality of the living
being with the Lord is also nescience.

In the field of nescience, activities are directed toward lording it over
the creation. In the material world, therefore, everyone is engaged in acquiring material opulence to lord it over the material world. Therefore
there is always clash and frustration, which are the symptoms of nescience. But in the field of knowledge, there is devotional service to the
Lord (*bhakti*). Therefore there is no chance of being contaminated by the
influence of nescience or forgetfulness (*avidyā*) in the liberated stage of

devotional activities. The Lord is thus the proprietor of the fields both of
nescience and of cognition, and it remains the choice of the living entity
to exist in either of the above regions.

TEXT 22

यस्मादण्डं विराड् जज्ञे भूतेन्द्रियगुणात्मकः ।
तद् द्रव्यमत्यगाद् विश्वं गोभिः सूर्य इवातपन् ॥२२॥

yasmād aṇḍaṁ virāḍ jajñe
bhūtendriya-guṇātmakaḥ
tad dravyam atyagād viśvaṁ
gobhiḥ sūrya ivātapan

yasmāt—from whom; *aṇḍam*—the universal globes; *virāṭ*—and the
gigantic universal form; *jajñe*—appeared; *bhūta*—elements; *indriya*—
senses; *guṇa-ātmakaḥ*—qualitative; *tat dravyam*—the universes and
the universal form, etc.; *atyagāt*—surpassed; *viśvam*—all the universes; *gobhiḥ*—by the rays; *sūryaḥ*—the sun; *iva*—like; *ātapan*—distributed rays and heat.

TRANSLATION

**From that Personality of Godhead, all the universal globes and
the universal form with all material elements, qualities and senses
are generated. Yet He is aloof from such material manifestations,
like the sun, which is separate from its rays and heat.**

PURPORT

The supreme truth has been ascertained in the previous verse as
puruṣa or the *puruṣottama*, the Supreme Person. The Absolute Person is
the *īśvara*, or the supreme controller, by His different energies. The
ekapād-vibhūti manifestation of the material energy of the Lord is just
like one of the many mistresses of the Lord, by whom the Lord is not so
much attracted, as indicated in the language of the *Gītā* (*bhinnā
prakṛtiḥ*). But the region of the *tripād-vibhūti*, being a pure spiritual
manifestation of the energy of the Lord, is, so to speak, more attractive to

Him. The Lord, therefore, generates the material manifestations by impregnating the material energy, and then, within the manifestation, He expands Himself as the gigantic form of the *viśva-rūpa*. The *viśva-rūpa*, as it was shown to Arjuna, is not the original form of the Lord. The original form of the Lord is the transcendental form of Puruṣottama, or Kṛṣṇa Himself. It is very nicely explained herein that He expands Himself just like the sun. The sun expands itself by its terrible heat and rays, yet the sun is always aloof from such rays and heat. The impersonalist takes into consideration the rays of the Lord without any information of the tangible, transcendental, eternal form of the Lord, known as Kṛṣṇa. Therefore Kṛṣṇa, in His supreme personal form, with two hands and flute, is bewildering for the impersonalists who can accommodate only the gigantic *viśva-rūpa* of the Lord. They should know that the rays of the sun are secondary to the sun, and similarly the impersonal gigantic form of the Lord is also secondary to the personal form as Puruṣottama. The *Brahma-saṁhitā* (5.37) confirms this statement as follows:

> ānanda-cinmaya-rasa-pratibhāvitābhis
> tābhir ya eva nija-rūpatayā kalābhiḥ
> goloka eva nivasaty akhilātma-bhūto
> govindam ādi-puruṣaṁ tam ahaṁ bhajāmi

"The Supreme Personality of Godhead, Govinda, the one who enlivens the senses of everyone by His personal bodily rays, resides in His transcendental abode, called Goloka. Yet He is present in every nook and corner of His creation by expansion of happy spiritual rays, equal in power to His personal potency of bliss." He is therefore simultaneously personal and impersonal by His inconceivable potency, or He is the one without a second, displaying complete unity in a diversity of material and spiritual manifestations. He is separate from everything, and still nothing is different from Him.

TEXT 23

यदास्य नाभ्यान्नलिनादहमासं महात्मनः ।
नाविदं यज्ञसम्भारान् पुरुषावयवानृते ॥२३॥

yadāsya nābhyān nalinād
aham āsaṁ mahātmanaḥ
nāvidaṁ yajña-sambhārān
puruṣāvayavān ṛte

yadā—at the time of; *asya*—His; *nābhyāt*—from the abdomen; *nalināt*—from the lotus flower; *aham*—myself; *āsam*—took my birth; *mahā-ātmanaḥ*—of the great person; *na avidam*—did not know; *yajña*—sacrificial; *sambhārān*—ingredients; *puruṣa*—of the Lord; *avayavān*—personal bodily limbs; *ṛte*—except.

TRANSLATION

When I was born from the abdominal lotus flower of the Lord [Mahā-Viṣṇu], the great person, I had no ingredients for sacrificial performances except the bodily limbs of the great Personality of Godhead.

PURPORT

Lord Brahmā, the creator of the cosmic manifestation, is known as Svayambhū, or one who is born without father and mother. The general process is that a living creature is born out of the sex combination of the male father and the female mother. But Brahmā, the firstborn living being, is born out of the abdominal lotus flower of the Mahā-Viṣṇu plenary expansion of Lord Kṛṣṇa. The abdominal lotus flower is part of the Lord's bodily limbs, and Brahmā is born out of the lotus flower. Therefore Lord Brahmā is also a part of the Lord's body. Brahmā, after his appearance in the gigantic hollow of the universe, saw darkness and nothing else. He felt perplexity, and from his heart he was inspired by the Lord to undergo austerity, thereby acquiring the ingredients for sacrificial performances. But there was nothing besides the two of them, namely the Personality of Mahā-Viṣṇu and Brahmā himself, born of the bodily part of the Lord. For sacrificial performances many ingredients were in need, especially animals. The animal sacrifice is never meant for killing the animal, but for achieving the successful result of the sacrifice.

The animal offered in the sacrificial fire is, so to speak, destroyed, but the next moment it is given a new life by dint of the Vedic hymns chanted by the expert priest. When such an expert priest is not available, the animal sacrifice in the fire of the sacrificial altar is forbidden. Thus Brahmā created even the sacrificial ingredients out of the bodily limbs of the Garbhodakaśāyī Viṣṇu, which means that the cosmic order was created by Brahmā himself. Also, nothing is created out of nothing, but everything is created from the person of the Lord. The Lord says in the *Bhagavad-gītā* (10.8), *ahaṁ sarvasya prabhavo mattaḥ sarvaṁ pravartate.* "Everything is made from My bodily limbs, and I am therefore the original source of all creations."

The impersonalists argue that there is no use in worshiping the Lord when everything is nothing but the Lord Himself. The personalist, however, worships the Lord out of a great sense of gratitude, utilizing the ingredients born out of the bodily limbs of the Lord. The fruits and flowers are available from the body of the earth, and yet mother earth is worshiped by the sensible devotee with ingredients born from the earth. Similarly, mother Ganges is worshiped by the water of the Ganges, and yet the worshiper enjoys the result of such worship. Worship of the Lord is also performed by the ingredients born from the bodily limbs of the Lord, and yet the worshiper, who is himself a part of the Lord, achieves the result of devotional service to the Lord. While the impersonalist wrongly concludes that he is the Lord himself, the personalist, out of a great gratitude, worships the Lord in devotional service, knowing perfectly well that nothing is different from the Lord. The devotee therefore endeavors to apply everything in the service of the Lord because he knows that everything is the property of the Lord and that no one can claim anything as one's own. This perfect conception of oneness helps the worshiper in being engaged in His loving service, whereas the impersonalist, being falsely puffed up, remains a nondevotee forever, without being recognized by the Lord.

TEXT 24

तेषु यज्ञस्य पशवः सवनस्पतयः कुशाः ।
इदं च देवयजनं कालश्चोरुगुणान्वितः ॥२४॥

teṣu yajñasya paśavaḥ
savanaspatayaḥ kuśāḥ
idaṁ ca deva-yajanam
kālaś coru-guṇānvitaḥ

teṣu—in such sacrifices; *yajñasya*—of the sacrificial performance; *paśavaḥ*—the animals or the sacrificial ingredients; *sa-vanaspatayaḥ*—along with flowers and leaves; *kuśāḥ*—the straw; *idam*—all these; *ca*—as also; *deva-yajanam*—the sacrificial altar; *kālaḥ*—a suitable time; *ca*—as also; *uru*—great; *guṇa-anvitaḥ*—qualified.

TRANSLATION

For performing sacrificial ceremonies, one requires sacrificial ingredients, such as flowers, leaves and straw, along with the sacrificial altar and a suitable time [spring].

TEXT 25

वस्तून्योषधयः स्नेहा रसलोहमृदो जलम् ।
ऋचो यजूंषि सामानि चातुर्होत्रं च सत्तम ॥२५॥

vastūny oṣadhayaḥ snehā
rasa-loha-mṛdo jalam
ṛco yajūṁṣi sāmāni
cātur-hotraṁ ca sattama

vastūni—utensils; *oṣadhayaḥ*—grains; *snehāḥ*—clarified butter; *rasa-loha-mṛdaḥ*—honey, gold and earth; *jalam*—water; *ṛcaḥ*—the Ṛg Veda; *yajūṁṣi*—the Yajur Veda; *sāmāni*—the Sāma Veda; *cātuḥ-hotram*—four persons conducting the performance; *ca*—all these; *sattama*—O most pious one.

TRANSLATION

Other requirements are utensils, grains, clarified butter, honey, gold, earth, water, the Ṛg Veda, Yajur Veda and Sāma Veda and four priests to perform the sacrifice.

PURPORT

To perform a sacrifice successfully, at least four expert priests are needed: one who can offer (*hotā*), one who can chant (*udgātā*), one who can kindle the sacrificial fire without the aid of separate fire (*adhvaryu*), and one who can supervise (*brahmā*). Such sacrifices were conducted from the birth of Brahmā, the first living creature, and were carried on till the reign of Mahārāja Yudhiṣṭhira. But such expert *brāhmaṇa* priests are very rare in this age of corruption and quarrel, and therefore in the present age only the *yajña* of chanting the holy name of the Lord is recommended. The scriptures enjoin:

harer nāma harer nāma
harer nāmaiva kevalam
kalau nāsty eva nāsty eva
nāsty eva gatir anyathā

TEXT 26

नामधेयानि मन्त्राश्च दक्षिणाश्च व्रतानि च ।
देवतानुक्रमः कल्पः सङ्कल्पस्तन्त्रमेव च ॥२६॥

nāma-dheyāni mantrāś ca
dakṣiṇāś ca vratāni ca
devatānukramaḥ kalpaḥ
saṅkalpas tantram eva ca

nāma-dheyāni—invoking the names of the demigods; *mantrāḥ*—specific hymns to offer to a particular demigod; *ca*—also; *dakṣiṇāḥ*—reward; *ca*—and; *vratāni*—vows; *ca*—and; *devatā-anukramaḥ*—one demigod after another; *kalpaḥ*—the specific scripture; *saṅkalpaḥ*—the specific purpose; *tantram*—a particular process; *eva*—as they are; *ca*—also.

TRANSLATION

Other necessities include invoking the different names of the demigods by specific hymns and vows of recompense, in accordance with the particular scripture, for specific purposes and by specific processes.

PURPORT

The whole process of offering sacrifice is under the category of fruitive action, and such activities are extremely scientific. They mainly depend on the process of vibrating sounds with a particular accent. It is a great science, and due to being out of proper use for more than four thousand years, for want of qualified *brāhmaṇas*, such performances of sacrifice are no longer effective. Nor are they recommended in this fallen age. Any such sacrifice undertaken in this age as a matter of show may simply be a cheating process by the clever priestly order. But such a show of sacrifices cannot be effective at any stage. Fruitive action is being carried on by the help of material science and to a little extent by gross material help, but the materialists await a still more subtle advancement in the process of vibrating sounds on which the Vedic hymns are established. Gross material science cannot divert the real purpose of human life. They can only increase the artificial needs of life without any solution to the problems of life; therefore the way of materialistic life leads to the wrong type of human civilization. Since the ultimate aim of life is spiritual realization, the direct way of invoking the holy name of the Lord, as mentioned above, is precisely recommended by Lord Caitanya, and people of the modern age can easily take advantage of this simple process, which is tenable for the condition of the complicated social structure.

TEXT 27

गतयो मतयश्चैव   प्रायश्चित्तं समर्पणम् ।
पुरुषावयवैरेते सम्भाराः सम्भृता मया ॥२७॥

gatayo matayaś caiva
prāyaścittaṁ samarpaṇam
puruṣāvayavair ete
sambhārāḥ sambhṛtā mayā

gatayaḥ—progress to the ultimate goal (Viṣṇu); *matayaḥ*—worshiping the demigods; *ca*—as also; *eva*—certainly; *prāyaścittam*—

compensation; *samarpaṇam*—ultimate offering; *puruṣa*—the Personality of Godhead; *avayavaiḥ*—from the parts of the body of the Personality of Godhead; *ete*—these; *sambhārāḥ*—the ingredients; *sambhṛtāḥ*—were arranged; *mayā*—by me.

TRANSLATION

Thus I had to arrange all these necessary ingredients and paraphernalia of sacrifice from the personal bodily parts of the Personality of Godhead. By invocation of the demigods' names, the ultimate goal, Viṣṇu, was gradually attained, and thus compensation and ultimate offering were complete.

PURPORT

In this verse, special stress is given to the person of the Supreme Lord, and not to His impersonal *brahmajyoti*, as being the source of all supplies. Nārāyaṇa, the Supreme Lord, is the goal of sacrificial results, and therefore the Vedic hymns are ultimately meant for attaining this goal. Human life is thus made successful by pleasing Nārāyaṇa and getting entrance into the direct association of Nārāyaṇa in the spiritual kingdom of Vaikuṇṭha.

TEXT 28

इति सम्भृतसम्भारः पुरुषावयवैरहम् ।
तमेव पुरुषं यज्ञं तेनैवायजमीश्वरम् ॥२८॥

iti sambhṛta-sambhāraḥ
puruṣāvayavair aham
tam eva puruṣaṁ yajñaṁ
tenaivāyajam īśvaram

iti—thus; *sambhṛta*—executed; *sambhāraḥ*—equipped myself well; *puruṣa*—the Personality of Godhead; *avayavaiḥ*—by the parts and parcels; *aham*—I; *tam eva*—unto Him; *puruṣam*—the Personality of Godhead; *yajñam*—the enjoyer of all sacrifices; *tena eva*—by all those; *ayajam*—worshiped; *īśvaram*—the supreme controller.

TRANSLATION

Thus I created the ingredients and paraphernalia for offering sacrifice out of the parts of the body of the Supreme Lord, the enjoyer of the sacrifice, and I performed the sacrifice to satisfy the Lord.

PURPORT

People in general are always anxious to have peace of mind or peace in the world, but they do not know how to achieve such a standard of peace in the world. Such peace in the world is obtainable by performances of sacrifice and by practice of austerity. In the *Bhagavad-gītā* (5.29) the following prescription is recommended:

> *bhoktāraṁ yajña-tapasāṁ*
> *sarva-loka-maheśvaram*
> *suhṛdaṁ sarva-bhūtānāṁ*
> *jñātvā māṁ śāntim ṛcchati*

"The *karma-yogīs* know that the Supreme Lord is the factual enjoyer and maintainer of all sacrifices and of the austere life. They also know that the Lord is the ultimate proprietor of all the planets and is the factual friend of all living entities. Such knowledge gradually converts the *karma-yogīs* into pure devotees of the Lord through the association of unalloyed devotees, and thus they are able to be liberated from material bondage."

Brahmā, the original living being within the material world, taught us the way of sacrifice. The word "sacrifice" suggests dedication of one's own interests for satisfaction of a second person. That is the way of all activities. Every man is engaged in sacrificing his interests for others, either in the form of family, society, community, country or the entire human society. But perfection of such sacrifices is attained when they are performed for the sake of the Supreme Person, the Lord. Because the Lord is the proprietor of everything, because the Lord is the friend of all living creatures, and because He is the maintainer of the performer of sacrifice, as well as the supplier of the ingredients of sacrifices, it is He only and no one else who should be satisfied by all sacrifices.

The whole world is engaged in sacrificing energy for advancement of learning, social upliftment, economic development and plans for total improvement of the human condition, but no one is interested in sacrificing for the sake of the Lord, as it is advised in the *Bhagavad-gītā*. Therefore, there is no peace in the world. If men at all want peace in the world, they must practice sacrifice in the interest of the supreme proprietor and friend of all.

TEXT 29

ततस्ते श्रातर इमे प्रजानां पतयो नव ।
अयजन् व्यक्तमव्यक्तं पुरुषं सुसमाहिताः ॥२९॥

tatas te bhrātara ime
prajānām patayo nava
ayajan vyaktam avyaktam
puruṣam su-samāhitāḥ

tataḥ—thereafter; *te*—your; *bhrātaraḥ*—brothers; *ime*—these; *prajānām*—of the living creatures; *patayaḥ*—masters; *nava*—nine; *ayajan*—performed; *vyaktam*—manifested; *avyaktam*—nonmanifested; *puruṣam*—personalities; *su-samāhitāḥ*—with proper rituals.

TRANSLATION

My dear son, thereafter your nine brothers, who are the masters of living creatures, performed the sacrifice with proper rituals to satisfy both the manifested and nonmanifested personalities.

PURPORT

The manifested personalities are the demigods like the ruler of the heavenly kingdom, Indra, and his associates; and the nonmanifested personality is the Lord Himself. The manifested personalities are mundane controllers of the material affairs, whereas the nonmanifested Personality of Godhead is transcendental, beyond the range of the material atmosphere. In this age of Kali the manifested demigods are also not to be seen, for space travel has completely stopped. So both the powerful

demigods and the Supreme Personality of Godhead are nonmanifested to
the covered eyes of the modern man. Modern men want to see everything
with their eyes, although they are not sufficiently qualified. Consequently, they disbelieve in the existence of the demigods or of the
Supreme God. They should see through the pages of authentic scriptures
and should not simply believe their unqualified eyes. Even in these days,
God can also be seen by qualified eyes tinged with the ointment of love
of God.

TEXT 30

ततश्च मनवः काले ईजिरे ऋषयोऽपरे ।
पितरो विबुधा दैत्या मनुष्याः क्रतुभिर्विभुम् ॥३०॥

*tataś ca manavaḥ kāle
ījire ṛṣayo 'pare
pitaro vibudhā daityā
manuṣyāḥ kratubhir vibhum*

tataḥ—thereafter; *ca*—also; *manavaḥ*—the Manus, the fathers of
mankind; *kāle*—in due course of time; *ījire*—worshiped; *ṛṣayaḥ*—great
sages; *apare*—others; *pitaraḥ*—the forefathers; *vibudhāḥ*—the learned
scholars; *daityāḥ*—great devotees of the demigods; *manuṣyāḥ*—
mankind; *kratubhiḥ vibhum*—by performance of sacrifices to please the
Supreme Lord.

TRANSLATION

**Thereafter, the Manus, the fathers of mankind, the great sages,
the forefathers, the learned scholars, the Daityas and mankind
performed sacrifices meant to please the Supreme Lord.**

PURPORT

The *daityas* are devotees of the demigods because they want to derive
the greatest possible material facilities from them. The devotees of the
Lord are *eka-niṣṭha*, or absolutely attached to the devotional service of
the Lord. Therefore they have practically no time to seek the benefits of
material facilities. Because of their realization of their spiritual identity,

they are more concerned with spiritual emancipation than with material comforts.

TEXT 31

नारायणे भगवति तदिदं विश्वमाहितम् ।
गृहीतमायोरुगुणः सर्गादावगुणः स्वतः ॥३१॥

nārāyaṇe bhagavati
tad idaṁ viśvam āhitam
gṛhīta-māyoru-guṇaḥ
sargādāv aguṇaḥ svataḥ

nārāyaṇe—unto Nārāyaṇa; *bhagavati*—the Personality of Godhead; *tat idam*—all these material manifestations; *viśvam*—all the universes; *āhitam*—situated; *gṛhīta*—having accepted; *māyā*—material energies; *uru-guṇaḥ*—greatly powerful; *sarga-ādau*—in creation, maintenance and destruction; *aguṇaḥ*—without affinity for the material modes; *svataḥ*—self-sufficiently.

TRANSLATION

All the material manifestations of the universes are therefore situated in His powerful material energies, which He accepts self-sufficiently, although He is eternally without affinity for the material modes.

PURPORT

The question put by Nārada before Brahmā concerning the sustenance of the material creation is thus answered. Material actions and reactions, as the material scientist can superficially observe, are not basically ultimate truth in regard to creation, maintenance and destruction. The material energy is a potency of the Lord which is displayed in time, accepting the three qualities of goodness, passion and ignorance in the forms of Viṣṇu, Brahmā and Śiva. The material energy thus works under the supreme spell of His Lordship, although He is always transcendental to all such material activities. A rich man constructs a big house by spending his energy in the shape of resources, and similarly he destroys a big house by his resources, but the maintenance is always under his personal care. The Lord is the richest of the rich because He is always fully complete in six opulences. Therefore He is not required to do anything personally, but everything in the material world is carried out by His wishes and direction; therefore, the entire material manifestation is situated in Nārāyaṇa, the Supreme Personality of Godhead. The impersonal conception of the supreme truth is due to lack of knowledge only, and this fact is clearly explained by Brahmājī, who is supposed to be the creator of the universal affairs. Brahmājī is the highest authority in Vedic wisdom, and his assertion in this connection is therefore the supreme information.

TEXT 32

सृजामि तन्नियुक्तोऽहं हरो हरति तद्वशः ।
विश्वं पुरुषरूपेण परिपाति त्रिशक्तिधृक् ॥३२॥

srjāmi tan-niyukto 'ham
haro harati tad-vaśaḥ
viśvaṁ puruṣa-rūpeṇa
paripāti tri-śakti-dhṛk

srjāmi—do create; *tat*—by His; *niyuktaḥ*—appointment; *aham*—I; *haraḥ*—Lord Śiva; *harati*—destroys; *tat-vaśaḥ*—under His subordination; *viśvam*—the whole universe; *puruṣa*—the Personality of Godhead; *rūpeṇa*—by His eternal form; *paripāti*—maintains; *tri-śakti-dhṛk*—the controller of three energies.

TRANSLATION

By His will, I create, Lord Śiva destroys, and He Himself, in His eternal form as the Personality of Godhead, maintains everything. He is the powerful controller of these three energies.

PURPORT

The conception of one without a second is clearly confirmed here. The one is Lord Vāsudeva, and only by His different energies and expansions are different manifestations, both in the material and in the spiritual worlds, maintained. In the material world also, Lord Vāsudeva is everything, as stated in the *Bhagavad-gītā* (7.19). *Vāsudevaḥ sarvam iti:* everything is Vāsudeva only. In the Vedic hymns also the same Vāsudeva is held to be supreme. It is said in the *Vedas, vāsudevāt paro brahman na cānyo 'rtho 'sti tattvataḥ:* in fact there is no greater truth than Vāsudeva. And Lord Kṛṣṇa affirms the same truth in the *Bhagavad-gītā* (7.7). *Mattaḥ parataraṁ nānyat:* "There is nothing above Me [Lord Kṛṣṇa]." So the conception of oneness, as overly stressed by the impersonalist, is also accepted by the personalist devotee of the Lord. The difference is that the impersonalist denies personality in the ultimate issue, whereas the devotee gives more importance to the Personality of Godhead. *Śrīmad-Bhāgavatam* explains this truth in the verse under discussion: Lord Vāsudeva is one without a second, but because He is all-powerful, He can expand Himself as well as display His omnipotencies. The Lord is described here as omnipotent by three energies (*tri-śakti-dhṛk*). So primarily His three energies are internal, marginal and external. This external energy is also displayed in the three modes of goodness, passion and ignorance. Similarly, the internal potency is also displayed in three spiritual modes—*saṁvit, sandhinī* and *hlādinī.* The marginal potency, or the living entities, is also spiritual (*prakṛtiṁ viddhi me parām*), but the living entities are never equal to the Lord. The Lord is *nirasta-sāmya-atiśaya;* in other words, no one is greater than or equal to the Supreme Lord. So the living entities, including even such great personalities as Lord Brahmā and Lord Śiva, are all subordinate to the Lord. In the material world also, in His eternal form of Viṣṇu, He maintains and controls all the affairs of the demigods, including Brahmā and Śiva.

TEXT 33

इति तेऽभिहितं तात यथेदमनुपृच्छसि ।
नान्यद्भगवतः किंचिद्भाव्यं सदसदात्मकम् ॥३३॥

iti te 'bhihitaṁ tāta
yathedam anupṛcchasi
nānyad bhagavataḥ kiñcid
bhāvyaṁ sad-asad-ātmakam

iti—thus; *te*—unto you; *abhihitam*—explained; *tāta*—my dear son; *yathā*—as; *idam*—all these; *anupṛcchasi*—as you have inquired; *na*—

never; *anyat*—anything else; *bhagavataḥ*—beyond the Personality of Godhead; *kiñcit*—nothing; *bhāvyam*—to be thought ever; *sat*—cause; *asat*—effect; *ātmakam*—in the matter of.

TRANSLATION

My dear son, whatever you inquired from me I have thus explained unto you, and you must know for certain that whatever there is (either as cause or as effect, both in the material and spiritual worlds) is dependent on the Supreme Personality of Godhead.

PURPORT

The complete cosmic situation, both in the material and in the spiritual manifestations of the energies of the Lord, is working and moving first as the cause and then as the effect. But the original cause is the Supreme Personality of Godhead. Effects of the original cause become the causes of other effects, and thus everything, either permanent or temporary, is working as cause and effect. And because the Lord is the primeval cause of all persons and all energies, He is called the cause of all causes, as confirmed in the *Brahma-saṁhitā* as well as in the *Bhagavad-gītā*. The *Brahma-saṁhitā* (5.1) affirms:

> *īśvaraḥ paramaḥ kṛṣṇaḥ*
> *sac-cid-ānanda-vigrahaḥ*
> *anādir ādir govindaḥ*
> *sarva-kāraṇa-kāraṇam*

And in the *Bhagavad-gītā* (10.8) it is said:

> *ahaṁ sarvasya prabhavo*
> *mattaḥ sarvaṁ pravartate*
> *iti matvā bhajante māṁ*
> *budhā bhāva-samanvitāḥ*

So the original primeval cause is *vigraha*, the personal, and the impersonal spiritual effulgence, *brahmajyoti*, is also an effect of the Supreme Brahman (*brahmaṇo hi pratiṣṭhāham*), Lord Kṛṣṇa.

TEXT 34

न भारती मेऽङ्ग मृषोपलक्ष्यते
न वै कचिन्मे मनसो मृषा गतिः ।
न मे हृषीकाणि पतन्त्यसत्पथे
यन्मे हृदौत्कण्ठ्यवता धृतो हरिः ॥३४॥

na bhāratī me 'ṅga mṛṣopalakṣyate
na vai kvacin me manaso mṛṣā gatiḥ
na me hṛṣīkāṇi patanty asat-pathe
yan me hṛdautkaṇṭhyavatā dhṛto hariḥ

na—never; *bhāratī*—statements; *me*—mind; *aṅga*—O Nārada; *mṛṣā*—untruth; *upalakṣyate*—prove to be; *na*—never; *vai*—certainly; *kvacit*—at any time; *me*—mine; *manasaḥ*—of the mind; *mṛṣā*—untruth; *gatiḥ*—progress; *na*—nor; *me*—mine; *hṛṣīkāṇi*—senses; *patanti*—degrades; *asat-pathe*—in temporary matter; *yat*—because; *me*—mine; *hṛdā*—heart; *autkaṇṭhyavatā*—by great earnestness; *dhṛtaḥ*—caught hold of; *hariḥ*—the Supreme Personality of Godhead.

TRANSLATION

O Nārada, because I have caught hold of the lotus feet of the Supreme Personality of Godhead, Hari, with great zeal, whatever I say has never proved to have been false. Nor is the progress of my mind ever deterred. Nor are my senses ever degraded by temporary attachment to matter.

PURPORT

Lord Brahmā is the original speaker of Vedic wisdom to Nārada, and Nārada is the distributor of transcendental knowledge all over the world through his various disciples, like Vyāsadeva and others. The followers of Vedic wisdom accept the statements of Brahmājī as gospel truth, and transcendental knowledge is thus being distributed all over the world by the process of disciplic succession from time immemorial, since the beginning of the creation. Lord Brahmā is the perfect liberated living being within the material world, and any sincere student of transcendental knowledge must accept the words and statements of Brahmājī as infallible. The Vedic knowledge is infallible because it comes down directly from the Supreme Lord unto the heart of Brahmā, and since he is the most perfect living being, Brahmājī is always correct to the letter. And this is because Lord Brahmā is a great devotee of the Lord who has earnestly accepted the lotus feet of the Lord as the supreme truth. In the *Brahma-saṁhitā*, which is compiled by Brahmājī, he repeats the aphorism *govindam ādi-puruṣaṁ tam ahaṁ bhajāmi:* "I am a worshiper of the original Personality of Godhead, Govinda, the primeval Lord." So whatever he says, whatever he thinks, and whatever he does normally in his mood are to be accepted as truth because of his direct and very intimate connection with Govinda, the primeval Lord. Śrī Govinda, who pleasingly accepts the loving transcendental service of His devotees, gives all protection to the words and actions of His devotees. The Lord declares in the *Bhagavad-gītā* (9.31), *kaunteya pratijānīhi:* "O son of Kuntī, please declare it." The Lord asks Arjuna to declare, and why? Because sometimes the declaration of Govinda Himself may seem contradictory to mundane creatures, but the mundaner will never find any contradiction in the words of the Lord's devotees. The devotees are especially protected by the Lord so that they may remain infallible. Therefore the process of devotional service always begins in the service of the devotee who appears in disciplic succession. The devotees are always liberated, but that does not mean that they are impersonal. The Lord is a person eternally, and the devotee of the Lord is also a person eternally. Because the devotee has his sense organs even at the liberated stage, he is therefore a person always. And because the devotee's service is accepted by the Lord in full reciprocation, the Lord is also a person in His complete spiritual embodiment. The devotee's senses, being engaged in the service of the Lord, never go astray under the attraction of false material enjoyment. The plans of the devotee never go in vain, and all this is due to the faithful attachment of the devotee for the service of the Lord. This is the standard of perfection and liberation. Anyone, beginning from Brahmājī down to the human being, is at once put on the path of liberation simply by his attachment in great earnestness for the Supreme Lord, Śrī Kṛṣṇa, the primeval Lord. The Lord affirms this in the *Bhagavad-gītā* (14.26):

mām ca yo 'vyabhicāreṇa
bhakti-yogena sevate
sa guṇān samatītyaitān
brahma-bhūyāya kalpate

Anyone, therefore, who is earnestly serious in heart and soul about being in intimate touch with the Personality of Godhead in the relationship of transcendental loving service will always be infallible in words and action. The reason is that the Supreme Lord is Absolute Truth, and anything earnestly dovetailed with the Absolute Truth attains the same transcendental quality. On the other hand, any amount of mental speculation on the strength of material science and knowledge without any bona fide touch with the Absolute Truth is sure to be a mundane untruth and failure, simply due to not being in touch with the Absolute Truth. Such godless, unfaithful words and actions, however materially enriched, are never to be trusted. That is the purport of this important verse. A grain of devotion is more valuable than tons of faithlessness.

TEXT 35

सोऽहं समाम्नायमयस्तपोमयः
प्रजापतीनामभिवन्दितः पतिः ।
आस्थाय योगं निपुणं समाहित-
स्तं नाध्यगच्छं यत आत्मसम्भवः ॥३५॥

so 'haṁ samāmnāyamayas tapomayaḥ
prajāpatīnām abhivanditaḥ patiḥ
āsthāya yogaṁ nipuṇaṁ samāhitas
taṁ nādhyagacchaṁ yata ātma-sambhavaḥ

saḥ aham—myself (the great Brahmā); *samāmnāya-mayaḥ*—in the chain of disciplic succession of Vedic wisdom; *tapaḥ-mayaḥ*—successfully having undergone all austerities; *prajāpatīnām*—of all the forefathers of living entities; *abhivanditaḥ*—worshipable; *patiḥ*—master; *āsthāya*—successfully practiced; *yogam*—mystic powers; *nipuṇam*—very expert; *samāhitaḥ*—self-realized; *tam*—the Supreme

Lord; *na*—did not; *adhyagaccham*—properly understood; *yataḥ*—from whom; *ātma*—self; *sambhavaḥ*—generated.

TRANSLATION

Although I am known as the great Brahmā, perfect in the disciplic succession of Vedic wisdom, and although I have undergone all austerities and am an expert in mystic powers and self-realization, and although I am recognized as such by the great forefathers of the living entities, who offer me respectful obeisances, still I cannot understand Him, the Lord, the very source of my birth.

PURPORT

Brahmā, the greatest of all living creatures within the universe, is admitting his failure to know the Supreme Lord despite his vast learning in the Vedic wisdom, despite his austerity, penance, mystic powers and self-realization, and despite being worshiped by the great Prajāpatis, the forefathers of the living entities. So these qualifications are not sufficient to know the Supreme Lord. Brahmājī could understand the Lord to a little extent only when he was trying to serve Him by the eagerness of his heart (*hṛdautkaṇṭhyavatā*), which is the devotional service mood. Therefore, the Lord can be known only by the sincere mood of eagerness for service, and not by any amount of material qualification as scientist or speculative philosopher or by attainment of mystic powers. This fact is clearly corroborated in the *Bhagavad-gītā* (18.54–55):

> *brahma-bhūtaḥ prasannātmā*
> *na śocati na kāṅkṣati*
> *samaḥ sarveṣu bhūteṣu*
> *mad-bhaktiṁ labhate parām*

> *bhaktyā mām abhijānāti*
> *yāvān yaś cāsmi tattvataḥ*
> *tato māṁ tattvato jñātvā*
> *viśate tad anantaram*

Only self-realization, by attainment of the above high qualifications of Vedic wisdom, austerity, etc., can help one on the path of devotional service. But failing in devotional service, one remains still imperfect because even in that position of self-realization one cannot factually know the Supreme Lord. By self-realization, one is qualified to become a devotee, and the devotee, by service mood (*bhaktyā*) only, can gradually know the Personality of Godhead. One should not, however, misunderstand the import of *viśate* ("enters into") as referring to merging into the existence of the Supreme. Even in material existence, one is merged in the existence of the Lord. No materialist can disentangle self from matter, for the self is merged in the external energy of the Lord. As no layman can separate butter from milk, no one can extricate the merged self from matter by acquiring some material qualification. This *viśate* by devotion (*bhaktyā*) means to be able to participate in the association of the Lord in person. *Bhakti*, or devotional service to the Lord, means to become free from material entanglement and then to enter into the kingdom of God, becoming one like Him. Losing one's individuality is not the aim of *bhakti-yoga* or of the devotees of the Lord. There are five types of liberation, one of which is called *sāyujya-mukti*, or being merged into the existence or body of the Lord. The other forms of liberation maintain the individuality of the particle soul and involve being always engaged in the transcendental loving service of the Lord. The word *viśate*, used in the verses of the *Bhagavad-gītā*, is thus meant for the devotees who are not at all anxious for any kind of liberation. The devotees are satisfied simply in being engaged in the service of the Lord, regardless of the situation.

Lord Brahmā is the first living being, who directly learned the Vedic wisdom from the Lord (*tene brahma hṛdā ya ādi-kavaye*). Therefore, who can be a more learned Vedāntist than Lord Brahmā? He admits that in spite of his perfect knowledge in the *Vedas*, he was unable to know the glories of the Lord. Since no one can be more than Lord Brahmā, how can a so-called Vedāntist be perfectly cognizant of the Absolute Truth? The so-called Vedāntist, therefore, cannot enter into the existence of the Lord without being trained in the matter of *bhakti-vedānta*, or *Vedānta* plus *bhakti*. *Vedānta* means self-realization, and *bhakti* means realization of the Personality of Godhead, to some extent. No one can know the Personality of Godhead in full, but at least to a certain extent one can know the Absolute Truth, the Personality of Godhead, by self-surrender and a devotional attitude, and by nothing else. In the *Brahma-saṁhitā* also, it

is said, *vedeṣu durlabham,* or simply by study of Vedānta one can hardly
find out the existence of the Personality of Godhead, but the Lord is
adurlabham ātma-bhaktau, very easily available to His devotee. Śrīla
Vyāsadeva, therefore, was not satisfied simply with compiling the
Vedānta-sūtras, but over and above this, by the advice of his spiritual
master, Nārada, he compiled the *Śrīmad-Bhāgavatam* in order to understand the real import of *Vedānta. Śrīmad-Bhāgavatam* therefore, is the
absolute medium by which to understand the Absolute Truth.

TEXT 36

नतोऽस्म्यहं तच्चरणं समीयुषां
भवच्छिदं स्वस्त्ययनं सुमङ्गलम् ।
यो ह्यात्ममायाविभवं स पर्यगाद्
यथा नभः स्वान्तमथापरे कुतः ॥३६॥

nato 'smy aham tac-caraṇam samīyuṣām
bhavac-chidam svasty-ayanam sumaṅgalam
yo hy ātma-māyā-vibhavam sma paryagād
yathā nabhaḥ svāntam athāpare kutaḥ

nataḥ—let me offer my obeisances; *asmi*—am; *aham*—I; *tat*
—the Lord's; *caraṇam*—feet; *samīyuṣām*—of the surrendered soul;
bhavat-chidam—that which stops repetition of birth and death; *svasti-
ayanam*—perception of all happiness; *su-maṅgalam*—all-auspicious;
yaḥ—one who; *hi*—exactly; *ātma-māyā*—personal energies; *vibhavam*
—potency; *sma*—certainly; *paryagāt*—cannot estimate; *yathā*—as
much as; *nabhaḥ*—the sky; *sva-antam*—its own limit; *atha*—therefore;
apare—others; *kutaḥ*—how.

TRANSLATION

**Therefore it is best for me to surrender unto His feet, which
alone can deliver one from the miseries of repeated birth and
death. Such surrender is all-auspicious and allows one to perceive
all happiness. Even the sky cannot estimate the limits of its own**

expansion. So what can others do when the Lord Himself is unable
to estimate His own limits?

PURPORT

Lord Brahmā, the greatest of all learned living beings, the greatest
sacrificer, the greatest observer of the austere life, and the greatest self-
realized mystic, advises us, as the supreme spiritual master of all living
beings, that one should simply surrender unto the lotus feet of the Lord
in order to achieve all success, even up to the limit of being liberated
from the miseries of material life and being endowed with all-auspicious
spiritual existence. Lord Brahmā is known as the *pitāmaha*, or the
father's father. A young man consults his experienced father about discharging his duties. So the father is naturally a good advisor. But Lord
Brahmā is the father of all fathers. He is the father of the father of
Manu, who is the father of mankind all over the universal planets.
Therefore the men of this insignificant planet should kindly accept the
instruction of Brahmājī and would do well to surrender unto the lotus
feet of the Lord rather than try to estimate the length and breadth of the
Lord's potencies. His potencies are immeasurable, as confirmed in the
Vedas. Parāsya śaktir vividhaiva śrūyate svābhāvikī jñāna-bala-kriyā ca
(*Śvetāśvatara Up.* 6.8). He is the greatest of all, and all others, even the
greatest of all living beings, namely Brahmājī, admits that the best thing
for us is to surrender unto Him. Therefore only those persons with a
very poor fund of knowledge claim that they themselves are lords of all
that they survey. And what can they survey? They cannot survey even
the length and breadth of a small sky in one small universe. The so-
called material scientist says that he would need to live forty thousand
years to reach the highest planet of the universe, being carried by a sput-
nik. This is also utopian because no one can be expected to live forty
thousand years. Besides, when the space pilot returned from his travel,
none of his friends would be present to receive him back as the greatest
astronaut, as has become fashionable for modern bewildered scientific
men. One scientific man, who had no belief in God, was very much enthusiastic in making plans for his material existence and therefore
opened a hospital to save the living. But after opening the hospital, he

himself died within six months. So one should not spoil his human life, which is obtained after many, many changes of bodies in 8,400,000 species of life, simply for the concocted material happiness of life through increasing artificial needs in the name of advancement of economic development and scientific knowledge. Rather, one should simply surrender unto the feet of the Lord to make a solution to all miseries of life. That is the instruction of Lord Kṛṣṇa directly in the *Bhagavad-gītā*, and that is the instruction of *Śrīmad-Bhāgavatam* by Brahmājī, the supreme father of all living beings.

Anyone denying this surrendering process as recommended both in the *Bhagavad-gītā* and in the *Śrīmad-Bhāgavatam*—and, for that matter, in all authorized scriptures—will be forced to surrender unto the laws of material nature. The living entity, by his constitutional position, is not independent. He must surrender, either unto the Lord or unto material nature. Material nature is also not independent of the Lord, since the Lord Himself has claimed material nature as *mama māyā*, or "My energy" (Bg. 7.14), and as *me bhinnā prakṛtir aṣṭadhā*, or "My separated energy in eight divisions" (Bg. 7.4). Therefore material nature is also controlled by the Lord, as He has claimed in *Bhagavad-gītā* (9.10). *Mayādhyakṣeṇa prakṛtiḥ sūyate sacarācaram:* "Under My direction only is material nature working, and thus are all things moving." And the living entities, being superior energy to matter, have choice and discrimination either to surrender unto the Lord or to surrender unto material nature. By surrendering unto the Lord, one is happy and liberated, but by surrendering unto material nature the living entity suffers. So the end of all suffering means surrendering unto the Lord because the surrendering process itself is *bhava-cchidam* (liberation from all material miseries), *svasty-ayanam* (perception of all happiness), and *sumaṅgalam* (the source of everything auspicious).

Therefore liberty, happiness and all good fortune can be attained only by surrendering unto the Lord because He is full liberty, full happiness and full auspiciousness. Such liberation and happiness are also unlimited, and they have been compared to the sky, although such liberation and happiness are infinitely greater than the sky. In our present position we can simply understand the magnitude of greatness when it is compared to the sky. We fail to measure the sky, but the happiness and liberty obtained in association with the Lord are far greater than the sky. That spiritual happiness is so great that it cannot be measured, even by the Lord Himself, not to speak of others.

It is said in the scriptures, *brahma-saukhyaṁ tv anantam:* spiritual happiness is unlimited. Here it is said that even the Lord cannot measure such happiness. This does not mean that the Lord cannot measure it and is therefore imperfect in that sense. The actual position is that the Lord can measure it, but the happiness in the Lord is also identical with the Lord on account of absolute knowledge. So the happiness derived from the Lord may be measured by the Lord, but the happiness increases again, and the Lord measures it again, and then again the happiness increases more and more, and the Lord measures it more and more, and as such there is eternally a competition between increment and measurement, so much so that the competition is never stopped, but goes on unlimitedly *ad infinitum.* Spiritual happiness is *ānandāmbudhi-vardhanam,* or the ocean of happiness which increases. The material ocean is stagnant, but the spiritual ocean is dynamic. In the *Caitanya-caritāmṛta,* (*Ādi-līlā,* Fourth Chapter) Kavirāja Gosvāmī has very nicely described this dynamic increment of the ocean of spiritual happiness in the transcendental person of Śrīmatī Rādhārāṇī, the pleasure potency of Lord Kṛṣṇa.

TEXT 37

नाहं न यूयं यदृतां गतिं विदु-
र्न वामदेवः किमुतापरे सुराः ।
तन्मायया मोहितबुद्धयस्त्विदं
विनिर्मितं चात्मसमं विचक्ष्महे ॥३७॥

nāhaṁ na yūyaṁ yad-ṛtāṁ gatiṁ vidur
na vāmadevaḥ kim utāpare surāḥ
tan-māyayā mohita-buddhayas tv idaṁ
vinirmitaṁ cātma-samaṁ vicakṣmahe

na—neither; *aham*—I; *yūyam*—all you sons; *yat*—whose; *ṛtām*—factual; *gatim*—movements; *viduḥ*—do know; *na*—nor; *vāmadevaḥ*—Lord Śiva; *kim*—what; *uta*—else; *apare*—others; *surāḥ*—demigods;

tat—by His; *māyayā*—by the illusory energy; *mohita*—bewildered; *buddhayaḥ*—with such intelligence; *tu*—but; *idam*—this; *vinirmitam* —what is created; *ca*—also; *ātma-samam*—by dint of one's personal ability; *vicakṣmahe*—observe.

TRANSLATION

Since neither Lord Śiva nor you nor I could ascertain the limits of spiritual happiness, how can other demigods know it? And because all of us are bewildered by the illusory external energy of the Supreme Lord, we can see only this manifested cosmos according to our individual ability.

PURPORT

We have many times mentioned the names of twelve selected authorities (*dvādaśa-mahājana*), of which Brahmā, Nārada and Lord Śiva head the list as the first, second and third in order of merit of those who know something of the Supreme Lord. Other demigods, semi-demigods, Gandharvas, Cāraṇas, Vidyādharas, human beings or *asuras* cannot possibly know fully about the potencies of the Absolute Lord, Śrī Kṛṣṇa. The demigods, semi-demigods, Gandharvas, etc., are all highly intelligent persons in the upper planets, the human beings are inhabitants of the intermediate planets, and the *asuras* are inhabitants of the lower planets. All of them have their respective conceptions and estimations of the Absolute Truth, as does the scientist or the empiric philosopher in human society. All such living entities are creatures of the material nature, and consequently they are bewildered by the wonderful display of the three modes of material nature. Such bewilderment is mentioned in the *Bhagavad-gītā* (7.13). *Tribhir guṇamayair bhāvair ebhiḥ sarvam idaṁ jagat:* every entity, beginning from Brahmā down to the ant, is individually bewildered by the three modes of material nature, namely goodness, passion and ignorance. Everyone thinks, in terms of individual capacity, that this universe, which is manifested before us, is all in all. And so the scientist in the human society of the twentieth century calculates the beginning and end of the universe in his own way. But what can the scientists know? Even Brahmā himself was once bewildered, thinking himself the only one Brahmā favored by the Lord, but later on, by the grace of the Lord, he came to know that there are innumerable more powerful Brahmās as well, in far bigger universes beyond this universe, and all of these universes combined together form *ekapād-vibhūti*, or one fourth of the manifestation of the Lord's creative energy. The other three fourths of His energy are displayed in the spiritual world, and so what can the tiny scientist with a tiny brain know of the Absolute Personality of Godhead, Lord Kṛṣṇa? The Lord says, therefore, *mohitam nābhijānāti mām ebhyaḥ param avyayam:* bewildered by such modes of material nature, they cannot understand that beyond these manifestations is a Supreme Person who is the absolute controller of everything. Brahmā, Nārada and Lord Śiva know about the Lord to a considerable extent, and therefore one should follow the instructions of these great personalities instead of being satisfied with a tiny brain and its playful discoveries such as spacecraft and similar products of science. As the mother is the only authority to identify the father of a child, so the mother *Vedas*, presented by the recognized authority such as Brahmā, Nārada or Śiva, is the only authority to inform us about the Absolute Truth.

TEXT 38

यस्यावतारकर्माणि गायन्ति ह्यस्मदादयः ।
न यं विदन्ति तत्त्वेन तस्मै भगवते नमः ॥३८॥

yasyāvatāra-karmāṇi
gāyanti hy asmad-ādayaḥ
na yaṁ vidanti tattvena
tasmai bhagavate namaḥ

yasya—whose; *avatāra*—incarnation; *karmāṇi*—activities; *gāyanti* —chant in glorification; *hi*—indeed; *asmat-ādayaḥ*—persons like us; *na*—do not; *yam*—whom; *vidanti*—know; *tattvena*—cent percent as He is; *tasmai*—unto Him; *bhagavate*—unto the Personality of Godhead Śrī Kṛṣṇa; *namaḥ*—respectful obeisances.

TRANSLATION

Let us offer our respectful obeisances unto that Supreme Personality of Godhead, whose incarnations and activities are chanted

by us for glorification, though He can hardly be fully known as
He is.

PURPORT

It is said that the transcendental name, form, quality, pastimes,
paraphernalia, personality, etc., cannot possibly be perceived by the
gross materialistic senses. But when the senses are purified by the process of hearing, chanting, remembering, and worshiping the lotus feet of
the holy Deity, etc., the Lord reveals Himself proportionately to the
advancement of the quality of devotional service (*ye yathā māṁ
prapadyante*). One should not expect the Lord to be an order-supplying
agent who must be present before us as soon as we desire to see Him. We
must be ready to undergo the prescribed devotional duties, following the
path shown by the predecessors in the disciplic succession from Brahmā,
Nārada and similar authorities. As the senses are progressively purified
by bona fide devotional service, the Lord reveals His identity according
to the spiritual advancement of the devotee. But one who is not in the
line of devotional service can hardly perceive Him simply by calculations
and philosophical speculations. Such a hard worker can present a jugglery of words before an audience, but can never know the Supreme Personality of Godhead in His personal feature. The Lord has clearly stated
in the *Bhagavad-gītā* that one can know Him only by devotional service.
No one can know the Lord by any puffed-up material process of
challenge, but the humble devotee can please the Lord by his earnest devotional activities. Thus the Lord reveals Himself proportionately before
the devotee. Lord Brahmā therefore offers his respectful obeisances as a
bona fide spiritual master and advises us to follow the process of *śravaṇa*
and *kīrtana*. Simply by this process, or simply by hearing and chanting
the glories of the activities of the Lord's incarnation, one can certainly
see within himself the identity of the Lord. We have already discussed
this subject in volume one of *Śrīmad-Bhāgavatam*, in connection with
this verse:

> *tac chraddadhānā munayo*
> *jñāna-vairāgya-yuktayā*
> *paśyanty ātmani cātmānaṁ*
> *bhaktyā śruta-gṛhītayā*
> (*Bhāg.* 1.2.12)

The conclusion is that one cannot know the Supreme Personality of Godhead fully by any method, but He can be seen and felt partially by the devotional service process of hearing, chanting, etc.

TEXT 39

स एष आद्यः पुरुषः कल्पे कल्पे सृजत्यजः ।
आत्मात्मन्यात्मनात्मानं स संयच्छति पाति च ॥३९॥

sa eṣa ādyaḥ puruṣaḥ
kalpe kalpe sṛjaty ajaḥ
ātmātmany ātmanātmānaṁ
sa saṁyacchati pāti ca

sah—He; eṣah—the very; ādyaḥ—the original Personality of Godhead; puruṣaḥ—the Mahā-Viṣṇu incarnation, a plenary portion of Govinda, Lord Kṛṣṇa; kalpe kalpe—in each and every millennium; sṛjati—creates; ajaḥ—the unborn; ātmā—self; ātmani—upon the self; ātmanā—by His own self; ātmānam—own self; saḥ—He; saṁyacchati—absorbs; pāti—maintains; ca—also.

TRANSLATION

That supreme original Personality of Godhead, Lord Śrī Kṛṣṇa, expanding His plenary portion as Mahā-Viṣṇu, the first incarnation, creates this manifested cosmos, but He is unborn. The creation, however, takes place in Him, and the material substance and manifestations are all Himself. He maintains them for some time and absorbs them into Himself again.

PURPORT

The creation is nondifferent from the Lord, and still He is not in the creation. This is explained in the *Bhagavad-gītā* (9.4) as follows:

mayā tatam idaṁ sarvaṁ
jagad avyakta-mūrtinā
mat-sthāni sarva-bhūtāni
na cāhaṁ teṣv avasthitaḥ

The impersonal conception of the Absolute Truth is also a form of the Lord called *avyakta-mūrti*. *Mūrti* means "form," but because His impersonal feature is inexplicable to our limited senses, He is the *avyakta-mūrti* form, and in that inexplicable form of the Lord the whole creation is resting; or, in other words, the whole creation is the Lord Himself, and the creation is also nondifferent from Him, but simultaneously He, as the original Personality of Godhead Śrī Kṛṣṇa, is aloof from the created manifestation. The impersonalist gives stress to the impersonal form or feature of the Lord and does not believe in the original personality of the Lord, but the Vaiṣṇavas accept the original form of the Lord, of whom the impersonal form is merely one of the features. The impersonal and personal conceptions of the Lord are existing simultaneously, and this fact is clearly described both in the *Bhagavad-gītā* and in the *Śrīmad-Bhāgavatam*, and also in other Vedic scriptures. Inconceivable to human intelligence, the idea must simply be accepted on the authority of the scriptures, and it can only be practically realized by the progress of devotional service unto the Lord, and never by mental speculation or inductive logic. The impersonalists depend more or less on inductive logic, and therefore they always remain in darkness about the original Personality of Godhead Śrī Kṛṣṇa. Their conception of Kṛṣṇa is not clear, although everything is clearly mentioned in all the Vedic scriptures. A poor fund of knowledge cannot comprehend the existence of an original personal form of the Lord when He is expanded in everything. This imperfectness is due, more or less, to the material conception that a substance distributed widely in parts can no longer exist in the original form.

The original Personality of Godhead (*ādyaḥ*), Govinda, expands Himself as the Mahā-Viṣṇu incarnation and rests in the Causal Ocean, which He Himself creates. The *Brahma-saṁhitā* (5.47) confirms this as follows:

> *yaḥ kāraṇārṇava-jale bhajati sma yoga-*
> *nidrām ananta-jagad-aṇḍa-saroma-kūpaḥ*
> *ādhāra-śaktim avalambya parāṁ sva-mūrtiṁ*
> *govindam ādi-puruṣaṁ tam ahaṁ bhajāmi*

Lord Brahmājī says in his *Brahma-saṁhitā*, "I worship the primeval Lord Govinda, who lies down in the Causal Ocean in His plenary portion as Mahā-Viṣṇu, with all the universes generating from the pores of hair on His transcendental body, and who accepts the mystic slumber of eternity."

So this Mahā-Viṣṇu is the first incarnation in the creation, and from Him all the universes are generated and all material manifestations are produced, one after another. The Causal Ocean is created by the Lord as the *mahat-tattva*, as a cloud in the spiritual sky, and is only a part of His different manifestations. The spiritual sky is an expansion of His personal rays, and He is the *mahat-tattva* cloud also. He lies down and generates the universes by His breathing, and again, by entering into each universe as Garbhodakaśāyī Viṣṇu, He creates Brahmā, Śiva and many other demigods for maintenance of the universe and again absorbs the whole thing into His person as confirmed in the *Bhagavad-gītā* (9.7):

> *sarva-bhūtāni kaunteya*
> *prakṛtiṁ yānti māmikām*
> *kalpa-kṣaye punas tāni*
> *kalpādau visṛjāmy aham*

"O son of Kuntī, when the *kalpa*, or the duration of the life of Brahmā, is ended, then all the created manifestations enter into My *prakṛti*, or energy, and again, when I desire, the same creation takes place by My personal energy."

The conclusion is that these are all but displays of the Lord's inconceivable personal energies, of which no one can have any full information. This point we have already discussed.

TEXTS 40–41

विशुद्धं केवलं ज्ञानं प्रत्यक् सम्यगवस्थितम् ।
सत्यं पूर्णमनाद्यन्तं निर्गुणं नित्यमद्वयम् ॥४०॥

ऋषे विदन्ति मुनयः प्रशान्तात्मेन्द्रियाशयाः ।
यदा तदेवासत्तर्केस्तिरोधीयेत विप्लुतम् ॥४१॥

> *viśuddhaṁ kevalaṁ jñānaṁ*
> *pratyak samyag avasthitam*

satyaṁ pūrṇam anādy-antaṁ
nirguṇaṁ nityam advayam

ṛṣe vidanti munayaḥ
praśāntātmendriyāśayāḥ
yadā tad evāsat-tarkais
tirodhīyeta viplutam

viśuddham—without any material tinge; *kevalam*—pure and perfect; *jñānam*—knowledge; *pratyak*—all-pervading; *samyak*—in fullness; *avasthitam*—situated; *satyam*—truth; *pūrṇam*—absolute; *anādi*—without any beginning; *antam*—and so also without any end; *nirguṇam*—devoid of material modes; *nityam*—eternal; *advayam*—without any rival; *ṛṣe*—O Nārada, O great sage; *vidanti*—they can only understand; *munayaḥ*—the great thinkers; *praśānta*—pacified; *ātma*—self; *indriya*—senses; *āśayāḥ*—sheltered; *yadā*—while; *tat*—that; *eva*—certainly; *asat*—untenable; *tarkaiḥ*—arguments; *tiraḥ-dhīyeta*—disappears; *viplutam*—distorted.

TRANSLATION

The Personality of Godhead is pure, being free from all contaminations of material tinges. He is the Absolute Truth and the embodiment of full and perfect knowledge. He is all-pervading, without beginning or end, and without rival. O Nārada, O great sage, the great thinkers can know Him when completely freed from all material hankerings and when sheltered under undisturbed conditions of the senses. Otherwise, by untenable arguments, all is distorted, and the Lord disappears from our sight.

PURPORT

Here is an estimation of the Lord apart from His transcendental activities in the temporary, material creations. Māyāvāda philosophy tries to designate the Lord as contaminated by a material body when He accepts forms of incarnation. This sort of interpolation is completely denied herein by the explanation that the Lord's position is pure and unalloyed in all circumstances. According to Māyāvāda philosophy, the spirit soul, when covered by nescience, is designated as *jīva*, but when freed from such ignorance or nescience he merges in the impersonal existence of the Absolute Truth. But here it is said that the Lord is eternally the symbol of full and perfect knowledge. This is His speciality: perpetual freedom from all material contaminations. This distinguishes the Lord from the individual, common living entities who have the aptitude for being subordinated by nescience and thus becoming materially designated. In the *Vedas* it is said that the Lord is *vijñānam ānandam,* full of bliss and knowledge. The conditioned souls are never to be compared to Him because such individual souls have the tendency to become contaminated. Although after liberation the living entity can become one with the same quality of existence as the Lord, his very tendency to become contaminated, which the Lord never has, makes the individual living entity different from the Lord. In the *Vedas* it is said, *śuddham apāpa-viddham:* the individual *ātmā* becomes polluted by sin, but the Lord is never contaminated by sins. The Lord is compared to the powerful sun. The sun is never contaminated by anything infectious because it is so powerful. On the contrary, infected things are sterilized by the rays of the sun. Similarly, the Lord is never contaminated by sins; on the contrary, the sinful living entities become sterilized by contact with the Lord. This means that the Lord is also all-pervading like the sun, and as such the word *pratyak* is used in this verse. Nothing is excluded from the existence of the Lord's potential expansions. The Lord is within everything, and He is all-covering also, without being disturbed by the activities of the individual souls. He is therefore infinite, and the living entities are infinitesimal. In the *Vedas* it is said that only the Lord alone exists, and all others' existences depend on Him. He is the generating reservoir for everyone's existential capacity; He is the Supreme Truth of all other categorical truths. He is the source of everyone's opulence, and therefore no one can equal Him in opulence. Being full of all opulences, namely wealth, fame, strength, beauty, knowledge and renunciation, certainly He is the Supreme Person. And because He is a person, He has many personal qualities, although He is transcendental to the material modes. We have already discussed the statement, *ittham-bhūta-guṇo hariḥ* (*Bhāg.* 1.7.10). His transcendental qualities are so attractive that even the liberated souls (*ātmārāmas*) are also attracted by them. Although possessed of all personal qualities, He is nevertheless omnipotent. Therefore, personally He has nothing to do, for everything is being carried out by His omnipotent energies. This is confirmed by the Vedic mantras: parāsya śaktir vividhaiva śrūyate svābhāvikī jñāna-bala-kriyā ca. This suggests His specific spiritual form, which can never be experienced by the material senses. He can be seen only when the senses are purified by devotional service (yam evaiṣa vṛnute tena labhyaḥ). As such, there are basic differences between the Lord and the living entities, in so many respects. No one can be compared to the Lord, as the Vedas declare (ekam evādvitīyaṁ brahma, dvaitād vai bhayaṁ bhavati). The Lord has no competitor, and He has nothing to fear from any other being, nor can anyone be equal to Him. Although He is the root of all other beings, there are basic differences between Him and other beings. Otherwise there would have been no necessity for the statement in the previous verse that no one can know Him one hundred percent as He is (na yaṁ vidanti tattvena). That no one can fully understand Him is explained also in this verse, but the qualification for understanding to some degree is mentioned here. Only the praśāntas, or the unalloyed devotees of the Lord, can know Him to a greater extent. The reason is that the devotees have no demands in their lives but to be obedient servants of the Lord, while all others, namely the empiric philosophers, the mystics and the fruitive workers, all basically have some demand, and as such they cannot be pacified. The fruitive worker wants reward for his work, the mystic wants some perfection of life, and the empiric philosopher wants to merge in the existence of the Lord. Somehow or other, as long as there is a demand for sense satisfaction, there is no chance for pacification; on the contrary, by unnecessary dry speculative arguments, the whole matter becomes distorted, and thus the Lord moves still further away from our understanding. The dry speculators, however, because of their following the principles of austerity and penance, can have knowledge of the impersonal features of the Lord to some extent, but there is no chance of their understanding His ultimate form as Govinda because only the amalātmanas, or the completely sinless persons, can accept pure devotional service to the Lord, as confirmed in the Bhagavad-gītā (7.28):

> yeṣāṁ tv anta-gataṁ pāpaṁ
> janānāṁ puṇya-karmaṇām
> te dvandva-moha-nirmuktā
> bhajante māṁ dṛḍha-vratāḥ

TEXT 42

आद्योऽवतार: पुरुष: परस्य
काल: स्वभाव: सदसन्मनश्च ।
द्रव्यं विकारो गुण इन्द्रियाणि
विराट् स्वराट् स्थास्नु चरिष्णु भूम्न: ॥४२॥

ādyo 'vatāraḥ puruṣaḥ parasya
kālaḥ svabhāvaḥ sad-asan-manaś ca
dravyaṁ vikāro guṇa indriyāṇi
virāṭ svarāṭ sthāsnu cariṣṇu bhūmnaḥ

ādyaḥ—first; *avatāraḥ*—incarnation; *puruṣaḥ*—Kāraṇārṇavaśāyī
Viṣṇu; *parasya*—of the Lord; *kālaḥ*—time; *svabhāvaḥ*—space; *sat*—
result; *asat*—cause; *manaḥ*—mind; *ca*—also; *dravyam*—elements;
vikāraḥ—material ego; *guṇaḥ*—modes of nature; *indriyāṇi*—senses;
virāṭ—the complete whole body; *svarāṭ*—Garbhodakaśāyī Viṣṇu;
sthāsnu—immovable; *cariṣṇu*—movable; *bhūmnaḥ*—of the Supreme
Lord.

TRANSLATION

**Kāraṇārṇavaśāyī Viṣṇu is the first incarnation of the Supreme
Lord, and He is the master of eternal time, space, cause and effects,
mind, the elements, the material ego, the modes of nature, the
senses, the universal form of the Lord, Garbhodakaśāyī Viṣṇu, and
the sum total of all living beings, both moving and nonmoving.**

PURPORT

That the material creation is not permanent has been discussed many
times hereinbefore. The material creation is but a temporary exhibition
of the material energy of the Almighty God. This material manifestation
is necessary to give a chance to the conditioned souls who are unwilling
to associate with the Lord in the relationship of loving transcendental
service. Such unwilling conditioned souls are not allowed to enter into
the liberated life of spiritual existence because at heart they are not willing to serve. Instead, they want to enjoy themselves as imitation Gods.

The living entities are constitutionally eternal servitors of the Lord, but some of them, because of misusing their independence, do not wish to serve; therefore they are allowed to enjoy the material nature, which is called *māyā*, or illusion. It is called illusion because the living beings under the clutches of *māyā* are not factually enjoyers, although they think that they are, being illusioned by *māyā*. Such illusioned living entities are given a chance at intervals to rectify their perverted mentality of becoming false masters of the material nature, and they are imparted lessons from the *Vedas* about their eternal relationship with the Supreme Lord Kṛṣṇa (*vedaiś ca sarvair aham eva vedyaḥ*). So the temporary creation of the material manifestation is an exhibition of the material energy of the Lord, and to manage the whole show the Supreme Lord incarnates Himself as the Kāraṇārṇavaśāyī Viṣṇu just as a magistrate is deputed by the government to manage affairs temporarily. This Kāraṇodakaśāyī Viṣṇu causes the manifestation of material creation by looking over His material energy (*sa aikṣata*). In the first volume of this book we have already discussed to some extent the explanation of the verse *jagṛhe pauruṣaṁ rūpam*. The duration of the illusory play of material creation is called a *kalpa*, and we have already discussed the creation's taking place in *kalpa* after *kalpa*. By His incarnation and potential activities, the complete ingredients of creation, namely time, space, cause, result, mind, the gross and subtle elements and their interactional modes of nature—goodness, passion and ignorance—and then the senses and their reservoir source, the gigantic universal form as the second incarnation Garbhodakaśāyī Viṣṇu, and all living beings, both moving and standing, which come out of the second incarnation, all became manifested. Ultimately, all these creative elements and the creation itself are but potential manifestations of the Supreme Lord; nothing is independent of the control of the Supreme Being. This first incarnation in the material creation, namely Kāraṇārṇavaśāyī Viṣṇu, is the plenary part of the original Personality of Godhead, Śrī Kṛṣṇa, described in the *Brahma-saṁhitā* (5.48) as follows:

> *yasyaika-niśvasita-kālam athāvalambya*
> *jīvanti loma-vilajā jagad-aṇḍa-nāthāḥ*
> *viṣṇur mahān sa iha yasya kalā-viśeṣo*
> *govindam ādi-puruṣaṁ tam ahaṁ bhajāmi*

All the innumerable universes are maintained only during the breathing period of Mahā-Viṣṇu, or Kāraṇārṇavaśāyī Viṣṇu, who is only a plenary part of Govinda, the original Personality of Godhead Lord Kṛṣṇa.

TEXTS 43–45

अहं भवो यज्ञ इमे प्रजेशा
दक्षादयो ये भवदादयश्च ।
खर्लोकपालाः खगलोकपाला
नृलोकपालास्तललोकपालाः ॥४३॥

गन्धर्वविद्याधरचारणेशा
ये यक्षरक्षोरगनागनाथाः ।
ये वा ऋषीणामृषभाः पितृणां
दैत्येन्द्रसिद्धेश्वरदानवेन्द्राः ।

अन्ये च ये प्रेतपिशाचभूत-
कूष्माण्डयादोमृगपक्ष्यधीशाः ॥४४॥

यत्किञ्च लोके भगवन्महस्व-
दोजःसहस्वद् बलवत् क्षमावत् ।
श्रीह्रीविभूत्यात्मवदद्भुतार्णं
तत्त्वं परं रूपवदस्वरूपम् ॥४५॥

aham bhavo yajña ime prajeśā
dakṣādayo ye bhavad-ādayaś ca
svarloka-pālāḥ khagaloka-pālā
nṛloka-pālās talaloka-pālāḥ

gandharva-vidyādhara-cāraṇeśā
ye yakṣa-rakṣoraga-nāga-nāthāḥ
ye vā ṛṣīṇām ṛṣabhāḥ pitṝṇāṁ
daityendra-siddheśvara-dānavendrāḥ
anye ca ye preta-piśāca-bhūta-
kūṣmāṇḍa-yādo-mṛga-pakṣy-adhīśāḥ

yat kiñca loke bhagavan mahasvad
ojaḥ-sahasvad balavat kṣamāvat
śrī-hrī-vibhūty-ātmavad adbhutārṇaṁ
tattvaṁ paraṁ rūpavad asva-rūpam

aham—myself (Brahmājī); *bhavaḥ*—Lord Śiva; *yajñaḥ*—Lord Viṣṇu; *ime*—all these; *prajā-īśāḥ*—the father of the living beings; *dakṣa-ādayaḥ*—Dakṣa, Marīci, Manu, etc.; *ye*—those; *bhavat*—yourself; *ādayaḥ ca*—and the bachelors (Sanat-kumāra and his brothers); *svarloka-pālāḥ*—the leaders of the heavenly planets; *khagaloka-pālāḥ*—the leaders of space travelers; *nṛloka-pālāḥ*—the leaders of mankind; *talaloka-pālāḥ*—the leaders of the lower planets; *gandharva*—the residents of Gandharvaloka; *vidyādhara*—the residents of the Vidyādhara planet; *cāraṇa-īśāḥ*—the leaders of the Cāraṇas; *ye*—as also others; *yakṣa*—the leaders of the Yakṣas; *rakṣa*—demons; *uraga*—snakes; *nāga-nāthāḥ*—the leaders of Nāgaloka (below the earth); *ye*—others; *vā*—also; *ṛṣīṇām*—of the sages; *ṛṣabhāḥ*—the chief; *pitṝṇām*—of the forefathers; *daitya-indra*—leaders of the atheists; *siddha-īśvara*—leaders of the Siddhaloka planets (spacemen); *dānava-indrāḥ*—leaders of the non-Āryans; *anye*—besides them; *ca*—also; *ye*—those; *preta*—dead bodies; *piśāca*—evil spirits; *bhūta*—jinn; *kūṣmāṇḍa*—a special type of evil spirit; *yādaḥ*—aquatics; *mṛga*—animals; *pakṣi-adhīśāḥ*—giant eagles; *yat*—anything; *kim ca*—and everything; *loke*—in the world; *bhagavat*—possessed of *bhaga*, or extraordinary power; *mahasvat*—of a special degree; *ojaḥ-sahasvat*—specific mental and sensual dexterity; *balavat*—possessed of strength; *kṣamāvat*—possessed of forgiveness; *śrī*—beauty; *hrī*—ashamed of impious acts; *vibhūti*—riches; *ātmavat*—possessed of intelligence; *adbhuta*—wonderful; *arṇam*—race; *tattvam*—specific truth; *param*—transcendental; *rūpavat*—as if the form of; *asva-rūpam*—not the form of the Lord.

TRANSLATION

I myself [Brahmā], Lord Śiva, Lord Viṣṇu, great generators of living beings like Dakṣa and Prajāpati, yourselves [Nārada and the Kumāras], heavenly demigods like Indra and Candra, the leaders

of the Bhūrloka planets, the leaders of the earthly planets, the
leaders of the lower planets, the leaders of the Gandharva planets,
the leaders of the Vidyādhara planets, the leaders of the
Cāraṇaloka planets, the leaders of the Yakṣas, Rakṣas and Uragas,
the great sages, the great demons, the great atheists and the great
spacemen, as well as the dead bodies, evil spirits, satans, jinn,
kūṣmāṇḍas, great aquatics, great beasts and great birds, etc.—in
other words, anything and everything which is exceptionally
possessed of power, opulence, mental and perceptual dexterity,
strength, forgiveness, beauty, modesty, opulence, and breeding,
whether in form or formless—may appear to be the specific truth
and the form of the Lord, but actually they are not so. They are
only a fragment of the transcendental potency of the Lord.

PURPORT

Those in the list given above, beginning from the name Brahmājī, the
first living creature within the universe, down to Lord Śiva, Lord Viṣṇu,
Nārada and other powerful demigods, men, supermen, sages, ṛṣis, and
other lower creatures of extraordinary strength and opulence, including
the dead bodies, satans, evil spirits, jinn, aquatics, birds and beasts, may
appear to be the Supreme Lord, but factually none of them is the
Supreme Lord; every one of them possesses only a fragment of the great
potencies of the Supreme Lord. The less intelligent man is surprised to
see the wonderful actions of material phenomena, as the aborigines are
fearful of a great thunderbolt, a great and gigantic banyan tree, or a
great lofty mountain in the jungle. For such undeveloped human beings,
merely the slight display of the Lord's potency is captivating. A still more
advanced person is captivated by the powers of the demigods and goddesses. Therefore, those who are simply astonished by the powers of anything in the creation of the Lord, without any factual information of the
Lord Himself, are known as śaktas, or worshipers of the great powers.
The modern scientist is also captivated by the wonderful actions and
reactions of natural phenomena and therefore is also a śakta. These
lower-grade persons gradually rise to become sauriyas (worshipers of
the sun-god) or gāṇapatyas (worshipers of the mass of people as
janatā-janārdana or daridra-nārāyaṇa, etc., in the form of Gaṇapati)
and then rise to the platform of worshiping Lord Śiva in search for the

ever-existing soul, and then to the stage of worshiping Lord Viṣṇu, the
Supersoul, etc., without any information of Govinda, Lord Kṛṣṇa, who is
the original Lord Viṣṇu. In other ways some are worshipers of race,
nationality, birds, beasts, evil spirits, satans, etc. The general worship of
Śanideva, the lord of distressful condition, and Śītalādevī, the goddess of
smallpox, is also common to the mass of people, and there are many
foolish men who worship the mass of people or the poor class of men. So
different persons, societies and communities, etc., worship some of the
potent manifestations of the Lord, wrongly accepting the powerful object
as God. But in this verse it is advised by Brahmājī that none of them is
the Supreme Lord; they are only borrowed plumes from the original
Almighty Lord Śrī Kṛṣṇa. When the Lord advises in *Bhagavad-gītā* to
worship Him alone, it is to be understood that worshiping Lord Kṛṣṇa includes worshiping all that is mentioned, because He, Lord Kṛṣṇa, includes everyone.

When the Lord is described as formless in the Vedic literatures, it is to
be understood that all these forms mentioned above, within the experience of universal knowledge, are different exhibitions of the Lord's
transcendental potencies only, and none of them factually represents the
transcendental form of the Lord. But when the Lord actually descends on
the earth or anywhere within the universe, the less intelligent class of
men also mistake Him to be one of them, and thus they imagine the
Transcendence to be formless or impersonal. Factually, the Lord is not
formless, nor does He belong to any of the multiforms experienced
within the universal forms. One should try to know the truth about the
Lord by following the instruction of Brahmājī.

TEXT 46

प्राधान्यतो यानृष आमनन्ति
लीलावतारान् पुरुषस्य भूम्नः ।
आपीयतां कर्णकषायशोषा-
ननुक्रमिष्ये त इमान् सुपेशान् ॥४६॥

prādhānyato yān ṛṣa āmananti
līlāvatārān puruṣasya bhūmnaḥ

āpīyatāṁ karṇa-kaṣāya-śoṣān
anukramiṣye ta imān supeśān

prādhānyataḥ—chiefly; *yān*—all those; *ṛṣe*—O Nārada; *āmananti*—worship; *līlā*—pastimes; *avatārān*—incarnations; *puruṣasya*—of the Personality of Godhead; *bhūmnaḥ*—the Supreme; *āpīyatām*—in order to be relished by you; *karṇa*—ears; *kaṣāya*—foul matter; *śoṣān*—that which evaporates; *anukramiṣye*—shall state one after another; *te*—they; *imān*—as they are in my heart; *su-peśān*—all pleasing to hear.

TRANSLATION

O Nārada, now I shall state, one after another, the transcendental incarnations of the Lord known as līlā-avatāras. Hearing of their activities counteracts all foul matters accumulated in the ear. These pastimes are pleasing to hear and are to be relished. Therefore they are in my heart.

PURPORT

As it was said in the beginning of *Śrīmad-Bhāgavatam* (1.5.8), one cannot be fully satisfied by hearing unless and until one is given a chance to hear of the transcendental activities of the Lord. So Brahmājī is also trying, in this verse, to stress the importance of narrating the transcendental pastimes of the Lord as He comes and manifests Himself here on the surface of the material planets. Every living entity has a tendency to hear pleasing messages, and as such almost every one of us is inclined to hear news and talks broadcast by the radio stations. But the difficulty is that no one is satisfied at heart by hearing all those messages. The cause of such dissatisfaction is the imcompatibility of the message with the innermost stratum of the living soul. This transcendental literature is especially prepared by Śrīla Vyāsadeva to give the utmost satisfaction to the people in general by narration of the activities of the Lord, as instructed by Śrī Nārada Muni to Śrīla Vyāsadeva. Such activities of the Lord are principally of two varieties. One concerns the mundane manifestation of the material creative force, and the other deals with His pastimes in the form of different incarnations in terms of the time and place. There are innumerable incarnations of the Lord, like the waves of the river flowing constantly in and out. Less intelligent persons take more interest in the creative forces of the Lord in the material world, and, being disconnected from their relationship with the Lord, they put forward many theories of the creation in the name of scientific research. The devotees of the Lord, however, know well how the creative forces work concurrently by the action and reaction of the material energy of the Lord. Therefore they take more interest in the transcendental activities of the Lord as He incarnates Himself on the surface of the material world. Śrīmad-Bhāgavatam is the history of such activities of the Lord, and people who take interest in hearing Śrīmad-Bhāgavatam clear their hearts of accumulated mundane filth. There are a thousand and one rash literatures on the market, but one who has taken interest in the Śrīmad-Bhāgavatam loses all interest in such filthy literatures. Śrī Brahmājī is thus attempting to narrate the principal incarnations of the Lord so that they may be drunk by Nārada as transcendental nectar.

Thus end the Bhaktivedanta purports of the Second Canto, Sixth Chapter, of the Śrīmad-Bhāgavatam, entitled "Puruṣa-sūkta Confirmed."

Appendixes

The Author

His Divine Grace A. C. Bhaktivedanta Swami Prabhupāda appeared in this world in 1896 in Calcutta, India. He first met his spiritual master, Śrīla Bhaktisiddhānta Sarasvatī Gosvāmī, in Calcutta in 1922. Bhakti-siddhānta Sarasvatī, a prominent religious scholar and the founder of sixty-four Gauḍīya Maṭhas (Vedic institutes), liked this educated young man and convinced him to dedicate his life to teaching Vedic knowledge. Śrīla Prabhupāda became his student, and eleven years later (1933) at Allahabad he became his formally initiated disciple.

At their first meeting, in 1922, Śrīla Bhaktisiddhānta Sarasvatī Ṭhākura requested Śrīla Prabhupāda to broadcast Vedic knowledge through the English language. In the years that followed, Śrīla Prabhu-pāda wrote a commentary on the *Bhagavad-gītā*, assisted the Gauḍīya Maṭha in its work and, in 1944, without assistance, started an English fortnightly magazine, edited it, typed the manuscripts and checked the galley proofs. He even distributed the individual copies and struggled to maintain the publication. Once begun, the magazine never stopped; it is now being continued by his disciples in the West and is published in nineteen languages.

Recognizing Śrīla Prabhupāda's philosophical learning and devo-tion, the Gauḍīya Vaiṣṇava Society honored him in 1947 with the title "Bhaktivedanta." In 1950, at the age of fifty-four, Śrīla Prabhupāda retired from married life, adopting the *vānaprastha* (retired) order to devote more time to his studies and writing. Śrīla Prabhupāda traveled to the holy city of Vṛndāvana, where he lived in very humble circum-stances in the historic medieval temple of Rādhā-Dāmodara. There he engaged for several years in deep study and writing. He accepted the re-nounced order of life (*sannyāsa*) in 1959. At Rādhā-Dāmodara, Śrīla Prabhupāda began work on his life's masterpiece: a multivolume trans-lation of and commentary on the eighteen-thousand-verse *Śrīmad-Bhāgavatam* (*Bhāgavata Purāṇa*). He also wrote *Easy Journey to Other Planets*.

After publishing three volumes of the *Bhāgavatam*, Śrīla Prabhupāda came to the United States, in 1965, to fulfill the mission of his spiritual master. Subsequently, His Divine Grace wrote more than sixty volumes

of authoritative translations, commentaries and summary studies of the
philosophical and religious classics of India.

In 1965, when he first arrived by freighter in New York City, Śrīla
Prabhupāda was practically penniless. It was after almost a year of great
difficulty that he established the International Society for Krishna Consciousness in July of 1966. Before his passing away on November 14,
1977, he guided the Society and saw it grow to a worldwide confederation
of more than one hundred *āśramas*, schools, temples, institutes and farm
communities.

In 1968, Śrīla Prabhupāda created New Vrindaban, an experimental
Vedic community in the hills of West Virginia. Inspired by the success of
New Vrindaban, now a thriving farm community of more than one thousand acres, his students have since founded several similar communities
in the United States and abroad.

In 1972, His Divine Grace introduced the Vedic system of primary and
secondary education in the West by founding the Gurukula school in
Dallas, Texas. Since then, under his supervision, his disciples have
established children's schools throughout the United States and the rest
of the world. As of 1978, there are ten *gurukula* schools worldwide, with
the principal educational center now located in Vṛndāvana, India.

Śrīla Prabhupāda also inspired the construction of several large inter-
national cultural centers in India. The center at Śrīdhāma Māyāpur in
West Bengal is the site for a planned spiritual city, an ambitious project
for which construction will extend over the next decade. In Vṛndāvana,
India, is the magnificent Kṛṣṇa-Balarāma Temple and International
Guesthouse. There is also a major cultural and educational center in
Bombay. Other centers are planned in a dozen other important locations
on the Indian subcontinent.

Śrīla Prabhupāda's most significant contribution, however, is his
books. Highly respected by the academic community for their authori-
tativeness, depth and clarity, they are used as standard textbooks in
numerous college courses. His writings have been translated into twenty-
eight languages. The Bhaktivedanta Book Trust, established in 1972 exclusively to publish the works of His Divine Grace, has thus become the
world's largest publisher of books in the field of Indian religion and
philosophy.

In just twelve years, in spite of his advanced age, Śrīla Prabhupāda circled the globe fourteen times on lecture tours that took him to six continents. In spite of such a vigorous schedule, Śrīla Prabhupāda continued to write prolifically. His writings constitute a veritable library of Vedic philosophy, religion, literature and culture.

References

The purports of *Śrīmad-Bhāgavatam* are all confirmed by standard Vedic authorities. The following authentic scriptures are specifically cited in this volume:

Bhagavad-gītā, 5, 9, 12, 23, 33, 38, 39, 42, 45, 48, 49, 53, 54, 59, 63, 66, 67, 75, 76, 77, 79, 85, 90, 92, 95, 98, 99, 102, 111, 120, 124, 126, 129, 140, 145, 147–148, 149, 154, 158, 159, 162, 163, 179–180, 184, 186, 189, 190, 191, 195, 197, 200, 201, 203, 205, 209–210, 213, 216, 220, 222, 223, 226, 230, 236, 245, 247, 251, 256, 260, 262, 266, 268, 271–272, 277, 278, 279, 283, 285, 286, 288, 293, 296, 302, 305–306, 307, 309, 315, 320, 325, 329–330, 330, 331, 333, 333–334, 335, 339, 341, 344, 346, 349

Brahma-saṁhitā, 54, 189–190, 247, 249, 318, 331, 333, 345–346, 351–352

Brahma-vaivarta Purāṇa, 163

Bṛhad-āraṇyaka Upaniṣad, 122

Caitanya-caritāmṛta, 136, 219

Īśopaniṣad, 206

Kaṭha Upaniṣad, 192, 206, 257

Mahābhārata, 214, 215

Muṇḍaka Upaniṣad, 206

Nārada-pañcarātra, 292

Padma Purāṇa, 217

Glossary

A

Ācārya—a spiritual master who teaches by example.

Acintya-bhedābheda-tattva—the Supreme Lord is inconceivably, simultaneously one with His material and spiritual energies and different from them.

Ārati—a ceremony for greeting the Lord with offerings of food, lamps, fans, flowers and incense.

Arcanā—the devotional process of Deity worship.

Āśrama—the four spiritual orders of life: celibate student, householder, retired life and renounced life.

Asuras—atheistic demons.

Avatāra—a descent of the Supreme Lord.

B

Bhagavad-gītā—the basic directions for spiritual life spoken by the Lord Himself.

Bhakta—a devotee.

Bhakti-yoga—linking with the Supreme Lord by devotional service.

Brahmacarya—celibate student life; the first order of Vedic spiritual life.

Brahman—the Absolute Truth; especially the impersonal aspect of the Absolute.

Brāhmaṇa—one wise in the *Vedas* who can guide society; the first Vedic social order.

Brahmavādīs—impersonalists among the transcendentalists.

D

Deva-dāsīs—female singers and dancers employed as servants of the Deity.

Dharma—eternal occupational duty; religious principles.

E

Ekādaśī—a special fast day for increased remembrance of Kṛṣṇa, which comes on the eleventh day of both the waxing and waning moon.

G

Goloka (Kṛṣṇaloka)—the highest spiritual planet, containing Kṛṣṇa's personal abodes, Dvārakā, Mathurā and Vṛndāvana.

Gopīs—Kṛṣṇa's cowherd girl friends, His most confidential servitors.

Gṛhastha—regulated householder life; the second order of Vedic spiritual life.

Guru—a spiritual master.

H

Hare Kṛṣṇa mantra—*See: Mahā-mantra*

J

Jīva-tattva—the living entities, atomic parts of the Lord.

K

Kali-yuga (Age of Kali)—the present age, characterized by quarrel; it is last in the cycle of four and began five thousand years ago.

Karatālas—hand cymbals used in *kīrtana*.

Karma—fruitive action, for which there is always reaction, good or bad.

Karma-kāṇḍa—sections of the *Vedas* prescribing rituals for material benefits.

Karma-yoga—(1) action in devotional service; (2) action performed by one who knows that the goal of life is Kṛṣṇa but who is addicted to the fruits of his activities.

Karmī—a person satisfied with working hard for flickering sense gratification.

Kīrtana—chanting the glories of the Supreme Lord.

Kṛṣṇaloka—*See:* Goloka

Kṣatriyas—a warrior or administrator; the second Vedic social order.

M

Mahā-mantra—the great chanting for deliverance:

Hare Kṛṣṇa, Hare Kṛṣṇa, Kṛṣṇa Kṛṣṇa, Hare Hare
Hare Rāma, Hare Rāma, Rāma Rāma, Hare Hare.

Mantra—a sound vibration that can deliver the mind from illusion.

Mathurā—Lord Kṛṣṇa's abode, surrounding Vṛndāvana, where He took birth and later returned to after performing His Vṛndāvana pastimes.

Māyā—illusion; forgetfulness of one's relationship with Kṛṣṇa.

Māyāvādīs—impersonal philosophers who say that the Lord cannot have a transcendental body.

Mṛdaṅga—a clay drum used for congregational chanting.

N

Nārāyaṇa-para—one who has dedicated his life to the Supreme Lord Nārāyaṇa, Kṛṣṇa.

P

Paramparā—the chain of spiritual masters in disciplic succession.

Prasāda—food spiritualized by being offered to the Lord.

S

Sac-cid-ānanda-vigraha—the Lord's transcendental form, which is eternal, full of knowledge and bliss.

Saṅkīrtana—public chanting of the names of God, the approved *yoga* process for this age.

Sannyāsa—renounced life; the fourth order of Vedic spiritual life.

Sarva-jña—one who knows everything, past, present and future.

Śāstras—revealed scriptures.

Sāttvika—in the mode of goodness.

Śravaṇaṁ kīrtanaṁ viṣṇoḥ—the devotional processes of hearing and chanting about Lord Viṣṇu.

Śūdra—a laborer; the fourth of the Vedic social orders.

Svāmī—one who controls his mind and senses; title of one in the renounced order of life.

T

Tapasya—austerity; accepting some voluntary inconvenience for a higher purpose.

Tilaka—auspicious clay marks that sanctify a devotee's body as a temple of the Lord.

V

Vaikuṇṭha—the spiritual world.

Vaiṣṇava—a devotee of Lord Viṣṇu, Kṛṣṇa.

Vaiśyas—farmers and merchants; the third Vedic social order.

Vānaprastha—one who has retired from family life; the third order of Vedic spiritual life.

Varṇa—the four occupational divisions of society: the intellectual class, the administrative class, the mercantile class, and the laborer class.

Varṇāśrama—the Vedic social system of four social and four spiritual orders.

Vedas—the original revealed scriptures, first spoken by the Lord Himself.

Veda-vāda-ratas—those who give their own explanations of the *Vedas*.

Virāṭ-rūpa—the conception likening the physical form of the universe to the Lord's bodily form.

Viṣṇu, Lord—Kṛṣṇa's expansion for the creation and maintenance of the material universes.

Viṣṇu-tattvas—the original Personality of Godhead's primary expansions, each of whom is equally God.

Vṛndāvana—Kṛṣṇa's personal abode, where He fully manifests His quality of sweetness.

Vyāsadeva—Kṛṣṇa's incarnation, at the end of Dvāpara-yuga, for compiling the *Vedas*.

Y

Yajña—sacrifice; work done for the satisfaction of Lord Viṣṇu.

Yogī—a transcendentalist who, in one way or another, is striving for union with the Supreme.

Yugas—ages in the life of a universe, occurring in a repeated cycle of four.

Sanskrit Pronunciation Guide

Vowels

अ a   आ ā   इ i   ई ī   उ u   ऊ ū   ऋ ṛ   ॠ ṝ
लृ ḷ   ए e   ऐ ai   ओ o   औ au

ं ṁ (anusvāra)   ः ḥ (visarga)

Consonants

Gutturals:	क ka	ख kha	ग ga	घ gha	ङ ṅa
Palatals:	च ca	छ cha	ज ja	झ jha	ञ ña
Cerebrals:	ट ṭa	ठ ṭha	ड ḍa	ढ ḍha	ण ṇa
Dentals:	त ta	थ tha	द da	ध dha	न na
Labials:	प pa	फ pha	ब ba	भ bha	म ma
Semivowels:	य ya	र ra	ल la	व va	
Sibilants:	श śa	ष ṣa	स sa		
Aspirate:	ह ha	ऽ ' (avagraha) – the apostrophe			

The numerals are: ० -0 १ -1 २ -2 ३ -3 ४ -4 ५ -5 ६ -6 ७ -7 ८ -8 ९ -9

The vowels above should be pronounced as follows:

a – like the *a* in org*a*n or the *u* in b*u*t
ā – like the *a* in f*a*r but held twice as long as short *a*
i – like the *i* in p*i*n
ī – like the *i* in p*i*que but held twice as long as short *i*

u – like the *u* in p*u*sh
ū – like the *u* in r*u*le but held twice as long as short *u*
ṛ – like the *ri* in *ri*m
ṝ – like *ree* in *ree*d
ḷ – like *l* followed by ṛ (*lṛ*)
e – like the *e* in th*ey*
ai – like the *ai* in *ai*sle
o – like the *o* in g*o*
au – like the *ow* in h*ow*
ṁ (*anusvāra*) – a resonant nasal like the *n* in the French word *bon*
ḥ (*visarga*) – a final *h*-sound: *aḥ* is pronounced like *aha*; *iḥ* like *ihi*

The vowels are written as follows after a consonant:

ा ā   ि i   ी ī   ु u   ू ū   ृ ṛ   ॄ ṝ   े e   ै ai   ो o   ौ au

For example: क ka   का kā   कि ki   की kī   कु ku   कू kū

कृ kṛ   कॄ kṝ   के ke   कै kai   को ko   कौ kau

The vowel "a" is implied after a consonant with no vowel symbol.

The symbol virāma (्) indicates that there is no final vowel: क्

The consonants are pronounced as follows:

k – as in *k*ite   jh – as in he*dgeh*og
kh – as in Ec*kh*art   ñ – as in ca*ny*on
g – as in *g*ive   ṭ – as in *t*ub
gh – as in di*g-h*ard   ṭh – as in ligh*t-h*eart
ṅ – as in si*ng*   ḍ – as in *d*ove
c – as in *ch*air   ḍha– as in re*d-h*ot
ch – as in staun*ch-h*eart   ṇ – as r*na* (prepare to say
j – as in *j*oy   the *r* and say *na*)

Cerebrals are pronounced with tongue to roof of mouth, but the following dentals are pronounced with tongue against teeth:

t – as in *t*ub but with tongue against teeth
th – as in ligh*t-h*eart but with tongue against teeth

d — as in *dove* but with tongue against teeth
dh— as in re*d-ho*t but with tongue against teeth
n — as in *nut* but with tongue between teeth

p — as in *pine*
ph— as in u*ph*ill (not *f*)
b — as in *bird*
bh— as in ru*b-h*ard
m — as in *mother*
y — as in *yes*
r — as in *run*

l — as in *light*
v — as in *vine*
ś (palatal) — as in the *s* in the German
　　　　word *sprechen*
ṣ (cerebral) — as the *sh* in *shine*
s — as in *sun*
h — as in *home*

Generally two or more consonants in conjunction are written together in a special form, as for example: **क्ष** kṣa **त्र** tra

There is no strong accentuation of syllables in Sanskrit, or pausing between words in a line, only a flowing of short and long (twice as long as the short) syllables. A long syllable is one whose vowel is long (ā, ī, ū, e, ai, o, au), or whose short vowel is followed by more than one consonant (including anusvāra and visarga). Aspirated consonants (such as kha and gha) count as only single consonants.

Index of Sanskrit Verses

This index constitutes a complete listing of the first and third lines of each of the Sanskrit poetry verses of this volume of *Śrīmad-Bhāgavatam*, arranged in English alphabetical order. The first column gives the Sanskrit transliteration, and the second and third columns, respectively, list the chapter-verse reference and page number for each verse.

so 'mṛtasyābhayasyeśo	6.18	307		taṁ nirvṛto niyatārtho bhajeta	2.6	76
śrī-hṛī-vibhūty-ātmavad adbhutārṇaṁ	6.45	353		tamo viśīryate mahyaṁ	4.5	186
śrī-lakṣaṇaḥ kaustubha-ratna-	2.10	82		taṁ satyam ānanda-nidhiṁ bhajeta	1.39	61
śriyaḥ patir yajña-patiḥ prajā-patir	4.20	220		tan-māyayā mohita-buddhayas tv idam	6.37	340
śrī-viṣṇu-padyā manujas tulasyāḥ	3.23	171		tapasvino dāna-parā yaśasvino	4.17	211
sṛjyaṁ sṛjāmi sṛṣṭo 'ham	5.17	255		tapo varāṣīṁ vidur ādi-puṁsaḥ	1.28	47
sṛjāmi tan-niyukto 'ham	6.32	329		taravaḥ kiṁ na jīvanti	3.18	159
śrotavyādīni rājendra	1.2	4		tasmād bhārata sarvātmā	1.5	8
śrotavyaḥ kīrtitavyaś ca	1.5	8		tasmād bhruvor antaram unnayeta	2.21	101
śrotavyaḥ kīrtitavyaś ca	2.36	130		tasmai namo bhagavate	5.12	248
śrotraṁ tvag-ghrāṇa-dṛg-jihvā	5.31	275		tasmāt sarvātmanā rājan	2.36	130
śrotreṇa copetya nabho-guṇatvam	2.29	114		tasya mātrā guṇaḥ śabdo	5.25	268
ṛtī vicakrame viśvaṅ	6.21	315		tasyāpi draṣṭur īśasya	5.17	255
sthiraṁ sukhaṁ cāsanam āsthito yatir	2.15	91		tasyārte yat-kṣaṇo nītā	3.17	157
sthiti-sarga-nirodheṣu	5.18	257		tataś ca manavaḥ kāle	6.30	327
sthitvā muhūrtārdham akuṇṭha-dṛṣṭir	2.21	101		tatas te bhrātara ime	6.29	326
sthūle bhagavato rūpe	1.23	40		tathā sasarjedam amogha-dṛṣṭir	2.1	65
śucau vivikta āsīno	1.16	29		tat-katyāṁ cātalaṁ klptam	5.40	286
surāsura-narā nāgāḥ	6.13	304		tato 'nusandhāya dhiyā manasvī	2.20	100
sva-dhiṣṇyaṁ pratapan prāṇo	6.17	306		tato viśeṣaṁ pratipadya nirbhayas	2.28	112
sva-lakṣaṇā prādurabhūt kilāsyataḥ	4.22	227		tatraikāvayavam dhyāyed	1.19	34
svalakṣita-gatir brahman	5.20	260		tavāpy etarhi kauravya	1.14	25
sva-pārṣṇināpīḍya gudaṁ tato 'nilaṁ	2.19	98		tāvat sthavīyaḥ puruṣasya rūpaṁ	2.14	89
svarlokaḥ kalpito mūrdhnā	5.42	289		tejasas tu vikurvāṇād	5.28	270
svarloka-pālāḥ khagaloka-pālā	6.43	352		tena khedayase nas tvaṁ	5.7	241
sva-viḍ-varāhoṣṭra-kharaiḥ	3.19	161				
				tenātmanātmānam upaiti śāntam	2.31	119
				tenedam āvṛtaṁ viśvam	6.16	304
				teṣāṁ pramatto nidhanaṁ	1.4	6
syād adhyavasyat kūṭastho	2.34	125		teṣu yajñasya paśavaḥ	6.24	321
sya ahaṁ te 'bhidhāsyāmi	1.10	16		tīvreṇa bhakti-yogena	3.10	143
syadā saṁhatya cānyonyaṁ	5.33	277		tvag asya sparśa-vāyoś ca	6.4	294
syad aśma-sāraṁ hṛdayaṁ batedam	3.24	174				
syad-bhrū-vijṛmbhaḥ parameṣṭhi-	1.30	50		U		
syad dravyam atyagād viśvam	6.22	317		udapadyata tejo vai	5.27	270
syad-gātraṁ vastu-sārāṇāṁ	6.4	294		udaraṁ viditaṁ puṁso	6.11	302
syad vijānīhi yaj jñānam	5.1	235		unnidra-hṛt-paṅkaja-karṇikālaye	2.10	82
syad viśva-nābhiṁ tv ativartya viṣṇor	2.25	107		upadhārya matiṁ kṛṣṇe	4.1	179
sijāsat tu vikurvāṇād	5.31	275		upakalpaya tat sarvaṁ	1.14	25
smaḥ-pradhānas tv abhavad	5.23	264		uraḥ-sthalaṁ jyotir-anīkam asya	1.28	47
smasād api bhūtāder	5.25	268		urugāya-guṇodārāḥ	3.16	156
sam eva puruṣaṁ yajñam	6.28	324		ūrvor vaiśyo bhagavataḥ	5.37	282

V

General Index

Numerals in boldface type indicate references to translations of the verses of *Śrīmad-Bhāgavatam*.

A

Ābhīra, 214

Ability in man, source of, 256

Aborigines, 42, 214, 354

Ābrahma-bhuvanāl lokāḥ
  verse quoted, 288

Abṛhad-vratas defined, 314

Absolute Truth
  as approached by "dovetailing" process, 36–37
  Caitanya's teaching of, 306
  Lord & His name as, 269
  Lord & His service as, 93
  oṁkāra represents, 32
  as personal, 260–261
  personal & impersonal view of, 36
  as realized in stages, 15
  via *Śrīmad-Bhāgavatam*, 337
  See also: Knowledge; Kṛṣṇa; Supreme Lord

Ācāryas
  as consulted for sacrifices, 58
  defined, 226
  Kṛṣṇa as accepted by, 42
  scientists vs., 109
  See also: Spiritual master

Acintya-bhedābheda-tattva, 62, 193, 306

Activities
  devotees transcendental to, 150
  of God. *See:* Supreme Lord, activities of; Supreme Lord, pastimes of
  instinctive, 264
  origin of, 263, 264
  as selfish or selfless, 213
  See also: Duty

Ādhāra-śaktim avalambya
  verse quoted, 345

Adhāyi mūrdhasu defined, 312

Adhibhūta, adhidaiva, adhyātma defined, 259, 265

Adhvaryu defined, 322

Ādi defined, 194

Aditi, **139**

Administrators. *See:* Government, leaders of; King

Advaita defined, 81

Ādyaḥ defined, 345

Affection of Lord for living beings, 77

Age of Kali. *See:* Kali-yuga

Ahaṁ sarvasya prabhavo
  quoted, 248, 283, 320
  verse quoted, 272, 331

Ahaṁ tvāṁ sarva-pāpebhyo
  verse quoted, 209

Ahaṅgrahopāsitā defined, 241–242

Air
  evolution of, **271**
  in body, disease caused by, 272
  of life, bodily outlets for, **101–102**, 103
  of life, *yogīs* control, 33, **99–102**

Airplanes in higher planets, **109**

Akāmaḥ defined, 144, 145

Akhila defined, 202

Akuṇṭha-dṛṣṭiḥ, 102

Alexander the Great, 214

Amalātmanas defined, 349

Ambarīṣa Mahārāja, 18, 198

America, discovery of, 256

Anādi defined, 194, 262

Anādir ādir govindaḥ
  verse quoted, 189, 249, 331

Analogies
  astronauts & child playing, 288
  banyan seeds & Lord's potencies, 248
  bellows & materialists, 161
  blood-sucking & material enjoyment, 162–163

C

F

Faith
faithlessness vs., 334
by hearing, 16, 17, 130–131
by knowing Lord's greatness, 191
renounced order for, 74, 75
False ego. *See:* Ego, false
Family life
bondage in, 29–30
charity given in, 74
Deity worship in, 169–170
"fallible soldiers" in, 7, 8
paraphernalia for, 181–182
retire from, at fifty, 313
sex pleasure in, 299–300
temporary relations in, 27
types of, 4–5
Farmers. *See:* Vaiśyas
Father & obedient son, analogy of, 297
Fear
of being alone, 75
causes & cures for, 309–312
at death, 27
freedom from, 9
Lord's feet remove, 298
renunciants beyond, 75
Fire
evolution of, 271
planet of demigod of, 107
priests kindle, 322
Fire consuming moth, analogy of, 95
Fire's by-products, analogy of, 252
Fire's energies, analogy of, 42, 262
Fish entering ocean, analogy of, 120
Food
for humans, 162
for mendicants, 73–75
vaiśyas supply, 283
Football, universe compared to, 44, 302
Forgetfulness
in living beings, 66
symbolized by bodies, 316
Forgetfulness in sleep, analogy of, 27–28

Freedom
to choose matter or spirit, 128
formula for, 8–9
of living beings, 128, 257, 277
from sex desire, 86–87
See also: Liberation
Friendship with the Lord, 97
Frog in well, analogy of, 244
Frog's tongue, analogy of, 165, 166
Fruitive activity. *See:* Work, fruitive

G

Gaṇapati, 354
Gāṇapatyas defined, 354
Gandharvas, 56, 139
Ganges River, 3, 320
Garbhodakaśāyī Viṣṇu
activities of, 279
Brahmā born from, 228
in creation, 346
sacrificial ingredients from, 320
Śiśumāra at navel of, 108
Gata-vyalīkas defined, 219, 221
Gati defined, 255
Gautama Muni, 18
Gāyatrī, origin of, 292
Genitals, pleasure for, 299–300
Germany, *Hūṇas* in, 214
Ghee (clarified butter) for sacrifice, 58
Ghosts, 172
Goal of life
beyond demigod worshipers, 147–148
as contacting Lord, 90
as detachment from sex life, 313
via duty, 56–57
as eternity, bliss & knowledge, 22
moment's notice to attain, 24, 25
questions & answers toward, 3
remembering the Lord as, 136, 283
by satisfying the Lord, 274, 275
self-realization as, 72
as spiritual values, 160, 163n

I

Prayer(s)
  speculation vs., 226
  by Śukadeva, **200-231**
Preaching Kṛṣṇa consciousness
  by being instrumental, 230
  defined, 282-283
  depend on Lord for, 199-200
  as duty of transcendentalists, 70
  impetus for, 243
  loudly, 166
  modern technology for, 58
  offenses in, 21
  to one & all, 216, 217
  for second-class devotees, 167
Prema defined, 175
Premānandīs defined, 203
Pride
  absent in *bhāva*, 176
  diminishing, 60
  of modern leaders, 164
Prītis tad-vasati sthale
  defined, 176
Prostitute's bad qualities, analogy of, 166
Protection by the Supreme Lord. *See:* Supreme
  Lord, protection by
Pseudodevotees, 97, 133, 176, 190-191
Psychic activities, Lord's presence in, 257
Pulindas, 214
Purification
  from designations, 292
  via devotional processes, 343
  as freedom from sex desire, 86, 87
  by glorifying the Lord, **207**
  from gross & subtle matter, **112-116**
  by hearing of Kṛṣṇa, 3, **132**
  by hearing *Śrīmad-Bhāgavatam*, 357
  of heart, 38-39
  via holy names, **19-21**, 23
  via Lord's lotus feet, 85-**88**, 225
  via mystic *yoga* process, **107, 108**
  via pure devotees, 216
  qualification for, 180
  by questioning about the Lord, 243
  by sacrifice, 222
  of senses, 116

Purification
  of soul, 348
  virāṭ-rūpa concept for, 42-43
  See also: Liberation
Pūrṇam defined, 306
Pūrṇasya pūrṇam ādāya
  quoted, 197
Puruṣa defined, 18
Puruṣāvatāras
  in creation, 197-201
  See also: Garbhodakaśāyī Viṣṇu; Mahā-
    Viṣṇu; Supersoul

Q

Questions
  about the Lord, effect of, **3**, 243
  to spiritual master, **235-236**

R

Rādhā-Dāmodara temple, 74
Rādhā-Kṛṣṇa worship, 89
Rādhārāṇī, Śrīmatī
  as foremost *gopī*, 222
  as happiness personified, 340
  mercy of, 173
Radio shows dissatisfying, 356
Rahūgaṇaitat tapasā na yāti
  verse quoted, 172-173
Rahūgaṇa Mahārāja, 172-173
Rājarṣis defined, 24
Rajas defined, 264
Rāmacandra, Lord
  Hanumān surpassed, 198
  Ikṣvāku as forefather of, 111
  in kingly role, 245-246
Rāmānanda Rāya, 176
Rāmānujācārya, 109
Rāmāyaṇa, 152-153n
Rāsa-līlā
  fine arts in, 232
  hearing about, 198
  purpose of, 221